HOW TO PROGRAM WELL

A Collection of Case Studies

HOW TO PROGRAM WELL

A Collection of Case Studies

Henry D. Shapiro

Associate Professor
The University of New Mexico

Adjunct Professor
Technische Universität Graz

IRWIN

Burr Ridge, Illinois
Boston, Massachusetts
Sydney, Australia

On the cover:
Routine of Cells, 1986 Elissa Dorfman   ©Elissa Dorfman/VAGA, New York 1993

We recognize that certain terms in this book are
trademarks, and we have made every effort to print
these throughout the text with the capitalization and
punctuation used by the holder of the trademark.

Senior sponsoring editor: *Tom Tucker*
Marketing manager: *Robb Linsky*
Project editor: *Susan Trentacosti*
Production manager: *Irene H. Sotiroff*
Designer: *Laurie Entringer*
Compositor: *Electronic Technical Publishing*
Typeface: *10/12 Palatino*
Printer: *Malloy Lithographing, Inc.*   1795454   1-27-95

Library of Congress Cataloging-in-Publication Data

Shapiro, H. D. (Henry D.),
    How to program well : a collection of case studies / Henry D.
Shapiro.
        p.   cm.
    ISBN 0-256-15150-4
    1. Electronic digital computers—Programming—Case studies.
    2. Structured programming—Case studies. I. Title.
QA76.6.S494   1994
005.1—dc20   93–7794

Printed in the United States of America
1 2 3 4 5 6 7 8 9 0 ML 0 9 8 7 6 5 4 3

To my father,
who has been teaching himself
to program for the last five years,
and to my mother,
who has become a
computer widow in the process.

PREFACE

TO THE STUDENT

The purpose of this book is to help you learn to write a well-structured computer program of moderate size. As with any skill that is a mixture of technique and artistry, it is best learned through practice under the watchful eye of a craftsman. As desirable as this approach may be, long gone are the days when a young person apprenticed for many years, practicing basic skills until they could be performed flawlessly time after time. In the modern world, the best alternative is to study the work of an experienced practitioner, hoping to gain in a short time the skills it has taken the professional many years to acquire. This is the approach taken here. The book consists of five case studies: programs of moderate length that solve what I believe are interesting problems. Each chapter revolves around the complete solution as I have coded it—the accompanying text explains the rationale behind the data structures and algorithms chosen, the special cases that had to be considered and dealt with, the little tricks and conventions that aren't part of any programming language but are part of the fabric of programming, and advanced topics that aren't always central to the main thread of the chapter.

The programs have not been edited for publication. They are as I wrote them for my own use—as sample solutions to projects assigned in various classes; sample solutions I did not originally intend to reveal. Thus, the comments were not added to the programs after the fact, out of fear that the programs would be scrutinized by teachers and students; they were, in fact, all present from the start. They also do not belabor points that might be new to students, but are well-known to more experienced programmers. This makes some of the comments quite terse, which is as I feel they should be. By publishing the solutions in this way, I hope you will find them an honest and vibrant example of a programming style that you might wish to emulate.

TO THE INSTRUCTOR

The impetus for writing this book came from my years of teaching the mainline programming sequence at the University of New Mexico. The intended audience is students who are learning to structure programs on the order of 500 lines. This skill is typically taught in either the course corresponding to ACM CS 2 or in a separate course taken after CS 2, a course with a title such as Programming Practicum or Introduction to Software Engineering; exactly where in the curriculum this skill is nurtured depends on the relative weights placed on theory and practice in the early courses, the number of credits allotted to these classes and whether they include a for-credit laboratory, and the preparation of incoming students. Over the years I have used many fine books for CS 2, but have always been dissatisfied with their lack of complete case studies. There are good reasons not to include case studies in books designed to cover the material of CS 2: including a complete case study would add many pages to books that already run to 600 pages, solutions to interesting problems often rely on system-specific details or utilize nonstandard language features, and dissecting a case study would consume valuable classroom time. It has always struck me as odd, however, that we expect students to learn to structure larger programs without ever giving them any examples to study—this is much like teaching writing without expecting students to read.

This book, designed as a supplemental text, attempts to remedy this situation. Basic material on the mechanics of pointers, linked lists, and recursion are assumed and not treated here; and, for this reason, the book is not a stand-alone text. While the main purpose of this book is to improve the programming skills of the student, this is not done at the expense of fundamental concepts of computer science. Each case study showcases an important data structure or algorithm. Abstract data types, functional programming, analysis of algorithms, recursive descent parsing, binary search trees, and graph search are all covered. Moreover, by studying data structures and algorithms within a case study framework, the student sees how theory is a component of successful programming and this is one of the book's key strengths. This style of presentation supports the recent curriculum recommendations of the ACM, which encourage better integration of fundamental concepts into the programming process.

The crucial question for an instructor considering the adoption of a supplemental text is undoubtedly: how will I use this book? Studying another person's code may be a worthwhile experience for the student—after all, modifying the code of others is what programmers do for a living most of the time—but lecturing on the details of someone else's program has to be unrewarding. As the experience of debugging shows, pouring over a program is a private activity, and this book has been designed for self-study. For this reason, the answers to the exercises are found at the back of the book and a $3\frac{1}{2}$-inch IBM-compatible diskette containing the programs is included. Except for the use of independent compilation and a few system calls, the programs are all in standard Pascal. The diskette contains both UNIX and Turbo Pascal versions of the case studies; if you are using a different Pascal compiler, porting the programs should be a matter of minutes.

Today, the most difficult question facing the author of a computer science text that is not innately language dependent is: what language should I write in? I have chosen to write in Pascal, even though standard Pascal is acknowledged to have many shortcomings. One reason for using Pascal is that while many schools are beginning to move away from teaching Pascal in their beginning courses, no consensus has arisen on a replacement and Pascal remains the predominant choice. Another reason for using Pascal is that it is very readable by programmers whose "native language" is not Pascal, something which cannot be said for C.

This is *not* a Pascal book—it is primarily a book about program design. The case studies are available in Ada, C, and C++ through anonymous `ftp`. The versions in these three languages are not just mechanical translations; the case studies have been rewritten in a style appropriate to the language and to take advantage of features that these languages provide. For those case studies where the design of the program is heavily influenced by Pascal's limitations, a version using both the Pascal-induced

design and a design tailored to Ada, C, and C++ is provided. Having the case studies available in alternate languages means that the project exercises that call for extensions to the programs remain appropriate in classrooms where Pascal is not being used. It also provides the Pascal-speaking student with a migration to other, more sophisticated programming languages—nothing beats good side-by-side examples when trying to learn another programming language.

The topics of the case studies have been chosen to be fun—that way students will want to study them. Although there are five case studies in this book, I never attempt to assign five projects in one semester, even in a class like Programming Practicum which is devoted solely to projects. To do so would be suicidal or murderous, depending on whether you look at it from the professor's or the student's perspective. In using this book you will need to pick and choose. With the exception of the introductory chapter and the material on independent compilation in Chapter 2, the chapters are self-contained. All the material in this book has been classroom tested—each of the case studies has been used as an assignment in the classes I teach at the University of New Mexico. The programs are my sample solutions, the accompanying text is an expanded version of my lecture material, and the annotations on the programs look suspiciously like the remarks I and my teaching assistants have scrawled in red ink on the programs submitted by students. For each case study, the design goals, data structures, and algorithms are thoroughly discussed. I do not expect students in a second or third course to have the skills to design the data structures themselves, only to understand why they were chosen and how they function. Their task is to convert the abstract description to code and integrate the various pieces into a complete, functioning program.

The organization of this book parallels the development found in many CS 2 books. This was done deliberately, so the book can be used as a supplemental text for that course. The first two chapters do not use pointers or recursion and fit into the beginning of the semester, in what is politely termed "review." The game of worm can be used to motivate true pointers, since it uses integers as pointers into one-dimensional arrays and ordered pairs of integers as pointers into two-dimensional arrays. True pointers and linked lists are the basis of the infinite precision arithmetic package, while recursion is the essence of the recursive lists case study and the Nero Project. Pointers and recursion are combined in an intimate way in the final case study. Some of the sections were written with the CS 2 audience specifically in mind and they extend the presentation usually found in CS 2 texts.

The leisurely pace of a book has allowed me to include some material of a more advanced nature. There is material on other programming languages (primarily, C/C++ and Ada, but also LISP), how random number generators work, how a parser handles the dangling `else` problem, and hashing. In curriculums where students are required to do an independent project as part of their graduation requirements, the project exercises can form the basis of any number of such projects—the calculator that sits in the upper right-hand corner of my X-windows terminal is really nothing more than the Nero Project, enhanced to accept mouse-driven input.

The main reason I delayed writing this book for so long is the issue of programming style. I have always heard deep within my psyche the remarks of my colleagues: "This book is great, except for . . . ," where . . . could be any of my choice of flow of control structures, commenting conventions, indenting style, or some other aspect of programming. While as readers we find differences in the use of language refreshing and enjoyable, we find deviations from our own programming style irritating. I purposely have not modified my programming style to suit either the marketplace or the typesetter. I think it is better that the programs be a reflection of how I program and not how someone else thinks I should program or, even worse, how a committee thinks I should program. I believe my coding style is robust enough to stand up to criticism and feel strongly that it is valuable for students to hear such criticisms; a good discussion of the issues will be of more benefit than the rote learning of any prescribed style. My style has served me well over 20 years, both in the commercial and academic worlds. This is not to say that my style has not evolved: I wince at some of the code I wrote 20 years ago, though the essence of my current style comes through even then.

OVERVIEW OF THE CASE STUDIES

Unlike the other five chapters, the introductory chapter does not revolve around a single case study, although the algorithm and code for binary search is a central theme. Preconditions, postconditions, and invariants are used to design the code and prove it correct. The language and techniques for analyzing the efficiency of algorithms is also introduced. Because a craftsman cannot produce a work of art if he or she is not intimately familiar with the tools of the trade, much of this chapter is devoted to a critical examination of Pascal. The issues raised are not specific to Pascal, and the lessons learned apply just as well to Ada, C, and C++.

The first case study, a program for a simple video arcade game, stresses the need for precise specifications and the need to anticipate special cases during the design phase of a project. It uses independent compilation as a project management and structuring tool. The theme of analyzing an algorithm is continued: since worm is an action game, it is desirable that each move be processed in constant time. This goal is achieved by a careful choice of data structures.

The second case study presents an implementation of an ADT for infinite precision integers. The user's and the implementor's view are kept strictly separate. It is only after some analysis that we settle on an implementation using circular, doubly linked lists, with a header cell containing a count of the number of digits. This choice, motivated in part by the limitations of Pascal, favors simplicity of the algorithms and efficiency of execution over economy of storage. The issue of memory management is addressed and the package can actually be used to solve significant problems. The chapter ends with a discussion of how the ADT might be implemented in C++; the facilities offered by that language permit a more natural representation and make the ADT totally transparent to the user.

The chapter on recursive lists is a bit different from the others. Its purpose is to give students plenty of practice with recursion and to get them to think abstractly. When I use this as an assignment in my classes I often do not reveal the internal workings of the ADT LIST. I want it to be a mystery— the student should think of LIST as an abstract data type, defined by the primitive operations that can be performed on LIST objects. The chapter is structured in the same manner, with the discussion of the implementation of the package put off until the end of the chapter and can be omitted if desired. Despite its abstract content, this assignment has always been a favorite of my students.

Nero—The Roman Calculator is a simple, infix calculator, only the input and output is in Roman numerals. There is considerable background material that must be absorbed to properly understand the program, a recursive descent parser for expressions. Both context-free grammars and recursive descent parsing are discussed at length. Students are always curious about how compilers work, and this chapter gives them an introduction to this important topic. The checking of Roman numerals for legality, if done in the straightforward way, can be a very messy piece of code. An elegant approach, for which I cannot claim the credit, makes this a very easy task. This shows, once again, that a little theory can go a long way.

The final case study, a `make` utility similar to the one found on UNIX systems, puts almost everything covered in this book together in a single place. It uses several data structures to provide an efficient implementation and uses independent compilation to interface with the operating system. It introduces graphs and provides a brief treatment of hashing. The need for a `make` utility is clearer to UNIX users than Turbo Pascal programmers, who have a `Compile|Make` option built in to their compiler and who may not have thought about how such a feature is implemented. Studying how Pascal compilers for UNIX systems implement independent compilation and studying `make` may help students leave the sheltered environment provided by Turbo Pascal and help prepare them for C programming.

ACKNOWLEDGMENTS

There are many people who I wish to thank for their assistance in writing this text. Jeff Van Dyke, our laboratory manager, helped with the C code for the screen manager for the UNIX version of the `worm` program, modifying the code of his predecessor, Lee Ward. He also assisted with the C code in the system interface portion of the `make` utility. The idea of using worm as an assignment in the second course in programming was due to Michael Wing, then a graduate student. Cleve Moler, at the time a faculty member in our department, used a much simplified version of Nero as a term project in our first course in programming. The idea of teaching recursion by treating the lists of LISP as an abstract data type in a Pascal environment restricted to `if ... then ... else ...` and recursion was

brought to my attention by Edgar Gilbert, a faculty member, now retired, who used it as an assignment in the second course. Sue Spaven of Sandia National Laboratories gave her time generously advising me on some of the fine points of Ada. And I must, of course, thank the countless students who labored over the projects discussed here, often proving to me that what I conceived of as a perfectly clear project specification was in fact subject to misinterpretation, and what I thought was adequate lecture coverage of the background material needed considerable amplification by my excellent teaching assistants.

Finally, I would like to acknowledge the efforts of people who reviewed the manuscript. They are Jack V. Briner, University of North Carolina—Greensboro; Pete Peterson, Texas A&M University; and Gregg Scragg, State University of New York—Geneseo.

Henry D. Shapiro

The actual compiler used to develop the UNIX versions of the programs was DEC Pascal for RISC. By moving the `#include` lines found in the main program modules inside the program heading, they all compile and run with the Berkeley Pascal compiler and on various Sun platforms.

The programs are also available by anonymous `ftp`. You should log into the Department of Computer Science network by typing `ftp ftp.cs.unm.edu` on your home machine and should respond to the request for a name by typing `anonymous`. At the password prompt, give your fully qualified mail address. You should then change directories to `pub/shapiro/CASE_STUDIES` and download the file `README` with a `get` command. This file contains further instructions.

Readers requiring other formats should contact the author.

`shapiro@cs.unm.edu`

CONTENTS

HOW TO PROGRAM WELL

A Collection of Case Studies

CHAPTER 1

PROGRAMMING WITH STYLE

Before delving into the five case studies that make up the bulk of this book, we examine a few shorter programs. The thrust of the discussion will be "style," that elusive quality that makes a program easy to read. Style is the accumulation of many small features—commenting conventions, use of white space, indenting, naming conventions for variables, choice of flow-of-control constructs, and many other small touches. Psychologists tell us that the language we speak affects the way we think. This applies to programming languages as well, and we will be better programmers if we keep the strengths and weaknesses of our programming language clearly in mind. For this reason we take a hard look at Pascal, learning about its inner workings and exposing some of its weaknesses. Lastly, because it impacts our case studies so heavily, we examine the fine details of processing input, both when it comes from a file and when it comes from the terminal. ◘

1.1 THE DESIGN AND ANALYSIS OF AN ALGORITHM

The first of our examples is one of the oldest well-solved problems in computer science—searching an ordered list for a particular value. Even if you haven't seen a procedure for solving this problem, it is a problem you encountered long ago and intuitively know how to solve—we have all looked up words in the dictionary and searched for a friend's phone number in the telephone book. An efficient procedure for solving this problem is given later on, but before examining the code, we should first make sure we understand the problem and its underlying algorithm. By an *algorithm* we mean a precisely stated method for solving a problem. It is natural, but incorrect, to equate an algorithm with a piece of code. An algorithm, though precise, is an abstract statement of the method of solution. The code that results is the embodiment of the algorithm in a programming language. The translation from algorithm to program may at times be mechanical and may at times be challenging, but it is always better to express

Don't run off and look at the code!

an algorithm abstractly, using a mixture of English, diagrams, and programming language constructs. The details that must be presented flawlessly in a computer program obscure the essence of the algorithm—extracting the algorithm from even a well-documented program can be a difficult chore.

The importance of precise specifications

Telling someone they "should understand the problem" before attempting to solve it seems like the height of silliness. Who would do otherwise? Yet, this crucial first step is often neglected. Even in a problem as simple as the one we are considering—searching an ordered list for a particular value—there are issues of design. We really should begin with some broad questions. Questions like

- How large are the lists we plan to search? This might affect our choice of algorithm. There is no point in developing a sophisticated algorithm to search lists containing only 10 values.
- We should ask *why* we are searching for the value. Do we just want to know if the value is present, as we might with an attendance roster, or do we need access to the data after we locate it, as we do when searching for a name in the telephone book?

These questions cannot be answered unless we know more about the context into which our procedure will fit. So that we have some environment in which to consider these questions, and since the problem we intend to solve arises often, we will create a **library routine**. A library routine must present to the user a well-defined interface, and we will jump ahead in our story by giving the interface now.

```
 1 const MAX = ...; (* something appropriate *)
 2
 3 type object = ...; (* Any type that can be compared with <. *)
 4      Data = array [1..MAX] of object;
 5
 6 procedure BinarySearch(var (* for speed *) A: Data; N: integer; X: object;
 7                        var Where: integer);
 8   (* Perform binary search on a SORTED (into increasing order) array.
 9
10      Input parameters:
11          A     -- sorted array to be searched.
12          N     -- effective size of array.
13          X     -- object for which to search.
14      Output parameter:
15          Where -- where  X  is located, or zero if absent.  In case of
16                   ties return any of the equally good choices.
17   *)
```

One decision that has been made in the above procedure declaration is the form that the input will take. While the problem statement said "search an ordered list...," it made no mention of arrays. Using an array is a natural choice, but it is not the only possible one: the data might be in a file, or it might be presented to our procedure as a linked list. This is not a superficial distinction: the algorithm we will examine is extremely efficient, but its efficiency depends on the ability to move about freely in the data. Neither files (at least Pascal files, which are *sequential files*) nor linked lists permit the necessary freedom of movement.

Another decision embedded in the procedure declaration is the nature of the result. The parameter `Where` returns the location within the array where `X` can be found. Other forms of output are possible. We might, for example, return a copy of the object. This seems a bit silly if our data is an array of `integer` or `real`, since then all we are returning is a copy of X, but we can easily imagine searching an array of records

```
record
  key: object;
  moredata: ...
end;
```

for the record whose `key` field matches X. Returning the *location* of X returns more information than just returning a copy of the record containing X. We are effectively granting access to the object. Since the calling procedure knows where X is located, it can modify it.

The comment associated with `Where` indicates that we have considered another design issue:

- What are we to do if the object we are searching for does not appear in the list at all or appears multiple times?

The way we resolve this design decision is not as important as the fact that we consider it in the first place. It is usually not too difficult to write a program that works most of the time. What is tricky is writing a program that works all of the time. And essential to writing bug-free code is planning for the exceptional cases. This is not a problem for humans—we are adaptable. When humans are given a task, they don't usually think about the special cases that can arise until they actually occur. When faced with an exceptional situation for the first time, a human stops, thinks, perhaps asks for advice, and finally makes a decision about what to do. Computers do not operate this way, and the programmer must anticipate all the special cases in advance. This is much harder.

As just remarked on, how we deal with special cases isn't nearly as important as the fact that we have identified them. Our solution would be no better and no worse if our interface was

```
procedure BinarySearch(var (* for speed *) A: Data; N: integer; X: object;
                       var Present: boolean; var Where: integer);
```

where `Present` indicates whether or not X occurs in the list, with `Where` containing a valid value only if it does. Instead, we have **overloaded** `Where`, making it serve two functions: the zero/nonzero status of this variable informs the caller whether X is present, and if it is, only then does it tell where the value actually is located.

The way in which we handle values that occur multiple times—returning the location of any of the equally good choices—is actually a reflection of the functioning of the algorithm. The algorithm simply returns the location of the first X it encounters. This may or may not be the first one in a left-to-right scan. While from the user's perspective it might be better to return the leftmost occurrence of X, at least the user is aware that we have thought about the possibility of multiple occurrences, and knows what to expect for an answer.

The comment   *Preconditions*

```
Perform binary search on a SORTED (into increasing order) array.
```

also informs the user of the **precondition** assumed to be true on procedure entry. Our procedure does *not* check this. Our precondition is precise: the array must be sorted and it must be sorted into increasing order. The precondition puts the user on notice. If the precondition is not met, then we do not guarantee that the routine returns the correct answer.

Binary Search

Now that we understand the problem, we can design the algorithm, although we are still not ready to program. Unlike with the five case studies that form the heart and soul of this book, we will not actually design the algorithm for solving this problem—it is well known, even to children, though they don't know that they know it. The algorithm, named **binary search**, is expressed in words as

■ Examine the element at the midpoint of the list.

■ If this element

– equals X, then X has been found. Quit.

– is greater than X, then X, if present at all, is in the first half of the list. Replace the list by the first half of the list and return to the first step.

– is less than X, then replace the list with the second half of the list and return to the first step.

Though vaguely phrased (how to detect when to stop if X is not present, how to "replace the list by...," and what value to return are not specified), and without any concern for how we might code it, this algorithm is highly effective, as the table of Figure 1–1 shows. If the array contains 1,000,000 entries, only 500,000 elements remain to be considered after one comparison, no matter which half is eliminated. After two comparisons, only 250,000 elements remain, and we can find out if any particular value is present in at most 20 comparisons. By generalizing the values given in the table to a list of length n, we see that cutting the size of the list in half at each step results in a maximum of $\lfloor \log_2 n \rfloor + 1$ comparisons.

"Big Oh" notation

When we are not concerned with the exact running time of a program—after all, what is the significance of one more or one less `if` test, especially when the exact running time depends on small details of coding and on how the compiler translates the program?—we use *"Big Oh"* notation to convey a sense of the overall running time. We say that the running time of binary search is $O(\log n)$, which we read aloud as "Big Oh of $\log n$." You can think of the notation as saying the algorithm takes "on the order of $\log n$ steps." We even let the $O(\ )$ hide multiplicative factors, so that an algorithm that takes $5n^2$ steps is still called $O(n^2)$. One reason to ignore constant multipliers is that the coefficient would be different if we counted machine code statements instead of Pascal statements. The notation $O(\log n)$ captures the essence of the performance of our algorithm. It will be significantly faster than simply searching through the list looking for X,

---

FIGURE 1–1   The Number of Comparisons Performed by Binary Search

Comparison	Size of Interval Remaining	Comparison	Size of Interval Remaining
initially	1,000,000	11	488
1	500,000	12	244
2	250,000	13	122
3	125,000	14	61
4	62,500	15	30
5	31,250	16	15
6	15,625	17	7
7	7,812	18	3
8	3,906	19	1
9	1,953	20	It's this one or
10	976		it's not present

irrespective of how good we are as programmers, what programming language we use, or on what computer we run our program.

Note that both the correctness of our algorithm and its efficiency rest on the precondition that the input is sorted. We make use of this property when we "replace the list by the ... half of the list." If the element at the midpoint is greater than X, there is no point in comparing X to elements further to the right, as they will be greater than X as well. Even though we do not explicitly consider these elements we know that they cannot equal X.

While our analysis of the number of comparisons performed by the algorithm is correct, to have an effective implementation we need to answer the questions

- How do we "replace the list by the ... half of the list?"
- How do we find the middle element of the list quickly?

as these affect both the running time and the details of implementation. We can solve both problems simultaneously if we represent the abstract notion of a list as the subarray A[l..r]. The original problem is just searching for X among the *n* entries of the "subarray" A[1..N]. With this representation, finding the middle element of the list just requires computing

```
m := (l + r) div 2
```

and consulting A[m]. Replacing the list by its first or second half involves nothing more than resetting one of l and r. Since each of these steps takes constant time and the loop iterates once for each comparison performed, we can truly say that our algorithm runs in $O(\log n)$ time. The crucial property of arrays that we are exploiting is the ability to examine any element of the array in constant time: it takes the same amount of time to examine A[1], A[N], or A[m], for any value of m. We can jump around in the array at will.

The point of presenting binary search in this top-down manner is to stress that

Summary of the design process

- Before designing an algorithm, make sure you understand the problem, paying particular attention to how the algorithm should respond to special cases.
- After you fully understand the problem, consider alternative algorithms and data structures. How efficient is your proposed method of solution? Are you getting the most out of any preconditions on the input? Does your algorithm affect how you detect and handle the special cases you have identified?

This design process may take several iterations, since a decision may shed new light on the problem, invalidate an earlier part of the solution, or reveal new trade-offs. The cardinal rule in designing algorithms to solve problems can be summarized in a few words: don't run off to program, think about the problem first. Follow the old adage about what to do when coming to a railroad crossing: stop, look, and listen.

We are finally in a position to look at the code for binary search. As with most algorithms that are noticeably better than their more obvious competitors, it is harder to correctly code binary search than it is to correctly code simple sequential search. While the first public discussion of the binary search algorithm occurred by 1946 and the algorithm was well known by the mid-1950s, the first published version that worked correctly in all cases did not appear until 1962. While the overall strategy is clear—compare X to the midpoint of the region of A[ ] that remains—this is difficult to interpret when the region has only one or two elements left. There doesn't seem to be a middle element in these circumstances. And we need to be careful that when we get down to one or two elements, and X is not in our list, we do not get into an infinite loop, checking

Invariants and correctness

the same element over and over again. We will write a bug-free program by establishing an *invariant*, which will guide us in translating our algorithm into Pascal and which will enable us to establish the correctness of the procedure. An invariant is a property of an algorithm, data structure, or collection of variables, that is true when we enter a piece of code and remains true upon exit from the piece of code, despite the fact that the values stored in the variables have changed. During the execution of the code, the invariant can be temporarily invalidated, but it must be reestablished before exiting. This is best illustrated with an example taken from the code of Figure 1–2. The invariant for the `while`

FIGURE 1–2   The Code for Binary Search

```
1  const MAX = ...; (* something appropriate *)
2
3  type object = ...; (* Any type that can be compared with <. *)
4       Data = array [1..MAX] of object;
5
6  procedure BinarySearch(var (* for speed *) A: Data; N: integer; X: object;
7                         var Where: integer);
8  (* Perform binary search on a SORTED (into increasing order) array.
9
10     Input parameters:
11       A     -- sorted array to be searched.
12       N     -- effective size of array.
13       X     -- object for which to search.
14     Output parameter:
15       Where -- where  X  is located, or zero if absent.  In case of
16                ties return any of the equally good choices.
17  *)
18     label 99;
19     var l, m, r: integer; (* left, middle, and right *)
20     begin
21       (* Invariant: If  X  is located in  A , it is at or to the right of
22          position  l  and at or to the left of position  r , and this range
23          is the narrowest consistent with our knowledge.
24       *)
25       l := 1;
26       r := N;
27
28       (* while there is still range left to search do *)
29       while l <= r do
30         begin
31           m := (l + r) div 2;
32           if A[m] < X
33             then l := m + 1
34           else if A[m] > X
35             then r := m - 1
36           else   begin (* A[m] = X -- found it *)
37                    Where := m;
38                    goto 99 (* return *)
39                  end
40         end;
41       (* The object is not in the list. *)
42       Where := 0; (* convention for not present in the sorted list *)
43  99:
44     end; (* BinarySearch *)
```

loop on lines 28–40 is

> *If* X *is located in* A, *it is at or to the right of position* l *and at or to the left of position* r, *and this range is the narrowest consistent with our knowledge.*

Phrased slightly differently: it is consistent with everything we have learned so far that X might be located in A[l], A[r] or in any location in-between, but it cannot lie outside of the subarray A[l..r].

This simple statement dictates the fine details of almost every line in the program. First, it forces the initialization on lines 25 and 26 to be

$$l := 1 \text{ and } r := N.$$

l cannot start at 0 nor can r start at N+1, the other natural choices, even if we pretend that the nonexistent A[0] and A[N+1] contain $-\infty$ and ∞. To start l at 0 or r at N+1 would violate the clause "this range is the narrowest consistent with our knowledge."

This clause also governs the assignment statements on lines 33 and 35. In the case of line 33,

$$l := m + 1$$

we have just compared A[m] to X and found that A[m] is strictly less than X. From this we can conclude that if X is present in A[ ], then it is located *to the right* of location m. It is incorrect to have line 33 read l := m. Assigning m to l does not take full advantage of what we learned from comparing A[m] and X. The invariant even dictates the stopping condition of the loop

```
while l <= r do
```

If l equals r we cannot terminate: the subarray A[l..r] will then be only one element wide, but that one element can still contain X.

Our invariant has guided us in writing the code. We can also use it to prove that the program is correct. It is clear that if the procedure returns via line 38, then it has found an m for which A[m] = X, and since the routine promises only to return *some* location where X is located, it will have done its job correctly. On the other hand, if the loop terminates normally, with l greater than r, then there is no range left in which X can lie. In other words, X must lie both at or to the right of l and at or to the left of r, but no location can satisfy these contradictory requirements. We can conclude that X is not present within A, which is what the algorithm returns.

While all that we have said is true, the argument just given is incomplete. There is one subtle point we have overlooked: does it always return? The answer is yes. We prove this final claim by showing that the width of the interval l..r, which is $r - l + 1$, shrinks with each iteration. Since the width is an integer, it cannot shrink forever without becoming zero, at which time the loop terminates. Why must the width of the interval shrink with each iteration? The intention of line 31

```
m := (l + r) div 2
```

is to set m to the midpoint of the interval l..r. Because m is an integer, this is possible only when there are an odd number of elements in the interval. But in all cases, even when the width of the interval is one or two, m lies within l..r. Because m is not less than l nor greater than r, line 33 definitely increases l, while line 35 definitely decreases r. Since one of these lines must execute, unless we happen to find X on the current iteration, the width of the interval must shrink. Notice that changing line 33 to l := m, in violation of our invariant, invalidates our proof of correctness. With this change, even though the routine will never return an incorrect answer, the interval of search does not necessarily become smaller with each iteration and the procedure may never return at all—it can get stuck in an infinite loop.

While it does not affect either the correctness or the "Big Oh" analysis of the running time, the ordering of the if tests in lines 32–39 is significant. It seems natural to test if A[m] = X first—after all, that is what we hope to find—but it is more efficient to place the case least likely to occur at the end. The loop as coded does an average of 1.5 tests per iteration. Making A[m] = X the first test raises the count to 2 tests per iteration, except on the final pass, when it does only 1.

EXERCISE 1–1   Construct an input to BinarySearch that will cause the procedure to get into an infinite loop if lines 33 and 35 are replaced by

l := m and r := m.

EXERCISE 1–2   Modify the procedure for BinarySearch so that it returns the location of the leftmost occurrence of X while incurring no loss of efficiency in "Big Oh" terms; that is, it should still run in $O(\log n)$ time. What is the most bizarre exceptional case you can think of to test this version of the program?

1.2 PROGRAMMING STYLE

So far our attention has been focused entirely on the algorithm. We have looked at a few lines of code, but not at their style. We have not been concerned that the lack of return in standard Pascal forces us into either writing a goto statement on line 38 or replacing line 29 with the commonly seen but less efficient

```
while not done and (l <= r) do
```

But programming languages do have personalities and we do have to adapt to them. And style is important, because a computer program communicates not only between the programmer and the computer, it is a vehicle of communication between people as well. Some aspects of style are universal, while others are peculiar to a particular programming language.

Variable names

An aspect of programming that exhibits both characteristics is the naming of variables. What is universal is the rule, which can be found in any beginning programming text, that "variable names should be meaningful." In many people's minds, "meaningful" often translates as "long," though this is incorrect. What it takes for a variable name to be meaningful depends on context. The longest name in our procedure is the name of the procedure itself, BinarySearch, which clearly conveys what the procedure is all about. The array is simply named A and the value being searched for is named X. Though these names are short, they are meaningful because of traditions that stem from mathematics. Mathematicians have long used x to signify an "unknown," and X is what we are searching for. Similarly, for centuries mathematicians have used a_i to denote the elements of a sequence and A has been used since the earliest days of computing to stand for

Rules Regarding Identifier Names

Systems differ

In standard Pascal, upper- and lowercase are not distinguished, except in strings, so `binarysearch`, `BINARYSEARCH` and `BinarySearch` are equivalent to the compiler, even if humans do not find them all equally readable. And while officially an identifier is an arbitrary length string of letters and digits beginning with a letter, many systems allow underscores in names. Turbo Pascal permits underscores after the initial letter. There is no single Pascal compiler for UNIX-based systems. Each hardware platform has its own, and though they tend to be similar, there are minor differences. The DEC Pascal for RISC compiler that runs on DECstations and the Sun Microsystems compiler allow underscores, whereas the Berkeley Pascal compiler running on VAXstations does not. On the other hand, both the Berkeley and Sun Microsystems compilers distinguish upper- and lowercase, while the DEC Pascal for RISC and Turbo Pascal compilers conform to the standard in this regard. (The DEC compiler has an option, `-casesense`, for turning on case sensitivity.)

Besides extensions, compilers sometimes impose restrictions. Instead of permitting identifiers of arbitrary length, a nuisance for compiler writers, many compilers impose a limitation on the maximum length of a name. If this length isn't too short, this is not a significant restriction. Turbo Pascal allows arbitrarily long identifiers, but only the first 63 characters are significant—hardly a serious limitation.

It is always safest to follow the standard, avoiding extensions (like underscore), but keeping common restrictions and limitations (like maximum identifier length) in mind. This makes for code that is easily ported to other systems.

---

an array. For this reason, control variables in loops like

```
for i := 1 to n do
```

should be named `i` and not `LoopCounter`. Variables whose functions are localized should have short names, to stress their *unimportance*. Another useful convention, with roots in mathematics, is that when loops are nested the outer loop is indexed by `i` and the inner loop is indexed by `j`. If three levels of nesting are needed, we continue alphabetically on to `k`. In programs that use both `integer` and `real` variables, names like `i`, `j`, `k`, `m`, and `n` are used for integers and `x`, `y`, and `z` are used for reals. `l` is generally avoided, though we used it in our binary search routine, because it looks too much like `1`. These rules stem partly from mathematics and were formalized in the earliest version of FORTRAN, where any variable whose name began with the characters `I` through `N` was taken to be `INTEGER` unless specifically declared to be of another type. The rule about not using `l` stems from the days of mechanical typewriters, which did not have a `1` key, using lowercase `l` to signify both the letter *l* and the number 1.

One reason not to glorify the names of loop control variables is that their very presence can be artificial. They are often needed only to translate an abstract algorithmic statement into a programming language construct. A loop like

```
for i := 1 to n do A[i] := 0
```

is better thought of as

```
set all the elements of A[ ] to zero
```

It is unimportant that `i` steps sequentially through the array—it is just a convenient way to translate the abstraction into Pascal.

Variables that are essential to the working of a procedure should be given names that immediately remind the reader of their function. This will become more evident in our case studies, where the programs span many pages and some procedures become intricate. Such variables should be used only for their intended purpose. Saving one or two memory locations by using a variable of importance as a temporary or loop control variable isn't worth the confusion that is likely to arise in the mind of the reader. Variables with related functionality should be declared together. This is better than having all the `integer` variables declared together, then all the `boolean` variables declared together, and so on. Sometimes just the organization of the declarations into lines is enough, while sometimes white space is needed. In our program for binary search, the input parameters are on one line and the output parameter is on another. `N` precedes `X` in the declarations because `N` acts as a qualifier on `A`. Because there are no conventions that suggest a name for the variable that returns the result of our search, the name `Where` was chosen. This is short enough that it is not offensive to read, but long enough that it informs the reader of its purpose.

As remarked on earlier, individual programming languages do have their own personalities. Ada and C permit the underscore character ("_") in names to improve their readability. The Ada reference manual suggests the convention that identifiers should be in all uppercase and keywords should be in all lowercase. The tradition in C is for variable and procedure names to be in all lowercase, while symbolic constants are in all uppercase. This convention is helpful, as it lets the reader know at a glance when a name is and isn't a variable. In standard Pascal, underscores are not permitted so we resort to capitalization to add stress, as in the name `BinarySearch`.

Indenting style

Indenting style is important because it lets the programmer see at a glance the flow of control. No one style of indenting has taken hold as "The Style" to use in Pascal and so it becomes very much a personal statement. Differences in indenting style show up most clearly in how the `if ... then ... else ...` construct is indented, especially when the ⟨statement⟩ following the `then` or the `else` is a compound statement. The most popular styles are

```
1. if ⟨condition⟩ then
       begin
         │ ...
         │
       end
     else
       begin
         │ ...
         │
       end
```

```
2. if ⟨condition⟩ then begin
       │ ...
       │
     end              (sometimes end else begin is written on one line)
     else begin
       │ ...
       │
     end
```

3. `if ⟨condition⟩`
```
    then begin
          │
          │ ...
          │
       end
    else begin
          │
          │ ...
          │
       end
```

The author of this book prefers the last of these styles. He likes it because

- The `end` lines up with the matching `begin`.
- The `else` lines up with the matching `then`.

The author almost never violates the rule that the `begin` and its matching `end` should line up. Furthermore, the textual material bracketed by the `begin` and the matching `end` is indented slightly. The motivation behind this rule is that

<code>begin ⟨statement_list⟩ end</code>

forges a group of statements into a unified whole. This is true both syntactically and metaphorically. It is as if a box were placed around the statements, shielding them from the outside world and converting them into a single concept. When crossing the barrier created by the `begin` and `end`, it is as if we are dropping from the outer world of ideas into the inner world of details. This is why the opening line of a `begin ... end` is often a comment—it expresses in one line of English the purpose of the several lines of Pascal that follow. This is just what procedures and functions are for: encapsulating larger ideas so that their purpose is evident, even as the details of implementation are hidden. `begin` and `end` serve a similar purpose, though on a smaller scale. The only exception the author allows is for very short compound statements, which express one logical operation and which can all fit on one line, such as in

```
if a < b
  then begin (* swap *) temp := a; a := b; b := temp end
```

The author likes the `else` to align with the `then`, and not with the `if`. While psychologically the `then` clause seems more important than the `else` clause— the `else` clause is often reserved to handle exceptional conditions—in a strict, formal sense they are of equal importance. The indenting should reflect that `true` and `false` are equally valid and that the `then` and the `else` clauses are both subordinate to the `if`.

If this logic seems irrefutable, then why is the second style, which also indents `while` loops as

```
        while ⟨condition⟩ do begin
              │
              │ ...
              │
        end
```

as opposed to the author's preferred style of

```
        while ⟨condition⟩ do
        begin
              │
              │ ...
              │
            end
```

so popular? One answer is that people who use it don't think of `then` as anything more than a dummy keyword. They view an `if` statement more as

```
if some condition is true do ...
otherwise the condition is false, so do ... instead
```

than as

```
case ⟨condition⟩ of
   true:  do ...;
   false: do ...
end
```

The second indenting style also closely matches the style used most widely in C

```
if ((⟨condition⟩) {
    |
    |...
} else {
    |
    |...

}
```

where the ⟨condition⟩ must be surrounded by parentheses, which makes the `then` superfluous, and where `begin` and `end` are replaced by the much shorter (and less visible) `{` and `}`.

An exception proves the rule   This rule concerning alignment of the `else` with the `then` is violated by our very first example program, the program for binary search! Why is this so? This is because the normal indenting, which would be

```
if A[m] < X
   then l := m + 1
   else if A[m] > X
           then r := m - 1
           else begin (* A[m] = X -- found it *)
                   Where := m;
                   goto 99 (* return *)
                end
```

is both hard to read and violates the spirit, if not the letter, of the rule. The algorithm for binary search is most naturally formulated as

```
case A[m] ? X of
   <: l := m + 1;
   >: r := m - 1;
   =: begin (* found it *)
         Where := m;
         goto 99 (* return *)
      end
end
```

Unfortunately, while this is what we may wish to write, it isn't even close to legal Pascal. However, one of the cardinal rules of elegant programming is

A cardinal rule of structured programming

> *Don't bend your thoughts to fit your programming language, bend your programming language to fit your thoughts.*

The indenting style used on lines 32–39 of `BinarySearch` suggests the `case` construct that really should have been in our minds all along.

Another situation in which the author violates his own rules is when there is no `else` clause and the `then` clause is very short. In this situation he sometimes writes the statement as

```
if ⟨condition⟩ then ⟨statement⟩
```

with all the text on one line. It is a little hard to categorize when to do this, but more often than not such lines have the flavor of "oops, we have a special situation we almost overlooked, correct it."

There are a few other fine points regarding the author's indenting style. Procedures are usually indented as

```
procedure ⟨proc_name⟩(⟨parameters⟩);
    type ...
    var  ...
    begin
       │ ...
       │
    end;  (* ⟨proc_name⟩ *)
```

instead of

```
procedure ⟨proc_name⟩(⟨parameters⟩);
type ...
var  ...
begin
   │ ...
   │
end;  (* ⟨proc_name⟩ *)
```

because the former makes the procedure heading stand out. The style is based on the same logic which dictates that the statements inside a `begin` ... `end` should be indented more strongly than the `begin` and `end` themselves—the box surrounding the contents should be more visible than the contents itself.

Finally, there is the question of how strongly to indent. Should each successive indentation move the text two columns to the right? Three columns? Four? One column is certainly not enough. The indenting style adopted by the author seems to work well when each successive indentation moves the text either two or three columns to the right. This makes for enough visible separation, without pushing the code too far to the right on the page. This can be a problem with the author's style when there are nested `if` ... `then` ... `else` ... constructs. For this reason, indenting four spaces each time another level of indentation is called for seems too much. A four-space indentation is popular with programmers who prefer the second style of indenting. Some advice:

> *A consistent indenting style is more important than the particular style adopted. It is easier for another programmer to adapt to your style than to deal with a program in which there is no consistent style at all. So, think over the choices, pick a style, and then stick with it.*

EXERCISE 1–3   Indenting can occasionally mislead the programmer into thinking that the code does something other than what it really does. The most common situation involves two nested `if` statements with only one `else` clause. The program fragment

```
if ...
    then if ...
            then ...
    else ...
```

is clear to another human, but the compiler interprets it as

```
if ...
    then if ...
            then ...
            else ...
```

How should this be coded so that the compiler understands the code the way the programmer intended it? There are two ways to accomplish this.

Commenting

Probably more energy has been expended trying to get students to comment their programs than on any other aspect of teaching programming. I know I have tried every trick I can think of to get students to comment better. Programs have even been written to take as input a Pascal program and report the average length of comments and the ratio of the number of comments to the number of Pascal statements, with the implied threat that if these numbers are too low, the student's grade will suffer. Unfortunately, these mechanical measures, while encouraging lots of long comments, don't encourage better comments. A tip:

Advice!

> *Comment your program while you are writing it, not afterwards.*

Almost nobody follows this advice at first. I urge you to try it. Not only will it make your code more bug-free, it will make your coding go faster.

General, expository comments

Comments come in two kinds: general, expository comments and "punch line" comments. The former usually occur immediately following the declaration of a procedure, at the beginning of a long block of code, or where a data structure that pervades the entire program is declared. They tend to be longer, to be written in proper English, and to explain at a high level what is going on inside the program. These should be written as the program is being developed because they help specify exactly what the preconditions and invariants are. If you cannot state these conditions precisely, then you probably can't write the code correctly either. And it is a lot more efficient to realize that you haven't developed a complete understanding of the problem or of the exact purpose of a piece of code before coding it, than to try to find the bug afterward. Once the ideas are crystal clear in your mind, the code will flow more easily. So, while general, expository comments are primarily included so that other humans can understand the algorithm, data structures, and implementation, they can also, if you write them as you code, help you to write better code.

Now for a few things that you *shouldn't* put in a comment. Assume that your reader is knowledgeable, though not intimately familiar with your particular piece of code. For example, don't try to explain the binary search algorithm in the code for binary search. In each of the case studies, there are long sections that describe the end user's view of the program, the algorithm and data structures found in the program, the design decisions that led to these algorithms, and why other choices were rejected. These should not be placed as comments in the code. The correct place to find this information is in the user's manual, the programmer's reference manual, and the requirements documents. A program with too many comments is just as hard to read and understand as a program with too few comments. The comments should remind the reader about important features (such as the fact that binary search is predicated on the data being sorted) or clarify specific features of the code itself (like the invariant on lines 21–24 or the description of N on line 12).

The other type of comment is the "punch line" comment. These comments are guides to yourself and other programmers who must become intimately familiar with the code. They point out little things that are easy to overlook, but, given the nature of programming, are crucial to the correct functioning of the program. They can be little reminders, like the comment

"Punch line" comments

```
Where := 0; (* convention for not present in the sorted list *)
```

or they can warn of some tricky and subtle situation. These comments can almost never be inserted correctly after the program is written and debugged. The insight that the code has to be just the way it is and not some other, ever so slightly different way must be captured the moment it occurs. Later, the situation will look obvious and the comment won't seem necessary. But the programmer who maintains the code won't have experienced the moment of inspiration, and might not see that the code has to be just the way it is and might modify it, making it incorrect. So when you write a line of code that is tricky or subtle, document it *on the spot*.

While we have explored briefly the whys and wherefores of comments, we have not said much about the mechanics of comments. You might have already noticed that the comments in the Pascal programs in this book are all delimited with a (* and *) instead of the more commonly used { and }. The reason is simple: a comment is useless if it isn't seen, and { and } don't show up well on either video displays or pieces of paper. A comment should jump out at the reader. In C and PL/I, comments are bracketed by /* and */, while in C++, comments are preceded by //, and in Ada they are preceded by --. These are more visible than the one-character delimiters allowed in Pascal.

The placement and exact layout of a comment can give subtle clues to its nature and importance. The author usually indents major comments, the expository comments that span several lines, this way

```
(*
 |...
*)
```

Other popular styles that serve the same purpose are

```
(*
 *
 * ...
 *
 *)
```

and

```
(**************************************************)
(*                                                *)
(*                      ...                       *)
(*                                                *)
(**************************************************)
```

At the other extreme, one-line comments associated with a specific Pascal statement are usually attached to the line they are meant to elucidate, like the punch line comment on line 3 or the comment on line 36

```
else begin (* A[m] = X -- found it *)
```

which informs the reader that while testing `A[m]` against `X` is needless, the code hasn't fallen through to this line by accident.

Comments like those of line 28, which express a programming construct in English or summarize the purpose of a few lines of code, are usually on a line by themselves. So are comments like the one on line 41, which describes a situation that can be deduced from the code. A good rule to follow is

> *The more important the comment, and the less tied it is to a specific line of code, the more visible the comment should be.*

A few final remarks. Comments are also used to delimit the ends of procedures, such as

```
end; (* BinarySearch *)
```

The `end` tells the Pascal compiler the code for the procedure has ended; the comment reminds the programmer. Lastly, when variables are referred to in a comment, they are usually surrounded by extra white space. This makes them stand out. If video terminals and inexpensive printers had many fonts, this would not be necessary. In many books, programs are printed so that keywords are in boldface, identifiers are in italic, and comments are in roman (the normal typeface), which serves the same purpose. In this book, programs are printed in an even-width typewriter font, as they appear in a listing or on a video screen.

1.3   THE GREAT goto CONTROVERSY

In 1968, Edsger Dijkstra, an early and well-known advocate of structured programming techniques, created a furor with his short article *"Go to statement considered harmful."* Since that time the teaching of introductory computer science has never been the same. The `goto` statement was banished from books and classrooms and some Pascal compilers banned it outright. Pascal never did fully endorse the `goto` statement: the `const` mechanism encourages the use of symbolic constants, which promotes readability, but labels are restricted to integers, which convey little information to the human reader.

Using a goto to simulate a missing control structure

The thrust of Dijkstra's article was correct: programmers had so abused the `goto` that they had made their code unreadable. Code was often a tangled web of `goto` statements and labels—unfathomable and unmaintainable. There are rare instances, however, where using a `goto` is actually clearer than not using it. In Pascal, many of these instances stem from the absence of a control structure that ought to be present in the language, but isn't. We have already seen an example of this in the code for binary search. Unlike other procedural languages, Pascal lacks a `return` statement. When executed from within a procedure or function, `return` immediately transfers control back to the caller. `return` behaves as if it causes the flow of control to pass to the final `end` of the procedure or function, an action performed in our program by the `goto 99`.

There are various ways to avoid this particular `goto`, and, in fact, it can be proven that a `goto` is *never* necessary. A popular approach is to add the declaration

```
var done: boolean;
```

and then write the body of the procedure as

```
done := false;
Where := 0; (* not present until proven otherwise *)
l := 1;
r := N;

(* while not found and there is still range left to search do *)
while not done and (l <= r) do
  begin
         :
         :
    else    begin (* A[m] = X -- found it *)
              Where := m;
              done := true
            end
  end
```

Though there is now no `goto`, there are a number of reasons why this code is inferior to the version presented earlier. First and foremost, it doesn't conform to the way we think. What we wanted to write on line 38 of the earlier version was `return`—it is not our fault that Pascal lacks this control structure, and we should make Pascal conform to our thinking and not the other way around. The `goto 99` mimics `return` more closely than the introduction of the extraneous `boolean` variable `done`. Is having a variable we didn't really want any better than having a `goto`? Secondly, there is the issue of efficiency. Based on running times measured on a DECstation 5000/200, the continual testing of `done` slows down the code by 20 to 25 percent.

The new version also treats the variable `Where` differently. In the original version, this variable is set once, when we know what it should be set to. In this version, it is initially set to "not present," and then corrected if we discover that `X` is indeed present. On philosophical grounds, it is generally better to set an output parameter when its value becomes known than to set it tentatively and then change it later. This is not a matter of efficiency, since in the modified procedure `Where := 0` executes only once; it is a matter of clarity. We cannot always avoid this "set and change" style of programming, but it is more confusing than "set it when you know it," and should be avoided if possible.

A number of minor modifications of this version, which all suffer from the same inefficiency and are no clearer, include

■ Removing the line `Where := 0` from before the loop and inserting

```
if not done then Where := 0
```

after the loop.

■ Changing the last alternative of the nested `if` to

```
else    done := true (* A[m] = X -- found it *)
```

and placing

```
if done
   then Where := m
   else Where := 0
```

after the loop.

- Using the fact that Where is overloaded to eliminate done entirely. Initialization of Where to zero is done before the loop is entered and the loop control is changed to

```
while (Where = 0) and (l <= r) do
```

If we want to scrupulously avoid goto statements, but don't want to suffer the loss of efficiency, the body of the procedure can be coded as

```
Where := 0; (* not present until proven otherwise *)
l := 1;
r := N;

(* while there is still range left to search do *)
while l <= r do
  begin
      ⋮

    else   begin (* A[m] = X -- found it *)
             Where := m;
             l := r + 1 (* force loop termination on next iteration *)
           end
  end
```

This bit of trickery may make the code just as efficient as before, but only by violating our invariant: l no longer always has the property that if X is present in A, it is at or to the right of l.

Do this exercise before reading further!

EXERCISE 1—4   Sometimes avoiding a goto can actually lead to bugs! Consider the simpler problem of searching an *unordered* list for a value, returning the location of the first occurrence if it is present multiple times and zero if it is not present at all. The body of this procedure can be written, using a goto, as

```
begin
  for i := 1 to N do
    if A[i] = X (* found first, and maybe only, occurrence *)
      then begin
              Where := i;
              goto 99 (* return *)
           end;
   Where := 0; (* convention for not present in the list *)
99:
  end; (* Search *)
```

Program a solution that works in all cases, does not use a goto, and does not suffer from the inefficiency of using an extraneous boolean variable.

exit/break *and* continue

A related control construct missing from Pascal is the exit of Ada. While return immediately terminates execution of a procedure and returns control to the caller, `exit` terminates execution of the smallest enclosing loop, sending the flow of control to the statement immediately following the loop. Like `return`, this construct is also easily simulated with a `goto`. C provides the same mechanism, but calls it `break`. C also provides `continue`, which causes the next iteration of the loop to begin immediately. It is equivalent to

```
for i := 1 to n do
   begin
      ... body of loop containing a goto 99 (* continue *) ...
 99: end
```

This construct is used far less often than `break`, but is useful on occasion.

Even with more extensive control structures, avoiding a `goto` is not always possible. When working with two-dimensional arrays, so that we have nested loops, it may be necessary to exit from both the inner and outer loops simultaneously as in:

```
for i := 1 to n do
  for j := 1 to n do
     begin
        ... body of nested loop containing a goto 99 ...
     end; (* inner and outer loop *)
 99: ...
```

This arises when, expressed abstractly, our algorithm is "`for` each element of a matrix, until some condition is detected, `do` ..." In our minds, we have a single loop—the nested loops are just an artifice of the programming language. A simple `exit` will get us out of the inner loop, but then we would just begin the next iteration of the outer loop, which is not what is intended. Our discussion so far can be summed up with the maxim:

> *Develop your program abstractly, using whatever control structures seem appropriate, whether they exist in your programming language or not. Then, when actually writing code, replace the abstract control structures with whatever control structures your programming language contains, bending the language to your intentions, and not the other way around.*

Advice!

We have used this maxim before: it was used to explain the abnormal indenting of the `if ... then ... else ...` statements of binary search. The real control structure we had in mind was a `case`, but the `case` labels were conditions, instead of constants.

Because it stares out at us, sometimes a `goto` should be used just to draw attention to an exceptional situation. Imagine a program that prompts the user for a yes or no answer. If the user times something other than a `y` or `n`, the input should be rejected, and the user prompted again. the `goto`-less solution in Pascal is to write

Using a goto *to grab the reader's attention*

```
write('Respond with yes or no (y/n): ');
repeat
  readln(ch);
  if (ch <> 'y') and (ch <> 'n')
    then write('Input error.  Retry: ')
until (ch = 'y') or (ch = 'n')
```

FOR YOUR
INFORMATION

Evaluation of Boolean Connectives

If your solution to Exercise 1–4 is similar to

```
i := 1;
while (i <= N) and (A[i] <> X) do i := i + 1;
if i <= N (* found first, and maybe only, occurrence *)
   then Where := i
   else Where := 0
```

then your solution is incorrect. The reason this solution is incorrect is due to the way Pascal evaluates the Boolean connectives and and or. The issue turns on what to do if the first operand of an and is false or the first operand of an or is true. In such a circumstance, the value of the second operand cannot affect the final outcome of the logical operation. There are three possible approaches to evaluating an expression like

$$(i <= N)\ \text{and}\ (A[i] <> X)$$

- The compiler can evaluate both operands in all cases. This is known as *full evaluation*, and is what Ada does. (Ada does not specify the order in which the two operands are evaluated.)
- The compiler can evaluate the operands in either order, *perhaps* stopping when the overall truth of the logical expression becomes known. This is what Pascal and FORTRAN do.
- The compiler can evaluate the operands from left to right, stopping when the overall truth of the logical expression is known. This is known as *short-circuited evaluation* and is what C does.

The first of these approaches corresponds to the mathematician's view of logical expressions. It is equivalent to evaluating the logical operator by picking a line out of the truth table for $p \wedge q$. To do this, it is necessary to know the value of both operands. The fact that the answer might be deducible from the value of one of the operands is not important: the model is one of table lookup, and the value of both operands must be known to reduce the choice to a single line of the table. The second approach is the compiler writer's view. By giving the compiler the freedom to do the evaluation in any which way, so long as the correct final answer is obtained, the compiler may be able to optimize the code. The third approach is the programmer's view. It makes the easy-to-read, five-line solution given earlier correct.

What is wrong with the solution proposed above and, more generally, how do the differences between the three approaches manifest themselves? In the absence of *side effects*, they behave identically. The difficulty is that the Pascal standard says that the behavior of a program is undefined if it makes an out-of-bounds array reference. If full evaluation is used, then executing

```
while (i <= N) and (A[i] <> X) do i := i + 1
```

when X is not present will eventually cause a reference to A[N+1], even though i <= N will be false. While the truth of the entire condition does not depend on whether or not the value stored in this memory location equals X, this reference may cause a subscript-out-of-range error, and the program may abort. This behavior occurs only in a rare conjunction of circumstances: X is

(continued)

not present in A, the effective length of the array, N, equals the true length of the array, MAX, and *range checking* is performed. Finding such an error can be very difficult, since the code will fail only occasionally.

Both full and short-circuited evaluation are consistent with the Pascal standard. In order to write a portable program, however, the programmer should assume nothing about the way in which Boolean connectives are evaluated. For historical reasons, most Pascal compilers use full evaluation. In Turbo Pascal, the default is short-circuited evaluation, though full evaluation can be specified by inserting the compiler directive {$B+} into the code. Statements of the form

```
while (condition1) and (condition2) do ... body of loop ...
```

where, because of an unwanted side effect, the second condition should not be evaluated if the first condition is false, should be written as

```
while (condition1) do
   if (condition2)
     then begin
             ... body of loop ...
          end
     else goto 99; (* exit *)
99: ... (* arrive here if either operand is false *)
```

Besides incorrectly assuming that Pascal does short-circuited evaluation of Boolean connectives and using the value stored in the control variable of a for loop when the loop terminates normally, two other sensitive spots in Pascal that cause careless programmers no end of trouble are

- Assuming variables are initialized when a procedure is entered. Many compilers initialize integer and real variables to zero, boolean variables to false, and pointer variables to nil, but the Pascal standard says that variables are uninitialized on procedure entry.

- Assuming the order of evaluation of arguments to a function or procedure is left to right. For technical reasons, many compilers evaluate arguments from right to left. The Pascal standard says that the order is undefined.

FOR YOUR INFORMATION

(concluded)

CAUTION

Systems differ

EXERCISE 1–5 Why is the code

```
i := 1;
while (i <= N) and (A[i] <> X) do i := i + 1;
if A[i] = X (* found first, and maybe only, occurrence *)
   then Where := i
   else Where := 0
```

incorrect, even if short-circuited evaluation is used?

EXERCISE 1–6 Design an experiment that will reveal in which order your compiler evaluates the arguments to a function.

This code contains two complex tests, one the negation of the other. Permitting ourselves license to use an `exit`, we might write this as

```
write('Respond with yes or no (y/n): ');
repeat
  readln(ch);
  if (ch = 'y') or (ch = 'n') then exit;
  write('Input error.  Retry: ')
until false (* infinite loop *)
```

But perhaps better still is

```
      write('Respond with yes or no (y/n): ');
99: readln(ch);
    if (ch <> 'y') and (ch <> 'n')
      then begin
            write('Input error.  Retry: ');
            goto 99
          end
```

The very presence of the `goto` emphasizes that we really do not expect the user to make an error, whereas the presence of a `repeat` suggests that iteration is the expected behavior. This code would read better if the label could be symbolic, like `TryAgain`.

Catastrophic error handling and the goto *statement*

So far our use of `goto` statements has been very limited—the flow of control has remained within one procedure. There is one common use of `goto` statements where the action isn't locally contained: catastrophic error handling. The model for this situation is shown in Figure 1–3: while deeply buried in some procedure, the program detects a condition from which it cannot recover. The program might, for example, detect an inconsistency in the data contained in a file. In a situation like this the program can do little but halt gracefully—the `goto` of Figure 1–3 is really mimicking another missing flow-of-control construct: the `stop` statement. Sometimes, halting the program is too extreme. It is easy to imagine an interactive program that repeatedly reads an entire line and processes it in some complex manner. If an error is detected while processing a line, the program should print an error message, abandon the current line, and return to the main read-process loop. This is really no different than the use of the `goto` in the respond-with-yes-or-no example, except now, because of the complex nature of the processing, the detection of the error is buried in a procedure nested several layers deep. This situation occurs in one of our case studies, Nero—The Roman Calculator. There we will repeatedly ask the user for an arithmetic expression to evaluate. If we detect an error while evaluating the expression, we will abandon the expression and use a `goto` to return to the outermost read-process loop.

There is a related problem, which might be called a "catastrophic success," involving recursive procedures and nonrecursive shells. The discussion of this use of the `goto` statement is deferred until it arises naturally.

Summary: Where a goto *is allowed*

There are only a few other, very special circumstances in which the author has found it necessary to use a `goto`. These involve simulating finite state machines and formally derecursing a recursive procedure—situations which do not occur in this book. Thus, we have a small catalog of cases where we find a `goto` useful.

- To simulate a control structure omitted from the language.
- To cut across whole pieces of code, in order to arrive at a "collecting point." There are two subcases here: handling catastrophic errors, and exiting cleanly from a recursive subprocedure to its nonrecursive shell.

Turbo Pascal and the `goto` Statement

Turbo Pascal does have a `return` statement, although it is called `exit`. Thus, the program of Figure 1–2 can be written in Turbo Pascal without the `goto`. As remarked on earlier, unless there is some real benefit to using an extension to standard Pascal, it is wiser to avoid these extra features. Avoiding a `goto` that is just mimicking a `return` isn't one of these situations.

Systems differ

While Turbo Pascal includes `exit` and some other nonstandard flow of control constructs that allow elimination of superfluous `goto` statements, it does place one serious restriction on the use of the `goto`. The Pascal standard has precise rules governing where a `goto` statement like the one used in Figure 1–3 can transfer control to. Despite what the standard says, Turbo Pascal does not permit `goto` statements to transfer control out of a procedure or function, and the code of Figure 1–3 will not compile. How do we get around this difficulty when programming in Turbo Pascal? The solution is to propagate the error outward, step by step. This is done by including an output parameter, `var error: boolean`, in the declaration of `procedure b` and testing it on the line immediately following the call. Other procedures that make calls to `procedure b` will have to be modified in a similar manner. The necessary modifications are shown in Figure 1–4. This clutters up the code with many tests, whose sole purpose is to propagate the error, but the translation is totally mechanical. The handling of `error` in Figure 1–4 is an example of where "set and change" is more natural than "set it when you know it."

FIGURE 1–3　A Model for Handling Catastrophic Errors

```
program ...

   procedure a(...);

      procedure b(...);

         if ... then goto 99; (* stop *)


      b(...);



   procedure ...



   a(...);

99: end. (* program ... *)
```

FIGURE 1—4   Modifications to the Code of Figure 1–3 Needed to Conform to Turbo Pascal

```
program ...
  var error: boolean;

  procedure a(...; var error: boolean);

    procedure b(...; var error: boolean);
      (* error  is false on entry -- maybe set it to true *)


      if ... then begin error := true; goto 99 (* return *) end;


    99: end; (* b *)


    (* error  is false on entry -- maybe set it to true *)


    b(...,error);
    if error then goto 99; (* propagate the error -- return *)


  99: end; (* a *)


  procedure ...



  error := false; (* until proven otherwise *)

  a(...,error);
  if error then goto 99; (* stop *)
99: end. (* program ... *)
```

- ■ To simulate a finite state machine.
- ■ To formally derecurse a recursive procedure.

The five case studies of this book use only 18 `goto` statements, 13 of the first type and 5 of the second.

1.4   A HARD LOOK AT PASCAL

When we design programs, we should think abstractly, but ultimately we must reduce our ideas to statements in some programming language. To do this well we must have a thorough understanding of both the semantics of our programming language and some knowledge of how its constructs are implemented at the machine-language level. In this section we take a close look at some of the aspects of Pascal that make the language what it is: static vs. dynamic scoping, strong typing, and parameter passing mechanisms. We pay particular attention to how arrays are handled, since this is often cited as a major weakness of Pascal.

The vastness of the topics covered in this section is almost overwhelming, and this section can serve only as an introduction.

Our first concern is how references to Pascal variables are understood during execution. It is natural to assume that the storage for the local variables of a procedure is somehow tightly tied to the procedure they are declared in. But if this were so, it is not obvious why we have the rule

Stack Frames

> *Variables in Pascal should be treated as uninitialized on procedure entry.*

Puzzling question #1: Why are variables uninitialized on procedure entry?

And why do variables not retain their values from one invocation of a procedure to the next?

EXERCISE 1–7   Predict the results of running the following program on your computer and then actually run it to see what you get.

```
1  program ExplainTheOutput(output);
2    var first: boolean;
3    procedure proc1;
4      var j: integer;
5      begin
6        if first then j := 2;
7        writeln('j = ',j:1)
8      end; (* proc1 *)
9    procedure proc2;
10     var k: integer;
11     begin
12       k := 1
13     end; (* proc2 *)
14   begin
15     first := true;
16     proc1; (* Prints  j = 2  *)
17     first := false;
18     proc1;
19     proc2;
20     proc1
21   end. (* ExplainTheOutput *)
```

Your computer most likely printed either 2, 2, and 1 or 2, 0, and 0. It almost certainly did not print 2, 2, and 2. Surprised? If the storage for the local variables of a procedure were allocated once and for all time when the program began executing, 2, 2, and 2 would be the correct answer. Somehow, especially if your output was 2, 2, and 1, you sense that j of proc1 and k of proc2 occupy the same storage at different times. This occurs because storage for the variables of a procedure is allocated not once, when the program starts execution, but is allocated every time the procedure is entered and deallocated when the procedure is exited. (The main program is just a procedure called by the operating system.) The history of the execution of this program is depicted in Figure 1–5. The variables of the currently active procedures are stored in a stack in a series of *stack frames*. Every time a procedure is called, a new stack frame is created on the top of the stack. This stack frame contains the storage for the parameters and local variables of the procedure, as well as other information, such as to where the procedure should return. When the procedure returns, the stack frame for the call to the procedure is destroyed.

FIGURE 1–5   A Sequence of Snapshots of Memory

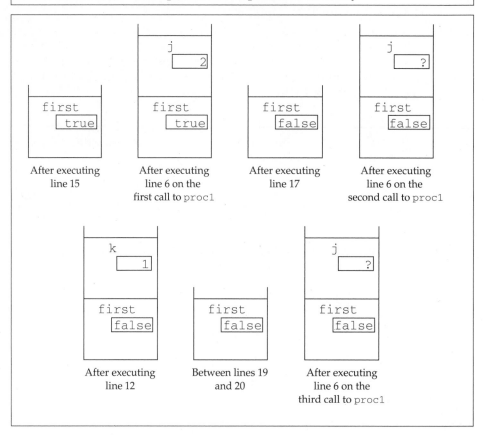

| After executing line 15 | After executing line 6 on the first call to proc1 | After executing line 17 | After executing line 6 on the second call to proc1 |

| After executing line 12 | Between lines 19 and 20 | After executing line 6 on the third call to proc1 |

If we had a more complex example, we would see more clearly that at any moment in time the ordering of the stack frames reflects the *sequence of calls at runtime*. This is a **dynamic property** of the program—it has nothing to do with the ordering of the procedures as the program is laid out on paper, which is a **static property**. Even in our simple example, we can see that only those procedures that are executing, even if currently in a suspended state, having called another procedure, have a stack frame on the stack. If a procedure is not executing, then no storage is allocated for its variables—they simply do not exist. Stack frames are not so much associated with procedures as with procedure *invocations*—when a procedure is called, a stack frame for this invocation is created, and when the procedure returns, the stack frame is destroyed. Also observe that when a procedure is actually active, the stack frame for this invocation is in the same relative, even if not absolute, position: the stack frame is on the top of the stack. When the currently active procedure calls another, a new stack frame is created and it becomes the top stack frame. The contents of the local variables in the new stack frame are unpredictable. They might contain whatever was left by the last invocation that just happens to have used the space (which is why 2, 2, and 1 is a possibility) or the Pascal compiler writer might, in an attempt to be helpful, initialize these locations to some convenient initial value (which is why 2, 0, and 0 is a possibility). The memory locations might even have been used by the operating system to store a temporary value, so the values might appear random. The Pascal standard makes no mention of how the storage occupied by a stack frame is supposed to be initialized. This is why local variables must be assumed to be uninitialized on procedure entry and, as a consequence, why they do not retain their values from one invocation to the next.

When a procedure returns, it is always the top stack frame that is eliminated. This stack regimen—push a new frame onto the top on a procedure call and pop a frame off on a procedure return—is just what is needed. It reflects an important property of the flow of control: the order in which the procedures return is exactly opposite to the order in which they were called.

The fact that Pascal behaves in this manner does not explain *why* it should behave this way. While it might seem more natural to tie the variables directly to the procedure, instead of to the invocation of the procedure, doing so makes it impossible to support **recursion**. Recursion is the ability of a procedure to call itself and it is the driving force behind the way memory is managed in Pascal. It is not at all obvious why we might want such a capability, as there are many thousands of useful programs that do not use recursion. We will explore the power provided by recursion later; for now it is enough to know that the simple approach of assigning a variable to a fixed location is inadequate.

Parameter Passing Mechanisms

Why is the declaration in `BinarySearch` written as

```
procedure BinarySearch(var (* for speed *) A: Data;...
```

and not as

```
procedure BinarySearch(A: Data;...
```

After all, the procedure `BinarySearch` does not modify `A` and the conventional wisdom is

> *If a procedure does not modify a variable, it should be passed by value.*

To understand why the `var` is appropriate, we must examine how parameters are passed. Pascal supports two parameter passing mechanisms: *call-by-value* and *call-by-reference*. The declaration of the parameter *in the procedure being called* dictates which mechanism is used. The default is call-by-value. To use call-by-reference the keyword `var` must be placed before the parameter in the argument list of the procedure declaration.

The following piece of code illustrates call-by-value:

```
procedure a(i: integer);
   begin
      ...
      i := 3;
      ...
   end; (* a *)
   :
j := 2;
a(j);
writeln(j);
   :
```

When `a` is called, the value of `j` is *copied* into the local variable `i` of `a`. On entry, the stack looks like

ABOVE
AND BEYOND   **case vs. if Statements**

In a formal sense, there is no need for the case statement in Pascal. It can always be replaced by a nested if ... then ... else .... The case statement is useful, however, for two reasons. First, it can make a program more readable. This is illustrated in Figure 1–6 a program that estimates the odds of winning at the game of craps. Running the program twenty times, playing 10,000 games each time, produced the following results: the player came out ahead three out of the twenty times, with the probability of winning varying from 48.25 to 50.39%—a reasonably even game, with the house appearing to have a slight edge. Analyzed mathematically, the odds of winning are 49.29%.

The case statement that forms the core of the program is more readable than the alternative

```
if (roll = 2) or (roll = 3) or (roll = 12)
  then (* lose *)
else if (roll = 7) or (roll = 11)
  then wins := wins + 1
else (* roll = 4, 5, 6, 8, 9, or 10 *)
      begin
        ...
      end
```

This is because if ... then ... else ... statements, especially nested if ... then ... else ... statements, leave the impression that the first alternative is more likely to be true than the others, with the last alternative being reduced almost to a special case. On the other hand, case statements leave the impression that all the alternatives are of equal importance, even if, as in our case, they are not all equally likely. This interpretation of nested if statements is all psychological: normally, important cases are treated first, less important ones are treated later.

The second reason for using a case statement is that the resulting machine code is more efficient. When a nested if ... then ... else ... is executed, the conditions are evaluated sequentially. This is equivalent to running down an unordered list searching for an item.

In contrast to the way nested if statements are handled, a case statement takes the same amount of time to begin executing the code associated with a case label no matter which one is selected. A case statement can be logically thought of as an array, CODE[ ], of code segments. After the ⟨expression⟩ in case ⟨expression⟩ of is evaluated, control is transferred to the code at CODE[⟨expression⟩]. As with all arrays, access to any element takes the same amount of time as access to any other.

The only problem with this explanation is it overlooks the fact that all the elements in an array of data take up the same amount of space—this is what allows the hardware to get to A[i] efficiently. With a case statement, however, the code segments at each case label can take up different lengths. This apparent difficulty is overcome as suggested in Figure 1–7. This approach works because all the goto statements in CODE[ ] occupy the same amount of space. Getting to the code associated with a case label now involves two successive jumps.

(continued)

FIGURE 1–6   A Program to Estimate the Odds of Winning at the Game of Craps

```pascal
1  program ProbabilityOfWinningCraps(input,output);
2  (* Experimentally determine the approximate probability of winning at the
3     game of craps.  Craps is played with a pair of dice.  The rules are:
4        The player rolls the dice.  If he/she gets a 7 or 11 the player wins.
5           If he/she gets a 2 (snake eyes), 3 (acey-deucey) or 12 (box cars)
6           the player loses.  Any other number becomes the player's "point".
7        The player continues to roll the dice until either the player gets
8           his/her point (player wins) or the player gets a 7 (player loses).
9  *)
10   uses RandomNumbers;
```

The program uses independent compilation to gain access to a random number generator. Independent compilation and random number generators are explained in Chapter 2. This is the Turbo Pascal version of the program. Randomize *starts the random number generator in a random place.* Random *is a function of no arguments that returns a random real number in the half-open interval* [0,1).

```pascal
11  var NumGames: integer; (* Play  NumGames  games to determine the approximate
12                            probability of winning. *)
13      wins,  (* number of games won *)
14      point, (* player's "point" if the first roll is not 2, 3, 7, 11, or 12 *)
15      roll,  (* result of rolling dice *)
16      i: integer;
17  begin
18    write('How many games should be played: '); readln(NumGames);
19
20    Randomize;
21    wins := 0;
22
23    for i := 1 to NumGames do
24      begin
25        roll := (trunc(6.0*Random) + 1)  +  (trunc(6.0*Random) + 1);
26        case roll of
27          2,3,12: ; (* lose *)
28          7,11:   wins := wins + 1;
29          4,5,6,8,9,10:
30                  begin
31                    point := roll;
32                    repeat (* roll until player gets 7 or point *)
33                      roll := (trunc(6.0*Random) + 1) +
34                              (trunc(6.0*Random) + 1)
35                    until (roll = 7) or (roll = point);
36                    if roll = point
37                      then wins := wins + 1
38                    (* else lose *)
39                  end
40        end
41      end;
42
43    writeln('The approximate probability of winning at the game of craps is: ',
44            100.0*wins/NumGames:1:2,'%.')
45  end. (* ProbabilityOfWinningCraps *)
```

This expression produces a uniformly distributed random integer between 1 and 6, that is, it simulates a die. This is explained in Above and Beyond: Random Number Generators.

The way in which a `case` statement is compiled explains several of the rules of Pascal.

- The ⟨expression⟩ must ultimately evaluate to an integer—you cannot write `case x of` where x is `real`. This is because the value is used as a subscript.
- The case labels must be distinct. This is because there is only one array element associated with each case label, and it can hold only one `goto` statement.
- Case labels must be constants. This is because the table of `goto` statements is built at compile time.
- The ordering of case labels, is irrelevant and labels can be grouped together in any arbitrary manner. The compiler sorts it all out. In Figure 1–7 there is one entry in `CODE[ ]` for case label 4 and one entry for case label 9, but they jump to the same place.
- While it is not illegal to have "holes" in the list of case labels, if the ⟨expression⟩ evaluates to a value for which no label has been specified, it is an error. This is why we need case labels for 2, 3, and 12, even though there is no code to execute when these cases arise.

This last rule includes the situation where the value of the ⟨expression⟩ falls outside the bounds of the array. Turbo Pascal does not consider branching to a missing case label an error; it treats missing labels as being logically followed by the null statement and simply goes on to the statement after the `case`. Some compilers, including Turbo Pascal, allow specification of a default option. It is typically introduced with a keyword like `else` or `otherwise`.

Now that we understand how a `case` statement is compiled, we can see that there are some pitfalls. What if the programmer writes

```
case i of
    1: ...;
    2: ...;
    10000: ...
end
```

Some compilers attempt to allocate space for an array of 10,000 `goto` statements. More sophisticated compilers consider the density of case labels and convert all or part of the `case` statement to a nested `if ... then ... else ...` structure. This is not a violation of the language standard—the standard describes the logical functioning of a `case` statement, not its implementation. Gaps in the case labels typically arise when the case labels are characters. The code usually looks something like

```
write('Input your option: '); readln(ch);
case ch of
    ...
end
```

where there are numerous options, each specified with one letter. Because the number of characters is limited, this isn't serious, even if the compiler does not optimize.

FIGURE 1–7   How a case Statement Is Compiled

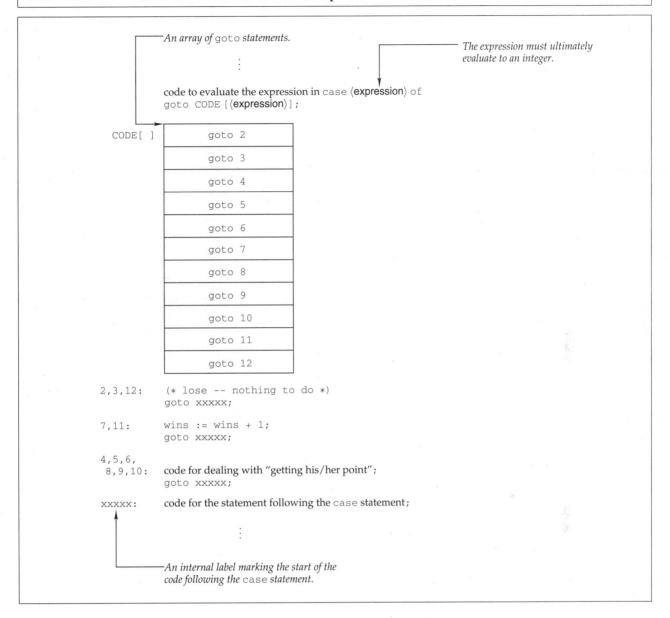

An array of goto *statements.*

The expression must ultimately evaluate to an integer.

code to evaluate the expression in case ⟨**expression**⟩ of
goto CODE [⟨**expression**⟩];

CODE[ ]

goto 2
goto 3
goto 4
goto 5
goto 6
goto 7
goto 8
goto 9
goto 10
goto 11
goto 12

```
2,3,12:    (* lose -- nothing to do *)
           goto xxxxx;

7,11:      wins := wins + 1;
           goto xxxxx;

4,5,6,
 8,9,10:   code for dealing with "getting his/her point";
           goto xxxxx;

xxxxx:     code for the statement following the case statement;
```

An internal label marking the start of the code following the case *statement.*

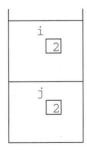

The variables j and i are completely decoupled. i is like any other local variable of procedure a, except that it is initialized on procedure entry, instead of being uninitialized. Any change made to i has no effect whatsoever on j. After execution of i := 3, memory looks like

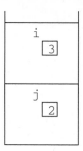

and after a returns, and the stack frame for the invocation of a is destroyed, memory looks like

The `writeln(j)` prints 2. With call-by-value, there is no way of modifying the actual argument.[1]

With call-by-reference, access is granted to the actual parameter and it can be changed. If the declaration of a had been

                    procedure a(var i: integer);

then the `writeln(j)` would have printed 3.

Puzzling question #2: Call-by-reference vs. call-by-value/result

EXERCISE 1—8   What will this Pascal program print?

```
 1 program Call(output);
 2   var n: integer;
 3   procedure Proc(var i, j: integer);
 4     begin
 5       i := i + 2;
 6       j := j + 1
 7     end; (* Proc *)
 8   begin
 9     n := 2;
10     Proc(n,n);
11     writeln(n:1)
12   end. (* Call *)
```

The correct answer is 5, not 3 (or 4), although, if you don't know how call-by-reference parameters are implemented, both 3 and 4 seem to be reasonable answers. One model of parameter passing that allows variables to be modified by the caller is *call-by-value/result* (also called *call-by-copy/restore*). This model is very easy to understand and is essentially the same model as call-by-value. When a procedure is called the actual arguments are first copied into the parameters of the called procedure. The called procedure then operates on these local variables. The only difference is that at the very last moment, right before the procedure

---

[1] This rule *appears* to be violated when pointer variables are passed by value. We will see, in Chapter 3, that this rule is *not* violated for pointer variables—but the rule must be properly understood in that context.

Sets in Pascal

Pascal's implementation of sets creates a lot of confusion, especially among beginning programmers. This is invariably caused by having a mental model of sets that is too closely tied to mathematics. The line of code which causes the difficulty is the innocent-looking

```
var LegalOptions: set of integer;
```

The intention of the programmer might be, at some point in the code, to provide the user with a sequentially numbered menu of choices.

Doesn't this declaration create an empty set, which will be filled later with lines like

```
LegalOptions := [1,3,5..10]
    (* Options 2 and 4 not currently implemented *)
```

If this is your mental model, the compile-time error on the line

```
var LegalOptions: set of integer;
```

comes as a rude shock. The problem is that in mathematics, we describe a set by listing its members surrounded by braces. We explicitly state which objects are in the set and all other objects are implicitly excluded. We also do not give the *base type* like we do in Pascal, and in mathematics a set can contain apparently unrelated items. The set containing the names of all people living in San Francisco, the positive integers less than 100, and the characters of the Chinese alphabet is a perfectly legal set, even if it seems to serve no purpose. There are some extremely useful sets, however, which also cannot be expressed in Pascal. You cannot declare sets of `real`. Another useful set is the *power set* of a set. Given a set S, the power set of S, written 2^S, is the set of subsets of S. As an example, if $S = \{1, 2, 3\}$, then the power set of S is $\{\emptyset, \{1\}, \{2\}, \{3\}, \{1, 2\}, \{1, 3\}, \{2, 3\}, \{1, 2, 3\}\}$. The notation 2^S is suggestive of the fact that if S is a finite set with n elements, then the number of elements in the power set is 2^n.

In Pascal, why does the line

```
var LegalOptions: set of integer;
```

produce an error and why can we not have a variable hold the power set of some other set? The answer is that the declaration

```
var A: set of ⟨base_type⟩;
```

allocates an array of bits, as shown in Figure 1–8, with one bit associated with each member of the base type. These bits exist whether or not a particular member of the base type is in the set. If the bit corresponding to the element is "turned on," meaning that it has a value of one, then the element is in the set, and if the bit is "turned off," it is not. The line

```
LegalOptions := [1,3,5..10]
```

assuming a proper declaration, like

```
var LegalOptions: set of 1..10;
```

(continued)

FIGURE 1–8   How Sets Are Implemented

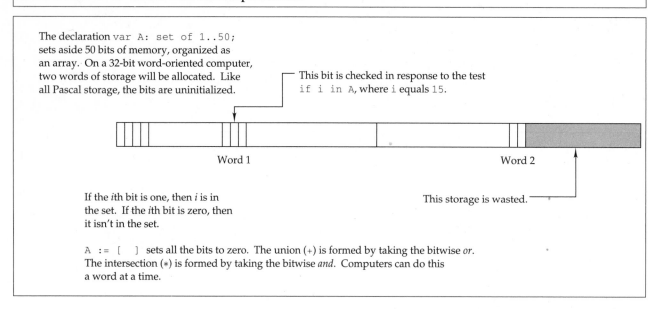

The declaration `var A: set of 1..50;`
sets aside 50 bits of memory, organized as
an array. On a 32-bit word-oriented computer,
two words of storage will be allocated. Like
all Pascal storage, the bits are uninitialized.

This bit is checked in response to the test
`if i in A`, where i equals `15`.

Word 1   Word 2

If the *i*th bit is one, then *i* is in
the set. If the *i*th bit is zero, then
it isn't in the set.

This storage is wasted.

`A := [   ]` sets all the bits to zero. The union (+) is formed by taking the bitwise *or*.
The intersection (∗) is formed by taking the bitwise *and*. Computers can do this
a word at a time.

**ABOVE
AND BEYOND**

(continued)

!
CAUTION

*Systems differ: Maximum set
size*

sets the bits in positions 1, 3, and 5 through 10 to one and those in positions
2 and 4 to zero. The line

                    `LegalOptions := [ ]`

logically sets `LegalOptions` to the empty set; inside the computer it sets all
the bits associated with `LegalOptions` to zero. This underlying model of
how sets are implemented explains why we get an error message when we
try to declare a set of `real`. What should be the bit position associated with
the number 2.3? The possibility of declaring a set of `integer` raises a more
interesting question. Abstractly, even though we can imagine a bit position for
each integer, we run into the practical problem that the integers are infinite in
number, so we would appear to be requiring an infinite number of bits. But
`integer` in Pascal isn't really the same as the integers of mathematics. It is
the subset of the mathematical integers in the range `-maxint..maxint`. So
in theory, and according to the standard,

              `var LegalOptions: set of integer;`

is legal. But each compiler has certain limitations built into it because of limitations in the underlying hardware. To expect a compiler to reserve space for
`2*maxint + 1` bits, especially on a computer that has $2^{31} - 1$ as its maximum
integer, is excessive. Systems vary considerably in how large a ⟨base_type⟩
they allow. UNIX Pascal compilers typically allow the ⟨base_type⟩ to contain
32,768 elements, while Turbo Pascal limits the size to 256 elements. This is
somewhat limiting, but fortunately is large enough to allow `set of char`,
which is one of the most frequent uses of sets.

The implementation of the operators on sets is now clear. The union operator, +, is nothing other than the bitwise *or* of the two sets and the intersection
operator, ∗, is the bitwise *and*. Most hardware can perform these operations a

(continued)

word at a time, so these operators, while theoretically taking time proportional to the size of the base type, are very fast if the base type is small. The `in` operator amounts to checking a specific bit to see if it is on or off.

Because sets do not model their use in mathematics, sets are not often used in Pascal programs, and other programming languages have not adopted the concept. There is one common use for them, however, brought about by the lack of a default option in `case` statements. Consider the example of letting a user select an option from a list of options, but suppose we wish to use mnemonics instead of the numbers 1 through 10. The code might look something like

```
writeln('Option menu');
writeln('   <A>dd a name to the database');
writeln('   <D>elete a name from the database');
writeln('   <C>hange the data associated with a name');
writeln('   <P>rint the database in alphabetical order');
writeln('   <Q>uit');
write  ('Select option: '); readln(ch);
case ch of
   'A','a': ...
   'C','c': ...
        ⋮
end;
```

The problem with this code is that if the user types a punctuation mark or a letter for which we have no option, the `case` statement will fail. In standard Pascal, we could attempt to specify an error option by including a line like

```
'B','b','E','e',...: ...
```

but this is ungainly and may not even be possible, since not every keystroke corresponds to a constant of type `char` (carriage return and tab are the most obvious examples). This effect can be achieved by writing

```
if ch in ['A','a', 'C','c', 'D','d', 'P','p', 'Q','q']
   then case ch of
           'A','a': ...
              ⋮
        end
   else perform error processing
```

returns, the values are *copied back* into the variables of the caller. If `var` in Pascal specified call-by-value/result, the history of the execution of `program Call` would be as shown in Figure 1–9. The value of `n` after `Proc` returns would be either 3 or 4, depending on the order in which the parameters are copied back—it need not be left to right. Pascal *does not use call-by-value/result*.

The implementation of call-by-reference is more subtle. Returning to our simple example of `procedure a`, the stack, after `a` is called, looks like

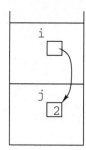

Despite the declaration var i: integer, i is not, deep down inside the computer, an integer variable. Storage for i is allocated in the stack frame for a, but what it contains is a *pointer to an integer variable*. Because of the var, whenever a references i the compiler actually generates a reference to where i is pointing; in this case, to j. Thus if a contains a line like

$$\ldots := i + 1$$

the reference to i actually fetches the current contents of j. Similarly, the line

$$i := 3$$

does not change i, which continues to point to j. It changes the memory location to which i points; namely j. We now see why the program of *Puzzling question #2* prints 5. The history of the program execution is given in Figure 1–10.

Notice that, unlike with call-by-value/result, a change to the var parameter is reflected back to the caller *immediately* and not just when the procedure returns. The line

$$i := i + 2$$

changes n from 2 to 4 right then and there. Thus the line

$$j := j + 1$$

finds that j, which is really n, is 4, which it changes to 5.

FIGURE 1–9   The Effect of Call-By-Value/Result

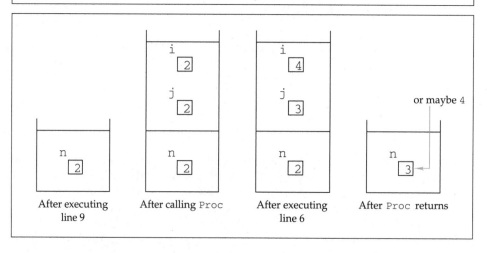

FIGURE 1–10 The Effect of Call-By-Reference

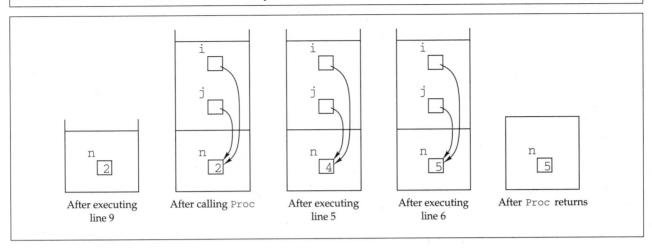

After executing   After calling Proc   After executing   After executing   After Proc returns
line 9   line 5   line 6

We can finally explain why the declaration for BinarySearch is

```
procedure BinarySearch(var (* for speed *) A: Data;...
```

The reason for var (* for speed *) *in* BinarySearch

and not

```
procedure BinarySearch(A: Data;...
```

If A is passed by value, the entire array has to be copied, which takes time proportional to the length of the array, even though the algorithm subsequently examines only a few locations within A. The running time would all be in the call to the procedure—it would take as long to complete the call as it would take to search the array sequentially, and the entire algorithm would take $O(n)$ time instead of the $O(\log n)$ that we expect. All the benefit of using binary search would be lost. On the other hand, passing A by reference is no more complicated than passing j to i by reference in procedure a. When an array is passed by reference all that is passed is a single pointer, which points to the first element of the array. The stack frame for BinarySearch looks like

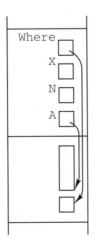

X and N are copied, but this takes little time because they are just integers. Where points back to the variable that is to receive the answer. It has to be passed by

reference because the answer must be passed back. A also points back into the stack frame of the caller. This allows references to be made to locations in the array without the expense, in both time and space, of copying the array. All `var` parameters take up the same amount of space, the space needed to hold a pointer.

In considering whether A should be passed by value or by reference, we have a classic conflict between the principles of software engineering and concerns about efficiency. Small gains in efficiency, with a concomitant loss of clarity, are to be studiously avoided, but this is one instance where the principles of software engineering must be violated—the gain is just too great. To stress the read-only nature of A, the code contains the comment (* `for speed` *), which at least alerts other programmers to our intentions.

Strong Typing

One of the great strengths of Pascal is **strong typing**. These words are often bandied about, and being strongly typed is regarded in the software engineering community as a "good thing," although, the original version of C was not strongly typed. Overzealous application of strong typing is also why Pascal is so often criticized as not being a "real" programming language—too many useful things are hard or impossible to do. Strong typing means that every variable has a type and that operations involving variables of two different types are strictly controlled. With the exception of the basic operations, like +, -, and < operating on the types `integer` and `real`, there isn't much interaction allowed between variables of different types.

Puzzling question #3: Passing expressions to parameters

EXERCISE 1—9 What is the result of compiling and running the following two programs? Respond to the `readln` with both `50` and `101`.

```
 1 program IntegerToSmall(input,output);
 2   type small = 1..100;
 3   var n: integer;
 4   procedure Proc(i: small);
 5     begin
 6       writeln(i:3)
 7     end; (* Proc *)
 8 begin
 9   readln(n);
10   Proc(n)
11 end. (* IntegerToSmall *)
```

```
 1 program IntegerToSmall(input,output);
 2   type small = 1..100;
 3   var n: integer;
 4   procedure Proc(var i: small);
 5     begin
 6       writeln(i:3)
 7     end; (* Proc *)
 8 begin
 9   readln(n);
10   Proc(n)
11 end. (* IntegerToSmall *)
```

If the results of running these two programs didn't conform to your expectations, you might examine the programs on page 41, after the intervening Above and Beyond box.

How Other Languages Handle Parameters

How do other procedural languages handle some of the issues raised in this section? Independent compilation, which is present in FORTRAN, C, and Ada, complicates type checking across the procedure interface, since the complete source code may not be available to the compiler at any one time. Consider the distinction that Pascal draws between call-by-value parameters and call-by-reference parameters. In an environment where independent compilation is permitted the declaration of a procedure may not even be available when the call is compiled. The compiler not only can't do type checking, it cannot even know which parameters are to be passed by value and which are to be passed by reference—it will not know what code to compile.

FORTRAN

This is the situation faced in FORTRAN. One solution is to support only the call-by-reference parameter passing mechanism, leaving the programmer of the calling routine with the burden of making sure that the parameters are of the correct type. If a call-by-value parameter is desired, the programmer of the called procedure can emulate the desired behavior by copying the parameter into a local variable and never referencing the parameter again. An interesting question is raised by the program `PassingExpressions`. Should such a program be legal in FORTRAN. Should we be able to pass expressions to parameters? If the only mechanism supported is call-by-reference, a simple solution is to require the actual arguments to be variables. This would be easy for the FORTRAN compiler to check. This approach places the burden on the writer of the calling procedure: if it is necessary to pass an expression, it can first be assigned to a temporary variable, and then this temporary variable can be passed. Passing an expression to a formal parameter is such a common occurrence, however, that FORTRAN allows it—the compiler creates an unnamed temporary, which is then passed to the called procedure. If the called procedure makes an assignment to the formal parameter, it just changes the unnamed temporary, which has no effect on any of the variables of the calling procedure. While execution proceeds without trouble, if an unnamed temporary is changed by the called procedure, it is a sure sign that there has been an error of communication—the called program is trying to return a result, but the result of the computation cannot be used by the calling procedure, because it cannot get to the unnamed temporary.

The very nature of the parameter passing mechanism makes unconstrained arrays a natural part of FORTRAN. The declaration of the binary search procedure in FORTRAN is

```
SUBROUTINE BSERCH(A,N,X,WHERE)
INTEGER A(*),N,X,WHERE
```

The asterisk in `A(*)` informs the compiler that `A` is an unconstrained array.

C and C++

C faces the same problems as FORTRAN, though it solves them quite differently. In C, the only parameter passing mechanism is call-by-value. This would seem to preclude the possibility of returning any results to the calling procedure, which would be a serious limitation. C gets around this difficulty by including a powerful operator known as the "address-of" operator (`&`). By passing the address of a variable to the called procedure, the stack frame looks exactly like it does when Pascal passes a parameter by reference. In C, the declaration of the binary search procedure is

(continued)

**ABOVE
AND BEYOND**

(continued)

```
void BinarySearch(int A[], int N, int X, int *Where);
```

and a typical call is

```
BinarySearch(B,len,obj,&loc);
```

`len` and `obj` are passed by value to `N` and `X`. The *address* of the integer variable `loc` is passed to `Where`, a variable that is declared to be a *pointer to an integer*. The ∗ before `Where` is the "keyword" that says that `Where` is a pointer to a "thing" and not a "thing" itself. References to `Where` in the body of `BinarySearch` must all be preceded by an ∗, which tells the compiler not to reference `Where`, but to address the location to which `Where` points, that is, to address `loc`. The issue of passing an expression to a call-by-reference parameter does not exist in C, because C does not have call-by-reference. But what if `&(2*n)` is passed to a variable declared as `int *i`? This is not legal. The address-of operator cannot be applied to an expression. Forcing every reference to `Where` to be preceded by an ∗ is ungainly and C++, an extension of C, includes call-by-reference parameters.

There is an intimate connection between arrays and pointers in C. Passing the array name `B`, as we have done in the call, can be thought of as a shorthand for passing `&B[0]`, that is, short for "passing the address of the first location in the array." (All arrays in C start at zero.) Like FORTRAN, unconstrained arrays are a natural part of C. The declaration `int A[]` says that `A` is to be viewed as an unconstrained array. (References to `A[m]` are not preceded by an ∗.)

C provides a mechanism for performing type checking when independent compilation is used. C allows, but does not require, the heading of a procedure to be separated from its body. By placing the heading, which is really the publicly visible interface to the procedure, in a separate file, other procedures which call the procedure can have access to the declaration for purposes of type checking. This "optionally available" philosophy is deeply ingrained in C. The attitude of the designers of C is that the programmer is responsible for his or her own actions. The language should not inhibit the programmer from doing what needs to be done, even if it is dangerous. A prize example of this is typeless parameters. It is possible to declare a formal parameter as having type `void *`. The parameter is effectively a call-by-reference parameter to a "typeless thing." This is needed to write generic sorting routines that can sort integers, reals, strings, or, in fact, anything at all. It is also needed to write a routine like the Pascal `readln`, which is capable of reading into variables

Turbo Pascal

that have different types. In recognition of the occasional need for untyped call-by-reference parameters and unconstrained arrays, Turbo Pascal follows the lead of C and allows untyped `var` parameters. In Turbo Pascal, we can write the declaration of `BinarySearch` as

```
procedure BinarySearch(var (* untyped *) A; N: integer; X: object;
                       var Where: integer);
```

The body of the procedure `BinarySearch` must contain the declaration

```
type Data = array [1..maxint] of object;
```

No variables are ever declared to be of type `Data`. A variable of this type would use more memory than is available on the computer. This declaration

(continued)

is needed so that the compiler can be informed that A is an array of integers. It is used as follows:

```
if Data(A)[m] < X
```

The expression Data(A), known as a *cast*, tells the compiler to treat A as an array (of great length) of object. This allows the address of A[m] to be computed correctly.

Ada

Ada has much the same underlying philosophy as Pascal. It is also a strongly typed language. With respect to parameter passing, there are two main differences. First, while the standard describes the internal mechanism used to pass parameters, the specification of a procedure heading is directed more toward expressing the programmer's intentions. A formal parameter can be declared to be in, out, or in out. A parameter declared in cannot be modified by the called procedure. This is more strict than saying modifications are not passed back to the caller. When a variable is declared in, the called procedure cannot assign a value to the variable—it simply cannot appear on the left-hand side of the assignment operator. Questions of implementation, "is it passed by value or is it passed by reference," do not arise. (C++ implements in as well, although the keyword is const.) An out parameter can be assigned to, but not used. It is for returning results. An in out parameter can be both read from and written to. The declaration of BinarySearch in Ada is

```
type DATA is array (INTEGER range <>) of OBJECT;
procedure BINARYSEARCH(A: in DATA; X: in OBJECT; WHERE: out INTEGER);
```

Because A is declared in, it cannot be accidentally modified, even though it is passed by reference. The range <> in the declaration of DATA specifies an unconstrained array. There is no need to pass the length of the array explicitly. When an array is passed, its characteristics are implicitly passed as well. The lower index can be retrieved with A'FIRST, while the upper index can be retrieved with A'LAST. This allows for subscript-out-of-range checking of unconstrained arrays. Ada requires the declaration of a procedure to be separated from the specification of its body. It also has an elaborate mechanism for performing type checking of independently compiled procedures.

```
1  program PassingExpressions(input,output);      1  program PassingExpressions(input,output);
2    var n: integer;                              2    var n: integer;
3    procedure Proc(i: integer);                  3    procedure Proc(var i: integer);
4      begin                                      4      begin
5        writeln(i:3)                             5        writeln(i:3)
6      end; (* Proc *)                            6      end; (* Proc *)
7    begin                                        7    begin
8      readln(n);                                 8      readln(n);
9      Proc(2*n)                                  9      Proc(2*n)
10   end. (* PassingExpressions *)                10   end. (* PassingExpressions *)
```

The first of these two programs performs as you might expect: it prints twice the value you type in. The second gives a *compilation* error. These results follow naturally from the mechanisms by which parameters are passed. In the first, the expression 2*n is evaluated and the result is assigned to the local variable i of Proc. Passing 2*n by value is like executing the assignment statement

$$i := 2*n$$

only `Proc` doesn't know that the right-hand side is `2*n` and the main program doesn't know that the left-hand side is `i`.

The difficulty with the second program is that the variable `i`, being a `var` parameter, is supposed to point back to the actual parameter in the stack frame for the main program. But what is the location of `2*n`? Expressions, unlike variables, aren't associated with memory locations, so there is no place for `i` to point back to, and the call is disallowed. Because in standard Pascal the entire program is available to the compiler at once—it is all contained between the `program` ... and the ... `end`.—this error can be detected at compile time.

The situation with the program `IntegerToSmall` is similar, but more subtle. In the first version the call effectively executes the line

$$i := n$$

Whether this is legal depends on the value of `n` *at runtime*. Assignment between variables whose types are subrange types of the same base type are allowed, but the value assigned is supposed to be checked to make sure it is in range. (Some compilers, for reasons of efficiency, allow this range checking to be disabled.) Thus the program prints `50` when the user inputs `50`, but it gives a runtime error when the user inputs `101`.

But what is wrong with the second version? Why does it give a *compile-time* error? The answer is that the type-checking rules for the call-by-reference parameter passing mechanism are stricter than for the call-by-value mechanism. The rule in Pascal is: the **actual parameter** and the **formal parameter** must have *exactly* the same type. `small` and `integer` are not the same type—the call is disallowed. The requirement that range checking be performed is the driving force behind Pascal's strict type-checking rule for call-by-reference parameters. The following program illuminates the issue.

```
 1  program SmallToInteger(input,output);
 2    type small1 = 1..100;
 3          small2 = -50..50;
 4    var i: small1;
 5        j: small2;
 6    procedure GetData(var k: integer);
 7      begin
 8        readln(k)
 9      end; (* GetData *)
10    begin
11      GetData(i);
12      GetData(j)
13    end. (* SmallToInteger *)
```

This program is not syntactically legal, but to see the difficulties that arise if we relax the strict type-checking rule for call-by-reference parameters, imagine for the moment that it is. If the user responds to the `readln` with `100`, then assignment to `k`, which is really an assignment to either `i` or `j`, would be legal in one case, but not in the other. The nature of the check that needs to be made here is different than the nature of the check that needs to be made in the first of the two `IntegerToSmall` programs. In `IntegerToSmall`, the information to perform the check is completely contained within the procedure `Proc`: the value about to be assigned to `i` has to be checked against the bounds specified by `small`. The issue is the *value* of `n`, not its *type*. In `SmallToInteger` the check depends not only on knowledge gleaned from the source code of `GetData`, it depends on where in the main program `GetData` is called from. The legal range of values is different for the calls on lines 11 and 12. Our model of how procedures should operate is that they are isolated and should not need to know from where they are called, except to perform the return. Allowing a variable of type subrange-of-`integer` to be passed by reference to a variable of type `integer` violates this software engineering principle and the language forbids it.

We need to consider the question "what does it mean to say that two variables have the same type?"

Puzzling question #4: Name vs. structure equivalence

EXERCISE 1—10   A program has these declarations.

```
const MAX = ...;
type IntVector = array [1..MAX] of integer;
     Data      = array [1..MAX] of integer;
var  A, B: IntVector;
     C:      Data;
     D:      Data;
     E, F: array [1..MAX] of integer;
     G:      array [1..MAX] of integer;
```

In Pascal, if two variables have the same type, they can be assigned one to the other. Thus A := B is a legal assignment statement, since they both have the type `IntVector`. Because A and B are arrays, the statement A := B means to copy every element of B into the corresponding location of A. It is as if we had written the loop

```
for i := 1 to MAX do A[i] : = B[i]
```

Which of these lines are legal assignment statements?

```
C := D;
A := C;
A := E;
E := F;
E := G;
```

Of these, only C := D and E := F are legal. The reason is that Pascal uses *name equivalence*, meaning that two types are the same only if they have the same name. It is not enough for them to have the same structure. So, while all seven variables have the same structure, which is

```
array [1..MAX] of integer
```

they cannot all be arbitrarily assigned one to the other. Since C and D both are of type `Data`, the assignment statement C := D is legal, even though they are not declared on the same line. But C cannot be assigned to A, since they have different types. The case of E := F and E := G is particularly tricky. E := F is legal, but E := G is not. The reason is that E and F have the same type. While the type names of E and F are anonymous, by being declared together, their type names are the same. On the other hand, by being declared in different declarations, E and G have different anonymous type names. An anonymous name can never be the same as an explicit name, so A := E also is not legal.

The statement

```
for i := 1 to MAX do A[i] := E[i]
```

is perfectly legal, however. The assignment statement, A[i] := E[i], is between two variables of the same type, the type integer. Because the type of a var parameter must be the same as the type of its actual argument, the type declaration in a procedure heading must be

var ⟨variable⟩: ⟨type_name⟩

All of this leads up to one of the great uglinesses of Pascal: it is essentially impossible to write library routines. The procedure for binary search makes this clear. The declaration of that procedure should really be

Library routines

```
type Data = array [1.. ] of object; (* no upper bound *)
procedure BinarySearch(var A: Data; N: integer; ...
```

Ignoring the syntax rules of Pascal, does this declaration make sense? Yes! Because A is passed by reference, A is just a pointer, and while the procedure needs to know the type of the elements that make up the array, so that it can correctly address A[m] and compile code for the comparisons of A[m] and X, it doesn't need to know how long the array is (except to do subscript-out-of-range checking). When, as in the case of binary search, the *algorithm* needs to know the length of the array, this information can be passed separately.

An array with unspecified bounds is called an **unconstrained array**. Restrictions have to be placed on the use of unconstrained arrays. While an appropriate type for formal call-by-reference parameters, it makes no sense to declare a variable as being of type unconstrained array. That is, we cannot have the declaration

var B: Data;

in either the main program or in the variable declaration sections of procedures. This restriction is needed because, when storage for a variable is actually allocated, the runtime support system needs to know how much space to allocate. When encountering an unconstrained array as a formal call-by-reference parameter, the compiler knows how much storage to allocate: one word for the pointer to the starting location of the array.

How serious is the lack of unconstrained arrays? After all, if a program needs a binary search routine we can just copy the *source code* from the library into the program and adjust the type declarations to suit our current situation. One drawback to physically copying and modifying the code is that this creates multiple copies (what if we find a bug or what if we improve the algorithm at a later time?), a situation that is error prone. To develop libraries properly we need both unconstrained arrays and another extension to standard Pascal: independent compilation, a topic discussed in Chapter 2. The lack of these capabilities in standard Pascal is a serious deficiency of the language.

Even if we are willing to copy the source code for a procedure into our program, overly strict adherence to strong typing and the lack of unconstrained arrays creates problems. Consider a program that needs, at different times, to search two sorted arrays of integers. If these arrays are of different types, we will need two copies of BinarySearch, one for each type. The two procedures will differ in only the most superficial way. One copy will have the declaration var A: Data1, while the other will have declaration var A: Data2. Except for the names of the procedures and this one change, the code of the two procedures will be *exactly* the same.

EXERCISE 1–11   What does the program in Figure 1–11 print when the user responds to the

Puzzling question #5: Visibility and scope

$$readln(ch)$$

on line 19 by typing a blank? Does it print 1 or does it print 2?

Your answer to this question depends on whether you think the reference to i in the writeln on line 7 refers to the i of the main program or the i of proc2. The answer is 1, even though the calling sequence is main calls proc2 calls proc1. The rule in Pascal is

When a variable is referenced, the compiler searches outward, using the static nesting of the procedures, starting with the current procedure and ending with the main program, looking for the innermost declaration of a variable with that name. If no declaration is found, the compiler issues an error message.

Scoping in Pascal

The important clause in this rule is "using the *static* nesting of the procedures." Since there is no variable named i in proc1 and since proc1 is nested within the main program, the reference to i on line 7 refers to the i declared in main.

This is the natural behavior for a compiled, block-structured, procedural language. The compiler, when it compiles the line writeln(i), cannot possibly

FIGURE 1–11   **Static vs. Dynamic Scoping**

```
1    program main(input,output);
2       var i: integer;
3           ch: char;
4
5       procedure proc1;
6          begin
7             writeln(i)
8          end; (* proc1 *)
9
10      procedure proc2;
11         var i: integer;
12         begin
13            i := 2;
14            proc1
15         end; (* proc2 *)
16
17      begin (* main *)
18         i := 1;
19         readln(ch);
20         if ch <> ' '
21            then proc1
22            else proc2
23      end. (* main *)
```

Suppose the user responds to this request with a blank.

main → proc2 → proc1

Calling sequence

Dynamically Allocated Arrays and Work Arrays

Suppose we want to write a library routine for sorting integers. This presupposes both independent compilation and unconstrained-arrays, which, while not available in standard Pascal, are both available in Turbo Pascal. We expect the declaration of the procedure to look like

```
procedure Sort(var (* untyped *) A; N: integer);
```

Because its worst-case running time is $O(n \log n)$ one of the most popular sorting algorithms for this task is mergesort. The algorithm has one drawback, however: it needs a second array the same size as A to hold data on a temporary basis. This is not an isolated example. Many algorithms involving matrices and vectors require an auxiliary matrix or vector of the same size. What is needed is a facility where we can declare, inside the procedure Sort, a second array, B, of sufficient size. We cannot do this in Turbo Pascal. Declaring B to be of type Data, where

```
type Data = array [1..maxint] of integer;
```

would make B sufficiently large, but it demands too much storage from the computer. But if we place some limit, like 1000, on the size of Data, while it will have no effect on references to Data(A)[i] (as long as subscript-out-of-range checking is turned off), B might be of insufficient length. What we desire is the ability to declare an array whose size is determined at runtime. Neither Pascal nor FORTRAN 77, the traditional language of science and engineering, provide any way of declaring arrays whose size is not known at compile time. Arrays whose bounds are specified at runtime are known as *dynamically allocated arrays*. Ada and PL/I have this capability built into

(continued)

determine whether proc1 will ultimately be called by proc2 or directly by main. If the dynamic behavior of the program were used to resolve references to nonlocal variables, the compiler would have to generate considerably more complex code. Consider, for example, the effect of a slight modification to the program of Figure 1–11: declare an integer variable j in proc1, replace the writeln on line 7 by j := i, and change the declaration of i on line 11 to real. If the dynamic behavior of the program were used to resolve references to i in proc1, then the very legality of the line j := i cannot be determined until the line executes. In the calling sequence where main calls proc1 directly, j := i would assign an integer to an integer variable, whereas in the calling sequence where main calls proc2 calls proc1, j := i would attempt to assign a real to an integer variable, which is illegal in Pascal. Static scoping allows type conflicts to be detected at compile time, which makes for more efficient code. Moreover, it is easier for humans to understand programs that use static scoping rules—after all, when we stare at a page of code we see its static structure, not its dynamic behavior.

Looking at the situation more abstractly, we see that we need to clarify the relationship between the concepts of *lifetime*, *scope*, and *visibility*. In our discussion of stack frames we saw that the lifetime of a variable is related to the program's dynamic behavior: a variable comes into existence when the procedure in which it is declared is entered and it ceases to exist upon exit from that procedure.

the language, and while C does not, dynamically allocated arrays can be obtained by using the powerful memory management routine `malloc` found in the standard C library. C++ has dynamically allocated arrays built-in, but the implementation is more C-like than Ada-like.

How can we handle this problem in Pascal and FORTRAN 77? The problem isn't so much that the size of B isn't known until runtime; it is that the size of B isn't known to `Sort` until runtime. The size of the auxiliary array is certainly known to the caller of `Sort`. After all, it declared the array passed to A in the first place. The standard solution to this problem, even if it is somewhat inelegant, is to change the declaration of `Sort` to

```
procedure Sort(var (* untyped *) A, B; N: integer);
```

and let the caller declare and pass in both the array to be sorted and the temporary array. This temporary array is known as a ***work array***. This solution is inelegant because it meddles with the interface to `Sort`. The user of a library routine shouldn't be concerned with the algorithm it employs, and certainly not with the details of its implementation. In an environment that allows precompiled procedures, if the declaration of `Sort` remains

```
procedure Sort(var (* untyped *) A; N: integer);
```

we can change the body of `Sort` and recompile it and the user will be none the wiser. We can change the algorithm to something better or fix bugs, and the user's program is not affected. By including the declaration of B in the interface, if we change our underlying algorithm to one that no longer needs extra storage, the user will have to change the calling program, which defeats the purpose of libraries.

Scope and visibility relate to the program's static structure. Scope is that portion of the program in which a variable can *potentially* be referenced. Visibility is that portion of the program where the variable can *actually* be referenced. The difference between the two concepts is illustrated in Figure 1–12. Inside `proc2`, references made to `i` refer to the variable named `i` that is local to that procedure and not to the variable of the same name declared in the main program. If the local variable of `proc2` were renamed `j`, then the `i` of the main program would become visible.

The automatic importation of variables to an inner procedure, as implied by the scope and visibility rules of Pascal, can lead to hard-to-find bugs. It is easy to write a line like

```
for i := 1 to n do ...
```

in an inner procedure, while forgetting to include the corresponding declaration for `i`. If, by chance, there is a variable named `i` in the main program, the compiler will find nothing wrong. When the inner procedure is called, the value of `i` in the main program will be changed, a side effect that is easily overlooked. For this reason, it would be advantageous if inner routines that reference variables declared in outer routines were required to state their intention to do so explicitly. The syntax might look something like

```
import i: integer;
```

which would allow for type checking. Referring to the structure of the nested procedures in Figure 1–11, such a declaration would be necessary within `proc1` if that procedure wished to access the `i` of the main program.

FIGURE 1–12   **The Difference Between Visibility and Scope**

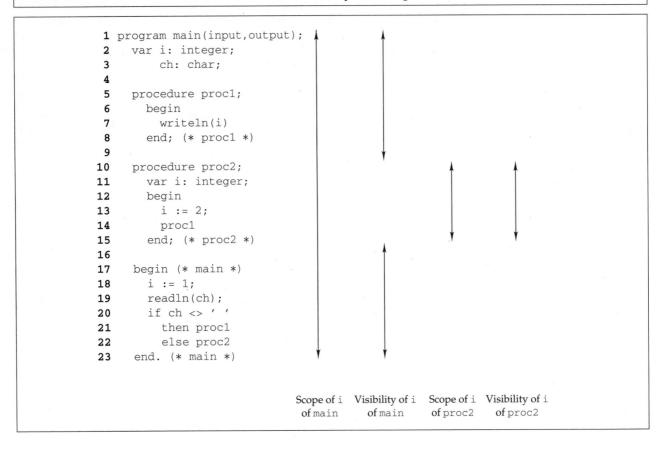

```
 1  program main(input,output);
 2     var i: integer;
 3         ch: char;
 4
 5     procedure proc1;
 6       begin
 7         writeln(i)
 8       end; (* proc1 *)
 9
10     procedure proc2;
11        var i: integer;
12        begin
13          i := 2;
14          proc1
15        end; (* proc2 *)
16
17     begin (* main *)
18        i := 1;
19        readln(ch);
20        if ch <> ' '
21          then proc1
22          else proc2
23     end. (* main *)
```

Scope of i   Visibility of i   Scope of i   Visibility of i
of main   of main   of proc2   of proc2

1.5 eoln AND eof

eoln and eof, two small functions that shouldn't even be in the Pascal language, cause an endless amount of trouble and Turbo Pascal's nonstandard handling of end-of-line and end-of-file just adds to the confusion. By looking at why these functions are in the language and how they work, maybe the confusion they create can be laid to rest. To jump right into the fray, let us consider which, if any, of the three programs of Figure 1–13 correctly echoes input to output, where the input is redirected to come from a file through the command line

echo.exe < sampltxt.dat

The first program *ought* to do the job, and it will when compiled with Turbo Pascal, but the correct way to echo a text file, so that the program works when compiled with both Turbo and standard Pascal, is given in the third program. The first program is not correct, because in standard Pascal, read(ch) cannot read in a "carriage return." The reason for this is historical. The first Pascal compiler became available in 1970 and was developed for the CDC 6400 computer, a computer that at the time didn't even have interactive terminals. The program, as well as the data on which the program was to be run, was typed on punch cards. Every line was the same length, rounded out with trailing blanks. The character set of this computer was not even the *ASCII* character set that is common today, but a 64-character character set that did not include { or } or a code for carriage return. This is why Pascal has (* and *) as an alternate form of comment delimiters, and why it has eoln.

FIGURE 1–13   Echoing the Input

```
 1 program echo(input,output);
 2   (* Echo the contents of the file  input . *)
 3   var ch: char;
 4   begin
 5     while not eof do
 6       begin
 7         read(ch); (* get the next character *)
 8         write(ch) (* echo the character *)
 9       end
10   end. (* echo *)
```

Version 1

```
 1 program echo(input,output);
 2   (* Echo the contents of the file  input . *)
 3   var ch: char;
 4   begin
 5     while not eof do
 6       begin
 7         read(ch); (* get next character *)
 8         if eoln   (* if the character is a carriage return *)
 9           then writeln   (* write out a carriage return *)
10           else write(ch) (* echo the character *)
11       end
12   end. (* echo *)
```

Version 2

```
 1 program echo(input,output);
 2   (* Echo the contents of the file  input . *)
 3   var ch: char;
 4   begin
 5     while not eof do
 6       if eoln (* if the next character is a carriage return *)
 7         then begin
 8                readln; (* throw it away,... *)
 9                writeln (* ...but don't forget to echo it *)
10              end
11         else begin
12                read(ch); (* get the next character,... *)
13                write(ch) (* ...and echo it *)
14              end
15   end. (* echo *)
```

Version 3

The situation is hardly better today. The hidden character at the end of a line displayed on a video screen, the logical end-of-line, may or may not be a single character. Many operating systems use the combination of ^M (control-M, an ASCII 13) and ^J (ASCII 10), which are officially known, respectively, as *carriage return* and *line feed*, to specify the logical end-of-line. Some use the same combination in the reverse order and some, use just one of these characters to signal the end-of-line. UNIX, for example, uses only ^J. The distinction between carriage return and line feed goes back to the days of mechanical typewriters, where returning the carriage and rolling the platen were separate operations.

FOR YOUR INFORMATION

eoln, eof, and Reading Integers

As confusing as `eoln` and `eof` are, the situation is made still more complicated by the decision to make the procedure `read` programmer-friendly. If the program declaration is

```
program ⟨program_name⟩(input,output,myfile);
```

where `myfile` is declared as

```
var myfile: file of integer;
```

`read` statements involving `myfile` must have the form `read(myfile,i)`, where `i` is an `integer` variable. In addition, the integers in `myfile` are not stored as we see them on paper or type them into a data file. They are not sequences of characters that humans interpret as integers. They are integers as the underlying computer represents them in hardware. Because such a file is not an ASCII file, it has to have been created by a previous run of a program, one that wrote `myfile` as a `file of integer`. If `myfile` is a file of `StudentRecord`, some complex `record`, the same holds true: `read` statements must have the form `read(myfile,Student)`, where `Student` is of type `StudentRecord`.

For the convenience of the programmer, Pascal has a special file type called `text`. It is almost, but not quite, a `file of char`. A `file of char` cannot contain logical end-of-line characters and can be read only with `read(⟨filename⟩,ch)`, where `ch` is of type `char`. A file of type `text` not only contains logical end-of-line characters, it allows characters, integers, and real numbers to be read from the same file. For example, the programmer can perform `read(i)` on the file `input`, where `i` is a variable of type `integer`. This exception to the strict rule that when reading a file of type ⟨type_name⟩ you can only read into a variable of type ⟨type_name⟩ makes it much easier to enter data into a program. You can type the *characters* 231 and have it interpreted as the *integer* two hundred thirty-one. But since a file of type `text` ultimately consists of characters, problems can arise: what if blanks and logical end-of-line characters precede the integer? What if some character that cannot be part of an integer precedes the integer? What if an English word is next in the file, where the programmer expected an integer? The rule is

Systems differ

> When performing `read(i)`, where `i` is of type `integer`, *blanks and logical end-of-line characters will be skipped until*
>
> ■ *The file becomes empty, at which time an error condition is raised (standard Pascal) or a zero is returned (Turbo Pascal).*
> ■ *A character that is not a blank or logical end-of-line is found.*

In the latter case, in standard Pascal, the longest sequence of characters that could comprise an integer is interpreted as an integer. Characters are read up to and including the last character that forms the integer, but not even one character beyond. Thus, an integer can abut a comma or period in the

(continued)

input. If no integer is present at all, say an English word appears next in the input stream, an error condition is raised. In Turbo Pascal, the runtime system attempts to interpret the sequence of characters up to, but not including, the next blank or end-of-line character as an integer. If these characters form a legal integer, the value is returned, otherwise an error condition is raised. In Turbo Pascal, an integer *cannot* abut a comma or period. The rule for reading real numbers is the same. These rules taken together work well, but have one unexpected consequence. In standard Pascal, will the program

```pascal
1 program SumOfIntegers(input,output);
2   (* Sum the numbers in the input stream. *)
3   var i, sum: integer;
4   begin
5     sum := 0;
6     while not eof do
7       begin
8         read(i);
9         sum := sum + i
10      end;
11    writeln('The sum was: ',sum:1)
12  end. (* SumOfIntegers *)
```

compute the sum of the integers in the input file and print the answer? No! It will produce a runtime error message about attempting to read past the end of the file. Why is this so? The answer is that when the last integer is read, the file is *not* empty. The programmer may have been thinking of the file as containing only integers, but what it really contains is characters, and after reading the last integer there is at least one more character in the file, the logical end-of-line after the last integer. Since the file is not empty, eof returns false, and the read(i) is executed. This call to read(i) begins by skipping the final logical end-of-line character and then, running out of characters to read, causes the error condition "attempt to read past end of file" to be raised. This problem can be fixed by changing the read(i) to a readln(i), but now the data must be entered one integer per line. readln(i) will read the integer and then throw away everything else on the line, including the logical end-of-line that marks the end of the line.

While in Turbo Pascal the program SumOfIntegers will return the correct answer, it does so more by luck than by design. In Turbo Pascal, instead of raising an error condition when the last read(i) is attempted, a zero will be returned. The final execution of sum := sum + i will thus add zero to sum, which will have no effect. But notice that if we were computing the product, or counting the number of integers in the file, instead of finding their sum, the program would not work correctly in either standard or Turbo Pascal. In standard Pascal we would continue to get "attempt to read past end-of-file," while in Turbo Pascal the product would come out as zero and the count would come out one too high.

(continued)

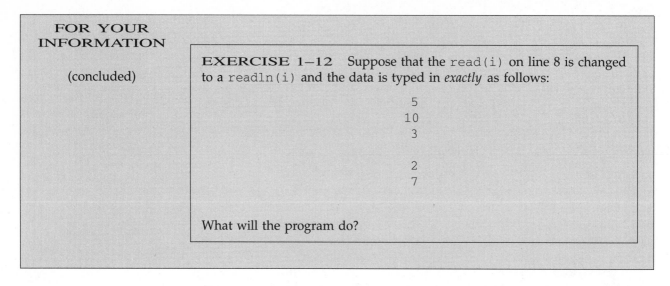

EXERCISE 1–12   Suppose that the `read(i)` on line 8 is changed to a `readln(i)` and the data is typed in *exactly* as follows:

5

10

3

2

7

What will the program do?

!
CAUTION

Systems differ: `read(ch)`

Pascal hides the system details concerning end-of-line from the programmer. In standard Pascal, when the program executes a `read(ch)` it reads the next character, but if that next character is the logical end-of-line, then `ch` is set to the blank character, no matter how the logical end-of-line is represented by the underlying computer. Thus, the first version of the program in Figure 1–13 echoes the input, except it converts all the logical end-of-line characters to blanks, and the output appears as one very long line. Turbo Pascal takes a more modern approach. It assumes that its input comes from an ASCII file and it reads each character exactly as it is stored in the file, with no internal translations. Thus when `read(ch)` encounters a ^M or a ^J it just reads in that character, and `write(ch)` simply echoes what was read.

`eoln`

Of course, in certain applications it is necessary to be able to tell when we have reached the end of a line. As an example, consider reading the response to the prompt

```
write('Type your name: ')
```

into an array. The user is supposed to respond by typing his or her name *followed by a carriage return*. The logical end-of-line at the end of the response indicates that the response is complete. The purpose of `eoln` is to detect the presence of the logical end-of-line. It answers the question: is the *next* character in the input stream the logical end-of-line character? It does this without actually reading the character. `eoln` does *not* tell us whether the character just read was the logical end-of-line. Once the character has been read, it is gone—in standard Pascal, it is then too late to determine if it was a logical end-of-line character. If it was, then `ch` is a blank and there is no longer any way to tell if it really was a blank or really was a logical end-of-line. In Turbo Pascal, we can compare the character read to `chr(13)` to see, after the fact, if we have read a carriage return, but our program will not be portable to other systems. And we will still have to read and discard the ^J that follows the ^M. Whether this rule is a good one, or whether it would have been better to have `eoln` return true if the character most recently read was the logical end-of-line (the rule that, in retrospect, most people seem to find more natural), is irrelevant. The rule is: `eoln` returns true if the *next* character in the input stream is the logical end-of-line character.

`readln` *and* `writeln`

The problems reflected by the presence of `eoln` explain why Pascal contains `readln` and `writeln`. `readln(...)` first performs any reading it needs to do, and then advances the input file until it is past the character or characters that comprise the logical end-of-line. After a `readln`, the next character read will be the first character of the next line. `writeln(...)`, after first writing out its arguments, writes the character or characters that comprise a logical end-of-line character. In this way, the burden of handling different system conventions for marking the end of a line is placed on the Pascal compiler and not on the programmer.

EXERCISE 1—13   The following version of `program echo` correctly echoes a file when compiled with compilers that adhere to the Pascal standard. Will it correctly echo the file when compiled with Turbo Pascal?

```
1 program echo(input,output);
2   (* Echo the contents of the file  input . *)
3   var ch: char;
4   begin
5     while not eof do
6       if eoln (* if the next character is a carriage return *)
7         then begin
8               read(ch); (* read it in (as a blank) and
9                             throw it away,... *)
10              writeln   (* ... but don't forget to echo it *)
11            end
12        else begin
13              read(ch); (* get the next character,... *)
14              write(ch) (* ... and echo it *)
15            end
16  end. (* echo *)
```

EXERCISE 1—14   What is the correct way to read in the name the user types in response to the prompt

```
write('Type your name: ')
```

The response should be read into the variable

```
var CustomerName: record
                    length: integer;
                    name: array [1..MAX] of char
                  end;
```

`eof` works similarly. It answers the question, "does anything remain in the file?" It doesn't answer the question, "did I just try to read something when nothing was there?" Like `eoln`, the history of `eof` is colored by the way systems implement files. The Pascal standard makes no mention of how files should be maintained by the operating system. Some systems, like MS-DOS, have an end-of-file character—in MS-DOS, it is ^Z. Other systems, like UNIX, don't. Instead they maintain a description of the file that includes the number of characters in the file. When that many characters have been read, the Pascal subsystem knows that there aren't any left and that the next call to `eof` should return `true`.

What should happen when an attempt is made to read from a file that is logically empty? The normal response is to generate the error message "attempt to read past end-of-file." This occurs in both standard Pascal and Turbo Pascal when reading from a `file of` ⟨type⟩. It also happens in standard Pascal when reading from a file of type `text`, such as `input`. In Turbo Pascal, however, a `read(ch)` performed on a text file when `eof` is `true` results in setting `ch` to ^Z. In addition, the file is *not* advanced over the ^Z and subsequent reads

Systems differ: `eof`

will also return a ^Z—it is as if the file ends with an infinite string of these characters.

Reading from a terminal poses additional problems. When Pascal was first developed, this possibility, which we take as the norm today, was uncommon. The program and its data were punched on cards, and both were read into the computer. The program was compiled, and if there were no errors, the program executed. For some kinds of computing applications, this style of computing is still used today, though the program is kept in one file and the data in another. For example, when simulating the airflow over an aircraft wing, the description of the wing is placed in a file. Given the amount of data involved, this is the only practical way to input it—nobody could flawlessly type in the amount of data demanded by such a program. But many computing tasks involve interacting with the user. Making an airline reservation or playing a computer game are examples of applications where the response to the next request for input depends on the most recent output.

One problem is: when does eof become true when a program is reading from the terminal? Does it *ever* become true? Though there may not be any data currently waiting to be processed, there is always the possibility that the user will type some more. When reading from a file, a call to eof will either return true or false. When reading from a terminal, a call to eof can either return true, return false, or can cause the system to sit there and wait for input. The interface between Pascal and the operating system must provide some mechanism for letting the user indicate that there is no more input. In UNIX systems, this is done by typing a ^D, which stands for *end of transmission*. MS-DOS systems have the user type a ^Z (followed by a carriage return), since ^Z is the normal MS-DOS signal for end-of-file.

Reading from a terminal poses other problems. When reading from a file, the characters in the file are presumed to be correct—they are just read, one at a time. But when input comes from a terminal, users expect to be able to correct typing errors. We expect to be able to backspace and reenter data. Only when we hit the carriage return key are we committing ourselves to what we have typed. This is known as **line buffering**. The terminal handler of the operating system sits between us and our Pascal program. The terminal handler is not very sophisticated. It just sits there and collects a whole line of characters, passing it on, lock, stock, and barrel, to Pascal. The terminal handler does, however, have a small amount of knowledge. It understands that a few special characters, like backspace, carriage return, and perhaps ^X, which stands for *kill the line* on some systems, require special processing. Line buffering is helpful in applications where the user is responding to queries like

Type your name:

while some applications, like visual editors and computer games, require that line buffering be turned off. These programs must respond to each keystroke as it is typed. This is not a Pascal issue per se, though it does affect how we write our programs. Pascal does not even know when line buffering is on or off. When a Pascal program performs a read, it is just making a procedure call. If the data is there waiting, then the procedure call returns quickly. If there is no data available, the procedure just waits, and so the entire program just waits, until data is typed in. The program for the game of worm in Chapter 2 assumes that the input is coming from a terminal without line buffering, whereas the program for Nero—The Roman Calculator assumes that the input is coming from a terminal with line buffering. The program for the simple make utility assumes that its input comes from a file.

While a Pascal program cannot tell if its input is line buffered, it is important, when we write the program, to know if the input is coming from a file or a terminal. When data is read from a file, it is traditional to echo the input. The results of simulating the behavior of an aircraft wing aren't very meaningful if we don't have a description of the wing and the conditions under which the plane was flying. On the other hand, when input comes from a terminal, the terminal handler typically echoes the input and the Pascal program does not need to do this. When line buffering is turned off, we often don't want the input echoed at all, either by the terminal handler or the Pascal program. The programs for our case studies will have to deal with these issues.

CHAPTER 2

THE GAME OF WORM

Before Nintendo captured the hearts and minds of young people everywhere, seven-year-olds and users new to the UNIX operating system often played the game of worm. Worm is a typical one-person arcade game: you match your wits and manual dexterity against the computer, only, unlike real arcade games, the graphics are primitive. You start life out as a little worm. Your goal is to grow longer, which you do by eating the food that is placed randomly on the screen by the computer. The motion of the worm is controlled by cursor control keys. If the worm bumps into either itself or the wall that surrounds the game board, it dies and the game is over. In this case study we develop an interactive program that lets others play this game. ◘

2.1 THE RULES OF THE GAME

The appearance of the screen during a typical game is shown in Figure 2–1. The screen is 23 rows high and 80 columns wide, with each square capable of holding one character.

- Asterisks form the wall. They fill the second and last rows and the first and last columns.
- The "at" sign (@) represents the head of the worm.
- The letter "o" shows where the body segments are.
- A digit in the range 1 through 9 indicates the location and nutritional content of food. There is exactly one piece of food on the game board at all times. When the piece of food is eaten, a new one miraculously appears.
- Any square not occupied by the worm, food, or the wall is blank.

In addition, the first row of the screen displays the name of the game and the current score.

Keystrokes direct the worm to move its head one square to the left, up, right, or down. The keys used are lowercase h, k, l, and j. (These are the cursor

FIGURE 2–1   A Typical Game of Worm in Progress

```
            Increasing y direction
         ┌──────────────────────────────────────────────────▶
  Worm                                                              Score: 208
  ********************************************************************************
  *
  *   ooo                                 oooooooooooooo      ooooooooooo         *
  *   o o                                 o            o    o            o        *
  *   o o                                 o oooooooooo o    o            o        *
  *   o o                                 o o        o o    o            o        *
  *   o o  oooooooooooooooooooo@          o o        o ooooo             o        *
  *   o                                   o o        o                   o        *
  *   o                                 ooooo o          ooooooooooo     o        *
  *   o                                       o                   o    ooo        *
  *   o                                       o                   o    o          *
  *   o                                       o                   o    o          *
  *   o                                       o                   o    o          *
  *   o                                       o                   o    o          *
  *   o                                       o                   o    oo         *
  *   o                                       o                   o    o          *
  *   o                                       o                   o    o          *
  *   o                                       o                   o    o          *
  *   o                                       o                   o    o          *
  *   oooooooooooooooooooooooooooooooooooooo  o         4         o    o          *
  *                                                     oooooooooooo               *
  ********************************************************************************
```

control keys of the popular UNIX editor `vi`.) The idea is to make it appear as if the worm inches forward. It *appears to the eye* as if the worm moves its last body segment onto its next to last body segment, its next to last body segment onto its next to next to last body segment, and so on, until the segment right behind the head moves to the square containing the head and the head moves to its new position. This is more or less the way a real earthworm or caterpillar moves. If the head of the worm strikes either itself or the wall, the worm dies.

The immediate goal is to direct the worm to the piece of food, because when the worm eats the food, the worm gets to grow. Growth is slow and orderly. After eating food of value n, the worm grows in length by one body segment for the next n moves. Though growth looks like it occurs at the head, it really occurs at the tail. When the worm is just inching along and not growing, the last segment is moved onto the next to last segment by switching the o marking its tail segment to a blank. But during the growth phase this square retains its o, as does every other segment of the worm, with the old head becoming a regular body segment and the new location of the head becoming the @. The current score is the sum of all the food eaten; the final score is the score at the time the worm dies.

While in theory it is possible to fill the screen with the worm, lack of patience or fatigue takes over long before then. Initially, the worm is in row 14, with its tail in column 3 and its head in column 10, and there is a piece of food in some random, unoccupied square.

One additional refinement makes the interface a little more friendly and makes the game a bit more difficult. Once started, the worm moves at regular intervals, come what may. While the worm responds instantly to keystrokes, if the player does not to strike a key, the worm continues to move in the direction it last moved at the rate of one square per second. If the user types an `l`, and nothing more, the worm moves steadily to the right until it hits the wall.

At this point, if you are unfamiliar with worm, you should trot off to the computer and play it for a bit, just to get the feel of the game. The complete code, in both Turbo and UNIX Pascal, is on the disk accompanying this book. Just compile it and run it. (Many UNIX systems already have this game installed in `/usr/games/worm` or some similar place.)

Go play the game!

Special Cases

Good programming practice says that you should think about all the special cases that can arise in a program and design your data structures before rushing off to program. But, if you are like most readers, something akin to the following thought probably has already popped into your head: "How on earth am I going to get Pascal to let me treat the screen like a rectangular array of cells, how am I going to suppress the echo of the user's keystrokes and, above all, how am I going to implement the automatic keystroke repetition?" The answer is that we will not use the standard input/output mechanisms of Pascal; we will use a set of system routines instead. Turbo Pascal already provides most of what we need in its `Dos` and `Crt` libraries and in the UNIX environment we can get to the necessary library routines through a C language interface. The Turbo and UNIX Pascal programs for worm are virtually identical and our worm program requires little or no modification to port to other systems as long as they support the commonly available but nonstandard Pascal feature of *independent compilation*. Independent compilation lets us separate the *declaration* of a procedure from its *definition*. We discuss the philosophy and mechanics of independent compilation in a later section. For now, a quick glance at the file `pscr.h` on page 101, which contains the declarations and header comments of a set of routines to manage the screen—procedures we can call from our main program just like any others— should allay any concerns. We can get on with the business of thinking about the game.

More than any other case study in this book, the program for worm has the potential for undetected bugs. Because the oddball situations in this game occur so rarely in actual play, we are unlikely to uncover bugs by just haphazardly testing the program. Forethought is all-important. All of the special cases are easily dealt with—the trick is catching them all in the first place.

If you have access to the UNIX-supplied version of the game of worm, the program that our program is trying to mimic, you will see that while the word `Worm` is placed in columns 2 through 5 of the top row when the game starts up, the word `Score` does not appear until there is a score to display. Another small programming problem is displaying the score the way the UNIX-supplied version displays the score: as `Score:` *ddd*, where *d* stands for a digit. If the score is less than one hundred the leading digits are written as blanks, while if the score reaches 1000, the score is displayed as `Score:` *dddd*, which puts the final digit in the very last column. Exactly how we handle this situation is of no great importance and `Score:`*dddd*, while not as elegant looking, might do just as well. What we don't want is a bug in our program—one that might not turn up for a very long time.

Displaying the score

Yet another detail requires that we consult the original version of the game: is the score the amount of food consumed or is it the worm's current length? These two are not the same when the worm is in a growth phase. Playing the UNIX-supplied version for a few moves reveals that the score is the amount of food consumed.

Is the score the length of the worm or the amount of food eaten?

A related question is what to do if the worm eats some food while it is growing. Given that the score is updated all at once, the only natural decision is to credit the worm with the sum of the amount of growth it is still due and the value of

Eating while growing

what it has just eaten. To do otherwise would mean that even after the worm stops growing the score and the length would be out of sync. *Failure to think of this possibility could very easily lead to a bug!* Just making line 315 of `worm.p`

```
NumToGrow := Food.Value;
```

instead of

```
NumToGrow := NumToGrow + Food.Value;
```

is all it takes to get it wrong.

The head lands on the tail

Yet another possible source of difficulty is illustrated in Figure 2–2. What should happen if the worm is not growing and the player types j? If you read the rules of the game very carefully you will know that the worm should still live, because logically it moves its tail onto the next to last segment as it starts inching forward, only moving its head as the last step of the process. This means that the head lands in the square that the tail just vacated, and the worm does not bump into itself.

The worm fills the screen

A related, and even more remote, possibility is having the entire screen fill with the worm. This is a very dangerous boundary condition for our program. If you think about the situation carefully you will see that this can occur only at the moment the worm eats. This is so because if there is a piece of food on the board, while it might come close, the worm does not actually fill the screen completely. To be truly precise, the screen can become filled by the worm only if the worm eats a piece of food while in growth mode. If the worm is not in growth mode when it eats, the square formerly occupied by the tail becomes free. The reason this situation is so dangerous is that, if the screen is full, no location exists in which to place a new piece of food. Without some care our program could get into an infinite loop searching for a free space, get a subscript-out-of-range error, place a piece of food in the middle of the worm, or exhibit some other bizarre behavior.

FIGURE 2–2   The Head of the Worm Lands on the Tail

```
    Worm                                                          Score:   26
    ***********************************************************************
    *                                                                     *
    *                                                                     *
    *                                                                     *
    *                                                                     *
    *             oooooooooo                                              *
    *             o        o                                             *
    *             @        o                                             *
    *             o        o                                             *
    *             o      ooo                                             *
    *             o      o                                               *
    *             o      o                                               *
    *             o      o                                               *
    *             oooooooo                                               *
    *                                                                     *
    *                      5                                              *
    *                                                                     *
    *                                                                     *
    ***********************************************************************
```

Problems can occur on input as well, though the situation is simpler here.
The only valid inputs are h, j, k, and l. All other characters should be ignored.
Unfortunately, certain keystrokes, like control-C and control-Z, are intercepted
by the operating system and not passed on to our program. We have no control
over this and we ignore this system problem.

Actually, the program presented in this chapter operates slightly differently
from the one supplied with UNIX. If you type an illegal character in the UNIX-
supplied version of the game, after the normal one-second delay, the worm keeps
on moving in the same direction it was moving in before. In our version, the
worm stops dead in its tracks until a valid character is typed. The code that
causes this discrepancy is carefully isolated. It is all in procedure GetMove at
lines 118–120:

```
repeat
   Direction := Inchr
until Direction in ['h', 'j', 'k', 'l']; (* ignore typing errors *)
```

When the code reaches line 119, the program calls the function Inchr declared
in pscr.h. This line behaves just like

```
                   read(Direction)
```

except that after one second Inchr stops waiting for the player to type something
and returns the last character typed. read, on the other hand, waits indefinitely
for a keystroke. In our version of worm, if the player types an illegal character,
the loop iterates and the program returns to line 119, where Inchr repeats the
illegal character. The program is prepared to sit in the repeat loop forever, executing it once every second, waiting for a legal character. Since it is our program
that makes the worm move (by writing blanks, o's and @'s to the screen—it's
not a bit of magic), the worm just stops.

This can be corrected by defining a global variable, LastDirection, which
stores the last valid character typed, and changing the loop to

```
repeat
   Direction := Inchr;
   if not (Direction in ['h', 'j', 'k', 'l'])
     then Direction := LastDirection (* repair typing errors *)
until Direction in ['h', 'j', 'k', 'l'];
LastDirection := Direction;
```

The code now substitutes the last valid character for the illegal one. (Even with
this change, the UNIX-supplied version of the program behaves slightly differently than ours. The UNIX-supplied version waits for the remainder of the
second to elapse before substituting the last valid character for the illegal one,
whereas our program makes the substitution immediately.)

There is actually an advantage to us as programmers in allowing this discrepancy to remain: during debugging we can stop the action and study the
game board, though, for the same reason, it also makes the game easier for a
seven-year-old willing to cheat.

---

*All the special cases covered in this section are really examples of the need for
precise problem specifications. In most cases, how we handle the situation isn't
that important. What is important is that the situations are thought of before
sitting down to program.*

> **EXERCISE 2–1**   Why must `LastDirection` be global? Why can it not be declared on line 112 and be local to `GetMove`? After all, no other procedure needs to refer to it.

> **EXERCISE 2–2**   Why do we still need the `repeat` loop? Why can't we just have
>
> ```
> begin
>    Direction := Inchr;
>    if not (Direction in ['h', 'j', 'k', 'l'])
>      then Direction := LastDirection; (* repair typing errors *)
>    LastDirection := Direction;
>    case Direction of
>      ⋮
> ```

2.2   DATA STRUCTURE SUPPORT FOR CONSTANT-TIME OPERATIONS

Now that we have thoroughly examined the problem, we are ready to design the data structures needed to program the solution—learning about them is really what makes this problem worth studying. If we had all the time in the world to process a move and an infinite amount of space, we could write the program easily. As suggested in Figure 2–3, we could have an infinitely long array of type `CoordType` in which to store the segments of the worm. Only a small part of this array would be in use at any one time. The cells between the indices `HeadPos` and `TailPos` would describe the worm as it is currently. Cells to the left of the tail would hold information about where segments of the worm once were but are no longer, and cells to the right of the head would be virgin territory to be used as the worm continues to move about. If the worm isn't growing, a move would consist of first erasing the tail segment from the screen and advancing the tail by executing

```
GotoXY[WormSeg[TailPos].Col,WormSeg[TailPos].Row];
write(' ');
TailPos := TailPos + 1;
```

and then scanning the array between `TailPos` and `HeadPos` to determine if the worm is about to bump into itself. The new location of the head also needs to be checked to see if the worm has bumped into the wall. Because the location of the wall is fixed, this can be done without reference to `WormSeg`. Assuming all is well, `HeadPos` is advanced, the new location of the head is stored in the array, and the screen is updated.

Circular buffers

Actually, the problem of needing infinite storage is easily solved. Since the maximum length of the worm is limited by the size of the board, if we just treat `WormSeg` as if it were circular, with the last array element followed by the first one, as shown in Figure 2–4, we never run out of storage. This data structure is known as a *circular buffer* or *circular queue*. We only have to be careful that in advancing `HeadPos` and `TailPos` we do our arithmetic modulo `BUFFERSIZE`.

The need for constant-time operations

Given the speed of modern computers, we can probably afford the time required to search the portion of `WormSeg` containing the worm to determine if the worm has bumped into itself, especially since the game usually doesn't last too

FIGURE 2–3   A Simple Implementation of the Game of Worm

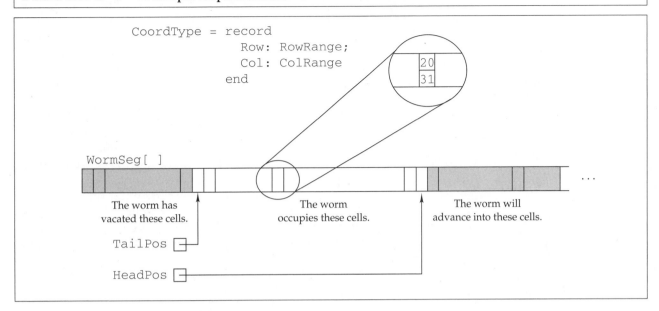

```
CoordType = record
              Row: RowRange;
              Col: ColRange
            end
```

WormSeg[ ]

The worm has vacated these cells.

The worm occupies these cells.

The worm will advance into these cells.

TailPos

HeadPos

long and the worm remains relatively short. Still, this approach is inefficient and ugly. Our goal is to make every worm-related action (determining if the worm lives or dies, moving the tail, moving the head, and placing a new piece of food) a *constant-time operation*. The phrase "constant time" means that the number of steps to process an operation is independent of the length of the worm. Our program should take the same number of steps to process a keystroke irrespective of whether the worm is short or long. In "Big Oh" notation, constant time is written $O(1)$. The lack of n in the formula inside the parentheses (and 1 is about as simple a formula as you can get) implies the running time is independent of n.

The motivation for developing a constant-time-per-move implementation is the interactive nature of the game; users can type quickly and we don't want

FIGURE 2–4   A Circular Buffer

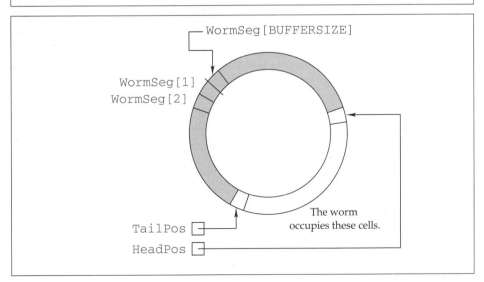

WormSeg[BUFFERSIZE]

WormSeg[1]
WormSeg[2]

TailPos

HeadPos

The worm occupies these cells.

them to outtype our program when the worm gets long. This is an example of *real-time processing*. Interactive games and software for visual editors and word processors must respond in real time if the user isn't to get hopelessly confused or frustrated. Programs that read sensors and control mechanical devices must also respond in real time. In real-time applications, by using carefully designed data structures we can reduce the time for each operation from what it takes using a simple approach and guarantee that our processing will be faster than the maximum possible data rate.

With the data structures we have described so far, the time it takes to process a move is linear in the worm's length; if the worm doubles in length, the time it takes to process a move doubles as well. An even worse situation arises when we need to place a new piece of food on the board. The naive approach to doing this is to generate a random location (using a random number generator) and then search `WormSeg` to see if this location is currently free. If it isn't, we simply iterate until we find a free location. Though unlikely to be a serious problem when the worm is short, when the worm is long this process might have to be repeated many times, and at least in theory we might be incredibly unlucky and never find a free location—we might get stuck in an infinite loop.

STOP

> **EXERCISE 2–3** Before going on, stop to think about how the code would look if we do nothing other than store the worm in a circular buffer. The text describes how to determine if the worm has bumped into itself and how to place a piece of food. How would you determine if the worm has hit the wall or eaten the food? How would you detect if the worm fills the screen? How long would these tests take? How should `WormSeg` be initialized?

Achieving Constant-Time Operations

We achieve constant-time-per-more performance by improving our data structures. By adding a two-dimensional array, `Board`, that mirrors the contents of the screen, we can determine with a simple `if` test whether the worm should die. If our program marks those cells of `Board` that are occupied by either the worm or the wall with a flag, then when the worm attempts to move its head to row r and column c, all we need do is perform the test

            if Board[r,c] = NOTFREEFLAG then ... (* worm died *)

to determine if the worm should die. Unlike on the physical screen, there is no need to distinguish between the wall, an internal segment of the worm, and the head of the worm, since they are all obstacles. Recording a move is a bit more complex than before. Not only do we need to modify the screen and update `WormSeg`, `TailPos`, and `HeadPos`; we also need to update `Board`, which can involve modifying either one or two locations depending on whether or not the worm is growing. The contents of `WormSeg[TailPos]` and `WormSeg[HeadPos]` tell us which elements of `Board` to modify. The data structures, as described so far, are depicted in Figure 2–5.

The small increase in the number of steps performed is more than made up for by our not having to search a portion of `WormSeg` looking for a collision. While updating `Board` takes constant time, initializing this array takes time proportional to the size of the game board, as every cell must be initially classified as occupied or free. But this operation occurs before the game really begins, so it is not offensive.

While we have made progress toward our goal of constant-time-per-move performance, we have not achieved it. The problem that remains is finding a

We are not there yet

FIGURE 2–5   The Effect of Adding the Two-Dimensional Array Board to Our Data Structures

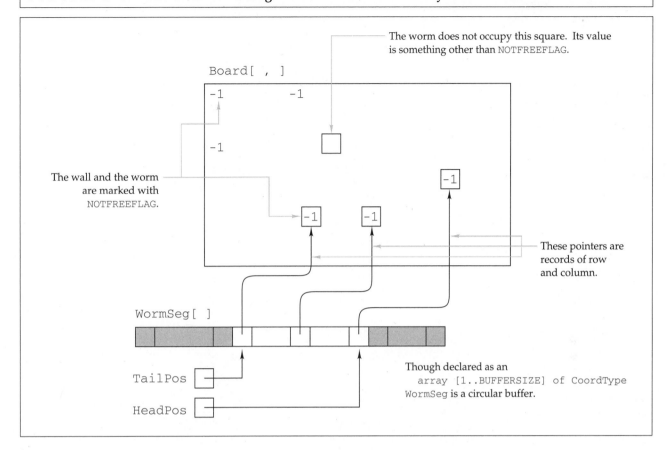

The worm does not occupy this square. Its value is something other than NOTFREEFLAG.

Board[,]

The wall and the worm are marked with NOTFREEFLAG.

These pointers are records of row and column.

WormSeg[ ]

TailPos

HeadPos

Though declared as an
array [1..BUFFERSIZE] of CoordType
WormSeg is a circular buffer.

place for a new piece of food in constant time. The inclusion of Board changes the task of checking if a proposed location is free from a linear-time search of WormSeg to a constant-time check of Board, but when the worm almost fills the screen we still might be unlucky and have to search a long time before finding a free square. Getting around this difficulty is harder and uses a generalization of the approach to efficiently shuffling a deck of cards discussed in For Your Information: How to Shuffle a Deck of Cards. We store, in yet another array, FreePool, all the free squares of the game board. The type of this array is the same as that of WormSeg,

Go read **For Your Information** *now!*

$$\text{array [1..BUFFERSIZE] of CoordType}$$

Every square of the game board, except those occupied by the wall, is always in exactly one of WormSeg and FreePool, though the distribution of the squares changes as the worm moves. Figure 2–7 shows our complete data structure.

While the data types of WormSeg and FreePool are the same, they are maintained quite differently. The worm occupies a contiguous section of WormSeg (at least if we view WormSeg as circular), which is continually shifting to the right. In addition, the data is kept in order: by scanning WormSeg from HeadPos to TailPos we can trace out the worm. The active region of FreePool, on the other hand, while also occupying a contiguous portion of the array, is always jammed up against the left edge, occupying positions 1 through LastFree. Furthermore, the data is in no particular order. This fits naturally with how we plan

FOR YOUR INFORMATION

How to Shuffle a Deck of Cards

When faced with the task of shuffling a deck of cards for the first time, most programmers usually write a piece of code similar to

A deck of cards has been standardized at 52 playing cards for a long time, so using a hardwired constant is reasonable.

Encoding a standard deck of cards as `0..51` is efficient, because the suit can be calculated as `n div 13` and the value as `n mod 13 + 2` (ace is high).

```
1  type Card = 0..51;  (* ace of spades = 51; king of spades = 50; ...
2                           three of clubs = 1; two of clubs = 0 *)
3       Deck = array [0..51] of Card;
4
5  procedure Shuffle(var A: Deck);
6    (* Shuffle a deck of cards by swapping pairs of them lots of times. *)
7    const NUMTIMES = 10000; (* This ought to mix 'em up real good! *)
8    var i, j1, j2: integer;
9        temp: Card;
10   begin
11     for i := 0 to 51 do A[i] := i;
12     for i := 1 to NUMTIMES do
13       begin
14         j1 := trunc(52*Random);
15         j2 := trunc(52*Random);
16         (* Ignore the possibility that j1 = j2, since swapping a card with
17            itself doesn't hurt, except to lower the number of actual swaps
18            a little -- about 2%. *)
19         temp := A[j1]; A[j1] := A[j2]; A[j2] := temp (* swap *)
20       end
21   end; (* Shuffle *)
```

See Stretching a random number generator in Above and Beyond: Random Number Generators.

Grouping the statements of an operation like swap together on one line emphasizes their logical structure.

There is actually a much better way to shuffle, one which takes considerably less time, requires the same amount of code, and mixes up the deck just as thoroughly. The idea behind the method is that the contents of a random location in a sorted array is no more or less random than the contents of a random location in a partially sorted or totally unordered array. Figure 2–6 illustrates the algorithm in action. Effectively, it partitions the deck into two parts. The right-hand part of the array contains the cards that are shuffled. These will not be touched again. The left-hand part contains the remaining cards in some, possibly nonrandom, order. Any ordering that might exist among these unshuffled cards is of no consequence to the algorithm. The two parts abut somewhere in the middle and, taken together, always fill the entire array. At each step the algorithm increases the size of the shuffled part and decreases the size of the unshuffled part by randomly selecting one unshuffled card, A[i], to incorporate into the shuffled portion. The requirement that the array be partitioned into an unshuffled and a shuffled part forces us to move A[i] into A[last]. The fact that the algorithm is oblivious

(continued)

**FOR YOUR
INFORMATION**

(concluded)

to any ordering in the unshuffled portion allows us to do this efficiently: we just swap the two elements. The shuffled part grows toward the left, as the unshuffled part shrinks from the right. The code that implements this algorithm is

```
1  type card = 0..51; (* ace of spades = 51; king of spades = 50; ...
2                      three of clubs = 1; two of clubs = 0 *)
3     Deck = array [0..51] of Card;
4
5  procedure Shuffle(var A: Deck);
6    (* Shuffle a deck of cards in an efficient manner. *)
7    var last, (* the index of the last card in the unshuffled portion *)
8        i: integer;
9        temp: Card;
10   begin
11     for i := 0 to 51 do A[i] := i;
12     for last := 51 downto 1 (* the final card is shuffled by default *) do
13       begin
14         i := trunc((last+1)*Random); (* pick a random unshuffled card *)
15         temp := A[i]; A[i] := A[last]; A[last] := temp (* swap *)
16       end
17   end; (* Shuffle *)
```

The method takes time proportional to the number of cards in the deck, or constant time per card.

FIGURE 2–6   The Strategy Behind Shuffling a Deck of Cards

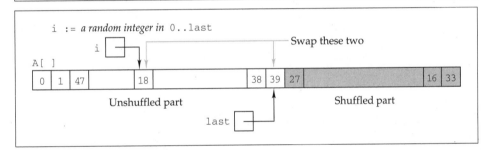

on using `FreePool`, which we don't do very often—just when we need to place a new piece of food. The code

$$\text{FoodLoc} := \text{FreePool[rand(LastFree)]}$$

which we find on line 280 of `worm.p`, returns, in constant time, a random, free location. (The function call `rand(LastFree)` returns a random integer in the range 1 through `LastFree`, inclusive. Because this value is random, even if the data in `FreePool` happens to be ordered, as it is initially, `FoodLoc` is a random location.)

One problem remains. When we shuffle a deck of cards, the contents of the array changes only as a result of dealing out the cards. Here, because the worm moves about, the contents of `FreePool[1..LastFree]` is constantly changing. When the tail vacates a cell, that cell becomes unoccupied. This is really no

FIGURE 2–7   **The Data Structures Needed to Implement the Game of Worm**

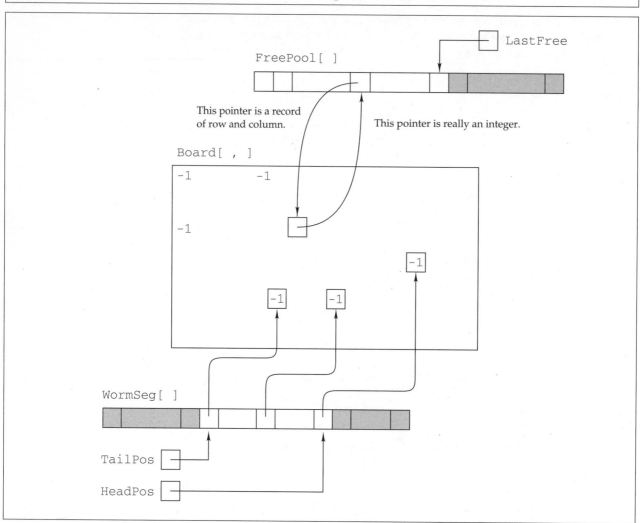

problem. Since the collection of cells stored in `FreePool` is unordered, we can simply tack the location of the vacated cell on to the end of the array. The code looks like

```
LastFree := LastFree + 1;
FreePool[LastFree] := WormSeg[TailPos];
...  write a blank to the screen and adjust
     Board[WormSeg[TailPos].Row,WormSeg[TailPos].Col];
TailPos := TailPos + 1;
if TailPos > BUFFERSIZE then TailPos := 1;
```

Unfortunately, the flip side of this problem is more difficult—the square the head lands on changes status from free to occupied. As the data in `FreePool` is unordered we have no efficient way of finding this location, although eliminating it from the middle of the array once we have found it takes constant time using the technique employed in shuffling. If we search `FreePool` looking for the element to delete, we are back to linear time per move, though now we are searching through a different array. What is worse, the search is usually lengthy, because the worm is typically short while the number of free cells is typically large.

We need a way of finding the element to delete in constant time. As shown in Figure 2–7, we do this by storing, in each unoccupied element of `Board`, the location in `FreePool` of the corresponding element.

> *The important invariant is the circularity of the pointers connecting* `FreePool` *and* `Board`. *Maintaining this circularity as the worm moves about and food is placed is crucial to the correct functioning of the program.*

Locating and deleting the new location of the head from the middle of `FreePool` is now a long-winded, but constant-time process:

- We use `HeadPos` to look up, in `WormSeg`, the current location of the head.
- Next, we calculate the new position of the head, which we store in `r` and `c`, based on the input from `Inchr`.
- We determine from `Board[r,c]` if the cell is occupied and, if it is not, where in `FreePool` to find the element we should delete.
- We then mark `Board[r,c]` as occupied, move the value at the end of `FreePool` into the hole created by the deletion, and decrement `LastFree`.
- Lastly, we reestablish the circle of pointers for the location that was moved into the hole.

The effect of the last two steps is illustrated in Figure 2–8. It is hard to see the need for the last of the five steps, the one that maintains the circularity invariant. Failure to perform this step will not be noticed right away. The problem will show up only much later, when the head of the worm lands on the newly freed square and the entry in `Board` points to the wrong place in `FreePool`.

> *This is typical of programs that use sophisticated data structures: bugs rarely reveal themselves until millions of additional instructions have executed. The location of an error can be far away from where the error is revealed. This makes the programs very hard to debug. Careful maintenance of invariants when the program is first coded is the best preventive medicine.*

If we trace the code in `worm.p` carefully, we see that a normal movement of the worm is accomplished in 27 Pascal statements. When the worm eats a piece of food, placing a new piece of food takes another 12.

The Organization of the Code

Armed with an understanding of the data structures, the code of `worm.p` should be easy to understand. Lines 17–59 declare a number of constants and types that make the program more readable. The only constant requiring special mention is `NOTFREEFLAG`. Because elements of `Board` not occupied by the worm point into `FreePool`, the value of this constant cannot lie in the range `1..BUFFERSIZE`.

The variables declared in lines 61–80 correspond to the data structures described in this section. Among the smaller variables declared in lines 82–94, the one we must treat most carefully is `Food`. This variable allows us to determine in constant time (line 312) if the food has been eaten. We need to decide: Should the square containing the food be in `FreePool`? Should it be marked in some special way in `Board`? How should we handle this one special location? As long

FIGURE 2–8   Changes to `Board` and `FreePool` due to Moving the Head of the Worm

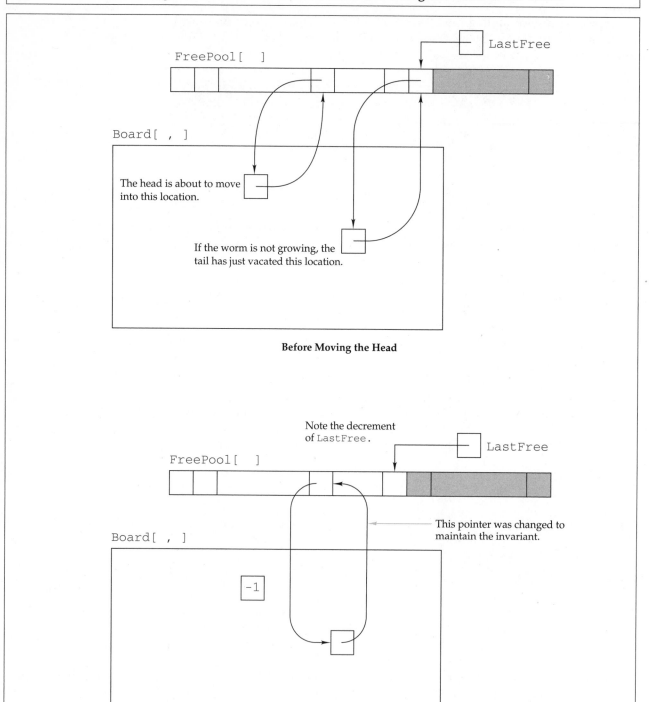

Before Moving the Head

After Moving the Head

as we carefully document our decisions and stick to them, at worst we will need to sprinkle some special-case testing throughout the code. The decision made in `worm.p` is to treat the square containing the food just like any other unoccupied location. From the perspective of the main data structures, food does not even exist. The only record of its presence is kept in `Food`. This makes for more uniform handling. After moving the worm, the program checks to see if the worm landed on the food, and if so it places a new piece of food on the board (lines 312–323).

Most of the procedures in `worm.p` are small, easy-to-write service routines (`WriteChar`, `rand`, `GetMove`, and `UpdateScore`) or routines that deal with initialization (`InitScreen`, `InitDataStructures`, and `InitWorm`). The five crucial procedures are `MakeLocFree`, `MakeLocInUse`, `MoveTail`, `MoveHead`, and `CreateNewFood`. These manipulate the data structures. The major decision in their design is the decoupling of the movement of the tail from the movement of the head. There are no procedures `MoveNormal` and `MoveGrowing`. If the worm is growing we just don't move the tail. `MakeLocFree` and `MakeLocInUse` maintain the circularity invariant between `Board` and `FreePool`. The first adds a location to the end of `FreePool` and the other finds and deletes a location from the middle of this array. These procedures are called by `MoveTail` and `MoveHead`. `MoveTail` and `MoveHead` also update the screen and `WormSeg`. Because of our decision to treat the location of the food no differently than any other free location, `CreateNewFood` references `FreePool`, but makes no adjustments to it.

The generality of `MakeLocFree` and `MakeLocInUse` makes initialization easy. The routine `InitDataStructures` makes *every* location free. This allows the circularity invariant to be established easily—there are no special tests to skip over locations occupied by the worm initially. Then `InitWorm` gives birth to the worm. All it has to do is call `MakeLocInUse`—`FreePool` and `Board` get updated automatically—and place the worm in `WormSeg` and on the screen.

The heart of the main program is about 25 lines long (lines 298–324) and is nothing other than a careful sequencing of calls to `GetMove`, `MoveTail`, `MoveHead`, and `CreateNewFood`.

PROJECT 2–1   A well-structured program should be easy to modify. The UNIX-supplied version of worm has an additional feature. The uppercase H and L keys are the equivalent of nine very rapidly typed lowercase h's and l's, except when the distance to the piece of food is less than nine cells. Then H and L are equivalent to rapidly typing just enough h's or l's to reach the food. Uppercase K and J work the same way, only the distance traveled is five cells. Modify the program for worm to implement the H, K, L, and J keystrokes. As always, it is wise to think about special situations before you go off to code. What should be the effect of automatic keystroke repetition for these uppercase letters? Should it be the same when the worm reaches the food as when it doesn't? (If it is available on your computer you can compare your answers to the UNIX-supplied version by performing some simple tests.)

PROJECT 2–2   Develop a program that, while operating in a boring, mechanical way, generates a series of keystrokes that will ultimately fill the screen with the worm.

FOR YOUR
INFORMATION

Displaying the score

Handling the Special Cases

Now that we have studied the data structures used in our implementation of the game of worm and have a good feel for the program, we should go back and see how easy it is to handle all the special cases. Not displaying the word `Score` until there is a score to display can be solved by using a `boolean` variable that indicates whether the word `Score` has been written to the screen, testing this variable each time the score is updated. Because it has virtually no effect on the efficiency of our program, we adopt a simpler approach: we simply write the word `Score` every time. The first time, it replaces the blanks on the message line, while on subsequent executions it overwrites the word `Score` with the word `Score`, which has no visual effect. This is done in `worm.p` on line 168, where the blanks are written in the first place, and on line 274, where `Score:` overwrites whatever is in columns 70–76.

Pascal's optional field width specification is just the tool we need for displaying the score the way the original designers of worm intended. The field width specification in the code on line 274

```
writeln('Score: ',Score:3)
```

writes the number right-justified in a field of width three, but does this only if it fits. Otherwise, it writes the number in the minimum number of spaces needed to hold it, which in our case is four.

Is the score the length of the worm or the amount of food eaten?

Defining the score as the amount of food eaten and not the length of the worm determines the placement of the call to `UpdateScore`. It is placed inside the `then` clause of the test on line 312

```
if (r = Food.Row) and (c = Food.Col)
```

which checks to see if the head has landed on the food, rather than inside the `then` clause of the test on line 305

```
if NumToGrow > 0
```

which separates the processing of the tail segment into two cases based on whether the worm is growing or not.

The head lands on the tail

Correct handling of the situation pictured in Figure 2–2 is easy because our program decouples moving the tail from moving the head. By placing the test

```
if Board[r,c] = NOTFREEFLAG then goto 99; (* worm died *)
```

on line 308, after moving the tail but before moving the head, we get the desired effect. As usual, any difficulty comes from not thinking of the potential problem in the first place.

The worm fills the screen

Since the screen can become full only at the moment the worm eats, this condition should be checked in the `then` clause of the code of lines 312–323. The test

```
if LastFree = 0
```

on line 317 prevents the call to `CreateNewFood` from attempting to place a piece of food when no space remains. The code branches to `99`, where the end-of-game message is printed.

> **PROJECT 2–3**   Extend the game of worm so that the game board includes barriers that the worm has to avoid and so that multiple pieces of food can appear at the same time, with pieces of food disappearing if they have not been eaten after a period of time.

2.3   INDEPENDENT COMPILATION

A large program cannot be managed as a single, monolithic entity. Keeping unrelated pieces of code physically together interferes with modular thinking, as it makes it too easy to cross the line from functionality to implementation. Besides, placing functionally related routines in their own file enhances portability and reusability, and encourages programmers to work together by permitting different pieces of a large program to be coded simultaneously. For this reason, C, Ada, FORTRAN, and most dialects of Pascal support *independent compilation*. Independent compilation allows individual files to be compiled and debugged separately, with the compiled files eventually *linked* into a complete, executable program. Independent compilation allows for prototyping of software products. Procedures can be programmed quickly, possibly using inefficient algorithms or incorporating only limited error checking, and then refined at a later date. If the interface does not change, then the code of the calling program should be unaffected by improvements made to the called procedures. Independent compilation is essential to the development of libraries. It can also speed compilation. Without this capability, if one line of a small procedure is changed, the whole program needs to be recompiled. On the other hand, if the small procedure is separate, only that procedure needs to be recompiled, although the entire program still needs to be relinked. The mechanics of independent compilation vary from programming language to programming language and even among various dialects of Pascal, but the principles remain the same.

This is the most system-dependent section in the entire book. Your system may differ slightly from what is described here.

When the Pascal compiler compiles a call to a procedure, like the call on line 171 of `worm.p`, `GotoXY(2,1)`, what does it really need to know? It doesn't need to know anything about the internal workings of `GotoXY`, but it does need to know the order, type, and parameter passing mechanism of each of the parameters. This is given by the declaration on line 34 of `pscr.h`

```
procedure GotoXY(col, row: integer);
```

The declaration provides sufficient information for the compiler to check the legality of the call, and to generate most of the code for the call as well. The only piece of information that it is missing is the address of the start of the code for `GotoXY`, the address to which the flow of control transfers. Because all addresses are the same size, the compiler can even leave space for this address— it will be filled in by the *linker* at the last minute when the executable module is formed.

The internal approaches to independent compilation taken by UNIX and Turbo Pascal are vastly different. UNIX Pascal follows the C model, whereas Turbo Pascal looks more like Ada. One reason for the difference in approach is that Turbo Pascal presents the programmer with an *integrated development environment*, whereas UNIX does not. In the UNIX environment, a programmer who wishes to create a Pascal file first uses an editor, like `vi` or `emacs`, to create the file `filename.p`. Both `vi` and `emacs` are general-purpose editors that can edit any ASCII file: Pascal programs, C programs, FORTRAN programs, little reminder notes, data files, basically any file that is a collection of ASCII characters. The file extension `.p` is a UNIX convention to indicate that the file contains a Pascal program. The editor doesn't use this information and would be just as happy with any other file name. The file can even be edited with one editor at one time and with another editor at another time. Later, when ready to compile the Pascal program, the programmer invokes the Pascal compiler with the line

pc filename.p -o filename2

pc is unaware how the program was created, but if any errors are reported, the file will have to be corrected using the editor and then recompiled. Once the program has been successfully compiled, the executable version (often referred to as "the executable," as if *executable* were a noun) can be run by typing the command filename2 after a UNIX prompt. (The most popular convention is to give the executable the same name as the .p file, but without the .p extension. That way, we can tell at a glance where the original Pascal is located.) The three steps, editing, compiling, and running, are completely separate and are each invoked from the operating system level.

On the other hand, once inside the Turbo Pascal environment, the programmer thinks of the computer as a Pascal machine and has no need to interact with the operating system directly again. The programmer faces a screen like that shown in Figure 2–9. The program in the window can be edited using a limited number of keys to control cursor movement and insertion and deletion of text. Then it can be run. Any compilation errors are highlighted, and the program can be immediately edited and rerun. Once the program is working satisfactorily, it can be saved. All this is done without leaving the Pascal environment. An explanation of all the features of the Turbo Pascal development environment would run to many pages; if you are using Turbo Pascal you already know most of them, whereas if you are using UNIX, you would simply get lost in the mass of detail. Some programmers, especially novices, love integrated environments, since on-line help is usually available and it isn't necessary to learn a myriad of operating system commands. Experienced programmers move freely between the two types of programming environments.

FIGURE 2–9   The Turbo Pascal Integrated Development Environment

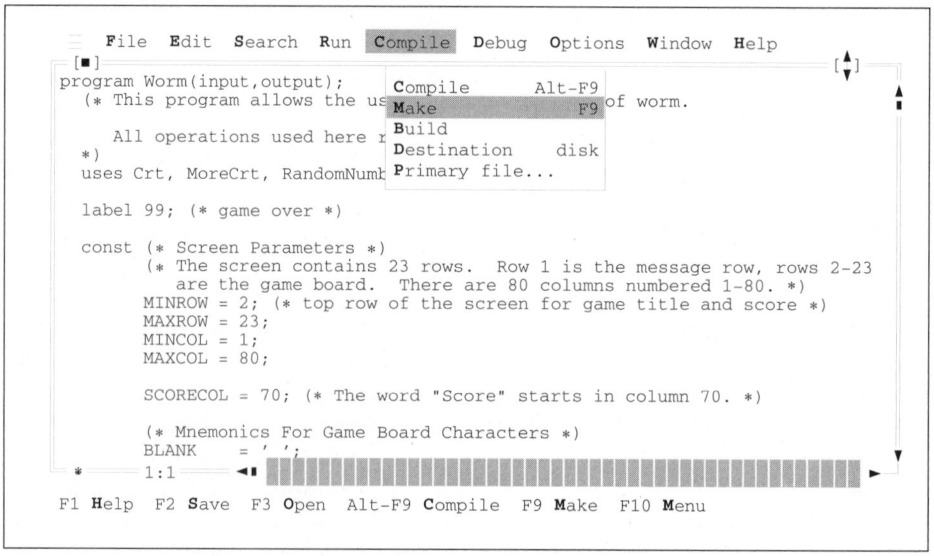

Two aspects of integrated environments concern us in the present context. First, integrated environments hide from the programmer the boundaries of tasks that are essentially distinct. The programming process flows naturally from editing (the normal mode and the **F**ile and **E**dit menu-bar options), to compiling (the **C**ompile menu-bar option), to linking (integrated into the **C**ompile menu-bar option), to executing (the **R**un menu-bar option).

The second aspect of integrated environments that concerns us is that an integrated environment can incorporate knowledge from the task domain; it can "understand" Pascal and take advantage of that understanding. Some integrated environments have built-in editors that automatically insert `end` when you type `begin` or insert `then` when you type `if`. Turbo Pascal has a built-in project management tool, as part of its **C**ompile menu-bar option, that prevents the programmer from editing a file and then forgetting to recompile it. Because it is easier to understand independent compilation if we examine each of the tasks separately, we will begin our discussion by considering how independent compilation is done in the UNIX environment.

In both systems, procedures that work together to implement a larger task can be grouped together and placed in files of their own, completely separate from the main program. Such a grouping is known as a `package` in Ada and a `unit` in Turbo Pascal. There is no special name associated with such a grouping in UNIX Pascal; the procedures are simply placed together in a file of their own, with the procedure declarations kept physically separate from their bodies. For example, in the program for worm `random.h` and `random.p` define the interface and body of the routines that deal with random number generation, while `pscr.h` and `pscr.c` (a C language file) do the same for the screen handling package. In Turbo Pascal, the interface and body are kept in the same file, `RANDOMNU.PAS` in our example. If the interface is carefully defined, the differences between the UNIX `worm.p` and the Turbo Pascal `WORM.PAS` will be minimal and are present only because the syntax of independent compilation is different. The modifications needed to convert a UNIX Pascal program to one that runs under Turbo Pascal and vice versa can be performed in a matter of minutes.

The UNIX Pascal and UNIX operating system approach to independent compilation is based on

The UNIX Pascal Approach

- Separating a procedure heading from its body.
- Separating the compilation of the packages and the main program from the linking together of the pieces.
- Adding to Pascal a nonstandard compiler directive.

`#include "filename.h"`

for reading in text during compilation.

The last of these concepts is the most straightforward. When the compiler is compiling a file like `worm.p` and encounters the directive

`#include` *files*

`#include "random.h"`

on line 8 (with the # required to be in column 1), the compiler simply replaces the line with the text found in the file `random.h` and continues compiling. The included file can be a Pascal comment, like a copyright notice or the name and affiliation of the programmer, or it can contain type, variable, and procedure declarations. The use of the extension `.h` for `include` files is traditional—it stands for *header*. The replacement occurs at compile time; it is as if the programmer had actually typed in all the lines in the included file at the point where the `#include` is encountered. If there are any Pascal errors, the compiler reports them, since it is in the process of compiling. One obvious advantage of using `#include` files is that if multiple `.p` files include the same `.h` file, they will incorporate exactly the same text. There is no possibility of a typing error.

The primary purpose of `#include` files is to have the `.h` files contain the declarations of procedures and functions. This is what you see if you look in `pscr.h`, `random.h`, and `clock.h`. There are lines like

```
procedure GotoXY(col, row: integer);
```

and

```
function Random: real;
```

but there are no procedure bodies. This creates a minor syntactic difficulty; Pascal normally expects the procedure declaration to be followed by the procedure body. There must be some mechanism for telling the compiler that the procedure body is found elsewhere. This is done in UNIX Pascal by replacing the body with the new keyword `external`, which informs the compiler that the procedure body is in another file, to be compiled at a different time.

Refer to **random.p** *while reading this.*

The bodies of the procedures declared in `random.h`, `pscr.h`, and `clock.h` are in the files `random.p`, `pscr.c`, and `clock.c`. (The code for the two `.c` files is not shown and is treated later, since the ability to combine Pascal and C code in the same program raises additional questions.) The file `random.p` contains few surprises. The procedure bodies are about as we would expect them to be, and look like standard Pascal. There are just a few details to be noted. We expect the file `worm.p` to contain

```
#include "random.h"
```

as the main program calls both `Randomize` and `Random` and so needs to have access to their declarations. And we expect the file `random.p` to contain

```
#include "clock.h"
```

as the procedure `Randomize` calls `clock`. But why does `random.p` contain

```
#include "random.h"
```

on line 2? Furthermore, where the actual procedure body is defined, the full declaration is not repeated; only the name of the procedure is given as

```
(* procedure Seed(iseed: integer); *)
procedure Seed;
  begin
    ... the code ...
  end; (* Seed *)
```

Why is this so? The reason is historical. The nonrepetition of the full declaration employs the syntax used for a similar, esoteric feature of the standard Pascal language: `forward` declarations. Being forced to include `random.h` also has the practical advantage that the declarations as `worm.p` sees them cannot get out of sync with the declarations as `random.p` sees them. It is good practice to repeat the full declaration, even if this can be done only as a comment, since a human looking at the `.p` file does not see the declarations tucked away in the `.h` file.

An important consequence of separating the declaration of a procedure from its body is that `worm.p` can be written and compiled while the bodies of the procedures in `random.p` are still just a gleam in some programmer's eye. Only the interface, specified in `random.h`, needs to have been composed. Of course, if the code in `random.p` has not been written, we cannot form a complete, executable program. We can, however, proceed by writing `random.p` using a very crude random number generator, debug our program for worm and then replace the procedure bodies in `random.p` with the code for a more sophisticated algorithm. (`Randomize` and `Seed` could even be stubs doing nothing, and `Random`, on successive calls, could return 0.1, 0.2, ..., 0.9, 0.1, 0.2, ...) While `random.p` will need to be recompiled when it is replaced, and the entire executable will need to be relinked, the code of `worm.p` will not even need to be recompiled.

Procedure declarations are not the only Pascal constructs we find in .h files. If a procedure declared in a .h file is passed an array or record, the type declaration for the array or record also needs to be placed in the .h file, as will any constant or type declarations on which this declaration depends. This is a consequence of Pascal's use of name equivalence, which forces the parameters of procedures to be declared using type names. Global variables that need to be accessed by both the main program and the called procedure can also be placed in the .h file. Because in the program for worm all our parameters are Pascal predefined types and we do not need to share any global variables, we do not see type or variable declarations in the .h files.

There is, however, a variable, `xsubk`, found on line 4 of `random.p`, that is outside of any procedure. This variable is visible only to the procedures `Seed` and `Randomize` and the function `Random`. It seems neither local nor global. To understand how this variable interacts with the other components of our Pascal program, we need to fit variables like this one, as well as those declared in .h files, into the stack frame model of memory management that was presented in Section 1.4. We take up this very interesting topic in the next section.

At this point, all the components have been accounted for. Figure 2–10 shows the structure of the `worm` program as it exists in the UNIX world.

A small syntactic problem can develop if one .p file includes several .h files that all contain type, variable, and procedure declarations. Standard Pascal expects the ordering of declarations to be labels, constants, types, variables, and procedures and functions, with these latter two intermingled. But if two .h files each contain both type and procedure declarations, the type declarations in the second .h file will follow the procedure declarations in the first .h file. Pascal implementations that support independent compilation accept this violation of the standard. The real concern is that a constant, type, variable, or procedure must be declared before it can be subsequently referenced. Without this constraint, the compiler cannot do type checking, but as long as this rule isn't violated, declarations can be in any order.

Linking

We now turn from the look of the Pascal code, which is not that different from standard Pascal, to how it is compiled and assembled into an executable program. Because a standard Pascal program is monolithic, the problem of assembling the pieces does not arise. A standard Pascal program is compiled with

`pc` filename`.p` `-o` filename2

Building an executable program when independent compilation is involved is a two-stage affair. First, each piece of the program is compiled separately. This is done with the first two lines and part of the third line of

```
cc -c pscr.c clock.c
pc -c random.p
pc worm.p pscr.o random.o clock.o -ltermlib -o worm
```

The first line invokes the C compiler on the files `pscr.c` and `clock.c`. The second invokes the Pascal compiler on `random.p`. The `-c` option to Pascal and C informs the compiler that only a piece of an entire program is being compiled.

FIGURE 2–10　The Structure of worm in UNIX Pascal

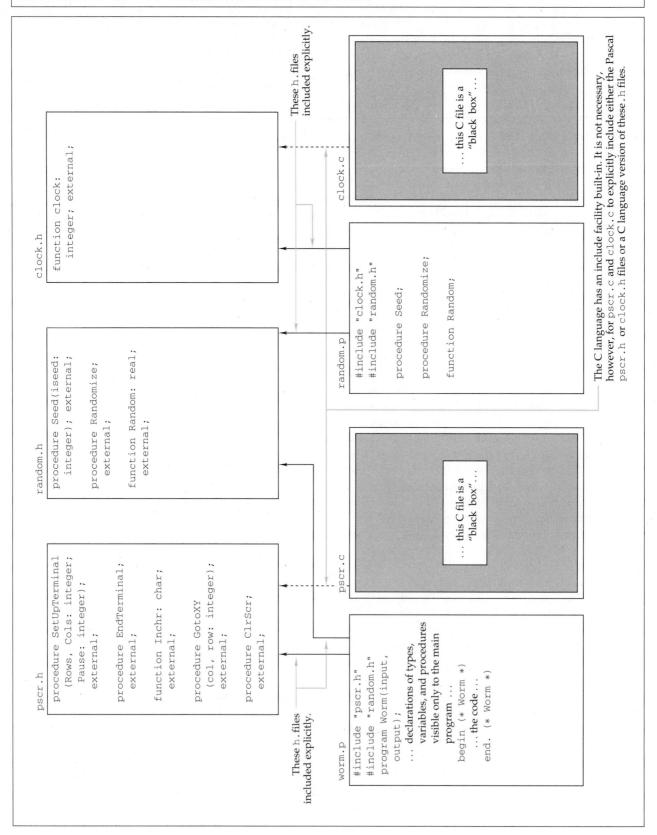

Compiling `pscr.c`, `clock.c`, and `random.p` creates the files `pscr.o`, `clock.o`, and `random.o`. The `.o` stands for **object code** file. In general, the file filename.`o` is the machine language code for filename.`p` with a few things left out and a few things added. When compiling calls to procedures defined elsewhere, like the call to `clock` on line 24 of `random.p`, the compiler simply leaves space for the address of the start of the code of the called procedure. It also places information within the `.o` file equivalent to: "I've got a call to the function `clock` at location ... in this `.o` file and I've left space for the correct address, which I don't yet know." For procedures, whose bodies are defined in the `.p` file, the compiler includes the information: "I contain the body of external procedure `Randomize` and its code begins at location ... in this `.o` file." The situation for the main program is only slightly more complex. We can also explicitly compile this file separately, invoking `pc -c worm.p`. The code in `worm.p` is identified as the main program by the presence of the `program` declaration. This causes `pc` to place additional information into the file `worm.o`. It take the form: "I'm the main program and execution should begin at location ... in this `.o` file."

After compiling all the individual pieces, we have a collection of `.o` files, each corresponding to a `.p` or `.c` file. In the second stage of building an executable program, the `.o` files are linked together into a single executable by a program known as a linker (`ld` on UNIX systems). This program takes all the pieces and, using the extra information stored in the `.o` files by `pc` and `cc`, pastes the program together into a single executable. If any piece called for does not exist, or if there is no main program, or more than one, the linker produces an error message. The linker is invoked with

```
ld worm.o pscr.o random.o clock.o -ltermlib -o worm
```

All the `.o` files needed to build a complete program must be specified. (The `-ltermlib` causes the linker to search a library named `termlib` for yet more already-compiled procedures—`termlib` stands for *terminal library*.) The line

```
pc worm.p pscr.o random.o clock.o -ltermlib -o worm
```

is just shorthand for

```
pc -c worm.p
ld worm.o pscr.o random.o clock.o -ltermlib -o worm[1]
```

The philosophy behind independent compilation is captured here: if at a later time we develop a better random number generator or find and correct a bug in `worm.p`, all we need to do is recompile that one file and then relink the pieces.

We now see why it is easy to combine packages written in both Pascal and C into a single program. Once the `.p` and `.c` files have been compiled into `.o` files, the knowledge that the original source language was Pascal or C becomes irrelevant; the linker simply doesn't care. As long as both language processors understand the internal format used by the linker, the linker can combine the `.o` files into a single executable. (Actually, they must agree on more than just the format used by the linker. When Pascal compiles a call to one of the routines in `pscr.c`, it thinks it is calling a Pascal routine. After all, what it finds in `pscr.h` is a Pascal declaration. It builds the stack frame for the call accordingly. If C were to organize its stack frames differently, then although the linker can still patch the Pascal

---

[1] While philosophically correct, this isn't quite true. On UNIX systems, doing the compilation and linking as indicated will not work. The reason is that Pascal includes some additional libraries that are passed along to `ld`, libraries that are not included when the compiling and linking is done separately. The correct two-step sequence is

```
pc -c worm.p
pc worm.o pscr.o random.o clock.o -ltermlib -o worm
```

code to contain the address of the C routine, things would go awry after the transfer of control. To successfully allow calls between routines written in different languages, the compiler writers must agree to observe conventions regarding the organization of memory, the format of external names, and a number of other matters. If this is done, the linker will have no trouble building an executable.)

Note that the `.h` files are never explicitly compiled themselves. They are compiled only indirectly, by being included in various `.p` files. This is reasonable. After all, they are just collections of declarations, and never contain procedure bodies or other code.

The Turbo Pascal Approach

Apart from the fact that Turbo Pascal is an integrated environment and `pc` is not, there are three main differences between the way Turbo Pascal and UNIX Pascal approach independent compilation.

- The syntax is different.
- A `unit` can have initialization code that is not part of any of the procedures in the package and is executed once before the main program begins execution.
- The programmer is protected against the error of forgetting to recompile a changed procedure body after making a correction.

Figure 2–11 shows the code for the Turbo Pascal version of the random number generator package.

The Turbo Pascal version of the main program, `WORM.PAS`, differs from `worm.p` in only the most minor of ways: the comment on how to compile and link the program, which is UNIX-specific, no longer applies (and is deleted) and the two `#include` lines are replaced by the line

```
uses Crt, MoreCrt, RandomNumbers;
```

which goes immediately *after* the `program` declaration, and not before, as in `worm.p`.

By examining Figure 2–11, we see that the `.h` and `.p` files of UNIX Pascal are now in one file, `RANDOMNU.PAS`. From the heading

```
unit RandomNumbers;
```

on line 1, it is clear that these routines form a reusable package instead of a main program. The keyword `unit` informs both us and the compiler of this fact.

At first sight, it would appear that putting both the declarations and the procedure bodies in the same file destroys our ability to

- Modify the bodies of the procedures in the package without having to recompile `WORM.PAS`.
- Provide the user with the interface (the `.h` files) and object code (the `.o` files) while keeping the Pascal source (the `.p` files) secret.

We will see that this is not so.

Syntax of a `unit`

Refer to Figure 2–11 while reading this.

A `unit` is divided into three parts

- The interface part.
- The implementation part.
- The initialization part.

The first of these parts is set off by the keyword `interface` on line 2. The contents of the interface part correspond to what is in the `.h` file. This is where we place constants, types, variables, and procedure declarations that we want to make visible to other routines. The bodies of the procedures and any variables that need to be visible throughout the package, like `xsubk`, but which do not need to be visible outside the package, are placed in the implementation portion, which is set off by the keyword `implementation`. The code in the implementation portion corresponds to what is in the `.p` file. By looking at line 22, we see that Turbo Pascal allows the declarations of procedures that appear in the interface part to be repeated, so they are no longer just comments.

Inclusion of a unit is done with the statement

```
uses unit_name, unit_name,...;
```

We have such a line in `WORM.PAS`, as well as one on line 20 of `RANDOMNU.PAS`

```
uses Dos; (* GetTime *)
```

This is the equivalent of

```
#include "clock.h"
```

in `random.p`.

Translating between UNIX and Turbo Pascal

Mechanically, translating a UNIX Pascal program that uses independent compilation into a Turbo Pascal program is an easy affair—the possibility of having initialization code within a `unit` doesn't really make going in the opposite direction any more complicated. A Turbo Pascal `unit` ends with an initialization section. This section can be empty, in which case all that is needed to mark the end of the package is the keyword `end` followed by a period. Or there can be a `begin` and some code before the `end`, as there is in `RANDOMNU.PAS`. The code in the initialization section executes once, before the main program begins execution. This allows variables like `xsubk` to be initialized to a default value. Setting the seed to a default value of 1 changes the comment of `procedure Seed` slightly; we no longer *have* to call `Seed` once before calling `Random` for the first time. When converting a Turbo Pascal program that uses units to a UNIX Pascal program, if a `unit` contains a nonempty initialization part, the code in the initialization part should be placed in a procedure with a name like `Init`. This procedure takes no parameters, is declared in the `.h` file, and should have the header comment

```
(* This routine should be called once, before any other routine
   in this package. *)
```

The call to `Init` is placed at the very beginning of the main program.

The Turbo Pascal method of handling initialization is the better of the two approaches. It is easy to forget to include the call to `Init` in the main program—in Turbo Pascal the initialization is performed automatically. Philosophically, UNIX Pascal places the burden on the user of the package, while Turbo Pascal places it on the writer of the package.

EXERCISE 2—4   By including a `boolean` variable, `SeedSet`, in the implementation portion of the random number generator package, it is possible to detect when the user of the package is using the package improperly, that is, when `Seed` or `Randomize` is called after the first call to `Random` or when these routines are called more than once. Modify the random number generator package to have this additional level of protection. What should the package do if the user does use it improperly?

The Turbo Pascal model of independent compilation

The difference between `uses` and `#include` is not just one of syntax—internally, the two approaches couldn't be more different! `uses` does *not* cause Turbo Pascal to go out and read the text of a `.PAS` file, replacing the `uses` statement with the Pascal code found there. When a `program` is compiled, the resulting machine

---

FIGURE 2–11   The Random Number Generator in Turbo Pascal—The File `RANDOMNU.PAS`

> *This header identifies the code in this file as an independently compiled package. In the main program or another unit, access to the publicly visible constants, types, variables, and procedures is gained by including the statement* `uses RandomNumbers`.

```
1   unit RandomNumbers;
```

> *The contents of the* `interface` *part dictates what is visible to the outside world.*

```
2   interface
```

> *Turbo Pascal recognizes different size integers. This reflects the reality that computer hardware and the mathematician's view of integers don't correspond.* `longint` *is a 32-bit integer, whereas* `integer` *is only a 16-bit integer. Since these parameters are call-by-value, there will be no problem if the caller passes in a constant or a variable of type* `integer`.

```
3   procedure Seed(iseed: longint);
4      (* Seed the random number generator with a user-specified seed.
5
6      This routine should be called at most once, either directly or indirectly
7      (by calling procedure  Randomize  below), before any calls to the
8      random number generator are made.
9      *)
```

> *See line 4 of* `random.h`. *Because Turbo Pascal units have an initialization part, the unit can set* `xsubk` *to a default value and* `Seed` *need not be called.*

```
10
11  procedure Randomize;
12     (* Start the random number generator stream in a random place.
13     Effectively, this routine calls  Seed  with the time of day.
14     *)
15
16  function Random: real;
17     (* Return a pseudorandom real number in the half-open interval [0,1). *)
18
```

> *The* `implementation` *part, besides giving the code for the procedures declared in the* `interface` *part, can declare constants, types, variables, and procedures that cannot be accessed by the outside world.*

```
19  implementation
```

> `xsubk` *is visible to* `Seed`, `Randomize` *(which doesn't actually use it), and* `Random`, *but not outside the unit.*

```
20  uses Dos;  (* GetTime *)
```

> *The full declaration can be repeated. It is a good idea to do so.*

```
21  var xsubk: longint;  (* previous random number in integer form *)
22  procedure Seed(iseed: longint);
23     (* Seed the random number generator with a user-specified seed.
24
25     This routine should be called at most once, either directly or indirectly
26     (by calling procedure  Randomize  below), before any calls to the
27     random number generator are made.
28     *)
29     begin
30        xsubk := iseed
31     end; (* Seed *)
32
```

> *Because* `Randomize` *needs to read the clock,* `unit RandomNumbers` *includes an even more basic, system-supplied package,* `Dos`. *A uses statement can go in one of three places:*
> 1. *Immediately after the* program *heading of the main program.*
> 2. *Immediately after the keyword* `interface` *in a unit.*
> 3. *Immediately after the keyword* `implementation` *in a unit.*

FIGURE 2–11   Concluded

In Turbo Pascal, unlike in UNIX Pascal, the interface *and* implementation *parts must be in the same file. Because the* uses *statement is not a read-and-replace, a change in the* implementation *part does not necessitate a recompile of those units that use the changed unit. When a program is recompiled using the* Compile|Make *option, the following rules are applied:*

1. *Any module whose source has changed is recompiled.*
2. *Any module that uses a unit whose* interface *has changed is recompiled.*
3. *If a compiled unit has no source code version it is deemed to be up to date. This allows proprietary object code to be delivered without the source code.*

```
33  procedure Randomize;
34    (* Start the random number generator stream in a random place.
35       Effectively, this routine calls  Seed  with the time of day.
36    *)
37    var Hours, Minutes, Seconds, Hundredths: word ;
```

— word *is another of Turbo Pascal's integer types. It is a 16-bit unsigned quantity* (0..65536), *whereas* integer *is a 16-bit signed quantity* (-32768..32767). *Since the parameters to* GetTime *are call-by-reference, these variables must be declared* word.

— *read the clock*

```
38    begin
39      GetTime(Hours,Minutes,Seconds,Hundredths);
40      Seed( longint(Hours)*60*60*100 + Minutes*60*100 + Seconds*100 + Hundredths )
41    end; (* Randomize *)
```

time of day in 1/100ths of seconds ——

```
42
43  function Random: real;
44    (* Return a pseudorandom real number in the half-open interval [0,1). *)

         ... the same code as on lines 30–61 of random.p ...


77    end; (* Random *)
```

— *Variables declared in both the interface and implementation parts are visible inside the initialization part.*

```
78  begin
79    xsubk := 1 (* The default seed is 1. *)
80  end. (* RandomNumbers *)
```

— *The initialization part is optional. If present, it executes once, before the main program begins execution. This allows variables, like* xsubk, *to be initialized. This capability, missing in UNIX Pascal, aids in avoiding errors. While the same effect can be had in UNIX Pascal by having a procedure named* Init *in the package, with the main program calling* Init *as its first executable statement, this places the burden on the user of the package, who might forget to do this. The ability to initialize variables before beginning execution of the main program is reflected in the change to the comment on line 6.*

When Turbo Pascal encounters
    uses *unit_name ;*
it searches for the file unit_name . TPU, *with unit_name truncated to eight letters (the length of file names in MS-DOS). If the file* unit_name . TPU *is not found, and there is no* unit_name . PAS *to compile, an error is reported.*

language program is placed in a file with the extension `.EXE`, whereas when a `unit` is compiled, the object code is placed in a file with the extension `.TPU`, which stands for "Turbo Pascal Unit." Just like a `.o` file in UNIX, the `.TPU` file contains information on the starting addresses of the procedures defined in the unit. But it contains more. It contains, in an internal form, the information found in the Pascal text of the interface portion of the unit. When Turbo Pascal encounters a `uses` statement, it looks for the `.TPU` file with the same name, not the `.PAS` file. It incorporates the information about the interface portion into its current compilation. Since the compiled code for the bodies of the procedures is also available in the `.TPU` file, it can do the necessary linking as well.

The `Compile|Make` *option*

That Turbo Pascal uses the internally formatted version of the information found in the `.TPU` file, instead of the raw Pascal found in the `.PAS` file, isn't that revolutionary. What makes Turbo Pascal essentially different is the protection the `Compile|Make` option in the `Compile` menu offers the programmer. When using the `Compile|Make` option on a main program, Turbo Pascal tracks down all the units used by the main program as well as all the units that are used indirectly. It tracks down everything that it needs to build a complete program, including `.PAS` versions of the units. Besides compiling the main program and linking all the pieces together, Turbo Pascal

- Recompiles any unit for which the source has been modified since the corresponding `.TPU` file was created.
- Recompiles any unit that depends on a unit whose `interface` part has changed.
- Treats `.TPU` files for which there is no corresponding `.PAS` file as up to date.

The first two points show that Turbo Pascal eliminates the problem of forgetting to recompile a file that was modified. Everything that needs recompiling will be recompiled. Notice that while Turbo Pascal does not physically separate the interface from the implementation, it effectively does make this separation, because units that depend on a unit that has been changed are recompiled only if the interface part has been changed. Just changing the implementation or initialization parts doesn't cause *other* units to be recompiled. The significance of the final point is that the object file of a proprietary software package can be turned over to the customer without having to turn over the source.

The dependencies for the Turbo Pascal version of the program `worm` are shown in Figure 2–12. The `.TPU` files for the system-supplied `Dos` and `Crt` packages have no corresponding `.PAS` files.

2.4 MORE ON LIFETIME, SCOPE, AND VISIBILITY

In Section 1.4 we explored the lifetime, scope, and visibility of variables in standard Pascal. C, FORTRAN, Ada, and both UNIX and Turbo Pascal give the programmer greater control over these basic properties of variables. Having a greater variety of options results in better-structured programs.

Automatic variables

The most significant separation, because it affects what we can easily do, involves the lifetime of variables. The "local" variables declared within a Pascal procedure are often referred to as *automatic variables*. Their lifetime is ephemeral. They come into existence with no guaranteed initial value when the procedure is called, and they disappear when it returns. These are really the only kind of variables supported by standard Pascal. Even the "global" variables of the main program are automatic. Their existence, which spans the entire execution, and their scope, which spans the entire program listing, are consequences of the scope rules of the language and not a reflection on their lifetime.

FIGURE 2–12   The Structure of worm in Turbo Pascal

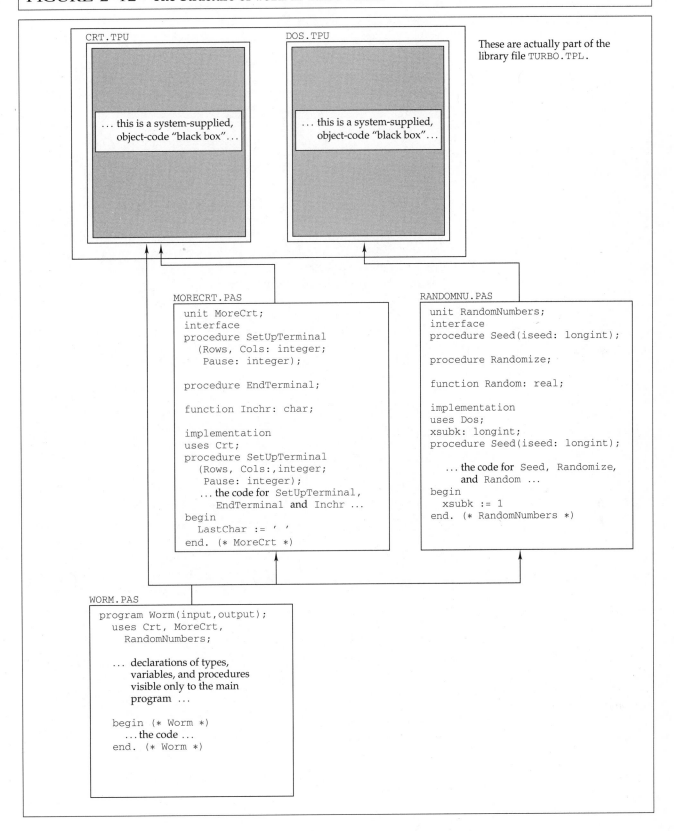

CRT.TPU

... this is a system-supplied, object-code "black box"...

DOS.TPU

... this is a system-supplied, object-code "black box"...

These are actually part of the library file TURBO.TPL.

MORECRT.PAS

```
unit MoreCrt;
interface
procedure SetUpTerminal
   (Rows, Cols: integer;
    Pause: integer);

procedure EndTerminal;

function Inchr: char;

implementation
uses Crt;
procedure SetUpTerminal
   (Rows, Cols:,integer;
    Pause: integer);
   ... the code for SetUpTerminal,
      EndTerminal and Inchr ...
begin
   LastChar := ' '
end. (* MoreCrt *)
```

RANDOMNU.PAS

```
unit RandomNumbers;
interface
procedure Seed(iseed: longint);

procedure Randomize;

function Random: real;

implementation
uses Dos;
xsubk: longint;
procedure Seed(iseed: longint);

   ... the code for Seed, Randomize,
      and Random ...
begin
   xsubk := 1
end. (* RandomNumbers *)
```

WORM.PAS

```
program Worm(input,output);
   uses Crt, MoreCrt,
      RandomNumbers;

   ... declarations of types,
      variables, and procedures
      visible only to the main
      program ...

   begin (* Worm *)
   ...the code ...
   end. (* Worm *)
```

FOR YOUR
INFORMATION

All UNIX systems aren't the same.

Fine Details of UNIX Systems

Unlike Turbo Pascal, which is a single commercial product, there is no such thing as UNIX Pascal. UNIX systems usually come with a Pascal compiler, but there are as many different dialects as there are hardware platforms. Because independent compilation is a nonstandard feature, each dialect has implemented it slightly differently, even if they all have adopted the same general philosophy.

While the read-and-replace nature of the include mechanism would seem to imply that a #include can go anywhere and contain anything, some dialects of UNIX Pascal place restrictions on where such lines can be placed and on what the .h files can contain. This is in line with their use as headers. In the dialect of Pascal available from Digital Equipment Corporation for the DEC-station, the #include "filename.h" lines can appear only at the outermost level, outside of procedures. For packages like our random number generator, this means that the #include "filename.h" lines must appear first in the .p file and can contain only declarations.

The situation with respect to the main program is more complex. On the DECstation the #include can appear either before or after the program statement, but the two placements have different effects. If the #include is outside the main program, then the names in the .h file are treated as external names, whereas if the #include is placed inside the the main program, right after the program statement, then the names are local to the main program and variables are not shared. This confusing detail is illustrated in Figure 2–13. In Berkeley Pascal for the VAXstation and in Pascal for various Sun platforms, the #include must be inside the program statement, but it is treated in the same way that Pascal for the DECstation treats it when it is on the outside.

Protection against programmer errors

One of the major benefits associated with the include mechanism is more reliable program maintenance. By not physically repeating the text of the .h file in each of the .p files, the possibility that they might become different over time is eliminated. But, what about the following scenario? First, the programmer defines the interface in random.h and scurries off to program random.p. Following good software engineering practice, the programmer next compiles it with a simple driver and thoroughly tests the routines. Suppose that sometime later, while working on worm.p, the programmer decides that the function Random would be more useful if the range of values returned by the function could be specified. Accordingly, the programmer changes the declaration in random.h to

```
function Random(low, high: real): real;
 (* Return a pseudorandom number in the half open interval [low,high). *)
```

And now, horror of horrors, after changing the body of Random in random.p, the programmer forgets to recompile this file. When the parts of the program are linked together, the references to Random in worm.o are based on the

(continued)

declaration in the new version of `random.h`

```
function Random(low, high: real): real;
```

whereas the code in `random.o` is based on the old version of `random.h`, where `Random` was declared

```
function Random: real;
```

What will happen? The linker won't care; it is quite capable of building an executable program, but since the caller's and callee's views of `Random` are different, the program will exhibit bizarre behavior. Furthermore, no amount of staring at the source program will find the error! The source is completely correct. What is wrong is that `random.o` is older than `random.p`. The `Compile|Make` option in Turbo Pascal prevents this error, because if notices that the `.TPU` file is older than the `.PAS` file and it automatically recompiles the `.PAS` file. Does UNIX Pascal prevent this error? Can it prevent this error?

Because the include mechanism need not simply be a read-and-replace, and because we link the `.o` files with `pc` and not directly with `ld`, there exists the possibility that Pascal can afford us some measure of protection by building into the `.o` files additional information that can be checked when we invoke

```
pc worm.o pscr.o random.o clock.o -ltermlib -o worm
```

Berkeley Pascal for the VAXstation incorporates into the `.o` files a copy of the `.h` files used. If two references to the same `.h` file don't agree, an error is reported. Other UNIX Pascal implementations do not perform this consistency check. As an aside, UNIX provides a language-independent project management tool, known as the `make` utility, for preventing just these sorts of errors. This utility is the subject of our last case study.

EXERCISE 2–5   If you have access to a UNIX system, test the Pascal compiler to see what protection is offered in the scenario just described.

Initialization

In Pascal for the DECstation it is possible to initialize static variables that occur in `.h` and `.p` files. For example, the declaration on line 4 of `random.p` can be

```
var xsubk: integer := 1;
```

The effect is the same as placing

```
xsubk := 1
```

in the initialization part of the Turbo Pascal unit `RandomNumbers`. The UNIX Pascal programs in this book do not use this extension.

FIGURE 2–13   The Effect of Placement of `#include` in DEC Pascal for RISC

vars–and–procs.h

```
1 var i: integer;
2
3 procedure SetI; external;
4 procedure PrintI; external;
```

main.p

```
1 program main(input,output);
2 #include "vars–and–procs.h"
3   begin
4     SetI;
5     i := 3;
6     PrintI
7   end.
```

The i *declared in* main.p *and the* i
declared in vars–and–proc.p
are not the same and the program prints 2.

vars–and–procs.p

```
1 #include "vars–and–procs.h"
2
3 procedure SetI;
4   begin
5     i := 2
6   end; (* SetI *)
7
8 procedure PrintI;
9   begin
10    writeln(i:1)
11  end; (* PrintI *)
```

With the `#include` Inside the Main Program

vars–and–procs.h

```
1 var i: integer;
2
3 procedure SetI; external;
4 procedure PrintI; external;
```

main.p

```
1 #include "vars–and–procs.h"
2 program main(input,output);
3   begin
4     SetI;
5     i := 3;
6     PrintI
7   end.
```

The i *declared in* main.p *and the* i
declared in vars–and–procs.p
are the same and the program prints 3.

vars–and–procs.p

```
1 #include "vars–and–procs.h"
2
3 procedure SetI;
4   begin
5     i := 2
6   end; (* SetI *)
7
8 procedure PrintI;
9   begin
10    writeln(i:1)
11  end; (* PrintI *)
```

With the `#include` Outside the Main Program

A rather natural alternative is to have variables whose lifetime extends over the entire run of the program. The term used to describe these variables is *static*. These variables do not reside in a stack frame and do *not* necessarily have to be "global"—their scope is an entirely different matter. In both UNIX and Turbo Pascal the variables that are external to any procedure are static. Both lifetime regimens are useful; automatic variables support recursion, whereas static variables allow information to be retained from one procedure invocation to the next. This latter attribute is very important when we have a data structure (like a stack) that is operated on by different procedures (PUSH and POP), but rightfully belongs to none of the procedures and must outlive a single call.

Static variables

The only sensible scope rule for automatic variables is to have the scope extend to the end of the procedure in which the variable is declared. This scope rule implies that access to an automatic variable is limited to nested subprocedures and the procedure itself, and we are guaranteed that when an automatic variable is referenced, a stack frame containing the variable exists. Since static variables have an independent existence, there are a greater variety of possible scope rules. There are three places where a static variable can be declared, and all of them are useful.

Scope rules for static variables

- In a procedure.
- In the interface portion of a package.
- In the implementation portion of the package, but external to any procedure.

Sometimes it is advantageous to have a variable whose scope is limited to a procedure, but whose value is retained from one invocation of the procedure to the next. We have already seen the need for such a variable. The variable `LastDirection`, used in fixing the discrepancy between our program and the UNIX-supplied program for worm, needs to be visible only within the procedure `GetMove`. But unlike the temporary variable `Direction`, the value of `LastDirection` must be retained from call to call. In standard Pascal, such a variable has to be declared in the main program and referenced globally. The disadvantage of this approach is that the variable `LastDirection` then becomes visible to all the procedures of the program. The issue is one of software engineering: in a large program, worked on by many people, it is too easy to accidently reference such a variable. The language gives us no protection against our own careless errors or sloppy programming practices; we must rely on our own good intentions. It would be better to have a storage class that fulfills this need. Other languages do: ALGOL 60 called variables in this class **own** *variables*. FORTRAN and C also have this storage class.

"`own`" Variables

The discussion of this discrepancy is on p. 61

We must be able to initialize static variables, or they are of no use. The issue is made clear by considering `LastDirection`, which must be initialized to a blank or some other invalid character before the procedure `GetMove` is entered for the first time. We cannot do this by placing the line

```
LastDirection := ' '
```

at the start of the routine, for while this works the first time, it destroys the very values we are trying to retain on subsequent invocations. On the other hand, we cannot initialize it at the start of the body of the main program because, if its scope is limited to `GetMove`, it is not visible there. All that is needed is a small amount of additional syntax, something like

```
var LastDirection: static char := ' ';
```

The keyword `static` would inform the compiler that storage for this variable should be allocated outside the stack and the `:= ' '` would say how `LastDirection` should be initialized. Conceptually, this initialization is done

Random Number Generators

Random number generators are short mathematical routines that produce a sequence of numbers, $x_1, x_2, \ldots$, that appear random to the eye and pass certain statistical tests. More properly, they should be called *pseudorandom number generators*, because while the numbers generated appear random, there is really nothing random about them at all. Typically, when a random number generator becomes popular it undergoes intense scrutiny and eventually some correlation is found among the elements of the sequence it produces, and it becomes discredited. Still, high quality random number generators are widely available and a body of theory about them has been developed. Turning the theory into practice is complicated by the goal of making random number generation fast as well as statistically reliable. This means taking advantage of hardware features, like performing modular arithmetic in modulus `maxint + 1` by simply performing integer arithmetic while ignoring overflow. For these reasons, the coding of random number generators should be left to specialists; here we treat the theory only in the most general terms. We have already discussed the software engineering aspects of random number generation, such as encapsulation of the routines in a package, the use of static variables to retain values, and the detection of misuse. Here we concentrate on the method itself, expressed in lines 31–61 of `random.p`.

Random number generators are based around a function, $f(\ )$, that generates the sequence by repeatedly applying the function to the previous term to get the next term:

$$x_{n+1} = f(x_n)$$

While the result returned by `Random` is a real number in the half-open interval $[0, 1)$, the x_i are typically integers in the closed interval $[0, m - 1]$. Integer arithmetic is used internally because it is better understood and more uniform in its behavior across machines. The value $m - 1$ is often the largest positive integer representable on the machine and the result is converted to a real number in the range $[0, 1)$ by dividing by m. This division must be performed carefully, since m is not representable as an integer and integers close to m may lose precision when converted into floating-point numbers. In languages like C and FORTRAN, which support both single- and double-precision numbers, the division is done in double precision. The care that needs to be taken can be seen on lines 52–61. Because the method relies on integer overflow to perform the `mod` operation, it is crucial that the calculation on line 53 be done with range checking turned off.

Because there are only a finite number of integers in the range 0 through $m - 1$, eventually there will come a time when a term in the sequence is repeated. Because the value of $f(\ )$ depends only on `xsubk`, from this point on, the sequence will keep on repeating. The length of the repetitive cycle is called the *period* of the generator. The initial choice, x_0, is called the *seed* of the generator. Typically it has a default setting (1 in the Turbo Pascal implementation), can be set explicitly by the user (`procedure Seed`), or can be set "randomly" (`procedure Randomize`) by setting the seed to some "random"

(continued)

physical event, like the time of day. One advantage of pseudorandom number generators over truly random natural processes is that their results are reproducible—if the seed is the same, the sequence of number produced will be the same.

Clearly, the heart of the matter is in choosing $f(\ )$. One popular approach is to use the ***linear congruential method***. In this method $f(\ )$ is

$$x_{n+1} = ax_n + c \quad (\text{mod } m)$$

Here a is called the ***multiplier***, c is called the ***increment***, and m is called the ***modulus***. The choices made for a, c, and m are important in ensuring a long period and statistically random behavior. The choices given on lines 45–50 are designed to work on a computer with 32-bit, two's-complement arithmetic that does not initiate an interrupt on integer overflow. The body of function Random is based on a more general FORTRAN function, URAND, found in *Computer Methods for Mathematical Computations*, by Forsythe, Malcolm, and Moler, which is itself based on a long discussion in *The Art of Computer Programming: Volume 2—Seminumerical Algorithms*, by Donald E. Knuth. The URAND routine is hardware independent and computes a, c, and m when called for the first time.

Often what is desired is a random integer in the range $[1, n]$ or a random real number taken from some other distribution. In the program for worm, random numbers are used in generating and placing food. We need random integers in the range 1 to 9 for the value and random integers in the continuously shrinking range 1 to LastFree in order to find a free location. Figure 2–14 illustrates the process by which a uniformly distributed random real number in $[0, 1)$ can be converted into a uniformly distributed random integer in the range $[1, n]$. This is implemented in worm.p as the function rand on lines 102–106.

Not only do applications need to manipulate the stream of random numbers so that they have different characteristics, they often need more than one stream. It is bad practice to do what we have done in the program for worm: use one stream for two purposes. In our program, x_1, x_3, x_5, ... are used for selecting the free locations and x_2, x_4, x_6, ... are used for determining the nutritional value. While every other element of a truly random sequence will be random, every other element of a pseudorandom sequence may not have the same statistical properties as does the sequence as a whole. It is better to have two independent streams. Because xsubk is associated with the random number generator package, and not with the stream of random numbers, having multiple streams is not possible with our implementation. The traditional way to have multiple streams is to make the variable xsubk part of the main program, passing it into function Random. The declaration of the function then becomes

```
function Random(var xsubk: integer): real;
```

In Ada terminology, xsubk is an in out parameter. There is now no need for the procedure Seed and the user can call the function clock directly,

ABOVE
AND BEYOND

(concluded)

using the value returned to set xsubk and, hence, start the random number generator in a random place. To have multiple streams, the user just maintains multiple seeds. While traditional, this is not a wholly satisfactory solution as it violates good software engineering practice by distributing the parts of the random number generator over the entire program. An alternative, also not fully satisfactory because, while it has more than one stream it still has a fixed number, is to declare xsubk as an array and to have Seed, Randomize, and Random have a parameter indicating which stream is being accessed. Both Ada and C++ have language features that allow the user to create multiple streams of random numbers, each with its own xsubk, without giving the user access to the variable.

EXERCISE 2–6   Explain why the line of code

```
round((n-1)*Random) + 1
```

does *not* produce a uniformly distributed random integer in the range $[1, n]$.

FIGURE 2–14   **Converting a Uniformly Distributed Random Real Number in the Range $[0, 1)$ into a Uniformly Distributed Random Integer in the Range $[1, n]$**

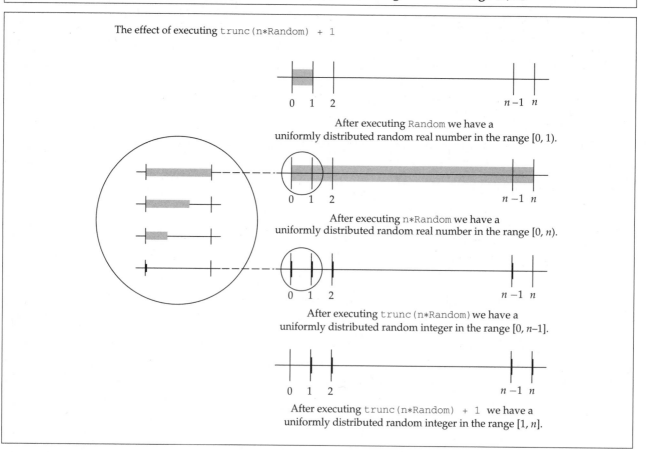

The effect of executing `trunc(n*Random) + 1`

After executing `Random` we have a uniformly distributed random real number in the range $[0, 1)$.

After executing `n*Random` we have a uniformly distributed random real number in the range $[0, n)$.

After executing `trunc(n*Random)` we have a uniformly distributed random integer in the range $[0, n-1]$.

After executing `trunc(n*Random) + 1` we have a uniformly distributed random integer in the range $[1, n]$.

once, right before the main program begins execution. Restrictions placed on what is allowed in the expression to the right of the assignment operator reflect how this concept is implemented. The conservative approach, which is adopted by C, is, in effect, to perform initialization at compile time and to allow the expression to be only a constant—a value the compiler can know. A more liberal view is to treat the initialization as an executable statement that executes before the main program starts. Not every expression can be legal, however—the expression certainly cannot refer to automatic variables in containing procedures, since they do not yet exist. Unfortunately, neither UNIX nor Turbo Pascal supports own variables.

Constants, types, and variables declared in the interface part of a package are visible throughout the package as well as in any other package that includes the package. On the other hand, constants, types, and variables declared in the implementation part, but external to any procedure, are visible only within the implementation part of the package and, in the case of Turbo Pascal, also within the initialization part. Though they are not present in standard Pascal, we use these external static variables extensively in our case studies.

FILE   worm.p   Page 1

See the section *Independent Compilation* for an explanation.
In Berkeley Pascal for the VAXstation and on Sun Microsystem platforms the lines
    #include "pscr.h"
    #include "random.h"
should be placed inside the main program, right before label 99.
In Turbo Pascal these two lines are replaced by
    uses Crt, MoreCrt, RandomNumbers;
which also goes immediately before label 99.

```
 1 (* Compile as:
 2    cc -c pscr.c clock.c
 3    pc -c random.p
 4    pc worm.p pscr.o random.o clock.o -ltermlib -o worm
 5 *)
 6
 7 #include "pscr.h"
 8 #include "random.h"
 9
10 program Worm(input,output);
11    (* This program allows the user to play the game of worm.
12
13       All operations used here run in constant time.
14    *)
15    label 99; (* game over *)
16
17    const (* Screen Parameters *)
18          (* The screen contains 23 rows.  Row 1 is the message row, rows 2-23
19             are the game board.  There are 80 columns numbered 1-80. *)
20          MINROW = 2; (* top row of the screen for game title and score *)
21          MAXROW = 23;
22          MINCOL = 1;
23          MAXCOL = 80;
24
25          SCORECOL = 70; (* The word "Score" starts in column 70. *)
26
27          (* Mnemonics For Game Board Characters *)
28          BLANK    = ' ';
29          HEADCHAR = '@';
30          BODYCHAR = 'o';
31          WALLCHAR = '*';
32
33          MAXFOOD = 9; (* it has to fit in one character *)
34
35          PAUSE = 1;    (* the delay before automatic keystroke repeat, in
36                           whole seconds *)
37
38          BUFFERSIZE = 1560; (* (MAXROW-3)*(MAXCOL-2) -- enough space to hold a
39                               worm that fills the screen *)
40
41          NOTFREEFLAG = -1; (* used to indicate cell occupied by worm or wall *)
42                            This value cannot lie in 1..BUFFERSIZE.
43    type RowRange = MINROW..MAXROW;
44         ColRange = MINCOL..MAXCOL;
45
46         CoordType = record
47                        Row: RowRange;
48                        Col: ColRange
49                     end;
50
```

*Unfortunately, standard Pascal does
not allow constant expressions.*

This value cannot lie in 1..BUFFERSIZE.

FILE   worm.p   Page 2

```
51          MoveType = record
52                        DeltaX, DeltaY: -1..1
53                     end;
54
55          FoodType = record
56                        Row: RowRange;
57                        Col: ColRange;
58                        Value: 1..MAXFOOD
59                     end;
60
```

The variables associated with each data structure are grouped physically together. The alternative, grouping all variables of the same Pascal type together, is inferior, because it does not put the emphasis on the logical structure of the program.

```
61  var (* Note: every cell of the game board (excluding the wall) is always
62              in exactly one of  WormSeg  and  FreePool . *)
63          (* Description Of The Worm *)
64          WormSeg:  (* A circular buffer containing the coordinates of each
65                        segment of the worm. *)
66            array [1..BUFFERSIZE] of CoordType;
67          HeadPos, TailPos: integer; (* pointers to head and tail in  WormSeg  *)
68
69          (* Description Of The Free Cells *)
70          FreePool: (* A randomly ordered list of the free cells on the game board.
71                        The cell with the piece of food is treated as free. *)
72            array [1..BUFFERSIZE] of CoordType;
73          LastFree: 0..BUFFERSIZE; (* index of last valid element of  FreePool  *)
74
75          (* Description Of The Game Board *)
76          Board: (* For free cells, the array element contains a back pointer to
77                     the corresponding location in  FreePool .  The  NOTFREEFLAG
78                     indicates the absence of a back pointer, that is, the presence
79                     of a worm segment or the wall. *)
80            array [MINROW..MAXROW,MINCOL..MAXCOL] of integer;
81
82          (* Description Of The Current Move *)
83          Move: MoveType;
84
85          (* Location And Value Of The Current Piece of Food *)
86          Food: FoodType;
87
88          NumToGrow, (* The number of segments the worm is to grow -- zero implies
89                        that the worm  is moving at both ends. *)
90          Score: integer;
91
92          r: RowRange;
93          c: ColRange;
94          FilledScreen: boolean;
95
```

The component type is overloaded. The sign tells us if the cell is occupied/unoccupied. If the cell is unoccupied, the value serves as a pointer into FreePool. *This takes less space, and, if well documented, is no less clear than having the component type defined as*
```
                  record
                     Occupied: boolean;
                     BackPtr: integer (* back pointer into  FreePool  *)
                  end;
```

```
96  procedure WriteChar(row, col: integer; ch: char);
97     (* Place the cursor in  [row,col]  and write a character. *)
98     begin
99        GotoXY(col,row); write(ch)
100    end; (* WriteChar *)
101
```

— See the annotation at line 34 of pscr.h.

```
102   function rand(n: integer): integer;
103     (* Return a random integer in the range [1..n]. *)
104     begin
105       rand := trunc(n*Random) + 1
106     end; (* rand *)
107
108   procedure GetMove(var Move: MoveType);
109     (* Get and return, in a form related to physical movement, a single
110        move of the worm.
111     *)
112     var Direction: char;
113     begin
114       (* Note: initially, because  Inchr  returns a blank until a key
115                 is struck, the program will hang here, waiting for the
116                 first valid user input.
117       *)
118       repeat
119         Direction := Inchr
120       until Direction in ['h', 'j', 'k', 'l']; (* ignore typing errors *)
121       case Direction of
122         'h': begin Move.DeltaX := 0;  Move.DeltaY := -1 end; (* left  *)
123         'j': begin Move.DeltaX := 1;  Move.DeltaY := 0  end; (* down  *)
124         'k': begin Move.DeltaX := -1; Move.DeltaY := 0  end; (* up    *)
125         'l': begin Move.DeltaX := 0;  Move.DeltaY := 1  end  (* right *)
126       end
127     end; (* GetMove *)
128
129   procedure MakeLocFree(Loc: CoordType);
130     (* Update data structures to indicate that a location is free,
131        that is, it is not occupied by a worm segment.
132     *)
133     begin
134       LastFree := LastFree + 1; (* place  Loc  at end of free pool *)
135       FreePool[LastFree] := Loc;
136       Board[Loc.Row,Loc.Col] := LastFree (* set back pointer *)
137     end; (* MakeLocFree *)
138
139   procedure MakeLocInUse(Loc: CoordType);
140     (* Update data structures to indicate that a location is in use,
141        that is, it is occupied by a worm segment.
142     *)
143     var p: integer;
144         r: RowRange;
145         c: ColRange;
146     begin
147       (* Move the last element of  FreePool  into the hole created by making
148          the cell at  Loc  occupied.  Update the back pointers to keep the
149          data structures consistent.  *)
150       p := Board[Loc.Row,Loc.Col];
151       r := FreePool[LastFree].Row;
152       c := FreePool[LastFree].Col;
153       FreePool[p] := FreePool[LastFree];
```

See Stretching a random number generator *in* Above and Beyond: Random Number Generators.

Create a "circle" at the end of FreePool.

Maintain the invariant of Figure 2–7.

FILE   worm.p   **Page 4**

```
154        (* When  p = LastFree  the order of the next two statements
155           is critical. *)
156        Board[r,c] := p;
157        Board[Loc.Row,Loc.Col] := NOTFREEFLAG;
158        LastFree := LastFree - 1
159      end; (* MakeLocInUse *)
160
```

— *These are the most subtle lines of the entire program.*

```
161   procedure InitScreen;
162      (* Draw the game board and write the title, but do not place the
163         worm or the initial piece of food.
164      *)
165      var r: RowRange;
166          c: ColRange;
167      begin
168        ClrScr;
169
170        (* Write Title Information *)
171        GotoXY(2,1); write('Worm');
172
173        (* Initialize Border *)
174        for c := MINCOL to MAXCOL do
175          WriteChar(MINROW,c,WALLCHAR);
176        for r := MINROW+1 to MAXROW-1 do
177          begin
178            WriteChar(r,MINCOL,WALLCHAR);
179            WriteChar(r,MAXCOL,WALLCHAR)
180          end;
181        for c := MINCOL to MAXCOL do
182          WriteChar(MAXROW,c,WALLCHAR)
183      end; (* InitScreen *)
184
```

The code on lines 173–182 is better than
```
      for r := MINROW to MAXROW do
        for c := MINCOL to MAXCOL do
          if (r = MINROW) or (r = MAXROW) or
             (c = MINCOL) or (c = MAXCOL)
            then WriteChar(r,c,WALLCHAR)
```
because running around the border takes
$O(n)$ *time, while this alternative takes*
$O(n^2)$ *time (on a square board that is $n \times n$).*

— *While these loops taken together still take $O(n^2)$ time, at the expense*
of a small amount of code we avoid $O(n^2)$ if *statements.*

```
185   procedure InitDataStructures;
186      (* Initialize the data structures to reflect the presence of the wall,
187         but not the initial placement of the worm or the initial piece of food.
188      *)
189      var r: RowRange;
190          c: ColRange;
191      begin
192        (* Indicate the presence of the wall in the back pointers array. *)
193        for c := MINCOL to MAXCOL do
194          Board[MINROW,c] := NOTFREEFLAG;
195        for r := MINROW+1 to MAXROW-1 do
196          begin
197            Board[r,MINCOL] := NOTFREEFLAG;
198            Board[r,MAXCOL] := NOTFREEFLAG
199          end;
200        for c := MINCOL to MAXCOL do
201          Board[MAXROW,c] := NOTFREEFLAG;
202
```

FILE   worm.p   Page 5

```
203        (* Indicate that every other cell in the game board is unoccupied. *)
204        LastFree := 0;
205        for r := MINROW+1 to MAXROW-1 do
206          for c := MINCOL+1 to MAXCOL-1 do
207            begin
208              LastFree := LastFree + 1;
209              Board[r,c] := LastFree;
210              FreePool[LastFree].Row := r;
211              FreePool[LastFree].Col := c
212            end
213      end; (* InitDataStructures *)
214
```

This implicit mechanism for relating Board[r,c] *to* FreePool[LastFree]
is less error prone than trying to find a formula for LastFree *in terms of* r
and c. LastFree *starts at zero and is incremented before use, as opposed to
starting at one and being incremented after use, as this way it has the correct
value on loop termination.*

See the related comment and annotation in procedure MoveHead.

```
215    procedure InitWorm;
216      (* The worm is initially placed in row 14, columns 3-10, with the
217          head in column 10.
218      *)
219      const WORMLEN  = 8;    (* procedure  MoveHead  assumes  WORMLEN >= 2  *)
220            STARTROW = 14;
221            STARTCOL = 3;
222      var i: integer;
223      begin
224        for i := 1 to WORMLEN-1 do
225          begin
226            WormSeg[i].Row := STARTROW;
227            WormSeg[i].Col := STARTCOL + (i - 1);
228            WriteChar(WormSeg[i].Row,WormSeg[i].Col,BODYCHAR);
229            MakeLocInUse(WormSeg[i])
230          end;
231        WormSeg[WORMLEN].Row := STARTROW;
232        WormSeg[WORMLEN].Col := STARTCOL + (WORMLEN - 1);
233        WriteChar(WormSeg[WORMLEN].Row,WormSeg[WORMLEN].Col,HEADCHAR);
234        MakeLocInUse(WormSeg[WORMLEN]);
235        TailPos := 1;
236        HeadPos := WORMLEN
237      end; (* InitWorm *)
238
```

*It might be better to place these constants with the others, at the outermost
level. Though used only here, they would become more visible.*

*Our standard mechanisms are used to place the worm initially.
This is better than complicating the data structure initialization
procedure to treat these squares separately.*

Some programmers prefer
```
       TailPos := TailPos mod BUFFERSIZE + 1
```
although a mod *is generally slower than an* if. *This modification allows*
TailPos *to be declared* 1..BUFFERSIZE *instead of* integer.

```
239    procedure MoveTail;
240      (* Move the tail of the worm -- the worm is not in growth mode. *)
241      begin
242        (* Erase the old tail. *)
243        WriteChar(WormSeg[TailPos].Row,WormSeg[TailPos].Col,BLANK);
244        MakeLocFree(WormSeg[TailPos]);
245        TailPos := TailPos + 1;
246        if TailPos > BUFFERSIZE then TailPos := 1
247      end; (* MoveTail *)
248
```

FILE   worm.p   Page 6

This line would incorrectly place an o on the screen if the worm initially had length 1.

```
249   procedure MoveHead(r: RowRange; c: ColRange);
250      (* Move the head of the worm to [r,c].
251         Preconditions: move does not involve the death of the worm
252                        worm has length >= 2 (initially)
253      *)
254      begin
255         (* Convert current head to normal body element. *)
256         WriteChar(WormSeg[HeadPos].Row,WormSeg[HeadPos].Col,BODYCHAR);
257
258         WriteChar(r,c,HEADCHAR);
259         HeadPos := HeadPos + 1;
260         if HeadPos > BUFFERSIZE then HeadPos := 1;
261         WormSeg[HeadPos].Row := r;
262         WormSeg[HeadPos].Col := c;
263         MakeLocInUse(WormSeg[HeadPos])
264      end; (* MoveHead *)
265
266   procedure UpdateScore(var Score: integer; Amount: integer);
267      (* As a result of eating a piece of food, update and print the score. *)
268      begin
269         Score := Score + Amount;
270         (* Normally the score is placed so that the last column contains a
271            blank, but for scores greater than 1000, use the last column
272            as well.  This happens automatically due to the rules of
273            field widths in Pascal. *)
274         GotoXY(SCORECOL,1); write('Score: ',Score:3)
275      end; (* UpdateScore *)
276
277   procedure CreateNewFood(var Food: FoodType);
278      var FoodLoc: CoordType;
279      begin
280         FoodLoc := FreePool[rand(LastFree)];
281         Food.Row := FoodLoc.Row;
282         Food.Col := FoodLoc.Col;
283         Food.Value := rand(MAXFOOD);
284         WriteChar(FoodLoc.Row,FoodLoc.Col,chr(Food.Value + ord('0')))
285      end; (* CreateNewFood *)
286
```

See the related comment on line 219.

This is a rare use of what Ada calls an in out *parameter.*

An apparently minor decision that affects many details of the code is whether or not to consider the cell containing the food a free cell. Doing so greatly simplifies the coding. The check to see if the worm dies and the code for moving the head, including the call to MakeLocInUse, *require no special cases.*

This trick for converting a one-digit number into a character works because the digits, as characters, are consecutive in the collating sequence. Unlike trunc *and assigning an integer value to a real variable, which involve changes to the internal format of numbers,* chr *and* ord *do very little. Basically,* ord *tells the Pascal compiler to change the amount of storage for the object from a byte to a word (if it isn't stored in a word already) and to change its internal notion of the type from* char *to* integer. chr *does just the opposite—the argument can have only a limited range, however.*

Uncoupling the movement of the head and tail, even though we normally call
MakeLocFree and then immediately call MakeLocInUse, is less error
prone than having two procedures, one for moving both the head and tail
under normal circumstances and one for moving just the head if the worm is in
a growth phase. Here, clarity is worth any slight inefficiency we might incur.

```
287  begin (* Worm *)
288    InitDataStructures;
289    Randomize;                (* initialize random number generator *)
290    SetUpTerminal(MAXROW,MAXCOL,PAUSE); (* set up the screen handling *)
291    InitScreen;               (* initialize game board *)
292    InitWorm;                 (* place the worm... *)
293    CreateNewFood(Food);      (* ...and the initial piece of food *)
294    Score := 0;
295
296    FilledScreen := false;
297    NumToGrow := 0; (* worm not growing initially *)
298    while true do (* escape from loop when worm dies or fills the screen *)
299      begin
300        GetMove(Move);
301        r := WormSeg[HeadPos].Row + Move.DeltaX;
302        c := WormSeg[HeadPos].Col + Move.DeltaY;
303        (* The head can legally go where the tail is currently, so move
304           the tail before moving the head. *)
305        if NumToGrow > 0
306          then NumToGrow := NumToGrow - 1
307          else MoveTail;
308        if Board[r,c] = NOTFREEFLAG then goto 99; (* worm died *)
309        MoveHead(r,c);
310        (* The worm can fill the board only at the exact same moment it
311           has eaten a piece of food, so delay test for this condition. *)
312        if (r = Food.Row) and (c = Food.Col)
313          then begin
314                 (* worm can eat a piece of food while it is growing *)
315                 NumToGrow := NumToGrow + Food.Value;
316                 UpdateScore(Score,Food.Value);
317                 if LastFree = 0
318                   then begin
319                          FilledScreen := true;
320                          goto 99
321                        end;
322                 CreateNewFood(Food)
323               end
324      end;
325
326 99: (* worm died or filled the screen *)
327    ClrScr;
328    if not FilledScreen
329      then writeln('Well, you ran into something and the game is over.')
330      else writeln('You have won the game of worm.');
331    writeln('Your final score was ',Score:1);
332    EndTerminal (* return terminal to normal behavior *)
333  end. (* Worm *)
```

This test and loop escape are needed to prevent calling CreateNewFood when there are no free
squares left—without it, CreateNewFood could place a piece of food on the head of the worm.

FILE

```
 1 procedure SetUpTerminal(Rows, Cols: integer; Pause: integer); external;
 2   (* Interface with the system to set up the terminal for special operation.
 3
 4      This routine should be called once, before any other routine in
 5      this package.  It allows  GotoXY  to place the cursor on the screen
 6      at the desired location and cancels line buffering and echoing of
 7      input from the keyboard.  Pascal's standard  write  procedure is
 8      not affected, except that the characters appear at the current
 9      location of the cursor and no buffering occurs.
10
11      Rows -- The number of rows and columns that form the window in which
12              worm is played.
13      Cols --
14      Pause -- The delay, in whole seconds, before the last character struck
15              will be restruck automatically.
16   *)
17
18 procedure EndTerminal; external;
19   (* Return the terminal to normal status -- cancels the effect
20      of  SetUpTerminal .
21
22      This routine should be called once.  No other routine in this
23      package should be called afterwards.
24   *)
25
26 function Inchr: char; external;
27   (* Get a character from the terminal, or the last character typed
28      if nothing has been typed within  Pause  seconds.
29
30      If  Pause  seconds elapse before the very first key is struck, blanks
31      are returned.
32   *)
33
```

> *The worm program is written to conform to the way programmers have been trained to think about arrays—row first and column second (here with lower numbered rows on the top and higher numbered rows on the bottom). The screen package, to conform to Turbo Pascal, specifies the column first and the row second.*

```
34 procedure GotoXY(col, row: integer); external;
35   (* Set the cursor to the [row,col] position on the screen.  Note that
36      [1,1] is "home" (the upper left hand corner of the screen).
37   *)
38
39 procedure ClrScr; external;
40   (* Clears the screen and homes the cursor. *)
```

> *The Turbo Pascal library unit* Crt *includes most of the capabilities described here, as well as many others. The procedures* GotoXY *and* ClrScr *are located in that unit, as is the function* ReadKey, *which reads a character from the keyboard without echoing it to the screen. The Turbo Pascal version of this package must still provide for the repetition of keystrokes—see the file* MORECRT.PAS *on the diskette that accompanies this book.*

FILE   random.h

> *Turbo Pascal has a random number generator with more or less the same interface already built-in. The only difference is that Seed is not a procedure. The same effect is achieved by having the longint variable RandSeed user visible. If we do not like the statistical properties of the system-supplied generator and wish to provide our own, the principles discussed in this chapter still apply—see the file RANDOMNU.PAS on the diskette that accompanies this book.*

```
1 procedure Seed(iseed: integer); external;
2   (* Seed the random number generator with a user specified seed.
3
4      This routine should be called once, either directly or indirectly
5      (by calling procedure  Randomize  below), before any calls to the
6      random number generator are made.
7   *)
8
9 procedure Randomize; external;
10   (* Start the random number generator stream in a random place.
11      Effectively, this routine calls  Seed  with the time of day.
12   *)
13
14 function Random: real; external;
15   (* Return a pseudo-random real number in the half open interval [0,1). *)
```

FILE   clock.h

```
1 function clock: integer; external;
2   (* Read the hardware clock and return the time elapsed from some
3      starting point (unspecified).
4   *)
```

> *The body of this routine will depend heavily on the nature of the operating system and hardware. The actual value returned is not as important as its having the appearance of randomness.*

FILE   random.p   Page 1

See the section More on Lifetime, Scope, and Visibility. *In the dialect of Pascal on the DECstation we can write*
```
var xsubk: integer := 1;
```
to give xsubk *a default value. The dialects of Pascal running on the VAXstation and Sun Microsystem platforms do not allow such initialization.*

```
 1  #include "clock.h"
 2  #include "random.h"
 3
 4  var xsubk: integer; (* previous random number in integer form *)
 5
 6  (* procedure Seed(iseed: integer); *)
 7  procedure Seed;
 8    (* Seed the random number generator with a user-specified seed.
 9
10     This routine should be called once, either directly or indirectly
11     (by calling procedure  Randomize  below), before any calls to the
12     random number generator are made.
13    *)
14    begin
15      xsubk := iseed
16    end; (* Seed *)
17
18  (* procedure Randomize; *)
19  procedure Randomize;
20    (* Start the random number generator stream in a random place.
21       Effectively, this routine calls  Seed  with the time of day.
22    *)
23    begin
24      Seed(clock)
25    end; (* Randomize *)
26
27  (* function Random: real; *)
28  function Random;
29    (* Return a pseudorandom real number in the half-open interval [0,1). *)
30
31    (* A linear congruential random number generator, that is, one where
32                x[k+1] = a*x[k] + c     mod m
33     Constants a, c, and m are based on the URAND Fortran routine discussed
34     in Chapter 10 of "Computer Methods for Mathematical Computations"
35     by Forsythe, Malcolm, and Moler, which is in turn based on the
36     discussion given in "The Art of Computer Programming:
37     Volume 2 -- Seminumerical Algorithms" by Donald E. Knuth.
38
39     The routine presented here has been specialized to work on 32-bit
40     two's-complement machines in which arithmetic is "well behaved".
41     In particular, it is assumed that interrupts do not occur on
42     integer overflow.  Other "abnormal" arithmetic behavior may invalidate
43     the behavior of this code.
44    *)
45    const (* m = 2^31, or one larger than the largest positive number
46             representable on the machine *)
47        halfm = 1073741824; (* m/2 = 2^30 = largest positive power of 2
48                                representable on the machine *)
49      a =  843314861;
50      c =  453816693;
```

See The UNIX Pascal Approach *in the section* Independent Compilation.

See Above and Beyond: Random Number Generators.

```
51   begin
52     (* Compute Next Random Number *)
53     xsubk := a*xsubk + c;
54
55     (* Due to the way overflow is handled in the hardware, the modulo m
56        has been done automatically, except the result can be negative. *)
57     if xsubk < 0
58       then xsubk := (xsubk + halfm) + halfm; (* xsubk + m, but done carefully *)
59
60     (* Return the answer as a real number in [0,1). *)
61     Random := xsubk/(2.0*halfm)
62   end; (* Random *)
```

If m *is a power of two, this computation returns* m *in floating-point format without any loss of precision.*

CHAPTER 3

COMPUTING 100 FACTORIAL

On February 6, 1989, the *Daily Lobo*, the student newspaper of the University of New Mexico, published as part of its weekly mathematics puzzle the following problem: how many terminal zeros are there in 100 factorial? This question can be answered by realizing that the only way to obtain a terminal zero is to have a factor of 10. So we really need to answer the question: how many factors of 10 are there in $100 \times 99 \times 98 \times \cdots \times 2 \times 1$? Since factors of 10 are composed of factors of two and factors of five, and since factors of two are more prevalent, the question boils down to: how many factors of five are there in $100 \times 99 \times 98 \times \cdots \times 2 \times 1$? The answer is 24—each of the 20 multiples of five contributes one, except 25, 50, 75, and 100, which contribute two. But what is the actual value of 100 factorial? You certainly cannot compute it using variables of type `integer`, because you will quickly overflow the word size of any computer. To answer this question and others like it, we will augment Pascal with a new type, `LongInteger`, whose values are arbitrarily long, nonnegative integers. It is then an easy computation to discover that

$$100! = \begin{aligned} &93, 326, 215, 443, 944, 152, 681, 699, 238, 856, 266, 700, 490, 715, \\ &968, 264, 381, 621, 468, 592, 963, 895, 217, 599, 993, 229, 915, 608, \\ &941, 463, 976, 156, 518, 286, 253, 697, 920, 827, 223, 758, 251, 185, \\ &210, 916, 864, 000, 000, 000, 000, 000, 000, 000, 000 \; \blacksquare \end{aligned}$$

3.1 ABSTRACT DATA TYPES

The ideal solution to this problem is to redefine `integer`, changing it from a type that matches what the underlying hardware supports, to a type that conforms to the mathematician's view of what integers are, with no limitations on the range of values. We would then be able to write the obvious program:

The way the program for n! ought to look.

```
 1  program NFactorial(input,output);
 2    (* Compute  n! . *)
 3    var i, n, NFact: integer;
 4    begin
 5      write('For what  n  do you wish to compute  n! : '); readln(n);
 6      NFact := 1;
 7      for i := 2 to n do
 8        NFact := NFact * i;
 9      writeln(n:1,'! = ',NFact:1)
10    end. (* NFactorial *)
```

Of course, the new version of `integer` must be implemented as some complicated data structure, and simple lines like

$$NFact := NFact * i$$

will now take much longer to execute than limited-range multiplication using the computer's multiplication instruction.

What we want to do is define an ***abstract data type*** (an "ADT") for the true integers.

> *An abstract data type is a collection of values and a set of operations that can be performed on them, bundled together into a package.*

The fundamental characteristic of an ADT is the total separation of the implementation of the data type from its use in applications programs. The outside world is supposed to be completely ignorant of the mechanics of how the data is represented and how the operations are performed; the only access to objects of the abstract data type is through the user-visible operations the ADT exports.

Of course, inside the package, the nitty-gritty of the representation must be known—otherwise, how will the developer program the ADT? Abstract data types are now universally recognized as one of the fundamental tools for developing correct, maintainable, reusable code. A key feature of languages like Ada, which grew out of the Pascal tradition, and C++, which evolved from C, is the built-in language support for implementing ADTs.

Actually, as farfetched as the idea of redefining `integer` might seem at first glance, you may know the fine details of Pascal well enough to be aware that `integer` is a ***predefined type*** and not a ***reserved word***. Thus, we can change `integer` to something like

```
type integer = record
                 ...
               end;
```

Unfortunately, while this type declaration is perfectly legal and the variable declaration

```
var i, n, NFact: integer;
```

compiles just fine, the line

```
NFact := NFact * i
```

produces the error message "cannot multiply records," because while the name of the type is integer, NFact and i aren't really integers.

Since we aren't about to monkey with the compiler, we will have to be a little less ambitious. Nevertheless, we will develop a useful tool, a package to manipulate infinite precision integers[1] that provides the same functionality as the Pascal predefined integer type. Using this package the program to compute *n!* is

The way it actually looks.

See the file Long_Arithmetic.h *for the procedure declarations used in this program.*

```
 1  #include "Long_Arithmetic.h"
 2
 3  program NFactorial(input,output);
 4    (* Compute  n!  using an infinite precision arithmetic package. *)
 5    var one,     (* the constant  1  in infinite precision format *)
 6        IInLong, (* the variable  i  in infinite precision format *)
 7        NFact: LongInteger;
 8        i, n: integer;
 9    begin
10      InitializeMemoryManagement;
11
12      Declare(one); Declare(IInLong); Declare(NFact);
13
14      MakeLong(one,1);
15
16      write('For what  n  do you wish to compute  n! : '); readln(n);
17      Assign(NFact,one);        (* NFact := 1         *)
18      Assign(IInLong,one);      (* i := 1             *)
19      for i := 2 to n do
20        begin
21          Add(IInLong,IInLong,one); (* i := i + 1          *)
22          Mult(NFact,NFact,IInLong) (* NFact := NFact * i *)
23        end;
24      writeln(n:1,'! =');  WriteNum(NFact)
25    end. (* NFactorial *)
```

While perhaps not as clear as the earlier ten-line program, this twenty-five-line program certainly gets the job done.

3.2 DATA STRUCTURES FOR REPRESENTING INFINITE PRECISION INTEGERS

Many intertwined issues affect the representation of infinite precision integers and the conventions that must be observed by programmers who use the package we are going to develop. At first, it is difficult to see the need for some of the procedures declared in Long_Arithmetic.h. For example, why is there a need for Declare? Don't the lines

```
var one,     (* the constant  1  in infinite precision format *)
    IInLong, (* the variable  i  in infinite precision format *)
    NFact: LongInteger;
```

declare these variables? And why is there the need for Assign? The line

```
                    NFact := one
```

---

[1] The phrase *infinite precision* is a misnomer, since any particular integer has only finitely many digits. Better terms might be *unlimited, indefinite,* or *arbitrary precision*. But *infinite precision* has been used in this context for a long time and the name, however inappropriate, has stuck.

will not cause the compiler to complain, since both `NFact` and `one` have the same type and it is a fundamental rule of Pascal that two variables of the same type can be assigned one to the other. The need for procedures like `Add`, and in fact all the arithmetic operations, is more obvious, though there is the question: why do we use procedures, and not functions, since functions are more in the spirit of operators like `+`, `-`, `*`, and `div`? The answers are intimately tied up with the details of how we will represent infinite precision integers.

EXERCISE 3–1   Using the program `NFactorial` as a model, write a program to compute the *n*th Fibonacci number. The Fibonacci numbers are defined by the sequence

$$0, 1, 1, 2, 3, 5, 8, 13, \ldots$$

Each term is the sum of the preceding two terms; formally, they are generated by the recurrence

$$F_n = F_{n-1} + F_{n-2}$$

with $F_0 = 0$ and $F_1 = 1$.

Do this exercise now to get a feel for the infinite precision arithmetic package.

Always think of the special cases first!

Before thinking about possible representations, we note that very little can go wrong in the mathematics of an infinite precision arithmetic package. About the only mishap that can occur is an attempt to divide by zero. There really is no good response if this should happen, but it doesn't seem like the sort of error that ought to affect our choice of data structure. Also, since our package supports only nonnegative integers, we must deal with the possibility that a subtraction yields a negative result. There is also the related problem of the user calling `MakeLong` with a negative second parameter. We define the subtraction problem away by making `Sub` perform **proper subtraction**. Proper subtraction is defined to be $a - b$ if a is greater than or equal to b, and zero otherwise. There might be some discussion of how to treat an illegal call to `MakeLong`, but the condition certainly is easy to detect. One of the projects in this chapter asks you to extend the package to include negative numbers as well; this extension makes these last two problems disappear, leaving only the divide-by-zero error.

There is another problem as well: the numbers might get so large that the computer does not have enough memory to hold them, no matter how compact our representation. Here we are at the mercy of Pascal and our operating system, so we just keep the concern in the back of our minds.

Coming to a decision on how to represent infinite precision integers is a wonderful example of engineering design. We have to consider the limitations of Pascal, as well as trade-offs between time and space. Deciding how to balance the trade-offs, in turn, depends on what operations we think will be performed most frequently, as some representations may allow an efficient implementation of one operation, but force the implementation of others to be inefficient. We begin by looking at addition, since it is the most basic of the arithmetic operations.

Representing Infinite Precision Integers—Using Arrays

Conceptually, it is simplest to think of an infinite precision integer as stored in an infinitely long array, with each element containing one base 10 digit. The least significant digit is stored in `A[1]`, since this is the digit we process first when performing addition. Pictorially, we view `A[1]` as drawn on the right, with `A[2]` drawn to its left, as shown in Figure 3–1, instead of the way we normally draw arrays, which is with `A[1]` on the left and the array stretching to the right. We now just perform addition in the natural manner, which is sometimes referred to as "schoolboy addition": we just add the digit pairs one by one, keeping track

FIGURE 3–1   Adding Infinite Precision Integers Stored in Arrays

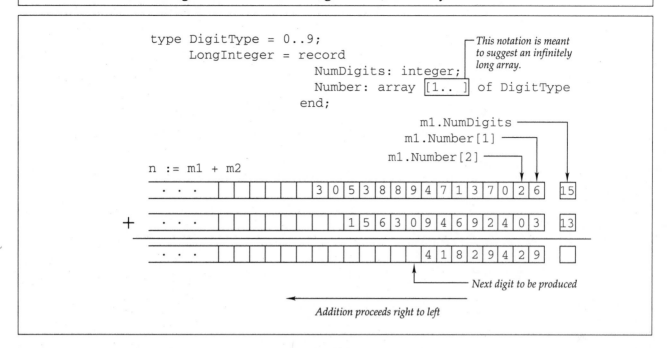

of carries. The code for this is given in Figure 3–2. Of course, this isn't legal Pascal, since Pascal does not support infinite length arrays, but the algorithm is quite clear.

Scanning from least significant digit to most significant digit seems natural for most of the arithmetic operations. Subtraction certainly works this way as well, and so does multiplication, though the algorithm is a bit harder to see. We again use schoolboy arithmetic. The fundamental step is multiplying an infinite precision integer by a single digit, forming one of the partial products that are ultimately summed. The entire procedure for multiplication is outlined in Figure 3–3. The "shifting over" that we do when we multiply on paper can be accomplished by shifting the digits in the array to the left and filling in the vacated elements with zeros as is done in procedure `ShiftingOver`.

Scanning right to left

```
1  procedure ShiftingOver(var n: LongInteger; e: integer);
2     (* Shift a  LongInteger  e  places to the left so that the
3        partial product of a  LongInteger  and a digit can be aligned
4        properly for the addition required during a multiplication.
5     *)
6     var i: integer;
7     begin
8        for i := n.NumDigits downto 1 do n.Number[i+e] := n.Number[i];
9        for i := e downto 1 do n.Number[i] := 0;
10       n.NumDigits := n.NumDigits + e
11    end; (* ShiftingOver *)
```

Note carefully the direction of this loop. The loop
```
for i := 1 to n.NumDigits do
   n.Number[i+e] := n.Number[i]
```
does not work correctly.

A difference between what we will implement and what we do on paper is that on paper we form all the partial products first and then go through a complicated

FIGURE 3–2   Performing Schoolboy Addition

```
1  function Add(m1, m2: LongInteger): LongInteger;
2    var n: LongInteger;
3      d: 0..19; (* 9 + 9 + 1 *)
4      carry: 0..1;
5      i: integer;
6  begin
7    carry := 0; (* no "carry in" initially *)
8    i := 1;
9        while i <= max(m1.NumDigits,m2.NumDigits) do
           begin
             if i <= m1.NumDigits
               then d1 := m1.Number[i]
               else d1 := 0;
             if i <= m2.NumDigits
               then d2 := m2.Number[i]
               else d2 := 0;
             d := d1 + d2 + carry;
             if d >= 10
               then begin n.Number[i] := d - 10; carry := 1 end
               else begin n.Number[i] := d;       carry := 0 end;
             i := i + 1
           end
10   (* while both numbers have digits left do... *)
11   while i <= min(m1.NumDigits,m2.NumDigits) do
12     begin
13       d := m1.Number[i] + m2.Number[i] + carry;
14       if d >= 10
15         then begin n.Number[i] := d - 10; carry := 1 end
16         else begin n.Number[i] := d;       carry := 0 end;
17       i := i + 1
18     end;
19   (* One or both numbers are exhausted. *)
20
21   while i <= m1.NumDigits do (* loop skipped if m1 exhausted *)
22     begin
23       d := m1.Number[i] + carry;
24       if d >= 10
25         then begin n.Number[i] := d - 10; carry := 1 end
26         else begin n.Number[i] := d;       carry := 0 end;
27       i := i + 1
28     end;
29
30   while i <= m2.NumDigits do (* loop skipped if m2 exhausted *)
31     begin
32       d := m2.Number[i] + carry;
33       if d >= 10
34         then begin n.Number[i] := d - 10; carry := 1 end
35         else begin n.Number[i] := d;       carry := 0 end;
36       i := i + 1
37     end;
38
39   (* Both m1 and m2 are now exhausted, but there can still be a carry. *)
40   if carry = 1
41     then begin n.Number[i] := 1; i := i + 1 end;
42
43   n.NumDigits := i - 1;
44   Add := n
45 end; (* Add *)
```

This approach is more elegant and efficient than the loop

Since the body of a while *loop can be executed zero times there is no need to guard entry into the loop with an* if *statement.*

If there is no final carry, i *is one greater than the number of digits in the sum.*

This is done for consistency so that the line
n.NumDigits := i - 1
is correct in all cases.

FIGURE 3–3   Performing Schoolboy Multiplication

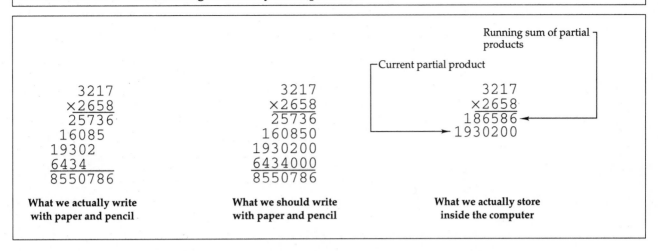

What we actually write with paper and pencil	What we should write with paper and pencil	What we actually store inside the computer

addition process in which we add them up all at once. On a computer, it is more natural to keep a running sum that starts at zero and is updated as each partial product is calculated.

EXERCISE 3–2   Assuming the existence of

```
function MultByDigit(n: LongInteger; d: DigitType): LongInteger;
```

the procedure `ShiftingOver`, and the function `Add`, sketch

```
function Mult(m1, m2: LongInteger): LongInteger;
```

The process of shifting over the partial product suggests that the ability to perform a left-to-right scan is also important, although this apparent need might be just an artifice of the program structure. Instead of two procedures   *Scanning left to right*

```
function MultByDigit(n: LongInteger; d: DigitType): LongInteger;
procedure ShiftOver(var n: LongInteger; e: integer);
```

we can combine them into one

```
function MultByDigit(n: LongInteger; d: DigitType; e: integer): LongInteger;
```

which computes $n \cdot d \cdot 10^e$ all in one step by first placing e zeros in n.Number starting at index 1, and then placing $n \cdot d$ in n.Number starting at index e+1.

While we don't need the ability to scan from left to right in multiplication after all, it is necessary, or at least handy, for some of the other operations. The most obvious is `WriteNum`. A more subtle case is illustrated by the six relational operators, which all operate in much the same manner. Just scanning left to right, looking for the first place where the two numbers differ, isn't correct—one number may have fewer digits than the other. But our proposed representation, illegal though it may be, solves this problem nicely. All we need to do is first compare the number of digits in the two numbers; if they are equal, we then go to the trouble of scanning the two numbers from left to right, looking for the first place they differ. This approach works, as long as we store our numbers   *Leading zeros* without leading zeros, except possibly in the representation of zero itself.

But our proposed representation is illegal. What can we do to get around this problem? We could, of course, just decide on a maximum length for the array `Number`. That would limit our integers to some finite range, just like the predefined type `integer`, only our range would be much larger. If we did this by using a `const` declaration to define the size of the array, a programmer using our package could increase the range if the one we provided was too small for the intended application. All the programmer would need to do is change the constant and recompile. This really isn't a very good solution, however. First, we would have to include checks in all our procedures to make sure that the capacity of a `Number` is not exceeded. Otherwise, the unsuspecting user of our package might just get garbage for answers. Secondly, even if we print an error message when this situation arises, the programmer might not have a very good idea of the size of the numbers used in the computation. Did you have any idea how many digits there were in 100 factorial? Thus, the programmer might have to change the constant and recompile several times before finding the right value. Lastly, the representation wastes a lot of the computer's memory. All numbers would have the same length, the length of the longest intermediate result, even though most numbers used in the computation might require far fewer digits.

Pascal is very limiting in this respect. Because the bounds of an array must be integer constants, the size of an array is fixed at compile time. The dynamically allocated arrays of Ada, PL/I, C, and C++ make these languages better suited for implementing this ADT. But we are writing our package in Pascal, so we are forced to abandon the use of large arrays to represent infinite precision integers.

See **Above and Beyond: Dynamically Allocated Arrays and Work Arrays** *in Chapter 1 and* **Our Package in C, Ada, and C++** *in this chapter.*

Representing Infinite Precision Integers—Using Linked Lists

In Pascal, the natural way to store indefinite length objects is to use linked structures. For our current needs, two distinctly different approaches suggest themselves, although there are minor variations: a singly linked list that links the digits together from least significant digit to most significant digit or a circular, doubly linked list. These alternatives are shown in Figure 3–4. (That both representations store the length of the number itself is a design decision, one we will return to shortly.) The immediate reaction is to discard the first alternative because it appears impossible to scan a number from left to right when we require this capability. But since the singly linked representation takes only two-thirds the storage (possibly less if the Pascal compiler uses only one byte for the `Digit` field), we should study this approach carefully before rejecting it. Another plus for the singly linked list representation is that there are fewer pointers to maintain, so at least some of the operations might be faster. This will be true for addition, which we expect to see used frequently in application programs, and is also used heavily, internally, during multiplication.

As already noted, the most obvious place where we need to scan from left to right is in procedure `WriteNum`. Suppose, however, we had a procedure that could reverse a singly linked list, making its first cell last and its last cell first. Then `WriteNum` could be implemented as

■ A call to `Reverse`.

■ If the digit count is not maintained as part of the data structure, a scan through the reversed list to count the number of digits—a necessary piece of information if we wish to increase readability by placing commas after every group of three digits.

■ A second scan through the reversed list to do the printing.

■ A second call to `Reverse` to restore the number to its original form.

While `WriteNum` using singly linked lists takes roughly three times as long as it takes if we use circular, doubly linked lists, this might not be a significant

FIGURE 3—4   Two Ways to Store Infinite Precision Integers Using Linked Structures

```
type DigitType = 0..9;
     PtrToDigitCell = ^DigitCell;
     DigitCell = record
                    Digit: DigitType;
                    MoreSig: PtrToDigitCell
                 end;
     LongInteger = record
                      NumDigits: integer;
                      Number: PtrToDigitCell
                      (* pointer to least significant digit *)
                   end;

var n: LongInteger;
```

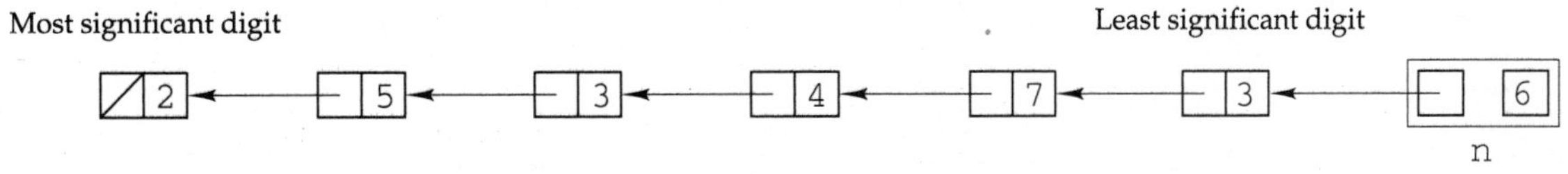

Most significant digit   Least significant digit

A singly linked, `nil`–terminated list representation of 253,473

```
type PtrToDigitCell = ^DigitCell;
     DigitCell = record
                    Digit: integer;
                    MoreSig, LessSig: PtrToDigitCell
                 end;
     LongInteger = PtrToDigitCell; (* To distinguish, logically, an entire
                                       number from one digit of a number. *)
```

This can no longer be `DigitType`, *since the number of digits will surely exceed* 9.

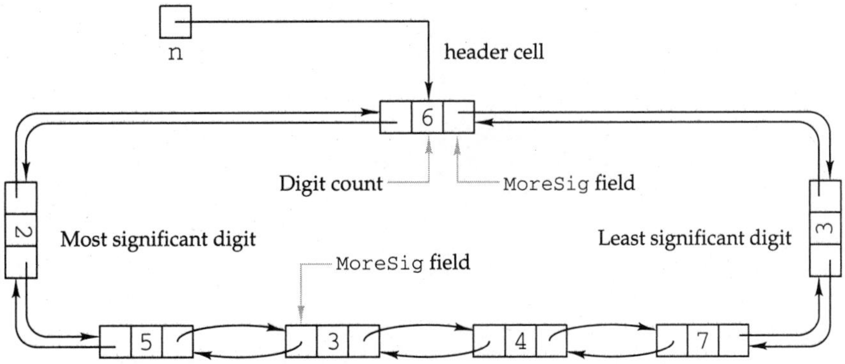

```
var n: LongInteger;
```

A circular, doubly linked list representation of 253,473

factor—we expect calls to WriteNum to be infrequent. Reverse is not hard to write either—the code is given in Figure 3–5.

The other procedures that need to scan from the most significant digit to the least significant digit are the relational operators, which can be viewed as calls to a generic Compare function

```
function Compare(m1, m2: LongInteger): Relation;
```

FIGURE 3–5 Reversing a Linked List

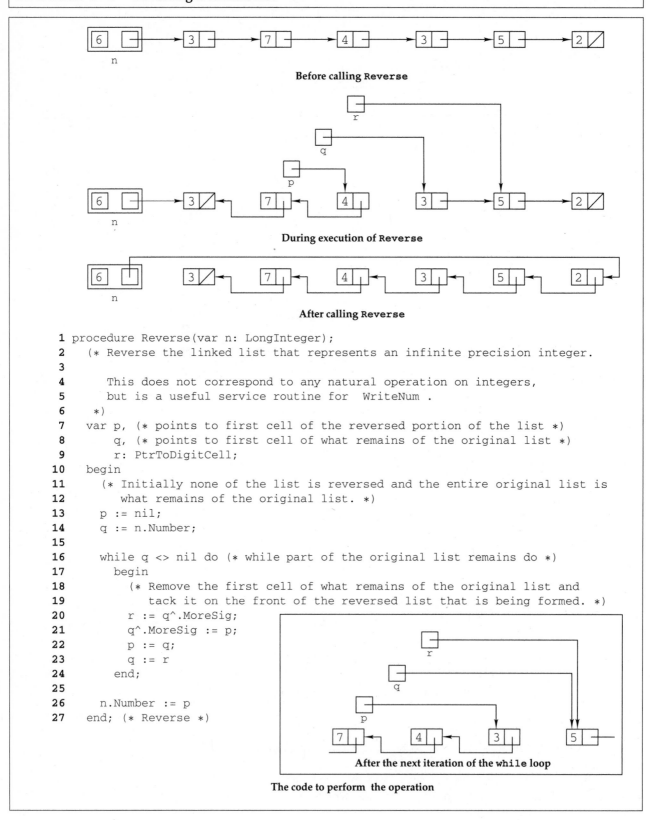

Before calling Reverse

During execution of Reverse

After calling Reverse

```
 1 procedure Reverse(var n: LongInteger);
 2   (* Reverse the linked list that represents an infinite precision integer.
 3
 4      This does not correspond to any natural operation on integers,
 5      but is a useful service routine for  WriteNum .
 6   *)
 7 var p, (* points to first cell of the reversed portion of the list *)
 8     q, (* points to first cell of what remains of the original list *)
 9     r: PtrToDigitCell;
10 begin
11   (* Initially none of the list is reversed and the entire original list is
12      what remains of the original list. *)
13   p := nil;
14   q := n.Number;
15
16   while q <> nil do (* while part of the original list remains do *)
17     begin
18       (* Remove the first cell of what remains of the original list and
19          tack it on the front of the reversed list that is being formed. *)
20       r := q^.MoreSig;
21       q^.MoreSig := p;
22       p := q;
23       q := r
24     end;
25
26   n.Number := p
27 end; (* Reverse *)
```

After the next iteration of the while loop

The code to perform the operation

that returns `LessThan`, `GreaterThan`, or `EqualTo`, members of the enumerated type `Relation`. The situation here is just as it was with our more intuitive, infinite-length array implementation. We don't want to scan simply left to right or right to left. We first need to determine which of the two numbers has more digits and, if both have the same number of digits, then we need to find the most significant digit at which they differ. The `Reverse` procedure can be used here as well. If the number of digits is maintained as part of the data structure, `Compare` reduces to nothing other than

- Compare the number of digits—if they differ, the situation can be resolved immediately.
- If the number of digits is the same, reverse both lists, and scan through the reversed lists, looking for the first place that they differ.
- Reverse the two lists a second time in order to restore the numbers to their original form.

Actually, with a little bit of tricky coding, we can determine the relationship between two numbers stored in this singly linked list format in a single pass without reversing the lists. The code is given in Figure 3–6. Comparing the running time of this version of `Compare` to one that uses a doubly linked

---

FIGURE 3–6   Implementing `Compare` in a Single Pass

```
 1  function Compare(m1, m2: LongInteger): Relation;
 2    (* Determine the relationship between  m1  and  m2 . *)
 3    var p1, p2: PtrToDigitCell;
 4    begin
 5      if m1.NumDigits < m2.NumDigits
 6        then Compare := LessThan
 7      else if m1.NumDigits > m2.NumDigits
 8        then Compare := GreaterThan
 9      else   begin
10            Compare := EqualTo; (* until proven otherwise *)
11            p1 := m1.Number;
12            p2 := m2.Number;
13
14            while (p1 <> nil) (* and (p2 <> nil) *) do
15              begin
16                (* If this pair of digits differs, a pair further left than
17                   any other pair examined so far, then the situation with
18                   respect to this pair overrides any information we have
19                   deduced up to this point.
20                *)
21                if p1^.Digit < p2^.Digit
22                  then Compare := LessThan
23                else if p1^.Digit > p2^.Digit
24                  then Compare := GreaterThan;
25                p1 := p1^.MoreSig;
26                p2 := p2^.MoreSig
27              end
28          end
29    end; (* Compare *)
```

Only one test is needed since both conditions become false at the same time.

This strategy of constantly changing our minds as we move left is tricky. At any moment, the value of `Compare` *is correct, under the assumption that the numbers agree in every place to the left of where we are at. This assumption is generally not true, but it is true when, unbeknownst to us, we compare the digits where the two equal-length numbers first disagree in a left-to-right scan. Notice that* `Compare` *cannot be reset to* `EqualTo` *once it has been set to either* `LessThan` *or* `GreaterThan`.

FOR YOUR
INFORMATION

Is It Really an Infinite Precision Arithmetic Package?

Have we really developed an infinite precision arithmetic package? By storing the number of digits, aren't we limiting the range of a `LongInteger`? Sure, the largest representable integer is huge, being a `maxint`-length string of nines, but still, haven't we just extended the range of integers from what is supported by the hardware to something much, much larger? From a purely theoretical point of view, this criticism is valid. If this troubles us, we can, at the expense of execution time in `Compare` and `WriteNum`, eliminate digit counts entirely. We already don't use them in `Add` and `Sub` and, while they make comparisons more efficient, we can always perform a comparison in linear time using a minor variation of the code in Figure 3–6. `WriteNum` doesn't really need the digit count either; it only needs to know the number of unprinted digits modulo 3, not the number of unprinted digits.

In multiplication, keeping track of the number of digits to shift over can be eliminated by a bit of careful programming. The number of places to shift over, which is really the number of zeros with which the partial product should be padded, equals the number of digits to the right of the digit passed to d. If, instead of the digit, we pass a pointer to the digit, we can scan back to the header cell, tacking on a zero for each digit we encounter. We can handle the padding of the divisor in division in the same manner. By scanning both the divisor and the dividend simultaneously, we can determine if the divisor runs out before the dividend, and if it does we can tack on one low-order zero for each digit of the dividend that remains unscanned. This "counting without counting" at first seems alien, but it is actually quite natural. It is the method used by small children. If two small children want to know who has more M&M's, they line them up next to each other and see which line is longer.

Refer to the code of procedure Mult, *starting at line 417 of* Long_Arithmetic.p.

(continued)

representation, we see that the running times are the same if the two numbers are unequal in length (in which case they are both very fast) or if the two numbers are equal (in which case every digit must be examined). Only when the two numbers differ but are of equal length does the doubly linked representation win out—we need only to scan until we find the first disagreement, whereas with the singly linked version we must scan the entire length every time. Is this situation so common that it favors one representation over the other?

Maintaining the digit count

We should stop at this point and carefully evaluate whether or not we really should keep a count of the number of digits. Having it around makes some operations easier to program, but it is another piece of information to maintain. The more code we have to write, especially when two parts of a data structure are interdependent, the more likely we are to make a mistake—redundant information must be maintained in a consistent state. Keeping `NumDigits` and the actual number of digits in sync is just another source of potential bugs. In a singly linked list implementation, `WriteNum` takes so long anyway that the extra time spent counting the number of digits doesn't really matter. We also don't need the digit counts to perform addition. Unlike in the array version of addition, where the digit counts are used to control termination of the loops, we can use the characteristics of linked lists to provide the control. In a singly linked

FOR YOUR
INFORMATION

(concluded)

While the objection that we have not truly developed an infinite precision arithmetic package is correct, it is of no practical importance: we can represent numbers of up to `maxint` digits. On a 32-bit computer, this means numbers of up to 2,147,483,647 digits in length. No computer in the world has enough memory to hold a number this large, though such a computer is at least conceivable. If our computer has 64-bit words, so that `maxint` is $2^{63} - 1$, then it certainly will not have enough memory to hold the largest representable integer—there probably aren't enough atoms in the universe to build a computer this large!

One last tidbit: since we reserve storage for an `integer` in the `Digit` field of a `DigitCell`, does it pay to store numbers digit by digit? Why not store numbers in three-digit blocks, effectively storing them in base 1000? This is a natural size, as `WriteNum` places commas after every block of three digits. We will have to be careful when writing out a block to print leading zeros, or we might print things like `23, 45,  7` when we mean to print `23,045,007`, but this is not a real difficulty. We also need to be a bit careful with `Divide`, because the loop on line 595

Improving the efficiency of
our package

```
while GreaterEq(tempr,m2) do
```

and the similar loop on line 623 might now execute up to 1000 times—we will need to develop a guessing algorithm.

See Project 3–3

If we adopt this approach to storing numbers, they will occupy one-third the space and more importantly, computations will be more efficient. Addition will be three times faster, whereas multiplication will be nine times faster. We can actually push this technique up to where each digit stores approximately the square root of `maxint`. We cannot push past this point because we don't want to overflow the size of an `integer` when we multiply two digits. Using a base other than a power of 10 greatly complicates `WriteNum`.

list implementation, the control of the three loops of procedure `Add` becomes

- Replace line 11 of Figure 3–2 with

```
while (p1 <> nil) and (p2 <> nil) do
```

- Replace line 21 with

```
while p1 <> nil do (* loop skipped if  m1  exhausted *)
```

- Replace line 30 with

```
while p2 <> nil do (* loop skipped if  m2  exhausted *)
```

The only real advantage of maintaining the digit count appears to be in implementing `Compare`, whose efficiency is noticeably improved. How do we decide this issue and how do we choose between the singly and doubly linked implementations? Maintaining the digit count isn't all that hard, and the gains in clarity and efficiency are real, so we adopt this approach. As to the question of singly linked versus doubly linked lists, how much weight should we put on clarity, on efficiency, and on storage utilization? We haven't even investigated whether storage limitations might be a problem. We also haven't investigated the algorithm for division. Perhaps this will tip the balance one way or the other.

FIGURE 3–7   Performing Schoolboy Division

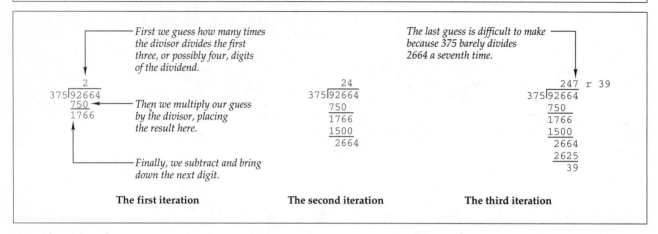

| The first iteration | The second iteration | The third iteration |

An Algorithm for Division

Because of all the guessing, schoolboy division, illustrated in Figure 3–7, does not seem to be a pleasant approach to implement. One thing is apparent, however: we probably don't want separate `div` and `mod` procedures, since the division process generates both simultaneously. Instead, we want a single internal procedure, `Divide`, which returns both the quotient and the remainder; we can then return whichever portion of the result is appropriate, discarding the other.

Multiplication as repeated addition and division as repeated subtraction

After staring at Figure 3–7 for a while, the reader might come up with a bright idea: isn't division just repeated subtraction, and for that matter, isn't multiplication just repeated addition? Why don't we write division as

```
 1  procedure Divide(var q, r: LongInteger; m1, m2: LongInteger);
 2    (* Perform division by repeated subtraction. *)
 3    var one, (* the constant  1  in infinite precision format *)
 4        tempq, tempr: LongInteger;
 5    begin
 6      (* If the divisor is zero, division is impossible. *)
 7      if m2.NumDigits = 0 (* m2 = 0 *)
 8        then begin
 9              writeln('Panic: division by zero.');
10              halt
11            end;
12
13      Declare(one); MakeLong(one,1);
14      Declare(tempr); Assign(tempr,m1); (* Make a copy of  m1  we can destroy. *)
15      Declare(tempq); MakeLong(tempq,0);
16
17      (* while  m2  divides  m1  at least one more time do *)
18      while GreaterEq(tempr,m2) do
19        begin
20          Add(tempq,tempq,one);
21          Sub(tempr,tempr,m2)
22        end;
23      DisposeNum(one);
24      DisposeNum(q); DisposeNum(r);
25      q := tempq; r := tempr
26    end; (* Divide *)
```

Ultimately, `if m2^.Digit = 0` in the doubly linked list version.

Multiplication, written in the same manner, would be even simpler—certainly far simpler than implementing the schoolboy algorithm described earlier. And another positive aspect of the simple algorithms just proposed is that they make heavy use of the more primitive procedures, `Add`, `Sub`, and `GreaterEq`. This is good software engineering practice: build complex algorithms out of simpler parts. This limits the amount of maintenance, and any improvements to the basic building blocks are automatically reflected in improved running times for the more complex routines—in fact, here, if we switch from a singly linked representation to a doubly linked representation, or vice versa, only one line of code needs to be changed: the error check for division by zero. This is a powerful argument, and we must provide good reasons for rejecting it, if we decide to do so.

Because it is easier to analyze, we focus our attention for the moment on multiplication. Suppose we can perform additions of infinite precision integers at the rate of one million per second. While the actual rate depends on the number of digits in the numbers added—after all, adding 100 to 100 involves only three digits, but adding 100 factorial to itself involves 158 digits—a rate of one million additions per second should provide a good ballpark estimate on the time it takes to perform a multiplication. Computing 100 factorial requires ninety-nine multiplications, which deep inside the bowels of our algorithm for multiplication by repeated addition would result in $2 + 3 + \cdots + 100$ additions. According to our estimate, these 5,049 additions should take about five milliseconds—not bad! But what if we were to multiply 100 factorial or a similarly sized number by itself? Since there are 86,400 seconds in a day and 31,536,000 seconds in a year, computing 100! × 100!, a 316-digit number, using this approach takes approximately 2.957×10^{142} *centuries*—not good at all! What has gone wrong here? If we assume that multiplying an infinite precision integer by a single digit takes about as long as adding two equal-length numbers, a reasonable assumption since we scan all the digits of the number in either case, then multiplying 100 factorial by itself, using the schoolboy algorithm, takes 316 basic operations; 158 multiplications of an infinite precision integer by a single digit and 158 additions. Even if our underlying hardware is capable of performing only one thousand of these basic operations per second, the resulting execution time, about one-third of a second, is quite reasonable. What we have seen here is the difference in size between n and $\log n$. More precisely, the running time of multiplication by repeated addition is roughly n, the *value* of the multiplier, whereas the running time of schoolboy multiplication is roughly $\log_{10} n$, the *number of digits* in the multiplier. If n is a big number, these quantities are vastly different.

Schoolboy division revisited

Since division by repeated subtraction is going to suffer for exactly the same reasons as multiplication by repeated addition, we have no choice but to figure out a way of doing schoolboy division. Actually, the process, illustrated in Figure 3–8, while more complicated than schoolboy multiplication, isn't really all that complex. The basic idea, as with schoolboy multiplication, is to work with powers of ten. The algorithm is roughly

- Make a copy of the dividend. This number will be systematically destroyed. What is left of it at the end is the remainder.

- Pad the divisor with enough zeros so that the divisor and the dividend have the same length.

- Determine how many times the zero-padded divisor divides the dividend. This determines the first digit of the quotient. This is where guessing is used in the way schoolchildren do division.

- Subtract, from the dividend, the product of the zero-padded divisor and the digit of the quotient just produced.

FIGURE 3–8   What Really Goes On In Schoolboy Division

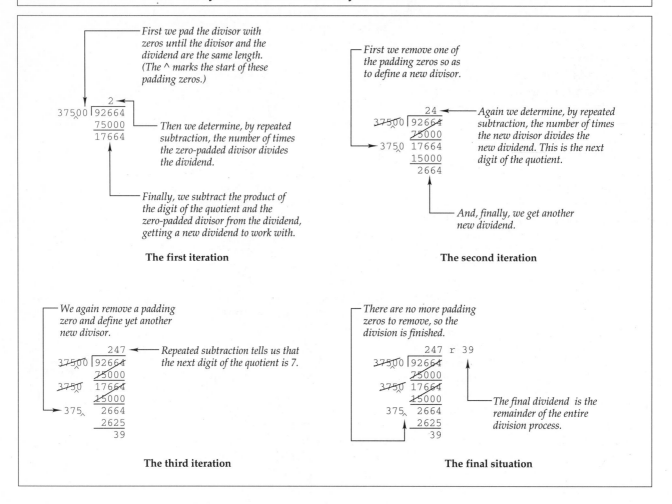

First we pad the divisor with zeros until the divisor and the dividend are the same length. (The ^ marks the start of these padding zeros.)

Then we determine, by repeated subtraction, the number of times the zero-padded divisor divides the dividend.

Finally, we subtract the product of the digit of the quotient and the zero-padded divisor from the dividend, getting a new dividend to work with.

The first iteration

First we remove one of the padding zeros so as to define a new divisor.

Again we determine, by repeated subtraction, the number of times the new divisor divides the new dividend. This is the next digit of the quotient.

And, finally, we get another new dividend.

The second iteration

We again remove a padding zero and define yet another new divisor.

Repeated subtraction tells us that the next digit of the quotient is 7.

The third iteration

There are no more padding zeros to remove, so the division is finished.

The final dividend is the remainder of the entire division process.

The final situation

■ If any padding zeros remain, remove one and repeat the third and fourth steps to obtain the next digit of the quotient. If there aren't any, then we have just computed the final digit of the quotient, the divisor is back in its original state, and what is left of the dividend is the remainder.

Special cases

There are a few difficulties that need to be ironed out. First, there is the possibility that the divisor is greater than the dividend to start with, so that the quotient is zero and the remainder is just the dividend. This is easily handled by a test before we enter the main body of the algorithm. Second, there is the possibility that, after padding the divisor with zeros so that the divisor and dividend have the same length, the divisor is larger than the dividend. The algorithm described above works correctly in this case, but it produces a leading zero as the first digit of the quotient. We have already seen that leading zeros need to be studiously avoided because of the way we intend to implement Compare. We can handle this by removing the leading zero after we create the quotient, but it is better not to produce it in the first place. This is easily accomplished by a slight modification to the second step: after padding the divisor with zeros, if the divisor is larger than the dividend, remove one of the padding zeros. If we have first checked that the original, unpadded divisor is less than or equal to the dividend, there will always be a zero to remove.

There is a little trap that the unwary programmer can fall into when implementing the fifth step. When we go to remove a padding zero, how do we know when there are none left? We cannot simply look at the rightmost digit and see if it is a zero! The divisor itself might end in a zero, and we don't want to remove that zero. There are two ways to handle this: either maintain a count of the number of padding zeros that still remain or maintain a marker that indicates the position of the true least significant digit of the divisor. And one other word of caution: the method of performing division outlined above and actually coded in lines 518–643 of `Long_Arithmetic.p` is a bit risky. This procedure, alone among all the procedures of our infinite precision integer package, modifies its input: it changes the divisor. Even though the algorithm ultimately restores the divisor to its original state, we do pass the modified version on to `Less`, `GreaterEq`, and `Sub` as part of the division process. We must be careful to maintain a valid number at all times; one whose digit count agrees with the number of digits in the number.

There is also still one gap in our description of the algorithm: how do we determine how many times the zero-padded divisor divides the dividend? This is the inverse operation of multiplying an infinite precision number by a single digit. This is where we as humans guess, though not always successfully. In dividing 375 into 92,664, the final iteration determines how many times 375 divides 2664. The quotient is seven, but just barely. If the dividend had been a little smaller, say 92,618, the correct guess would have been six. While we can devise a guessing algorithm, in which we just check the result and refine our guess if we guessed wrong, it is easier to just repeatedly subtract the zero-padded divisor from the dividend until it is greater than what is left. The number of times we successfully subtract the zero-padded divisor is the number of times it divides the current dividend. While this is slower than multiplying an infinite precision integer by a digit, which gets the correct answer without fail in a single pass, it isn't that much slower. The number of subtractions is limited to nine—after all, we are determining the next digit of the quotient. Thus, our implementation of division still executes in time proportional to the number of digits in the dividend, though it can be up to ten times slower than multiplication.

Avoiding guessing at the next digit

Unlike all the other routines in the package, `Divide` produces its answer from most significant digit to least significant digit. This is not a good argument for using doubly linked lists. Whereas in the singly linked list implementation of addition we keep tacking the next digit of the result onto the end of the singly linked list, here we just keep tacking it onto the beginning—the last digit we tack on is the least significant digit and that is the first `DigitCell` of the number when we look at the representation of Figure 3–4. Still, if we look closely at the workings of `Divide`, we see that the balance might be tipped slightly in favor of the circular, doubly linked list representation, at least if we place our emphasis on efficiency and clarity and not on storage utilization. The most frequently performed operations in `Divide` are the calls to `GreaterEq` and `Sub` on lines 595 and 597. These occur inside a loop, which is itself inside a loop. The number of times the outer loop is performed equals the difference between the number of digits in the dividend and the number of digits in the divisor, while the inner loop is performed an average of five times per outer-loop iteration. Furthermore, the two numbers passed to `GreaterEq` are roughly equal in value, and so will almost always have an equal number of digits. If we use a singly linked list representation, so that we have to scan all the way through the numbers when they have equal length, then the call to `GreaterEq` will take about the same amount of time as the call to `Sub`. But if we use the circular, doubly linked list representation, the chances are very great that the call to `GreaterEq` will resolve

Finally—a reason for using circular, doubly linked lists ... maybe

the matter very quickly. Thus, a doubly linked list representation will speed up division by almost a factor of two.

It is still a close call. We have done as much analysis as possible. We need to make a decision. We will implement our package with circular, doubly linked lists. They make `Compare`, `Divide`, and `WriteNum` faster, and the code for `Compare` and `WriteNum` clearer. The main drawback is that circular, doubly linked lists use about 50 percent more storage.

Fine details: representing zero and storing the digit count

Now that we have settled on a representation, there are still some fine details to consider. Should we use a dummy header cell, like the one pictured in Figure 3–4? How should we represent zero, keeping in mind that we don't want numbers to contain leading zeros, but that we normally represent zero as a single-digit number? And where should the count of the number of digits be kept? These decisions are not terribly fundamental, though the decisions we make will be reflected throughout the code. Circular, doubly linked lists usually are programmed with dummy header cells because experience shows that they make the coding more uniform. Zero will now be either just a dummy header cell, with its `LessSig` and `MoreSig` fields pointing to itself and with zero as the count of the number of digits, or it will contain a dummy header cell and one true `DigitCell`, whose `Digit` field is set to zero. While the second approach reflects how we do things as humans, inside a computer it makes better sense to be consistent. Consistency leads to fewer errors. We adopt the former representation—we *never* allow leading zeros, even in zero. The final issue is: where do we store the count of the number of digits? We actually have a handy place to do this: the `Digit` field of the dummy header cell is unused, although using this field in this way forces us to change the type of `Digit` to `integer`. This is the representation used in Figure 3–4 and the one used in our package.

STOP

It is time to go study most of the program in `Long_Arithmetic.p`.

The reader is now in a position to understand the code in the routines that implement all the relational operators, basic arithmetic operations, and input/output routines, except for the presence of occasional calls to `Declare`, `DisposeDigit`, and `DisposeNum`. This constitutes the vast majority of the project: about 630 of the 731 lines of `Long_Arithmetic.p`. The program, while long, is really a straightforward implementation of the algorithms described and is absorbed very quickly.

3.3   SOME HIDDEN SOFTWARE ENGINEERING ISSUES

So far, we have ignored the user of our package. While we ourselves might want to compute 100! or 2^{1000}, the point of developing this package is to let other people, who might have some real needs, perform these sorts of computations easily. Such users might be fairly inexperienced programmers. They might be physicists or mathematicians; they might not have worked much in Pascal. We need to provide them with a user's manual. It probably won't have to be very extensive— after all, they are familiar with integers. There doesn't seem to be much that can go wrong. Despite the warning in the comments of `Long_Arithmetic.h`, the user might forget to call `InitializeMemoryManagement` before calling any other routine in the package or might forget to call `Declare` before referencing a `LongInteger` for the first time. The user also might use a variable after it is declared, but before it is assigned a value, possibly by passing it to one of the call-by-value parameters of `Add`. (`Declare`, which we have not yet discussed, does not give its argument an initial value. It is the equivalent of the "colon operator" in the Pascal line

```
var i: integer;
```

which declares i, but leaves it uninitialized.) Of course, it is a mistake to use an uninitialized variable in any programming language.

Some other user errors will be caught automatically by the Pascal compiler. For example, if the user inadvertently writes

```
IInLong := IInLong + one    or    NFact := 1
```

instead of

```
Add(IInLong,IInLong,one)    or    MakeLong(NFact,1)
```

the compiler will report that "pointers cannot be added—line ..." or "integers cannot be assigned to pointers—line ...". These are not very informative error messages, since the user should not be concerned with the internal representation of infinite precision integers, but upon examining the offending line, the user will be able to identify the source of the problem.

There are, however, some inadvertent errors the user can make. These errors are quite serious, and will not be caught by the Pascal compiler or the routines of our package. What if the user forgets and accidentally writes

The need for Equal

```
if IInLong = JInLong ...
```

instead of

```
if Equal(IInLong,JInLong) ...
```

The type of both IInLong and JInLong is LongInteger, which is ultimately ^DigitCell. Pascal compares these two pointers for equality and returns false even if the two numbers agree digit for digit. This is because the = operator applied to pointers just compares the pointers, not the structures they point to, and is why we need to define Equal in the first place. The Pascal <> operator causes similar problems, though inadvertent use of < or the other three relational operators will be caught, since Pascal doesn't allow pointers to be compared in this manner, even though, deep down in the hardware, a pointer is just an integer.

The same difficulty exists with the assignment operator. Its use is perfectly legal Pascal, but it has an unexpected effect. We want an infinite precision integer to appear much like a Pascal integer—an undifferentiated blob that the hardware knows about and the user cannot readily take apart and examine. Thus

The need for Assign

```
Assign(JInLong,IInLong)
```

should have the same effect as

```
j := i
```

when j and i are of type integer. It should copy the contents of i into j, which is what Assign does. Notice, however that

```
JInLong := IInLong
```

has a very different effect: it makes two pointer variables point to the same linked list (see Figure 3–9). Having two pointers point to the same place is a form of *aliasing*. While there might be no adverse side effects to having two variables of type LongInteger point to the same storage, it is surely better to insist on the invariant:

> *Each circular, doubly linked list representing a number should be associated with only one variable of type* LongInteger.

FIGURE 3–9   The Effect of Executing `JInLong := IInLong`

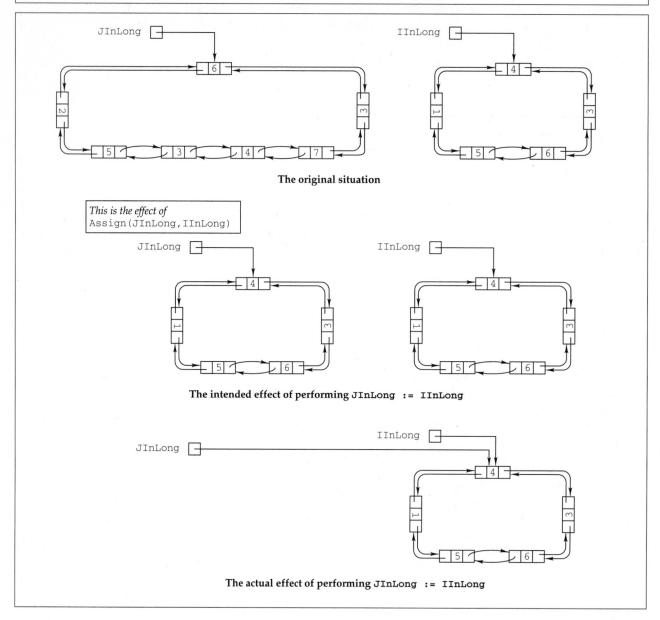

The original situation

This is the effect of
`Assign(JInLong,IInLong)`

The intended effect of performing `JInLong := IInLong`

The actual effect of performing `JInLong := IInLong`

Having two pointers point to the same number should be forbidden. Of course, if the user breaks this rule, accidentally or intentionally, there is nothing we can do to prevent it.

We attempt to reinforce the view that an infinite precision integer is an undifferentiated blob by giving `LongInteger` its own type declaration of line 17 of `Long_Arithmetic.h`:

$$LongInteger = PtrToDigitCell;$$

This has no effect other than the psychological one of separating an infinite precision integer viewed as a whole from an infinite precision integer viewed as a collection of digits. The user of our package has no need for variables of type `PtrToDigitCell`, though we, the writers of the package, do. Ada and

C++, unlike Pascal, allow us to make this separation in a more than superficial way. In these languages, the details of the implementation can be completely hidden from the user—the user's program simply cannot reference individual components of the data structure and the user's code cannot be dependent on the internal representation. This is the goal of using ADTs.

We are now in a position to examine the last issue in the design of our infinite precision arithmetic package: memory management. As motivation, consider the effect on computer memory of executing the line

Memory Management

$$\texttt{Add(IInLong,IInLong,one)}$$

Our addition procedure builds a new infinite precision integer that is the sum of `IInLong` and `one`, and then, on its very last line (`Long_Arithmetic.p`, line 331), assigns this number to the call-by-reference parameter n. This will, of course, make `IInLong` point to a totally new area of computer memory and, unless we do something about it, *nothing will point to any of the storage occupied by the number previously pointed to by* `IInLong`. As shown in Figure 3–10, this storage will be lost. Programs to compute quantities like 100! and 2^{1000} will quickly consume an enormous amount of memory. Not only do lines like

$$\texttt{Add(IInLong,IInLong,one)}$$

FIGURE 3–10   How Memory Can Become Permanently Unusable

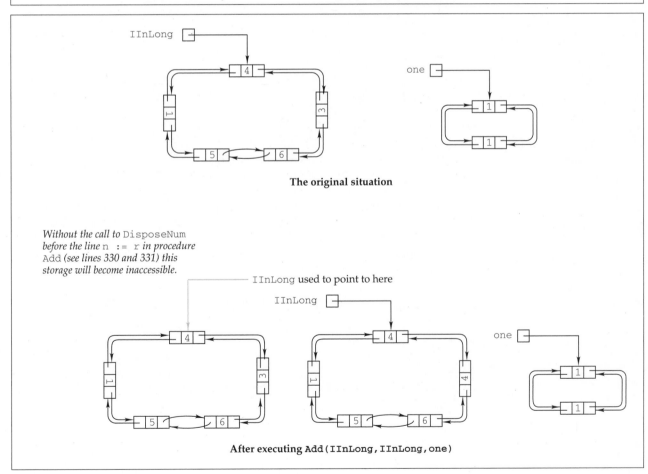

The original situation

Without the call to `DisposeNum` *before the line* n := r *in procedure* Add *(see lines 330 and 331) this storage will become inaccessible.*

`IInLong` used to point to here

After executing Add(`IInLong`,`IInLong`,`one`)

Dynamically Allocated Memory in Pascal

The development of this chapter assumes some familiarity with pointer variables and elementary linked data structures. In this For Your Information box, we look at some of the more subtle aspects of pointers. When they are first introduced, probably the most puzzling aspect of pointer variables is that call-by-value doesn't seem to be call-by-value anymore. The code

```
1  program Modifies(output);
2    type PtrToNode = ^Node;
3        Node = record
4                  data: integer;
5                  next: PtrToNode
6              end;
7  var L: PtrToNode;
8  procedure Change(p: PtrToNode);
9    begin
10       p^.data := 1          Note: p passed by value.
11     end; (* Change *)
12  begin
13    new(L);
14    L^.data := 0; L^.next := nil;
15    Change(L);
16    writeln(L^.data:1)
17  end. (* Modifies *)
```

prints 1, not 0. That this *should* happen, and that it is not an aberration, becomes crystal clear when you understand the manner in which pointer variables and dynamically allocated storage fit into the model of memory discussed in Section 1.4. First, all pointer variables are the same, even though they might be of type `PtrToNode`, `PtrToDigitCell`, or `PtrTo...`. Ultimately they all hold addresses; they occupy the same amount of memory whether what they point to is large or small. In this regard, pointer variables are very much like `var` parameters. The primary difference is syntactical—the syntax of `var` parameters makes us feel as if we really have the variable itself in the palm of our hands, whereas pointer variables place the "indirection operator," ^, between us and the variable.

An important distinction between "named" variables, which are explicitly declared, and "anonymous" variables, which are allocated with `new`, is where they are located. Named variables are all located on the stack, whereas dynamically allocated variables are kept in a separate area known as the *heap*. When line 13 of `Modifies` executes

■ The Pascal runtime support system uses a sophisticated algorithm to find a block of storage within the heap large enough to hold a variable of type `Node`.

■ It places the address of this block of storage in the named variable `L`, so that `L` "points" to the allocated storage.

(continued)

FOR YOUR INFORMATION

(continued)

The situation is depicted in the first part of Figure 3–11. Why line 10 changes `L^.data` is illustrated as well. When the main program calls `Change`, L is passed to p by value—*the value of* L *is copied*. But since L is a pointer, p and L point to exactly the same memory location and when `p^.data` is assigned 1, it changes it from the perspective of L as well. The parameter, however, is truly passed by value. If p itself is changed, with a line like `p := nil`, this change will not be reflected back to L; L will not become `nil`.

If L were passed to p by reference, then L, as well as what L points to, can be changed. Upon entry to `Change`, memory would look as shown in the lower right part of the figure. Just like with `integer` variables passed by reference, the compiler sorts out all the indirection necessary to handle a reference like `p^.data`.

One common error that is made when pointers are first introduced is to place lines like

new does not create pointer variables

```
new(p1);
new(p2);
```

at the start of procedure `Add` or right before the first use of p1 and p2 in lines 259 and 260. The two calls to `new` are not illegal, but they aren't needed and they demonstrate a lack of understanding. The call to `new` does *not* create p1. Storage for p1 is allocated (in the stack segment) the moment `Add` is entered. This storage is uninitialized, but p1 exists. The line `new(p1)` allocates a block of storage from the heap and places the address of this storage in p1. A few lines later, when the program executes

Refer to the opening lines of Add, *lines 244–260 while reading this.*

```
p1 := m1^.MoreSig
```

p1 is set to point somewhere else. Nothing points to the storage that was allocated with `new(p1)`—it is inaccessible for the remainder of the program's execution. If the line `new(p1)` is omitted, as it should be, then after executing

```
p1 := m1^.MoreSig
```

p1 will point to exactly the same place it points to when the `new(p1)` is present, and a small piece of storage will not have been wasted.

Scope, visibility, and lifetime don't play as big a role here as they do with named variables. The interesting question is: what is the lifetime of dynamically allocated storage? Half of the answer is fairly obvious: dynamically allocated storage comes into existence when the allocator `new` is called. Pascal does not define very carefully when dynamically allocated storage ceases to exist. It is better to ask the question: when does storage allocated in the heap become inaccessible? The answer is: when it cannot be reached from any named variable by any route, no matter how indirect.

Lifetime of dynamically allocated storage

A consequence of the way in which dynamically allocated storage functions is that a record stored in the heap can still be accessible after the named variable involved in its creation has long since ceased to exist. This is demonstrated by the program

(continued)

FOR YOUR
INFORMATION

(continued)

```
 1  program KeepAlive(output);
 2    type PtrToNode = ^Node;
 3       Node = record
 4                    data: integer;
 5                    next: PtrToNode
 6              end;
 7    var q: PtrToNode;
 8    procedure SetQ;
 9      var p: PtrToNode;
10      begin
11        new(p);
12        p^.data := 1; p^.next := nil;
13        q := p
14      end; (* SetQ *)
15    begin
16      SetQ;
17      writeln(q^.data:1)
18    end. (* KeepAlive *)
```

Although the variable p, declared on line 9 and used to allocate the storage on line 11, has ceased to exist by the time the program executes

writeln(q^.data:1)

the storage allocated by the call to new continues to exist, since the variable q still points to it. While this example is silly, we use this strategy all the time when working with linked lists. The procedure Add uses the variables q1 and q2 to insert nodes of type DigitCell into the sum. While these variables, and even r, disappear when Add returns, the LongInteger they have built outlives them, since the actual parameter associated with n points to the header cell of the circularly linked list, and so indirectly to all the nodes comprising the number.

By the same token, when no named variables point directly or indirectly to a dynamically allocated piece of storage, the storage is no longer accessible. This can happen in two ways. The more obvious is that the storage can be explicitly disconnected from the data structure of which it is a part. This is what happens when a node is deleted from the middle of a linked list. A more subtle situation occurs when a named variable that begins a chain of indirection disappears because of a procedure exit. This possibility exists in our infinite precision arithmetic package, which is why we need to make DisposeNum user visible if we are going to allow user-defined procedures and why we have calls to DisposeNum scattered throughout the package.

Losing access to large amounts of storage can make a program that works in theory fail in practice. In our infinite precision arithmetic package, if all the calls to DisposeNum and DisposeDigit are deleted, then every call to NewDigit will effectively be a call to new. We may still have enough

Refer to lines 261–280 in the code of procedure Add *while reading this.*

dispose

(continued)

memory to compute 100 factorial, but at some point, say at 1000 factorial, we will run out. There are only 2568 digits in 1000 factorial, so there really is no need to run out of memory, but the number of words of memory consumed if inaccessible storage is not reclaimed is beyond the capacity of many midsized computers—the `NFactorial` program would use 6,698,482 nodes of type `DigitCell` to compute 1000 factorial. For this reason, Pascal provides a mechanism for allowing the programmer to reclaim storage at the moment it is about to become inaccessible. The call `dispose(p)` returns the storage pointed to by p, storage necessarily allocated previously by a call to `new`, to the heap management system for reallocation at a later time. It makes the value of p undefined. In addition, the call to `dispose` makes the value of any other variable that points to the disposed block of memory undefined. This is true only in a formal sense; if p and q point to the same block of memory and `dispose(p)` is executed, q is not changed. However, subsequent references to q^.⟨field_name⟩ give unpredictable results and, if the program makes such a reference without first resetting q, the program is considered erroneous. Unfortunately, there is no way the compiler or runtime support system can detect the error of referencing memory through q when what q points to has been indirectly freed. For this reason, debugging programs that contain calls to `dispose` can be very difficult. Pointer variables can inadvertently point to storage that has been freed, or worse, point into the middle of some other record, since the storage may have been reallocated on a subsequent call to `new`.

> *It is a good idea when debugging programs that use pointers to not include calls to* `dispose` *until the program is working.*

A debugging tip—don't use `dispose`

A consequence of the intermingling of calls to `new` and `dispose` is that consecutive calls to `new` do not necessarily result in the allocated storage being contiguous in memory. Since the fundamental idea behind using linked data structures is that logically contiguous data need not be physically contiguous, this poses no problem.

Pointers and strong typing

Because pointers are so easily abused, Pascal takes a very strict view of them. Even though all pointer variables are essentially the same, they cannot be freely assigned one to the other. A pointer variable has a type and the type isn't "pointer," it is "pointer to something." Unless two pointers point to the same type of object, they are not assignment compatible.[2] The only exception is `nil`, which is a constant defined as belonging to all pointer types. Also, two pointers of the same type can be compared only with = and <>, not with <, even though addresses, deep down in the hardware, are just integers. Arithmetic also cannot be performed on pointers; specifying p+1 in a program produces a compile-time error, it does not refer to the next location in memory as it does in C. Even with all these restrictions, pointers are very

(continued)

---

[2] Turbo Pascal has a generic `pointer` type and an "address of" operator, @, similar to C's & operator. These features, like untyped `var` parameters, provide the Pascal user with some of the power that pointers have in C.

powerful, with many sophisticated and elegant data structures utilizing them. On the other hand, even with strong typing, because two pointers can point to the same location in memory, it is possible to create bugs that are very hard to find.

Neither `new` nor `dispose` can themselves be written in standard Pascal. This is because the type of the argument to these procedures is just "pointer." One program can have multiple pointer types (`PtrToNode`, `PtrToCell`, `PtrToStkElt`, `PtrTo...`) and yet it can call `new` with variables declared to be any of these types. Because of their strong type checking rules, the storage allocator in both Ada and C++ has a different syntax and is not a procedure.

FIGURE 3–11   Management of the Stack and the Heap

The heap segment is shown as an amorphous cloud to emphasize that it has no obvious structure.

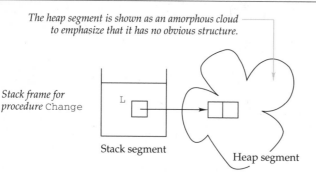

Stack frame for procedure Change

Stack segment   Heap segment

The situation after executing `new(L)`

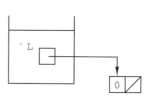

The situation after executing line 14

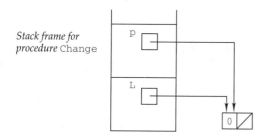

Stack frame for procedure Change

The situation after entry to procedure `Change`

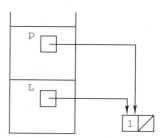

The situation after executing `p^.data := 1`

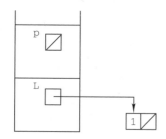

The situation as it would be if we were to execute `p := nil` after line 10

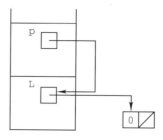

The situation as it would be after entering procedure `Change` if `p` were a call-by-reference parameter

and

$$\texttt{Mult(NFact,NFact,IInLong)}$$

use and discard memory, our multiplication routine consumes an enormous quantity of storage as well because of all the partial products that it creates. Even though the amount of memory in use at any one time might be small, at most a few thousand words when computing 100 factorial, the amount discarded will soon exceed the memory available on even a reasonably large computer.

Luckily, if the user of our package does not inadvertently write lines like

$$\texttt{JInLong := IInLong}$$

we can safely reclaim this storage just as it is about to become inaccessible, keeping our demands on memory to not much more than is actually required by the application program. Since our package, if used properly, maintains the invariant that each number is pointed to by only one variable of type `LongInteger`, we know that, after executing the final line of procedure `Add`, nothing will point to the number previously pointed to by our call-by-reference parameter. Thus, we can reclaim the storage for later use. This is why we have

$$\texttt{DisposeNum(n)}$$

immediately before `n := r`, and why we have similar lines at the end of nearly every procedure in the package.

The big issue, the need for memory management, has been placed on the table; once the principle is clear, there are just a lot of details to examine. The first detail is that `DisposeNum` does not conform to the model of `InternalDispose` outlined in the For Your Information box: A Simple Memory Management Package. `InternalDispose` is designed to return one node to the free storage pool, whereas here we wish to return an entire number. Just returning the dummy header cell won't return the entire number; each node will have to be returned separately. We do have a routine to return a single node, `DisposeDigit`, so we might expect `DisposeNum` to just loop through the linked list, disposing of the digits one at a time. Because our lists are circular and doubly linked, we can return an entire number much more efficiently, using just two Pascal statements:

```
(* Break open the circularly linked list and attach the
   entire number to the free storage list in one step. *)
n^.MoreSig^.LessSig := FreeNodeList;
FreeNodeList := n;
```

Now we can see the danger of lines like

$$\texttt{JInLong := IInLong}$$

If at some time after executing the above line we assign a new `LongInteger` to `IIinLong`, by a call to any one of `MakeLong`, `Assign`, or the five arithmetic operators, the call to `DisposeNum` in these routines will place what `JInLong` points to back on the free storage list. Subsequent uses of `JInLong` will go completely haywire.

This also explains why routines like `Add` have to be procedures and cannot be functions. While it might be more convenient to evaluate $y = ax^2 + bx + c$ by writing

$$\texttt{Assign(y,Add(Add(Mult(a,Mult(x,x)),Mult(b,x)),c))}$$

Read **For Your Information: A Simple Memory Management Package**

Refer to lines 27–102 of `Long_Arithmetic.p` *when reading this.*

Why `JInLong := IInLong` *is so dangerous*

Why `Add` *is a procedure*

A Simple Memory Management Package

Because new and dispose must be prepared to deal with requests for different size objects within the same program, memory management algorithms are very complicated and repeated calls to the Pascal-supplied memory management system can be very time consuming. Often a program has only one type of dynamically allocated record—in our infinite precision arithmetic package, only records of type DigitCell are allocated dynamically—and we can then provide our own simple, efficient memory manager. The Turbo Pascal version of the code is given in Figure 3–12. This code is really a template and must be modified slightly when it is used in a larger program; the type Node must be completed and should be given a name that is relevant to the larger application. Also, the next field is *not* a special field, present only for use by the memory management package. It should just be one of the pointer fields already defined in the record; the memory manager needs a pointer field to link all the free storage together, but any pointer field will suffice for this purpose.

The basic strategy of the memory manager is to maintain a linked list of all the records that have been freed by the application program. When a new record is requested, by a call to InternalNew, the memory manager returns one of these previously freed records when one is available. Otherwise it calls new to get truly never-before-used storage. The application program never calls dispose. All such calls are made to InternalDispose, which places the Node pointed to by p onto the free storage list. InternalNew and InternalDispose act in concert to manage the free storage list as efficiently as possible. Since one free Node is as good as any other, the free list is managed as a stack—InternalDispose just places the Node being freed on the front of the free storage list and InternalNew just grabs whatever Node happens to be first. So that we do not lose access to the free storage list between calls to these two procedures, we keep the pointer to the start of the list in a static variable in the private part of the package. On program start-up, the free storage list must be initialized to empty, since there aren't any free records of type Node yet, and the first call to InternalNew will get storage from the Pascal runtime system.

than by specifying the computation with the five-line sequence

```
Mult(y,x,x);
Mult(y,a,y);
Mult(temp,b,x);
Add(y,y,temp);
Add(y,y,c);
```

in the first version we cannot reclaim the storage that holds intermediate values. We can reclaim the storage used by the number pointed to by y, because of the call to Assign, but the result of Mult(b,x) is just passed to one of the call-by-value parameters of the inner Add and we will never be able to reclaim the storage used to hold this intermediate result. Add cannot reclaim the storage, since it does not know if its call-by-value parameters are user-defined variables, which cannot be reclaimed, or unnamed temporaries that the compiler creates to hold the value returned by a function. And once the inner Add returns, and the stack frame containing its parameters is destroyed, nothing points to the result returned by Mult(b,x), so we cannot get to it to reclaim the storage.

FIGURE 3–12   A Simple Memory Manager

```
 1  unit MemoryManager;
 2  interface
 3  type PtrToNode = ^Node;
 4      Node = record
                   ... other fields of Node
                        declared here ...
 5              next: PtrToNode
 6          end;
 7
 8  procedure InternalNew(var p: PtrToNode);
 9     (* If there are returned  Nodes  then use one, otherwise get a
10         fresh one from the Pascal memory management system.
11     *)
12
13  procedure InternalDispose(p: PtrToNode);
14     (* Return a  Node  to the memory management system. *)
15
16  implementation
17  var FreeNodeList: PtrToNode; (* Manage the returned storage as a stack,
18                                  linked through the  next  field. *)
19
20  procedure InternalNew(var p: PtrToNode);
21     (* If there are returned  Nodes  then use one, otherwise get a
22         fresh one from the Pascal memory management system.
23     *)
24     begin
25       if FreeNodeList <> nil
26         then begin
27                 p := FreeNodeList;
28                 FreeNodeList := FreeNodeList^.next
29             end
30         else new(p)
31     end; (* InternalNew *)
32
33  procedure InternalDispose(p: PtrToNode);
34     (* Return a  Node  to the memory management system. *)
35     begin
36       p^.next := FreeNodeList;
37       FreeNodeList := p
38     end; (* InternalDispose *)
39
40  begin
41    FreeNodeList := nil
42  end. (* MemoryManager *)
```

In our infinite precision arithmetic package this is specialized to
```
    type PtrToDigitCell = ^DigitCell;
         DigitCell = record
                         Digit: integer;
                         MoreSig, LessSig: PtrToDigitCell
                     end;
```
this is next

InternalNew *becomes* NewDigit *and* InternalDispose *becomes* DisposeDigit.

These two routines cooperate to manage the free storage pool as a stack.

Initially there isn't any storage to manage and all requests to InternalNew *will result in a call to* new.

Memory management is also the reason why we need the procedure Declare. Consider, for example, line 117 in MakeLong,

The need for Declare

$$DisposeNum(IInLong)$$

where we recover the storage used by the number currently pointed to by IInLong. There is a good chance that IInLong doesn't point to any number. It is very likely to be the first time anything is assigned to the variable passed to the call-by-reference parameter of MakeLong. With Add, it is even harder to tell. Sometimes, addition redefines a variable, as in i := i + 1, but at other times it defines it for the first time. The problem is: if a variable is being defined for the first time, something DisposeNum has no way of knowing, then DisposeNum shouldn't do anything. If Pascal initialized pointer variables to nil, we wouldn't need Declare, because we would have a way of determining if there was anything to reclaim. Declare does for us what Pascal should have done in the first place, which is why it should be called once per variable, before that variable is put to any use whatsoever. Overall, we see that memory management, a necessity if the application program is going to do any significant computation, conflicts with naturalness of use by forcing the user to call Assign, instead of writing :=, to call Declare once per variable, and to call InitializeMemoryManagement once, at the very start.

User-Defined Procedures and Functions

Are there any other operators besides assignment, equality, and declaration about which we need to warn the user? Suppose the user wishes to write a procedure that squares a number:

```
1  procedure Square(var y: LongInteger; x: LongInteger);
2    (* Effectively perform  y := x*x . *)
3    begin
4      Mult(y,x,x)
5    end; (* Square *)
```

STOP

If you haven't read **For Your Information: Dynamically Allocated Memory in Pascal,** *do so now.*

Can any harm come from letting the user do this? While this example is harmless, even if the call is of the form Square(i,i), call-by-value parameters violate the invariant that every number should be pointed to by only one variable. This is because call-by-value is really an implicit assignment statement to the formal parameter of the called procedure. When the called procedure returns, this second, temporary reference to the number disappears, and all is well again, *provided that nothing inside the called procedure changes what the parameter points to.* This is true for Square. But consider the procedure

```
1  procedure Factorial(var y: LongInteger; x: LongInteger);
2    (* Effectively perform  y := x! . *)
3    var one: LongInteger;
4    begin
5      Declare(one); MakeLong(one,1);
6
7      MakeLong(y,1);                 (* y := 1;                  *)
8      while Greater(x,one) do        (* while x > 1 do -- 0! = 1 *)
9        begin                        (*   begin                  *)
10         Mult(y,y,x);               (*     y := y * x;          *)
11         Sub(x,x,one)               (*     x := x - 1           *)
12       end;                         (*   end                    *)
13
14     DisposeNum(one)  ─────┐
15   end; (* Factorial *)    └── Without this call, the storage pointed to by
                                 one will be lost when Factorial returns.
```

The first execution of Sub(x,x,one) causes the call to DisposeNum at the end of Sub to return the storage originally pointed to by x to the free storage pool. Because x is a call-by-value parameter, the value of the pointer variable n in the call Factorial(m,n) is *not* changed, even though the value of the pointer variable x is changed by Sub. n still points to the DigitCell it pointed to when Factorial was entered, only this DigitCell is now on the free storage list or in the middle of some other number! This certainly isn't what the user expected, since n was passed by value and the user's mental image of a LongInteger is supposed to be that it is of type integer, only with lots more bits.

> *This example makes clear, in a graphic way, how pointers and call-by-value parameters interact: while the pointer cannot be changed, what it points to can be modified. Only the pointer is copied; the structure it points to is not copied.*

If we had used large arrays to represent infinite precision integers, both the assignment operator and call-by-value parameters would be perfectly safe, because the entire array would be copied.

On the other hand, call-by-reference parameters work just fine. While the call Factorial(m,...) appears to define two pointers to the same number, m and y, y really points to the pointer variable m itself and not to what m points to. Changing y doesn't actually change y, it changes m. So the call MakeLong(y,1) on line 7 of Factorial first reclaims what m points to and then resets m to point to 1 in infinite precision format. By the time Factorial exits, m points to the right answer.

Unfortunately, just changing x to a call-by-reference parameter won't make Factorial correct—at least from the user's perspective. The user does not want n destroyed in the process of computing n factorial. But the call to Sub on line 11 will do just that. When call-by-value parameters are needed, they can be faked with a simple trick. The correct way to write Factorial is

```
                                           Because the only use of x is in Assign(xcopy,x),
                                           x can actually be passed as a call-by-value parameter.

 1  procedure Factorial(var y: LongInteger; var x: LongInteger);
 2    (* Effectively perform  y := x! . *)
 3    var xcopy, one: LongInteger;
 4    begin
 5      Declare(xcopy); Assign(xcopy,x); (* simulate call-by-value *)
 6
 7      Declare(one); MakeLong(one,1);
 8
 9      MakeLong(y,1);                (* y := 1;                    *)
10      while Greater(xcopy,one) do (* while x > 1 do -- 0! = 1 *)
11        begin                      (*   begin                   *)
12          Mult(y,y,xcopy);         (*     y := y * x;           *)
13          Sub(xcopy,xcopy,one)     (*     x := x - 1            *)
14        end;                       (*   end                     *)
15
16      DisposeNum(one); DisposeNum(xcopy)
17    end; (* Factorial *)
```

DisposeNum, *which is private to the package, will have to be made user visible.*

While call-by-reference parameters can be allowed and call-by-value parameters can be faked, user-defined functions need to be prohibited for the same reason that Add has to be a procedure.

PROJECT 3–1   Implement the infinite precision arithmetic package using singly linked, `nil`-terminated lists. Compare the performance of your implementation with the circular, doubly linked list implementation given in the book.

PROJECT 3–2   Implement the fast multiplication strategy described in the annotations to `Long_Arithmetic.p`. The same technique improves the performance of division. How can this method be made effective even when the base is 1000?

PROJECT 3–3   It is possible to "guess" the next digit of the quotient very accurately. Consider, for example, determining the next digit when the current, zero-padded divisor is 3652400... and the current dividend is 21642865718.... (The dividend has one more digit than the divisor.) As a real number, the quotient of these two enormous integers lies between $216/37 = 5.837...$ and $217/36 = 6.027...$, so the next digit of the integer quotient is either 5 or 6. In general, if two digits of the divisor are used to predict the next digit of the quotient, the true next digit cannot be off by more than one. Turn this idea into an efficient division algorithm. This technique is especially important if numbers are stored in base 1000.

PROJECT 3–4   Upgrade the infinite precision arithmetic package by including negative integers (making `Sub` function the way we would expect), by including a `ReadNum` procedure that can read arbitrarily long integers containing commas (deal with errors in the input), and by storing numbers in base 1000. (If you are programming in Turbo Pascal, note that the product of 999 and 999 exceeds the capacity of an `integer`.)

PROJECT 3–5   Upgrade the infinite precision arithmetic package further by adding a type

```
fraction = record
             num, den: LongInteger;
               (*  den  cannot equal zero *)
           end;
```

with appropriate operators. It is important to keep fractions reduced to lowest terms; this gives a unique representation for each rational number, it keeps the numerators and denominators from growing excessively large (which affects both efficiency and storage requirements), and it conforms to the user's expectations. To do this, you will need to find the **greatest common divisor** of two numbers. There is a famous algorithm due to Euclid for doing this efficiently.

PROJECT 3–6   An alternative to adding fractions to the package is to allow numbers to have a decimal portion. This is a much larger project, involving both design and programming. You cannot simply allow infinite precision to the right of the decimal point because the results of divisions like one divided by seven are unending decimals ($1/7 = .142857142857...$).

PROJECT 3–7 Upgrade the infinite precision arithmetic package further, by combining it with the code of *Nero—The Roman Calculator*, to produce *Spock—The Calculator of the 23rd Century*. There is such a program available under UNIX, called `bc`. Read the manual page for `bc` and experiment with it.

Computing x^n

Every scientist and engineer considers exponentiation a basic arithmetic operation. This is reflected in the syntax of BASIC, FORTRAN, and Ada, all three of which include an exponentiation operator. C provides the equivalent capability through the standard library function

```
double pow(double x, double y);
```

and in Pascal we can write

```
exp(n*ln(x))
```

which is based on the sequence of equalities

$$x^n = (e^{\ln x})^n = e^{n \ln x}$$

But how is exponentiation performed? There is no hardware instruction for exponentiation, as there are for the other four basic arithmetic operations. If n is a real number, then the result can only be approximated anyway, and numerical approximation techniques are employed. On the other hand, if n is a nonnegative integer, x^n can be computed exactly by repeatedly multiplying by x.

```
1  function XToTheN(x: integer; n: integer): integer;
2    (* Compute  x^n  by repeated multiplication. *)
3    var prod: integer;
4        i: integer;
5    begin
6      prod := 1; (* x^0 = 1 *)
7      for i := 1 to n do prod := prod * x;
8      XToTheN := prod
9    end; (* XToTheN *)
```

The types of `x`, `prod`, and the value returned by the function need not be `integer`; they can all be `real`.

For small values of n, this code is reasonably efficient, and if `x` is restricted to type `integer`, only small values of `n` can meaningfully be passed in anyway. (Except when `x` equals zero or one, a value of `n` greater than or equal to 31 causes overflow on a 32-bit computer.) However, since we have an infinite precision arithmetic package at our disposal, it might pay to reexamine how to compute x^n, since n might no longer be small. As we saw in the discussion of how to implement multiplication and division, algorithms that run in time proportional to the *value* of n need to be avoided—and exponentiation by repeated multiplication is essentially the same as multiplication by repeated addition, except that the basic step, a multiply, takes a lot longer than an add.

Perhaps amazingly, x^n can be computed quite efficiently. The strategy is based on observing that $x^n = (x^{n/2})^2$. After $x^{n/2}$ is computed, x^n can be computed with just one additional multiply: simply multiply $x^{n/2}$ by itself. And the same approach can be used to compute $x^{n/2}$ in the first place! If, somehow, $x^{n/4}$ can be computed quickly, $x^{n/2}$ can be computed with just one

(continued)

more multiply. There is, however, one little problem: n might be odd, in which case $n/2$ is not an integer. But at least if n is even, this strategy ought to save us quite a few multiplies. Actually, when n is odd there is no particular problem. Instead of computing $x^{n/2}$, we compute $x^{\lfloor n/2 \rfloor}$, which is $x^{n \text{ div} 2}$. When we square this quantity, we get either x^n, if n is even, or x^{n-1}, if n is odd. In the latter case, we can correct the result by performing an additional multiplication by x. So we can go from $x^{\lfloor n/2 \rfloor}$ to x^n in either one or two multiplications; far fewer than the roughly $n/2$ needed by the simple iterative algorithm. While the concept is quite simple, this computation is difficult to organize in an iterative manner. It is, however, extremely easy to incorporate this approach into a recursive procedure!

```
1  function XToTheN(x: integer; n: integer): integer;
2   (* Compute  x^n  by repeated squaring and multiplication. *)
3   var XToTheNDiv2: integer;
4   begin
5     if n = 0
6       then XToTheN := 1
7       else begin
8             XToTheNDiv2 := XToTheN(x,n div 2);
9             if odd(n)
10               then XToTheN := XToTheNDiv2 * XToTheNDiv2 * x
11               else XToTheN := XToTheNDiv2 * XToTheNDiv2
12          end
13  end; (* XToTheN *)
```

This method is known as exponentiation by repeated squaring and multiplication. Though it might be a bit difficult to guess the running time of this program, it is $O(\log n)$. This is actually not hard to see if looked at the right way: the value of n is cut roughly in half with each recursive call, and thus the values taken on by n form a sequence something like 1338, 669, 334, 167, 83, 41, 20, 10, 5, 2, 1, and 0. As with binary search, because n is cut roughly in half at each step, the number of steps needed to reduce n to zero is approximately $\log_2 n$. For a value of n in the neighborhood of 10,000, this algorithm reduces the number of multiplications from 10,000 to a maximum of 25.

A word of caution. It is very tempting to get rid of the temporary variable XToTheNDiv2 and to write the code as

```
1  function XToTheN(x: integer; n: integer): integer;
2   (* Compute  x^n  by repeated squaring and multiplication. *)
3   begin
4     if n = 0
5       then XToTheN := 1
6       else if odd(n)
7             then XToTheN := XToTheN(x,n div 2) * XToTheN(x,n div 2) * x
8             else XToTheN := XToTheN(x,n div 2) * XToTheN(x,n div 2)
9   end; (* XToTheN *)
```

(continued)

**ABOVE
AND BEYOND**

(concluded)

This innocent-looking change is a disaster! The problem is that we now make two recursive calls to XToTheN, instead of one. This does *not* double the execution time—it changes it from $\log_2 n$ back to n. The reason is that each of the two recursive calls spawns two more recursive calls and all four of these spawns two more, for a total of eight, and so on. The situation is illustrated in Figure 3–13.

EXERCISE 3–3   By measuring the running times, show the effect of reducing the computation time from $O(n)$ to $O(\log n)$ by computing 2^{1000} using both repeated multiplication and the recursive algorithm of repeated squaring and multiplying.

EXERCISE 3–4   If $\log n$ is so much less than n, why are the timings in the answer to the previous exercise as close as they are? Because all hardware instructions take about the same amount of time, it is normally acceptable to simply count the number of basic operations (additions, multiplications, if tests, loop counter incrementations, etc.) performed by a program when calculating its running time. This is what we did in claiming that exponentiation by repeated multiplication took $O(n)$ time and that exponentiation by repeated squaring and multiplying took only $O(\log n)$ time. This reasoning does not apply to infinite precision arithmetic—the time to perform an addition is proportional to the number of digits in the two numbers and so all additions are not alike. Using this more precise method of accounting, how long does it take to perform a multiplication? How long for exponentiation using repeated squaring and multiplication?

FIGURE 3–13   The Calls Generated in Computing x^n Recursively

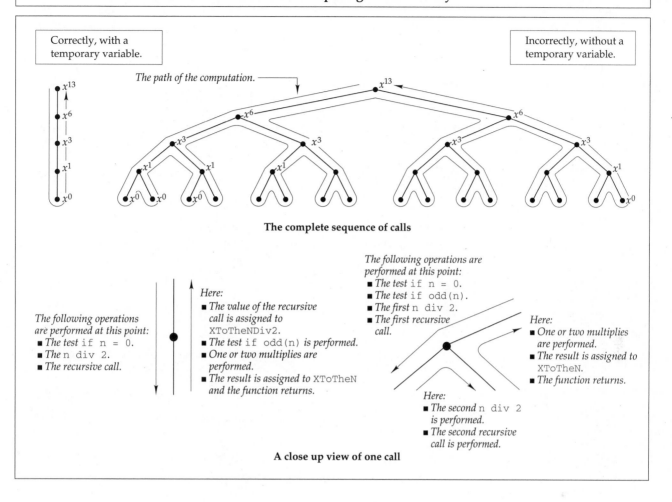

Correctly, with a temporary variable.

Incorrectly, without a temporary variable.

The path of the computation.

The complete sequence of calls

The following operations are performed at this point:
- *The test* if n = 0.
- *The n* div 2.
- *The recursive call.*

Here:
- *The value of the recursive call is assigned to* XToTheNDiv2.
- *The test* if odd(n) *is performed.*
- *One or two multiplies are performed.*
- *The result is assigned to* XToTheN *and the function returns.*

The following operations are performed at this point:
- *The test* if n = 0.
- *The test* if odd(n).
- *The first* n div 2.
- *The first recursive call.*

Here:
- *One or two multiplies are performed.*
- *The result is assigned to* XToTheN.
- *The function returns.*

Here:
- *The second* n div 2 *is performed.*
- *The second recursive call is performed.*

A close up view of one call

**ABOVE
AND BEYOND**   **Our Package in C, Ada, and C++**

While the engineering design process is unaffected by the language used to code the infinite precision arithmetic package, differences between languages do lead to vastly different implementations. The two issues are: how well does the language support the internal representation we, the package implementors, find most natural, and how well does it support a natural user interface? Pascal doesn't do a terribly good job of either. The implementation that is most natural is an array of digits of just the right size. Pascal's inability to allocate arrays whose bounds are defined at runtime forced us into an unnatural, linked implementation. In C, we find that this restriction disappears. While explicitly declared arrays must have compile-time bounds, just as in Pascal, arrays with runtime-specified bounds can be allocated on the heap. In C, we can declare the type `LongInteger` to be

—— *The C keyword for* `record`.

```
struct LongInteger {
    int NumDigits;
    char *Number; /* Actually a pointer to an array of digits. */
};
```

`byte` *would have been a better name than* `char`, *and in C, despite the type name, a character is actually viewed as a small integer.*

Refer to the code for **Add**, *starting at line 244 of* **Long_Arithmetic.p**, *for the counterpart in Pascal.*

Within `Add`, declaring the temporary variable that holds the sum of `m1` and `m2` is done with the line

```
                struct LongInteger r;
```

which allocates a record on the stack, but leaves both fields uninitialized. The first executable line of `Add`,

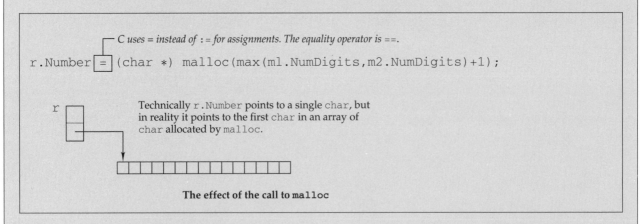

— *C uses = instead of :* = *for assignments. The equality operator is ==.*

```
r.Number = (char *) malloc(max(ml.NumDigits,m2.NumDigits)+1);
```

Technically `r.Number` points to a single `char`, but in reality it points to the first `char` in an array of `char` allocated by `malloc`.

The effect of the call to `malloc`

allocates sufficient storage to hold the sum, even if there is an overflow carry. `malloc` is essentially `new`, except its argument is the number of bytes to allocate. Unlike `new`, `malloc` returns a "generic pointer" (the actual type is `void *`, read as "pointer to `void`"). The type coercion operator `(char *)`

(continued)

changes this type into the type of the `Number` field—this has no effect inside the computer, since all pointers are really the same; it is needed to satisfy the compiler's type-checking rules. Within `Add`, we can now reference `r.Number[i]` and perform addition as described in Figures 3–1 and 3–2.

C does nothing to address the software engineering issues. As with Pascal, the internal representation cannot really be hidden from the user and assignment will copy the pointer stored in the `Number` field and not make a copy of the array pointed to. Our package will also need to manage memory. Because we no longer have equal-sized objects, the package will just rely on `malloc` and `free` (the `dispose` of C), and does

```
free((void *) n->number);
*n = r;
```

as the last steps of `Add`. (The `->` in `n->Number` and the `*` before the `n` are needed because `n` is a call-by-reference parameter.) `Add` will still need to be a procedure, and if user-defined procedures with local variables are permitted we will need to define a user-visible `DisposeNum` procedure, which is really just the call to `free` packaged with a nice interface. User programs will look much like they do in Pascal and the structure of our package is unchanged.

Both Ada and C++ designed after the lessons of Pascal and C had been learned, provide support for the software engineering issues raised by ADTs. The user program to compute *n*! in C++ is given in Figure 3–14. Except for the Pascal vs. C++ syntax, the program looks remarkably like the all-`integer` program with which the chapter opened. The only difference is that some variables are declared `LongInteger` instead of `int`. The two features that separate Ada and C++ from Pascal and C are the ability to hide the implementation details from the user and the ability to overload operators. In C++, the type declaration for infinite precision integers is

```
class LongInteger {
public:
    ... a long list of user-visible procedures and functions...

private:
    int NumDigits;
    char *Number; // Actually a pointer to an array of digits.
    ... a list of internal procedures and functions ...
};
```

While the internal representation is the same as the one used in C, the `private` specification means that procedures declared outside the package cannot examine these fields. (The user can, of course, personally examine the code by looking at a listing, but the compiler will prevent the user from accessing the fields of the `class` that are declared in the `private` part.)

The idea of "overloading operators" is essential to making ADTs seem natural. To achieve naturalness, the need for certain operators, like + on objects of type `LongInteger`, is clear. These operators are really functions; they just happen to be written in infix notation instead of in the more conventional functional notation. In both Ada and C++, we can define + for two objects of type `LongInteger`, `Vector`, `Matrix`, `String`, or what have you, all in

(continued)

the same program, and without overriding its meaning on normal integers. The compiler sorts out which version is appropriate based on the types of the operands. The meaning of + will vary from ADT to ADT. For `String`, it can mean concatenation. The two arguments don't even have to be of the same type. We might, for example, have a `class BST` for binary search trees. The + might be used as `Tree + item` to insert `item` into `Tree`. For `LongInteger`, we would like to be able to mix infinite precision integers and normal ones in lines like `i = 2*i`.

An important question is: what is an "operator"? To make overloading effective we need to take a broad view. Among the operators we need to overload are

- The assignment operator. We need to force the assignment operator, be it = or := , to allocate an array of appropriate size and copy the contents of the array on the right-hand side into the newly created array. If this is done, assignment has the correct meaning, the user can write `j = i`, and `Assign` is no longer needed. This is known as "specifying the copy semantics."

- The type coercion operator. While we could define three forms of +, one involving two `LongInteger` quantities and two for mixed `int` and `LongInteger` additions, it is better to define just one and let `i + 1` coerce the `1` into a `LongInteger`. In the Pascal implementation, type coercion is provided by procedure `MakeLong`. In the C++ implementation, it is invoked automatically when needed.

- The constructor operator. Whenever a variable of the type defined by an ADT is created, Ada and C++ implicitly call a "constructor" to initialize it. The package developer must write the constructor, which can do whatever is necessary and appropriate, but does not need to be concerned with its being called—this happens automatically when a variable of the type is declared.

- The destructor operator. This is also called implicitly, whenever a variable "goes out of scope." Like with the constructor, the responsibility of calling this procedure at the appropriate time is removed from both the user and the package implementor. When a procedure exits, the destructor will automatically be called for all the local variables declared in that procedure. The automatic nature of the call to the destructor, which is also applied to compiler-generated, unnamed temporaries, allows + to be a function without our having to give up control over memory management.

With these operators, we can not only provide a natural coding style for the user, but can remove the burden of calling `Declare` (the constructor) and `DisposeNum` (the destructor). User-defined procedures with call-by-value parameters and local variables come for free—`LongInteger` really looks like `integer` to the user.

FIGURE 3–14   Computing *n*! in C++

```
1 #include <iostream.h>
2 #include "Long—Arithmetic.h"
3
4 LongInteger Factorial(LongInteger n) {
5     // Compute  n! .
6     LongInteger NFact;
7     LongInteger i;
8
9     NFact = 1;
10    for (i = 2; i <= n; i++)
11        NFact = NFact * i;
12    return NFact;
13 } // Factorial
14
15 void main() {
16     int n;
17
18     cout << "For what  n  do you wish to compute  n! : "; cin >> n;
19
20     cout << n << "! = " << Factorial(n);
21 } // main
```

An implicit type coercion occurs here.

An implicit type coercion occurs here too, since the type of the actual parameter is int *and the type of the formal parameter is* LongInteger. *The parameter passing mechanism is call-by-value. Because the package implementor can specify the copy semantics, the entire array is copied, not just the pointer to the array—it operates as a call-by-value parameter from the user's perspective.*

The C/C++ way of writing
```
for i := 2 to n do ...
```

FILE   Long_Arithmetic.h Page 1

```
1  (* Store an infinite precision (nonnegative) integer in a circular, doubly
2      linked list with header cell.  If  p  points to the header cell, then the
3      least significant digit stored is in  p^.MoreSig  and the most significant
4      digit is stored in  p^.LessSig .  Numbers are stored in base 10, one digit
5      per cell.  No leading zeros are stored.  To conform to this rule, zero is
6      stored as just a header cell.  The header cell stores in its  Digit  field
7      the number of digits in the number.
8  *)
9  type PtrToDigitCell = ^DigitCell;
10      DigitCell = record
11                      Digit: integer; (* One digit of an infinite precision
12                                         integer, except in the header cell,
13                                         where it is the count of the number
14                                         of digits. *)
15                  MoreSig, LessSig: PtrToDigitCell
16              end;
17      LongInteger = PtrToDigitCell;   (* To distinguish, logically, an entire
18                                         number from one digit of a number. *)
19
20
21
22 (* Memory Management *)
23 procedure InitializeMemoryManagement; external;
24   (* Initialize the internal memory management system.  This routine should
25      be called once, before any calls to other routines in this package.
26   *)
27
28
29
30 (* Procedures That Apply To Infinite Precision Integers *)
31 (* Declarations *)
32 procedure Declare(var n: LongInteger); external;
33   (* Effectively, perform  n: LongInteger .
34
35      Call this procedure exactly once for every  LongInteger  declared,
36      before the number is used in any other operation.
37   *)
38
39
```

All the procedures in this package have a direct parallel with some operation that Pascal performs on variables of type integer*. This one corresponds to* var n: integer;—*the "declaration operator."*

This declaration psychologically reinforces the distinction between a LongInteger, *an object in "application programmer space," and a pointer to a single digit, an object in "package implementor space." The alternative of declaring* Digit *to be of type* DigitType, *leaving this field empty in the dummy header cell, and making*

```
            LongInteger = record
                            NumDigits: integer;
                            Number: PtrToDigitCell (* pointer to dummy header cell of
                                                      circular, doubly linked list *)
                          end;
```

is perhaps better, as it doesn't overload the meaning of Digit *and it reinforces more strongly the separation of the logical concept of a* LongInteger *and the details of its physical implementation—*LongInteger *and* PtrToDigitCell *are no longer the same type.*

```
40 (* Type Coercions *)
41 procedure MakeLong(var IInLong: LongInteger; i: integer); external;
42   (* Effectively, perform  IInLong := i  for  i >= 0 . *)
43
44
```

This procedure corresponds to the "type coercion operator"—it has the same effect as the line
    x := i
where x *is* real *and* i *is* integer.

```
45  (* Relational Operators *)
46  (* Effectively, perform  if  m1  relational—operator  m2  then ... . *)
47  function Equal(m1, m2: LongInteger): boolean; external;
48  function NotEqual(m1, m2: LongInteger): boolean; external;
49  function Less(m1, m2: LongInteger): boolean; external;
50  function LessEq(m1, m2: LongInteger): boolean; external;
51  function Greater(m1, m2: LongInteger): boolean; external;
52  function GreaterEq(m1, m2: LongInteger): boolean; external;
53
54
55  (* Assignment Operator *)
56  procedure Assign(var n: LongInteger; m: LongInteger); external;
57    (* Effectively, perform  n := m . *)
58
59
```

See **The need for** Assign *for why we cannot just allow the user to write*

$$n := m$$

even though it is syntactically legal Pascal.

```
60  (* Arithmetic Operators *)
61  procedure Add(var n: LongInteger; m1, m2: LongInteger); external;
62    (* Effectively, perform  n := m1 + m2 . *)
63
```

See **Why** Add **is a procedure** *for why we cannot provide the more natural*
function Add(m1, m2: LongInteger): LongInteger;

```
64  procedure Sub(var n: LongInteger; m1, m2: LongInteger); external;
65    (* Effectively, perform  n := m1 - m2 , where subtraction is understood
66       to mean proper subtraction, that is, the proper difference of two
67       numbers is zero if the first is less than the second.
68    *)
69
70  procedure Mult(var n: LongInteger; m1, m2: LongInteger); external;
71    (* Effectively, perform  n := m1 * m2 . *)
72
73  procedure Quotient(var n: LongInteger; m1, m2: LongInteger); external;
74    (* Effectively, perform  n := m1 div m2 . *)
75
76  procedure Remainder(var n: LongInteger; m1, m2: LongInteger); external;
77    (* Effectively, perform  n := m1 mod m2 . *)
78
79
80  (* I/O Operations *)
81  procedure WriteNum(n: LongInteger); external;
82    (* Effectively, perform  writeln(n)  with commas inserted in the
83       appropriate places for readability.
84    *)
```

No equivalent ReadNum *procedure is provided by our package (see Project 3–4).
Normal size integers can be read in with*
```
            procedure ReadNum(var n: LongInteger);
               var i: integer;
               begin
                 read(i); MakeLong(n,i)
               end; (* ReadNum *)
```

```
 1  (* Unreported Errors:
 2       Failure to call  InitializeMemoryManagement  before any other procedure
 3          in this package or a second call to this procedure.
 4       Reference to a  LongInteger  (used as a  var  parameter) before it
 5          is declared.
 6       Redeclaration of a  LongInteger .
 7       Use of a  LongInteger  (used as a value parameter) before it
 8          is given a value, even if it is declared.
 9       Improper use of :=, = or <> between  LongIntegers .
10       Storage lost due to local variables going out of scope -- make  DisposeNum
11          public if user-defined procedures are allowed.
12       Passing  LongIntegers  by value to user-defined procedures.
13
14    Reported Errors:
15       Passing a negative argument to  MakeLong .
16       Division by zero.
17       Subtractions that result in negative numbers -- this defined away by
18          making subtraction proper subtraction.
19  *)
20
21  #include "Long_Arithmetic.h"
22
23  type Relation = (LessThan, EqualTo, GreaterThan);
24
25
26
```

Such calls just discard memory. The application program would continue to function correctly as long as memory isn't exhausted.

See the internal function Compare *and the six user visible functions* Equal, NotEqual, ...

See For Your Information: A Simple Memory Management Package *for a discussion of the technique used here.*

```
27  (* Memory Management *)
28  var FreeNodeList: PtrToDigitCell; (* Manage the returned storage as a stack,
29                               linked through the  LessSig  field. *)
30
31  (* procedure InitializeMemoryManagement; *)
32  procedure InitializeMemoryManagement;
33    (* Initialize the internal memory management system.  This routine should
34       be called once, before any calls to other routines in this package.
35    *)
36    begin
37      FreeNodeList := nil
38    end; (* InitializeMemoryManagement *)
39
40  procedure NewDigit(var p: PtrToDigitCell);
41    (* If there are returned  DigitCells , use one.  Otherwise, get a
42       fresh one from the Pascal memory management system.
43    *)
44    begin
45      if FreeNodeList <> nil
46        then begin
47              p := FreeNodeList;
48              FreeNodeList := FreeNodeList^.LessSig
49           end
50        else new(p)
51    end; (* NewDigit *)
52
```

This routine is needed because UNIX Pascal does not provide a mechanism for initializing the variable FreeNodeList. *This procedure is not needed in the Turbo Pascal implementation.*

This routine corresponds to InternalNew.

```
53 procedure DisposeDigit(p: PtrToDigitCell);
54    (* Return a single digit to the memory management system. *)
55    begin
56      p^.LessSig := FreeNodeList;
57      FreeNodeList := p                    This routine corresponds to InternalDispose.
58    end; (* DisposeDigit *)
59
```

If users are permitted to define their own procedures, DisposeNum *needs to be made user visible.*
If this is not done, storage used by local variables cannot be reclaimed on procedure exit.

```
60 procedure DisposeNum(var n: LongInteger);
61    (* Return the storage used by the LongInteger  n  to our
62       internal memory management system, making  n  uninitialized.
63    *)
64    begin
65      (* The user can legitimately expect to write code like:
66           Declare(n);
67           Declare(m1);
68           Declare(m2);
69           ... set  m1  and  m2  to something by some calculation ...
70           Add(n,m1,m2);
71         The call to  DisposeNum  at the end of  Add  should not be allowed
72         to cause a problem.
73
74         See also  Declare( )
75      *)
```

n = nil *is the flag for determining if a* LongInteger *has been declared, but is uninitialized.*
If so, there is no storage to return to our memory management system. An alternative is to have
Declare *initialize* n *to zero. If that convention were adopted, this test would not be needed.*

```
76      if n <> nil
77        then begin
78                (* Break open the circularly linked list and attach the
79                   entire number to the free storage list in one step. *)
80                n^.MoreSig^.LessSig := FreeNodeList;
81                FreeNodeList := n;
82                n := nil
83             end
84    end; (* DisposeNum *)
85
86
87
```

We do this for safety. If we do not do this and there are two calls to DisposeNum *with the*
same actual parameter but without an intervening assignment to the variable, the free storage
list will be destroyed. By examining Long_Arithmetic.p *we see that this cannot happen,*
but building in such interprocedural dependencies for such a small gain is a bad idea. If we make
DisposeNum *user visible, this line becomes necessary.*

We take advantage of the circular, doubly linked representation to return an entire LongInteger
in constant time. The more structured alternative

```
      p := n; (*  p  points to  DigitCell  being disposed *)
      repeat
        q := p^.MoreSig; (* don't lose our place *)
        DisposeDigit(p);
        p := q (* advance to next cell *)
      until p = n (* until we reach the  DigitCell  we disposed of first *)
```

takes time proportional to the number of digits.

although
```
        DisposeDigit(p);
        p := p^.MoreSig
```
is safe, we should not use p *to reference memory after what it points to has been deallocated. It is safe because the free storage list is linked on the* LessSig *field and not on the* MoreSig *field, but taking advantage of such interprocedural dependencies is extremely dangerous.*

```
88  (* Procedures That Apply To Infinite Precision Integers *)
89  (* Declarations *)
90  (* procedure Declare(var n: LongInteger); *)
91  procedure Declare;
92    (* Effectively, perform  n: LongInteger .
93
94      Call this procedure exactly once for every  LongInteger  declared,
95      before the number is used in any other operation.
96    *)
97    (* This routine is needed because Pascal does not guarantee initialization
98      of variables.
99    *)
100   begin
101     n := nil
102   end; (* Declare *)
103
104
105 (* Type Coercions *)
106 (* procedure MakeLong(var IInLong: LongInteger; i: integer); *)
107 procedure MakeLong;
108   (* Effectively, perform  IInLong := i , for  i >= 0 . *)
109   var p1, p2: PtrToDigitCell;
110       j: integer; (* number of digits in  i  *)
111   begin
112     if i < 0
113       then begin
114             writeln('Panic: negative second argument to  MakeLong .');
115             halt
116           end;
117     DisposeNum(IInLong);
118     NewDigit(IInLong);
119     j := 0;
120     p1 := IInLong;
121     while i > 0 do
122       begin
123         (* Peel off the next least significant digit of  i . *)
124         NewDigit(p2);
125         j := j + 1;
126         p2^.Digit := i mod 10;
127         p1^.MoreSig := p2;
128         p2^.LessSig := p1;
129         p1 := p2;
130         i := i div 10
131       end;
132     p1^.MoreSig := IInLong;
133     IInLong^.LessSig := p1;
134     IInLong^.Digit := j
135   end; (* MakeLong *)
136
137
```

We explicitly make n *uninitialized from the user's perspective, but make it initialized (as a pointer) from ours.*

We don't "close the circle" until the very end. Moving these two lines inside the while *loop would keep the list circular at all times (a condition for which there is no need), but would make the routine about 10 percent slower. (With these lines placed inside the loop,* i *= 0 is a special case not handled correctly.) The same style is used in all the other arithmetic routines as well.*

This routine operates correctly when comparing zero to a positive integer.

```
138  (* Relational Operators *)
139  function Compare(m1, m2: LongInteger): Relation;
140    (* Determine the relationship between  m1  and  m2 . *)
141    var p1, p2: PtrToDigitCell;
142    begin
143      (* Because of its use in division, we want this routine to be as
144         fast as possible -- take advantage of the digit count stored in
145         the header cell and, in case of a tie, the double linking to scan
146         from the most significant to the least significant digit.
147      *)
148      if m1^.Digit < m2^.Digit
149        then Compare := LessThan
150      else if m1^.Digit > m2^.Digit
151        then Compare := GreaterThan
152      else (* m1^.Digit = m2^.Digit *)
153            begin
154              (* Compare the two numbers digit by digit, from most significant
155                 digit to least significant digit, until a difference is
156                 detected or the two numbers are exhausted.
157              *)
158              p1 := m1^.LessSig;
159              p2 := m2^.LessSig;
160              (* Scan, looking for a difference. *)
161              while (p1 <> m1) and (p1^.Digit = p2^.Digit) do
162                begin
163                  p1 := p1^.LessSig;
164                  p2 := p2^.LessSig
165                end;
166              if p1^.Digit < p2^.Digit
167                then Compare := LessThan
168              else if p1^.Digit > p2^.Digit
169                then Compare := GreaterThan
170              else (* p1 = m1 and p2 = m2 and they had the same digit count *)
171                    Compare := EqualTo
172            end
173  end; (* Compare *)
174
```

Making this routine as efficient as possible is one of the driving forces behind selecting circular, doubly linked lists as our representation for infinite precision integers. The others are clarity of the code and the lack of dynamically allocated arrays in Pascal.

p2 <> m2 as well. Since the two numbers have the same number of digits, there is no need to check this condition explicitly.

This routine operates correctly when comparing zero to zero—the while *loop is simply skipped.*

This is more elegant and efficient than the straightforward

```
while p1 <> m1 (* and p2 <> m2 *) do
  if p1^.Digit < p2^.Digit
    then begin Compare := LessThan;    goto 99 (* return *) end
  else if p1^.Digit > p2^.Digit
    then begin Compare := GreaterThan; goto 99 (* return *) end
  else (* p1^.Digit = p2^.Digit -- keep searching *)
        begin p1 := p1^.LessSig; p2 := p2^.LessSig end;
Compare := EqualTo
```

The loop at line 161 scans to the point of disagreement and then sorts out the situation. If the two numbers are equal, then the while *loop terminates with* p1 = m1, p2 = m2, *and* p1^.Digit = p2^.Digit.

```
175  (* Effectively, perform  if  m1  relational-operator  m2  then ... . *)
176  (* function Equal(m1, m2: LongInteger): boolean; *)
177  function Equal;
178    begin
179      Equal := Compare(m1,m2) in [EqualTo]
180    end; (* Equal *)
181
```

```
182 (* function NotEqual(m1, m2: LongInteger): boolean; *)
183 function NotEqual;
184   begin
185     NotEqual := Compare(m1,m2) in [LessThan, GreaterThan]
186   end; (* NotEqual *)
187
```

> *For reasons of efficiency we do not want to code this as*
>   NotEqual := (Compare(m1,m2) = LessThan) or (Compare(m1,m2) = GreaterThan)
> *The alternative,*
>   Comp := Compare(m1,m2);
>   NotEqual := (Comp = LessThan) or (Comp = GreaterThan)
> *which uses a temporary variable to hold the result of the comparison, is equally efficient, though perhaps less elegant.*

```
188 (* function Less(m1, m2: LongInteger): boolean; *)
189 function Less;
190   begin
191     Less := Compare(m1,m2) in [LessThan]
192   end; (* Less *)
193
194 (* function LessEq(m1, m2: LongInteger): boolean; *)
195 function LessEq;
196   begin
197     LessEq := Compare(m1,m2) in [LessThan, EqualTo]
198   end; (* LessEq *)
199
200 (* function Greater(m1, m2: LongInteger): boolean; *)
201 function Greater;
202   begin
203     Greater := Compare(m1,m2) in [GreaterThan]
204   end; (* Greater *)
205
206 (* function GreaterEq(m1, m2: LongInteger): boolean; *)
207 function GreaterEq;
208   begin
209     GreaterEq := Compare(m1,m2) in [GreaterThan, EqualTo]
210   end; (* GreaterEq *)
211
212
213 (* Assignment Operator *)
214 (* procedure Assign(var n: LongInteger; m: LongInteger); *)
215 procedure Assign;
216   (* Effectively, perform  n := m . *)
217   (* Make a copy of  m . *)
218   var r: LongInteger;
219       p, q1, q2: PtrToDigitCell;
220   begin
221     NewDigit(r);
222     r^.Digit := m^.Digit; (* The digit counts will ultimately be the same. *)
223     q1 := r;
224     p := m^.MoreSig;
```

```
225      while p <> m do
226        begin
227          (* Copy over another digit. *)
228          NewDigit(q2);
229          q2^.Digit := p^.Digit;
230          q1^.MoreSig := q2;
231          q2^.LessSig := q1;
232          q1 := q2;
233          p := p^.MoreSig
234        end;
235      q1^.MoreSig := r;
236      r^.LessSig := q1;
237
238      DisposeNum(n);
239      n := r
240    end; (* Assign *)
241
242
243  (* Arithmetic Operators *)
244  (* procedure Add(var n: LongInteger; m1, m2: LongInteger); *)
245  procedure Add;
246    (* Effectively, perform  n := m1 + m2 . *)
247    (* Perform the addition using "schoolboy arithmetic," that is, add the
248       digits one by one from least significant digit to most significant
249       digit, keeping track of the carry along the way.
250    *)
251    var r: LongInteger;
252        p1, p2, q1, q2: PtrToDigitCell;
253        carry: 0..1;
254        i: integer; (* number of digits in the sum *)
255    begin
256      NewDigit(r);
257      i := 0;
258      carry := 0; (* no "carry in" initially *)
259      p1 := m1^.MoreSig;
260      p2 := m2^.MoreSig;
261      q1 := r;
262
263      (* while both numbers have digits left do... *)
264      while (p1 <> m1) and (p2 <> m2) do
265        begin
266          NewDigit(q2);
267          i := i + 1;


268          q1^.MoreSig := q2;
269          q2^.LessSig := q1;
270          q2^.Digit := p1^.Digit + p2^.Digit + carry;
271          if q2^.Digit >= 10
272            then begin
273                   q2^.Digit := q2^.Digit - 10;
274                   carry := 1
275                 end
276            else carry := 0;
```

By placing this last and building a copy of m, *this routine works correctly even when faced with the absurd call* Assign(i,i).

Because the user can make calls like Add(IInLong,IInLong,one) *the call to* DisposeNum *(line 330) must occur after the sum of* m1 *and* m2 *has been computed. Otherwise, despite the fact that* m1 *and* m2 *are call-by-value, one or both of the arguments to* Add *might already have been placed on the free storage list. We would then start incorporating the freed cells into the sum before processing their data, resulting in a hard-to-find bug. For this reason, we build the result in a temporary and assign it to* n *at the last minute.*

See the annotations in Figure 3–2 for an explanation of this control structure.

It would be more efficient (constant time vs. time proportional to the number of digits in the sum) to set n^.Digit *to* max(m1^.Digit,m2^.Digit), *incrementing it by one if there is an overflow carry (line 315), but it is more in the spirit of "building the sum digit by digit" to count them as we go. The effect on the running time is a few percent—changing this might be worthwhile.*

If we define the type of Digit *to be* 0..9, *this sum will have to be stored in a temporary and then assigned to* q2^.Digit *after any necessary adjustments have been made.*

This can also be done as
    carry := q2^.Digit div 10;
    q2^.Digit := q2^.Digit mod 10;
but a div *and a* mod *are slower than an* if *and a subtract.*

```
277            p1 := p1^.MoreSig;
278            p2 := p2^.MoreSig;
279            q1 := q2
280          end;
281       (* One or both numbers are exhausted. *)
282       while p1 <> m1 do (* loop skipped if  m1  exhausted *)
283         begin
284           NewDigit(q2);
285           i := i + 1;
286           q1^.MoreSig := q2;
287           q2^.LessSig := q1;
288           q2^.Digit := p1^.Digit + carry;
289           if q2^.Digit >= 10
290             then begin
291                    q2^.Digit := q2^.Digit - 10;
292                    carry := 1
293                  end
294             else carry := 0;
295           p1 := p1^.MoreSig;
296           q1 := q2
297         end;
298       while p2 <> m2 do (* loop skipped if  m2  exhausted *)
299         begin
300           NewDigit(q2);
301           i := i + 1;
302           q1^.MoreSig := q2;
303           q2^.LessSig := q1;
304           q2^.Digit := p2^.Digit + carry;
305           if q2^.Digit >= 10
306             then begin
307                    q2^.Digit := q2^.Digit - 10;
308                    carry := 1
309                  end
310             else carry := 0;
311           p2 := p2^.MoreSig;
312           q1 := q2
313         end;
314       (* Both  m1  and  m2  are now exhausted, but there can still be a carry. *)
315       if carry = 1
316         then begin
317                NewDigit(q2);
318                i := i + 1;
319                q1^.MoreSig := q2;
320                q2^.LessSig := q1;
321                q2^.Digit := 1;
322                q1 := q2
323              end;
324
325       (* Link the number being formed into a circle. *)
326       q1^.MoreSig := r;
327       r^.LessSig := q1;
328       r^.Digit := i;
329
330       DisposeNum(n);
331       n := r
332     end; (* Add *)
333
```

FILE   `Long_Arithmetic.p` Page 8

```
334  (* procedure Sub(var n: LongInteger; m1, m2: LongInteger); *)
335  procedure Sub;
336    (* Effectively, perform  n := m1 - m2 , where subtraction is understood
337       to mean proper subtraction, that is, the proper difference of two
338       numbers is zero if the first is less than the second.
339    *)
340    (* Perform the subtraction using "schoolboy arithmetic," that is, subtract
341       the digits one by one from least significant digit to most significant
342       digit, keeping track of the borrow along the way.
343    *)
344  var r: LongInteger;
345      p1, p2, q1, q2: PtrToDigitCell;
346      borrow: 0..1;
347      i: integer; (* number of digits in the difference *)
348  begin
349    if LessEq(m1,m2)
350      then (* return result of zero *)
351           begin Declare(r); MakeLong(r,0) end
352      else begin
353           NewDigit(r);
354           i := 0;
355           borrow := 0; (* no "borrow from" initially *)
356           p1 := m1^.MoreSig;
357           p2 := m2^.MoreSig;
358           q1 := r;
359
```

The borrow can be treated in the same manner as the carry in addition. This is not how we subtract on paper, but once understood we see that the approach used here is easier to implement and doesn't destroy m1, *which would undoubtedly surprise the user.*

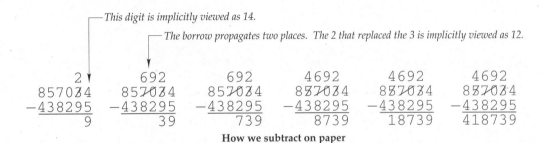

This digit is implicitly viewed as 14.

The borrow propagates two places. The 2 that replaced the 3 is implicitly viewed as 12.

How we subtract on paper

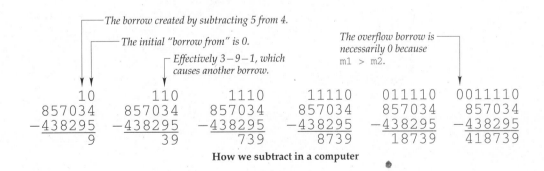

The borrow created by subtracting 5 from 4.

The initial "borrow from" is 0.

Effectively 3 − 9 − 1, which causes another borrow.

The overflow borrow is necessarily 0 because m1 > m2.

How we subtract in a computer

The loop control is slightly simpler than that of Add *because* m1 *is at least as long as* m2, *if not longer.*

```
360         (*  m1  has at least as many digits as  m2 .  *)
361         while p2 <> m2 do
362           begin
363             NewDigit(q2);
364             i := i + 1;
365             q1^.MoreSig := q2;
366             q2^.LessSig := q1;
367             q2^.Digit := p1^.Digit - p2^.Digit - borrow;
368             if q2^.Digit < 0
369               then begin
370                      q2^.Digit := q2^.Digit + 10;
371                      borrow := 1
372                    end
373               else borrow := 0;
374             p1 := p1^.MoreSig;
375             p2 := p2^.MoreSig;
376             q1 := q2
377           end;
378         (*  m1  might not yet be exhausted *)
379         while p1 <> m1 do  (* loop skipped if  m1  exhausted *)
380           begin
381             NewDigit(q2);
382             i := i + 1;
383             q1^.MoreSig := q2;
384             q2^.LessSig := q1;
385             q2^.Digit := p1^.Digit - borrow;
386             if q2^.Digit < 0
387               then begin
388                      q2^.Digit := q2^.Digit + 10;
389                      borrow := 1
390                    end
391               else borrow := 0;
392             p1 := p1^.MoreSig;
393             q1 := q2
394           end;
395         (* Post condition: borrow = 0.  *)
396
397         (* It is possible that some, but not all, of the digits of
398            the difference are zero.  Eliminate any leading zeros. *)
399         while q1^.Digit = 0 do
400           begin
401             i := i - 1;
402             q2 := q1^.LessSig;  (* don't lose our place *)
403             DisposeDigit(q1);
404             q1 := q2
405           end;
406
```

The overflow borrow is necessarily zero because m1 > m2.

The comment explains why the test is q1^.Digit = 0 *and not* (q1 <> r) and (q1^.digit = 0). *This gain in efficiency comes from using* LessEq *and not* Less *on line 349.*

```
407                    (* Link the number being formed into a circle. *)
408                q1^.MoreSig := r;
409                r^.LessSig := q1;
410                r^.Digit := i
411             end;
412
413     DisposeNum(n);
414       n := r
415     end; (* Sub *)
416
417  (* procedure Mult(var n: LongInteger; m1, m2: LongInteger); *)
418  procedure Mult;
419     (* Effectively, perform  n := m1 * m2 . *)
420     (* Perform the multiplication using "schoolboy arithmetic," that is, form
421        partial products by shifting over the product of  m1  and a digit
422        of  m2 , and then add the partial products up.  It is easier to
423        compute the sum of the partial products as we go along.
424     *)
425     var p: PtrToDigitCell;
426         r, r1: LongInteger;
427         shift: integer;
428
429     procedure MultByDigit(var n: LongInteger; m: LongInteger; d, e: integer);
430        (* Effectively, perform  n := m * d * 10^e . *)
431        (* Used to form partial products that have been shifted over the correct
432           number of places in "schoolboy arithmetic."
433        *)
434        (* Precondition:  m <> 0 . *)
435        var r: LongInteger;
436            p, q1, q2: PtrToDigitCell;
437            carry: 0..8; (* worst case is 9*9 with a previous carry of 8 *)
438            i, (* number of digits in result *)
439            j: integer;
440        begin
441          (* Multiplying by 0 is a bit of a special case as we do not want to
442             create leading zeros. *)
443          if d = 0
444            then begin Declare(r); MakeLong(r,0) end
445            else begin
446                  NewDigit(r);
447                  q1 := r;
448
449                  (* Place  e  zeros at the least significant end of the number. *)
450                  for j := 1 to e do
451                    begin
452                      NewDigit(q2);
453                      q1^.MoreSig := q2;
454                      q2^.LessSig := q1;
455                      q2^.Digit := 0;
456                      q1 := q2
457                    end;
458                  i := e;
459
```

(Precondition: m <> 0 . *)* ←——— *See line 499.*

This avoids constructing 000...00, *which, while it would work correctly when passed on to* Add, *violates our prohibition against leading zeros. Consistency aids the proof of program correctness and it should not be sacrificed needlessly.*

See **For Your Information: Is It Really an Infinite Precision Arithmetic Package?**

```
460                    carry := 0;
461                    (* There is at least one digit in  m . *)  ◄── Justification for a repeat instead of a while.
462                    p := m^.MoreSig;
463                    repeat
464                      NewDigit(q2);
465                      i := i + 1;
466                      q1^.MoreSig := q2;
467                      q2^.LessSig := q1;
468                      j := p^.Digit*d + carry;          Unlike in Add, here we use div and mod.
469                      q2^.Digit := j mod 10;
470                      carry := j div 10;
471                      q1 := q2;
472                      p := p^.MoreSig
473                    until p = m;
474                    if carry > 0
475                      then begin
476                              NewDigit(q2);
477                              i := i + 1;
478                              q1^.MoreSig := q2;
479                              q2^.LessSig := q1;
480                              q2^.Digit := carry;
481                              q1 := q2
482                           end;
483
484                    (* Link the number being formed into a circle. *)
485                    q1^.MoreSig := r;
486                    r^.LessSig := q1;
487                    r^.Digit := i
488                 end;
489
490        DisposeNum(n);
491        n := r
492      end; (* MultByDigit *)
493
494    begin (* Mult *)
495      (* The sum of the partial products starts at zero. *)
496      Declare(r); MakeLong(r,0);
497
498      (* We only have something to do if the multiplicand is not zero. *)
499      if m1^.Digit <> 0   ◄─────────  This is not just a matter of efficiency. MultByDigit does
500        then begin                    not work correctly if m1 is zero.
501            Declare(r1);
502            p := m2^.MoreSig;
503            shift := 0;
504            while p <> m2 do
505              begin
506                MultByDigit(r1,m1,p^.Digit,shift);
507                Add(r,r,r1);
508                p := p^.MoreSig;
509                shift := shift + 1
510              end;
511            DisposeNum(r1) (* last partial product needs to be disposed of *)
512          end;
513
514      DisposeNum(n);
515      n := r
516    end; (* Mult *)
517
```

r1 is a temporary variable of type LongInteger. *Though local to a routine of the package, there is no difference between it and a local variable of type* LongInteger *in an application program. While* MultByDigit *will dispose of* r1 *before assigning the partial product to* n *(line 490),* Mult *must dispose of the final partial product before returning or the storage pointed to by* r1 *will be lost.*

We can multiply more efficiently, at least in most cases, by taking advantage of two observations:
- *Ignoring the zeros that we add to the less significant end of a number to accomplish the shifting over, there are only 10 different partial products.*
- *If neither* m1 *nor* m2 *is zero, the length of the product is either the sum of their lengths or one less than this sum.*

The first observation suggests that we should precompute all ten partial products with calls to MultByDigit, *storing them in a temporary, locally declared array*

```
    var PartialProds: array [0..9] of LongInteger;
```

Then for each digit of m2, *when we process it we do not need the call to* MultbyDigit—*we can just look up the partial product.*

We first construct an illegal number of m1^.Digit + m2^.Digit *zeros to hold the running sum. This guarentees that when we add in a shifted partial product, the shifted partial product will run out first, even if there are overflow carries. The reason we do this is that we plan on doing the addition "in place," modifying the running sum as we add in the shifted partial product. This will be considerably more efficient, since it will involve no memory management after the construction of the original running sum of* m1^.Digit + m2^.Digit *zeros. We also do not shift the partial products to the left. The inner loop of our multiplication routine becomes*

```
          (*  r  consists of a header cell and  m1^.Digit + m2^.Digit  zeros. *)
          q1 := r^.MoreSig; (*  q1  accounts for the "shifting over" -- initially there
                                   is none. *)
      p := m2^.MoreSig;
      while p <> m2 do (* process another digit of the multiplier *)
        begin
          p1 := PartialProds[p^.Digit]; (*  p1  points to the header cell of the
                                               appropriate partial product. *)
          p2 := p1^.MoreSig;
          carry := 0;
          q2 := q1; (* the shifting over is free *)
          while p2 <> p1 do
            begin
              q2^.Digit := q2^.Digit + p2^.Digit + carry; (* do the addition "in place" *)
              if q2^.Digit >= 10
                then begin q2^.Digit := q2^.Digit - 10; carry := 1 end
                else carry := 0;
              q2 := q2^.MoreSig;
              p2 := p2^.MoreSig
            end;
          while carry = 1 do
            begin
              q2^.Digit := q2^.Digit + carry;
              if q2^.Digit >= 10
                then q2^.Digit := q2^.Digit - 10 (* carry := 1 *)
                else carry := 0;
              q2 := q2^.MoreSig
            end;
          q1 := q1^.MoreSig; (* The next partial product is shifted over one more place. *)
          p := p^.MoreSig
        end;
```

After all this, there may be a single leading zero that needs elimination.

It is hard to say exactly how much time is saved by this approach. If the multiplier is the shorter of the two numbers (this can be guaranteed with a simple test inside Mult), *then the improvement is all in eliminating the work done for the additions performed on the zeros inside the triangle (which is never more than a third of the work), having to call* MultByDigit *ten times (instead of* m2^.Digit *times), and the time saved doing memory management and pointer manipulations.*

A disadvantage is that multiplication now relies far more heavily on the internal representation of numbers than it did previously, so there is more to modify if we should switch to a different representation. Additionally, precomputing all the partial products and storing them for later use is effective only if the base of the number representation is less than the number of digits in the integers we expect to encounter (see Improving the efficiency of our package). *If we use base 1000, then precomputing the partial products does not pay unless the multiplier has 3000 or more base 10 digits. Building a running sum of* m1^.Digit + m2^.Digit *zeros and adding in place is still effective, however.*

```
518 procedure Divide(var q, r: LongInteger; m1, m2: LongInteger);
519    (* Effectively compute  q := m1 div m2
520                      and  r := m1 mod m2
521       at the same time.
522    *)
523    (* Perform the division using "schoolboy arithmetic."  The actual
524       implementation is done somewhat differently than what was learned
525       in school.  First, the divisor has to be padded with zeros, so that
526       the divisor and dividend are the same length -- children do this
527       implicitly.  Secondly, we do not guess the number of times the divisor
528       goes into the dividend.  We do repeated subtractions and actually
529       count the number of times the divisor goes into the dividend.  This
530       really isn't terribly inefficient -- if we were working in base two
531       it would be just the thing to do.
532    *)
533    (* Unlike all other routines in this package that perform arithmetic,
534       here the result is produced most significant to least significant
535       digit.
536    *)
537    var LastDigit, (* mark the location of the original last digit of  m2 . *)
538        tempq, tempr: LongInteger;
539        p, q1, q2: PtrToDigitCell;
540        i: integer;
541    begin
542      (* If the divisor is zero, division is impossible. *)
543      if m2^.Digit = 0
544        then begin
545             writeln('Panic: division by zero.');
546             halt
547           end;
548
549      Declare(tempr); Assign(tempr,m1); (* Make a copy of  m1  we can destroy. *)
550      if Less(m1,m2)
551        then (* If the divisor is greater than the dividend, then the quotient
552                is zero and the remainder is the dividend. *)
553             begin Declare(tempq); MakeLong(tempq,0) end
554        else begin
555             (* Caution: We tack on extra zeros to  m2 .  We must make sure to
556                         remove these before returning.  They are actually
557                         removed one at a time during the division process.
558                *)
```

> Modifying the input data, even though we restore it, is a dangerous practice. This is more efficient than the more structured alternative of making a copy of m2, padding the copy with zeros, and successively removing them until the copy and m2 become equal, at which time there would be one last digit of the quotient to calculate. A very subtle, potential bug, which turns out not to be one, is that we might be modifying the dividend indirectly when we modify the divisor, because of the rather silly call Quotient(n,m,m).

```
559             LastDigit := m2^.MoreSig;
560             for i := 1 to m1^.Digit - m2^.Digit do
561               begin
562                 (* Equalize the length of the divisor and the dividend. *)
563                 NewDigit(p);
564                 p^.Digit := 0;
565                 p^.LessSig := m2;
566                 p^.MoreSig := m2^.MoreSig;
567                 p^.MoreSig^.LessSig := p;
568                 m2^.MoreSig := p
569               end;
570             m2^.Digit := m1^.Digit;
```

> See **Schoolboy division revisited** *for a discussion of the algorithm*

—— See For Your Information: Is It Really an Infinite Precision Arithmetic Package?

> Since m2 *is passed to* Sub, *we need to maintain* m2 *as a legitimate number. For this reason, we adjust the digit count to reflect the added zeros; and do not just add the padding zeros surreptitiously.*

```
571        (* They now have the same length, but  m2  might be larger
572           than  m1 .  If so, correct this. *)
573     if Less(m1,m2)                    ┌── Because of the test on line 550, if m1 < m2 then m2 was padded with zeros.
574       then begin
575             ┌─────────────────────────────────────────────────┐
                │(* Remove the last zero we (necessarily) added. *)│
576             │m2^.Digit := m2^.Digit - 1;                       │
577             p := m2^.MoreSig;
578             p^.MoreSig^.LessSig := m2;
579             m2^.MoreSig := p^.MoreSig;
580             DisposeDigit(p)
581           end;
582
583     (* We are ready to do the division. *)
584     NewDigit(tempq); (* get the header cell for the quotient *)
585     tempq^.Digit := 0; (* the quotient has no digits at this time *)
586     q1 := tempq;
587    ┌────────────────────────────────────┐
       │while m2^.MoreSig <> LastDigit do    │
588       (* Calculate how many times the current zero-extended version
589          of the divisor goes into what is left of the dividend.  While
590          this can produce a zero, the previous code ensures that it
591          cannot the very first time through the outer  while  loop.
592       *)
593       begin
594         i := 0;
595         while GreaterEq(tempr,m2) do
596           begin
597             Sub(tempr,tempr,m2);
598             i := i + 1
599           end;
600         (*  i  cannot exceed 9. *)
601
602         (* Add the new digit to the end of the quotient being
603            formed. *)
604         NewDigit(q2);
605         tempq^.Digit := tempq^.Digit + 1; (* quotient has one more
606                                              digit *)
607         q1^.LessSig := q2;
608         q2^.MoreSig := q1;
609         q2^.Digit := i;
610         q1 := q2;
611
612         ┌──────────────────────────────────────────────────────────┐
           │(* Remove the least significant zero from the end of  m2 . *)│
613         │m2^.Digit := m2^.Digit - 1;                               │
614         p := m2^.MoreSig;
615         p^.MoreSig^.LessSig := m2;
616         m2^.MoreSig := p^.MoreSig;
617         DisposeDigit(p)
618       end;
619     (*  m2  is back to the way it was on procedure entry. *)
620
621     ┌────────────────────────────────────────────┐
        │(* Calculate the last digit of the quotient. *)│
622     │i := 0;                                       │
623     while GreaterEq(tempr,m2) do                  │
624       begin                                       ── Because of the removal of the low order
625         Sub(tempr,tempr,m2);                         digit, the final digit of the quotient must
626         i := i + 1                                   be computed separately.
627       end;
628
```

```
629              NewDigit(q2);
630              tempq^.Digit := tempq^.Digit + 1; (* the quotient has one more
631                                          digit *)
632           q1^.LessSig := q2;
633           q2^.MoreSig := q1;
634           q2^.Digit := i;
635
636           (* Link the number being formed into a circle. *)
637           q2^.LessSig := tempq;
638           tempq^.MoreSig := q2
639         end;
640
641     DisposeNum(q); DisposeNum(r);
642     q := tempq; r := tempr
643   end; (* Divide *)
644
645 (* procedure Quotient(var n: LongInteger; m1, m2: LongInteger); *)
646 procedure Quotient;
647   (* Effectively, perform  n := m1 div m2 . *)
648   var q, r: LongInteger;
649   begin
650     Declare(q); Declare(r);
651     Divide(q,r,m1,m2);
652     DisposeNum(r); (* don't need the remainder *)
653     DisposeNum(n);
654     n := q
655   end; (* Quotient *)
656
657 (* procedure Remainder(var n: LongInteger; m1, m2: LongInteger); *)
658 procedure Remainder;
659   (* Effectively, perform  n := m1 mod m2 . *)
660   var q, r: LongInteger;
661   begin
662     Declare(q); Declare(r);
663     Divide(q,r,m1,m2);
664     DisposeNum(q); (* don't need the quotient *)
665     DisposeNum(n);
666     n := r
667   end; (* Remainder *)
668
669
670 (* I/O Operations *)
671 (* procedure WriteNum(n: LongInteger); *)
672 procedure WriteNum;
673   (* Effectively, perform  writeln(n)  with commas inserted in the
674      appropriate places for readability.
675   *)
676   (* Ground rules for pretty printing:
677       Commas are printed after every block of three digits.
678       Numbers that take more than one line to print are justified so that
679        the commas line up.
680       The short line is last.  It holds the least significant digits.
681       " ...more" is used to indicate that a number continues on the next line.
682       Things can go haywire if the user has printed something on the line
683        before calling  WriteNum .
684   *)
```

We need to call DisposeNum *or we will lose the storage occupied by these local variables when we return from* Quotient *and* Remainder.

```
685    (* The maximum line length is  4*k + 8, where  k  is the number
686       of blocks of three that can appear on a line.  This formula is
687       used to calculate  MAXGROUPSOFTHREE .
688    *)
689    const MAXGROUPSOFTHREE = 17;    (* Don't push to column 80, as some terminals
690                                        and printers have trouble with this. *)
691    var p: PtrToDigitCell;
692        i, (* number of groups of three written on a line *)
693        j: (* number of digits left to write out -- used for comma placement *)
694           integer;
695
696    begin
697       (* Zero is a bit of a special case, since one digit gets written,
698          even though we record it as a zero-digit number. *)
699       j := n^.Digit;
700       if j = 0
701         then write(0:3)
702         else begin
703                 i := 0; (* no groups of three written on the line so far *)
704                 (* Write out any blanks needed to align commas on multiline
705                    numbers. *)
706                 case n^.Digit mod 3 of
707                   0: ;
708                   1: write('  ');
709                   2: write(' ')
710                 end;
711                 p := n^.LessSig; (* point to most significant digit *)
712                 while p <> n do
713                   begin
714                     write(p^.Digit:1);
715                     j := j - 1;
716                     if (j mod 3 = 0) (* finished a group of three *) and
717                        (j <> 0) (* didn't finish the number *)
718                       then begin
719                               write(',');
720                               i := i + 1;
721                               if i = MAXGROUPSOFTHREE
722                                 then begin
723                                         writeln(' ...more');
724                                         i := 0
725                                      end
726                            end;
727                     p := p^.LessSig
728                   end
729              end;
730       writeln
731    end; (* WriteNum *)
```

Some terminals and printers insert an automatic carriage return if a character is written in the rightmost column. This would be the e of . . .more. The carriage return of the writeln *(line 723) would make for double spacing.*

See For Your Information: Is It Really an Infinite Precision Arithmetic Package?

This strategy is more efficient than
```
    if i mod MAXGROUPSOFTHREE = 0
        then writeln(' ...more')
```
where now i *stands for the total number of groups written, as opposed to the number written on the current line.*

Generally, tests like this one, which are false only the last time through the loop, should be avoided. This can be accomplished by changing the condition of the outer loop to
```
    LeastSig := n^.Moresig;
    while p <> LeastSig do
```
eliminating the test j <> 0*, and printing the final digit outside the loop. Since we expect* WriteNum *to be called only occasionally, the loss of clarity is probably not worth the gain in efficiency.*

CHAPTER 4

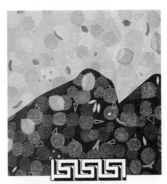

RECURSIVE LISTS

This case study differs from all the other case studies in this book. In the others, we develop programs to do something fun or practical—the programs play games, permit computations with infinite precision integers, implement a simple hand calculator, or provide a tool for managing large projects. In this case study we focus on abstract and recursive thinking, and the many small programs we develop using the abstract data type List have no practical significance. The List is the fundamental data type of the programming language LISP, one of the two languages that has attained a premier position in artificial intelligence research and the language used to develop MACSYMA, a tool for symbolic computation that is widely used by physicists and mathematicians. ◘

4.1 THE ADT List

A *list* is defined recursively by three rules:

- ( ) is a list.
- Any string of letters and digits that begins with a letter, and which is uninterrupted by punctuation marks or blanks, is a list.
- If $l_1, l_2, l_3, \ldots, l_n$ are lists, then so is

$$(l_1 \; l_2 \; l_3 \ldots l_n)$$

A list is anything derivable by repeated application of these three rules. Nothing else is a list. (A word of warning: despite the name, don't confuse the lists of the ADT List with a linked list.)

To make sure there is no confusion, we begin by looking at some examples of lists. Like virtually everything else in this chapter, the definition of a list is itself recursive. There are two *base cases* (also known as *terminal conditions* or *degenerate cases*):

- The first base case is the *empty list*. It is represented pictorially as

  ( )

  and is traditionally called NIL, which should not be confused with the Pascal `nil` pointer.
- The other base case is the *atom*. An atom is any string of letters and digits (with upper and lower case distinguished) that begins with a letter.

Typical atoms are

```
a
atom
AnEnormouslyLongImpossiblyDifficultToReadAtom
```

At least in theory, there are an infinite number of atoms. An atom is an indivisible quantity. The atom `abc` is *not* a list consisting of the three atoms `a`, `b`, and `c`. It is a single, unbreakable entity.

There is also a recursive building rule, which allows us to make complex lists out of simpler ones:

- If $l_1, l_2, l_3, \ldots, l_n$ are lists, then so is

$$(l_1 \; l_2 \; l_3 \; \ldots \; l_n)$$

Examples of Complex Lists

Some lists formed by use of this rule are

```
(a b)
(c)
( () a (b (c d)) ((e)) )
( ((a) b) (c b) )
(())
```

The blanks have no significance, except when necessary to separate adjacent atoms. The final list in the previous example could just as well have been written as `(( ))`, `( () )`, or `( ( ) )`.

It is instructive to see this list-building rule in action. For example,

```
( () a (b (c d)) ((e)) )
```

is a list because it can be formed by *repeated* application of the three rules.

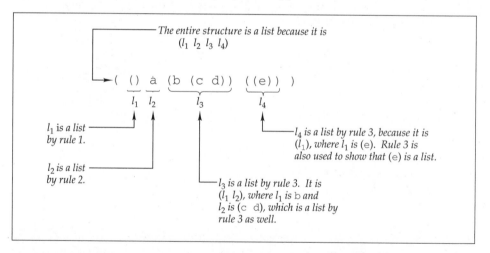

Note carefully that `(e)` is *not* an atom, because it is *not* a string of letters and digits. It is a list by virtue of the third rule; it has the form (l_1), where l_1 is a list, because l_1 is the atom `e`. Similarly, `(())` is not the empty list. It is a list containing one element, which just so happens to be the empty list. We call lists that are lists by virtue of the third rule *complex lists*.

STOP

If you don't understand this paragraph, read it again until you do!

An ADT is defined by its set of data values and its collection of primitive operations for manipulating these data values. This is not an alien concept—common objects like integers and their associated operations can be viewed as an ADT. This is effectively what we did in the case study of the previous chapter. Familiar data structures like stacks can also be described as ADTs. The data values are stacks of "atoms" (objects taken from a different ADT) and the primitive operations are PUSH, POP, and ISEMPTY. Relationships among these operations, like

$$\text{POP}(\text{PUSH}(x)) = x$$

which is true for any x, are independent of the implementation.

Declarations for the primitive list handling functions can be found on lines 23–66 of the file `Primitives.h`.

There are two functions in the ADT LIST that identify when a list is a list by virtue of its being a base case. These functions are used to stop procedures that manipulate lists from recursing forever.

- The function `null(p)` returns true or false depending on whether or not p is ( ).   `null`
- The function `atom(p)` returns true or false depending on whether or not p is an atom.   `atom`

In Pascal, these functions have, declarations

```
        function null(p: list): boolean;
```

and

```
        function atom(p: list): boolean;
```

It is an unfortunate aspect of Pascal that the declaration of `list` must appear in `Primitives.h` and in the interface portion of the Turbo Pascal unit `Primitives`. Ada and C++ are much better in this regard—they allow this declaration to be hidden from the program using the ADT. If you did look at these type declarations, you probably didn't gain much insight into how lists are implemented. For the present we prefer to think of lists abstractly, as objects of the form `(a (b a))`, though we aren't able to write

```
        if null( (a (b a)) )
            then ...
```

in a Pascal program, because this produces a syntax error.

Because we specifically don't want to look at the internal representation (we might want to change it later), we need yet another primitive function to sort out the bases cases. While there is only one empty list, ( ), there are an infinite number of atoms. The primitive function `eq` separates them.

- The function `eq(p,q)` returns true if p and q are the same atom. If p and q are different atoms, then `eq` returns false. If either argument is not an atom, we have an error.   `eq`

A similar situation arose in the infinite precision arithmetic package of Chapter 3, where it is discussed in great length in the section **Some Hidden Software Engineering Issues.**

This function raises a number of questions, and it is wise to clear them up immediately. First, if you peek at the type declarations that define a list, you will see that we are going to store an atom as a linked list of characters. The implementation of `eq` in `Primitives.p` does *not* check to see if the two Pascal pointers that point to these linked lists are equal as pointers. Two atoms are equal if their strings of characters are the same. Whether or not this translates into the more strict "whether or not their pointers point to the same location in memory" depends on the implementation. The high-level programs we develop should not depend on these internal details. Thus, it is wrong for high-level functions that manipulate lists to include tests like

```
        if p = q then ...
```

List Handling Primitives

While this line will compile, it will almost certainly give the wrong answer. If a high-level function needs to compare two atoms for equality, it should do this as

```
if eq(p,q) then ...
```

One of our first tasks will be to generalize `eq(p,q)` to `equal(p,q)`, a function that determines if two arbitrary lists are the same. Just like `eq`, `equal` should check to see if p and q are logically the same, not whether they occupy the same physical locations in memory. This is what we intend when we write

```
if i = j then ...
```

for variables of type `integer`—the equality check compares their *values*. We want `equal` to do the same thing. `equal(p,q)` should compare the logical structure of p and q for equality, not just the pointer variables p and q, which is what

```
if p = q then ...
```

tests. In Chapter 6 we will see a more sophisticated way to store atoms. If we have done our job properly, changing their internal representation will affect some of the routines in `Primitives.p`, but any high-level routines we have written should not change in even the slightest way.

The philosophy of error handling in LISP

A second issue raised by `eq` is the handling of errors. It is the responsibility of the caller to make sure that the arguments to `eq` are atoms. The implementation of `eq` checks that this precondition is met, but no error recovery is performed: if they are not atoms, then the entire program halts. `eq` could have returned false in this circumstance, but there are other primitive functions that cannot do anything sensible if their arguments do not meet their preconditions. While these functions could return a flag indicating that they have failed, leaving resolution of the problem up to the caller, it is not in the spirit of LISP to do this. The reason is twofold: the caller isn't likely to be able to recover anyway and, because our nonprimitive functions are going to be highly recursive, they would become cluttered with error processing. Cluttering up the code with error processing is particularly painful, since most of these nonprimitive functions are going to be only a *few lines long*—which shows just how powerful recursion is.

There is one error that the primitive functions cannot guard against: being passed an argument that has never been initialized. Pascal provides no mechanism to check for this condition, so we cannot bulletproof our program even if we wish to. (We faced this problem in the infinite precision arithmetic package as well—there we provided the procedure `Declare`, but could do nothing if the user did not call it.)

car, cdr, and cons

We now come to the three most interesting primitive LISP functions, `car`, `cdr`, and `cons`. While `cons` (pronounced as it is spelled) gets its name from "build the <u>cons</u>truct of," the names `car` and `cdr` (pronounced "could-er") are the names of registers in the computer on which LISP was first implemented. `car` and `cdr` take lists apart, while `cons` builds them up.

car

■ The function `car(p)` takes a complex list and returns its first element, that is

$$\text{car}(\ (l_1\ l_2\ \dots\ l_n)\ ) = l_1$$

p itself is not changed by taking its `car`.

`car` applied to the empty list or an atom is a error. `car` checks for this possibility and halts the program if p is one of these two types of lists.

Note that `car(AnAtom)` is an error, it is not `A`. For the five complex lists given earlier, the `car` of each of them is

```
a
c
()
((a) b)
()
```

The Pascal declaration of `car` is

```
function car(p: list): list;
```

A significant property of `car` is that it does not destroy its argument. When the primitive operations of an ADT don't change their arguments, we say the ADT is *immutable*. That `p` is passed by value is not sufficient assurance; by itself, this does not prevent what `p` points to from being changed. Even though we are not supposed to be concerned with the implementation of lists at this point, the possibility of changing the list is something to keep in mind. A correct implementation does not do this—we will have to wait and see whether or not this requires copying what `p` points to when constructing `car(p)`. *Immutability*

The function `cdr` is essentially the other half of `car`, in much the same way that `mod` is the other half of `div`.

■ The function `cdr(p)` takes a complex list and returns the list formed by deleting the first element, that is **cdr**

$$cdr((l_1 \ l_2 \ l_3 \ \ldots \ l_n)) \ = \ (l_2 \ l_3 \ \ldots \ l_n)$$

`p` itself is not changed by taking its `cdr`.

As with `car`, `cdr` applied to the empty list or an atom is a error. For the five complex lists given earlier, the `cdr` of each of them is

```
(b)
()
( a (b (c d)) ((e)) )
( (c b) )
()
```

The function `cons` puts together what `car` and `cdr` take apart.

■ The function `cons(p,q)` takes two arguments. The first can be any type of list, while the second can be either a complex list or the empty list, but cannot be an atom. `cons` returns a new list formed by inserting `p` as the new first element of `q`, that is **cons**

$$cons(p \ , (l_1 \ l_2 \ \ldots \ l_n)) \ = \ (p \ l_1 \ l_2 \ldots \ l_n)$$

Neither `p` nor `q` is changed by applying `cons`.

If `q` is an atom, then we have an error. Some examples of applying `cons` are

```
cons( a , (b c) ) = (a b c)
cons( (a (b)) , ((d) c) ) = ((a (b)) (d) c)
cons( a , () ) = (a)
cons( () , () ) = (())
cons( () , (()) ) = (() ())
```

Here is cons in action on the second example.

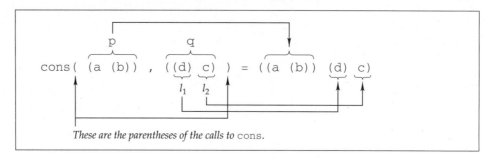

These are the parentheses of the calls to cons.

Pay particular attention to the third, fourth, and fifth examples—they follow the definition of cons completely—it is just a little difficult to see what is going on at first.

Do this exercise now!

EXERCISE 4–1   What is the result of performing each of the following operations?

```
cons( (a) , (b c) )
cons( (a) , ((b c)) )
cons( (a) , ((b) (c)) )
```

We can describe the relationship between Push and Pop in the ADT Stack with the equations

- Pop(Push(x)) = x, for any x.
- Push(Pop( )) leaves the stack unchanged for any nonempty stack.

Similarly, we can describe the relationship between car, cdr, and cons with the equations

- cons(car(p),cdr(p)) = p, for any complex list p.
- car(cons(p,q)) = p, for any lists p and q, with q not an atom.
- cdr(cons(p,q)) = q, for any lists p and q, with q not an atom.

NILL *and* readlist

While it certainly isn't obvious yet, the six primitive functions null, atom, eq, car, cdr, and cons are all we need to build an entire array of interesting programs. We do have one problem, however: how do we build lists in the first place? Placing cons(a,(b c)) in a Pascal program will produce error messages like "undefined variable a," "missing operator" (between b and c), and "type of (b c) not pointer." We need a way to convert our human-readable representation into the internal representation used in our implementation. The ADT List package provides only a limited capability to do this.

NILL

- The function NILL takes no arguments and returns the internal representation of ( ).

readlist

- The function readlist takes no arguments and returns the internal representation of a list that it reads from the terminal.

The inverse of readlist is writelist.

writelist

- The procedure writelist(p) writes out its argument in human-readable form.

The line writelist(readlist) echoes the list the user types in, although the spacing may be different. Project 4–1 discusses adding to our package a new primitive function, quote, similar to readlist, which will allow us to write

```
cons(quote('a'),quote('(b c)'))
```

`writelist` cannot fail, but `readlist` will fail when the input contains an illegal atom (due to illegal characters) or because the parentheses do not balance. (Actually, if there are insufficient right parentheses `readlist` will just wait for more input. Since `readlist` returns as soon as it finds a list, there cannot be too many right parentheses, unless the list begins with one. When faced with `(a b))`, `readlist` will return `(a b)` and leave the extra right parenthesis in the input, where it will cause an error on the *next* call to `readlist`.)

4.2   USING THE ADT List

From the small set of list handling primitives, we will build up a large number of complex functions using only

- The `if ... then ... else ...` construct.
- Recursive function calls.

We will use

- No loops.
- No variables (other than the function parameters).
- No Boolean connectives (`and`, `or`, and `not`).
- No `begin ... end` blocks.
- No labels and `goto` statements.

Limiting ourselves in this way might seem artificial, but pure LISP does not have the rich, but unnecessary (in the mathematical sense of their not being absolutely necessary, as opposed to convenient) set of programming language primitives we have come to expect. And having only a limited collection of language primitives will force us to think recursively, which is the main point of this chapter.

Before we charge off to do something interesting, we demonstrate the power of recursion by examining two very useful functions. These are not primitive functions, since writing them does not require any knowledge of the internal representation of lists.

`equal`

The first function is `equal(p,q)`, the extension of `eq` to arbitrary lists. This function is not all that difficult to write; it is mostly just a mass of cases. The overall strategy is

You may want to try your hand at writing `equal` *before looking at the solution given in the Figure 4-1.*

> `if` either of p or q is a base case
> > `then` sort out the details of whether they are `equal`
> > `else` both lists are complex lists and for two complex lists
> > to be `equal`, they must have the same number of sublists
> > and each pair of corresponding sublists must be `equal`.

The complete code for `equal` is given in Figure 4–1. Note that if only one of p and q is a base case, then the lists surely cannot be equal, and even if they are both base cases, one could be `( )` and the other could be an atom, or they could both be atoms, but different atoms. So there is a lot of sorting out to do, and it must be done in an order which ensures that none of the cases will be missed and none of the primitive functions will stop the program because they have invalid arguments. It is not hard, just a bit tedious, taking up lines 3–12 of a 16-line function.

More difficult is: how do we determine that two complex lists have the same number of sublists and, if they do, that each pair of corresponding sublists is the same? The answer to this question is *recursion, recursion, and more recursion.*

FIGURE 4–1   The Function equal

```
1    function equal(p, q: list): boolean;
2      begin
3        if null(p)
4          then equal := null(q)
5        else if null(q)
6          then equal := false
7        else if atom(p)
8          then if atom(q)
9                 then equal := eq(p,q)
10                else equal := false
11       else if atom(q)
12         then equal := false
13       else if equal(car(p),car(q))
14         then equal := equal(cdr(p),cdr(q))
15       else   equal := false
16     end; (* equal *)
```

If null(q) *returns true, then both are* ( ). *Otherwise,* p *is* ( ), *but* q *isn't, so* null(q) *alone is the right answer. This could have been coded less professionally as*
```
     if null(p)
        then if null(q)
              then equal := true
              else equal := false
     else if...
```

p *is not* ( ), *but* q *is.*

p *and* q *are both atoms. Are they the same atom? Notice how the Boolean connective* and *is avoided.*

p *is an atom, but* q *is not, so they cannot be equal.*

p *is not an atom, but* q *is, so they cannot be equal.*

Both p *and* q *are complex lists. For them to be equal,* car(p) *and* car(q) *must be equal.*

If car(p) *and* car(q) *are equal, then the equality of* p *and* q *rests on the equality of* cdr(p) *and* cdr(q).

car(p) *and* car(q) *are unequal, so there is no point in continuing.*

Testing the two lists comprising the first pair of corresponding sublists for equality is relatively straightforward. car applied to p and q returns l_1 from each of p and q, so the recursive call equal(car(p),car(q)) on line 13 tells us if these sublists are equal. Neither call to car can fail because, if the procedure reaches line 13, both p and q are complex lists. Now if equal(car(p),car(q)) is false, then there is no need to concern ourselves with whether the two lists have the same number of sublists or whether another corresponding pair happens to be different as well. The ultimate answer is that they are not equal, so we might as well return the result right now. This is done on line 15. While it might seem more natural to return the false in the then clause, this would require that we write the test

```
if not equal(car(p),car(q))
   then equal := false
   else ...
```

but Boolean connectives are not allowed—a minor inconvenience.

The most interesting line of the function is line 14. We *don't* explicitly check to see if the two lists have the same number of sublists, which might be hard to do without introducing both iteration (in the form of a while loop) and a variable to count their lengths. Instead, we simply ask "are the two lists that remain when we delete the known-to-be-equal first sublists the same?" We do this with a recursive call to equal, passing in the two lists that remain when the first sublists are dropped, that is, by passing in cdr(p) and cdr(q). Since cdr(p) and cdr(q) are smaller than p and q, the recursion will eventually terminate. If cdr(p) and cdr(q) are equal, the entire lists are equal, and if they are unequal, either because two corresponding sublists differ or because they have a different number of sublists, then the entire lists are unequal. If they are unequal, we really do not care to know why, and this information is not reported back.

EXERCISE 4–2   If each pair of corresponding sublists is equal, but the two lists are of different lengths, how will this be discovered?

An even more useful function is `append(p,q)`. `append` is like `cons`, but is more list-oriented. Both `p` and `q` are supposed to be lists that are not atoms, and the result of `append(p,q)` is

append

$$\text{append}(\ (l_1\ l_2\ \dots\ l_n),\ (k_1\ k_2\ \dots\ k_m)\ ) = (l_1\ l_2\ \dots\ k_m)$$

`append(p,q)` is one long list whose sublists are the n sublists of `p` followed by the m sublists of `q`. Some examples are:

```
append( (a b c) , (c a) ) = (a b c c a)
append( ((a) b (c d)) , (((c)) d) ) = ((a) b (c d) ((c)) d)
append( (a) , ( ) ) = (a)
append( ( ) , (a) ) = (a)
append( ( ) , ( ) ) = ( )
```

As is often the case, it is the base cases that are the most revealing. When forming the `append` of `(a)` and `( )`, we are to form a list (which accounts for the parentheses of the result) whose elements are the sublists of `p` (there is one, and it is `a`), followed by the sublists of `q`. In this case, `q` is `( )`, which means it does not have any *sub*lists. `( )` is *not* a sublist of `q`.

Note carefully that `append(p,q)` is *not* the same as `cons(p,q)`. For these five examples, `cons(p,q)` yields

```
((a b c) c a)
(((a) b (c d)) ((c)) d)
((a))
(( ) a)
(( ))
```

As unfathomable as it might at first appear, the complete function that implements `append` is only six lines long, including the function header and the `begin` and the `end`, which account for three of the six lines—such is the power of recursion once you fully understand it! Figure 4–2 shows how `append` works. Once you see the overall strategy, the details of `append` are not hard, but coming up with the overall strategy in the first place is difficult. For example, you might, quite naturally, think that the base case should be

$$\text{append}(\ (\ )\ ,\ (\ )\ )$$

even though, if you look at the code, you will see that the base case is the more general

$$\text{append}(\ (\ )\ ,\ (k_1\ k_2\ \dots\ k_m)\ )$$

The secret to seeing how to write `append`, and why this generalization is the correct base case, is the realization that, while `cons` doesn't quite do the job, it does tack things onto the front of a list. The reason that we focus our attention on `p`, and essentially ignore `q`, is that `q` is already in the correct form. All we really have to do to perform `append` is successively tack onto the front of `q` the lists $l_n, l_{n-1}, \dots, l_1$. Now it may not seem any easier to tack the elements of `p` onto the front of `q` in *reverse* order than it is to tack the elements of `q` onto the *tail* of `p` in normal order. After all, we don't have a way to either access the sublists of a list in reverse order or tack something on at the end of a list.

FIGURE 4–2 How append Works

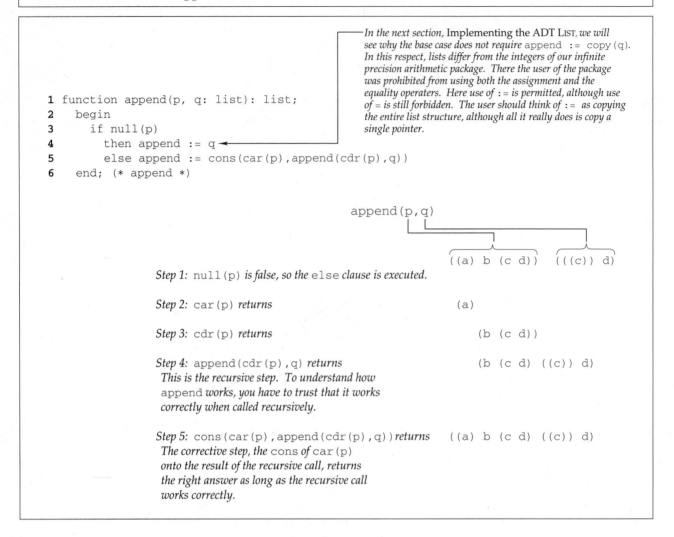

```
1  function append(p, q: list): list;
2    begin
3      if null(p)
4        then append := q
5        else append := cons(car(p),append(cdr(p),q))
6    end; (* append *)
```

In the next section, Implementing the ADT List, *we will see why the base case does not require* append := copy(q). *In this respect, lists differ from the integers of our infinite precision arithmetic package. There the user of the package was prohibited from using both the assignment and the equality operaters. Here use of* := *is permitted, although use of* = *is still forbidden. The user should think of* := *as copying the entire list structure, although all it really does is copy a single pointer.*

append(p,q)

((a) b (c d))   (((c)) d)

Step 1: null(p) *is false, so the* else *clause is executed.*

Step 2: car(p) *returns*   (a)

Step 3: cdr(p) *returns*   (b (c d))

Step 4: append(cdr(p),q) *returns*   (b (c d) ((c)) d)
This is the recursive step. To understand how
append *works, you have to trust that it works*
correctly when called recursively.

Step 5: cons(car(p),append(cdr(p),q)) *returns*   ((a) b (c d) ((c)) d)
The corrective step, the cons *of* car(p)
onto the result of the recursive call, returns
the right answer as long as the recursive call
works correctly.

Still, once we decide to tack the elements of p onto the front of q in reverse order, at least the base case becomes clear: if there are no elements to tack onto the front of q, we are done, and the answer is just q. This is what the fourth example was all about—append(( ) , (a)) returns (a), since there is nothing in ( ) to tack onto the front of the second list. The base case is handled by lines 3 and 4 of the program.

We now come to the hard part of writing append. One crucial aspect of recursive programs is that each recursive call should bring us closer to the base case. Thus, it should not surprise us to see, in line 5,

$$append(cdr(p),q)$$

Taking the cdr(p) brings us closer to the base case. We have replaced the task of performing

$$append(\ (l_1\ l_2\ \dots\ l_n)\ ,\ (k_1\ k_2\ \dots\ k_m)\ )$$

with

$$append(\ (l_2\ l_3\ \dots\ l_n)\ ,\ (k_1\ k_2\ \dots\ k_m)\ )$$

If we trust in recursion (and our ability to write `append` correctly), this call returns the list

$$(l_2 \ l_3 \ \ldots \ k_m)$$

The last step in any recursive procedure is the slight modification of the value returned from the recursive call to account for the fact that the call was passed parameters that were slightly closer to the base case. In `append`, all we have to do is insert l_1 as the new first element of $(l_2 \ l_3 \ \ldots \ k_m)$. Now `car(p)` returns l_1. If the input to `append` obeys the precondition that p is not an atom, this call cannot fail, since on line 3 we have already checked that p is not the empty list. How do we tack the l_1 returned by `car(p)` onto the front of $(l_2 \ l_3 \ \ldots \ k_m)$? Well, how do we tack *anything* onto the front of a list? We use `cons`. Thus, we get

```
append := cons(car(p),append(cdr(p),q))
```

Just a quick word about error checking. As mentioned, it is not in the spirit of LISP to check for errors, and `append` does not verify that the preconditions are satisfied. What will happen if they are not? Will the error eventually be caught? If p is an atom, it will be caught on line 5, when we attempt to take `car(p)`, which does check its input for validity. If q is an atom, the error *might* be caught.

EXERCISE 4–3   If q is at atom, under what circumstances will the error not be caught? When caught, where will it be caught?

EXERCISE 4–4   The following attempt at writing `append` does not work. What does it do?

```
1 function append(p, q: list): list;
2   begin
3     if null(p)
4       then append := q
5       else append := append(cdr(p),cons(car(p),q))
6   end; (* append *)
```

In answering the last two exercises, your first impulse might have been to run off to the computer to do a little testing. The preferred approach is to think about the two six-line routines for a while instead, trying to puzzle out their workings. But your impulse to test, if you had it, does raise the question: how are we to test any high-level procedures we might write? It would be useful to have a driver program that permits easy testing. Such a program is given in the file `Driver.p`. Its inner workings are quite simple. It is nothing other than a loop that repeatedly queries the user for the task to perform, initializes the input mechanism with a call to `InitIO` (see lines 70–73 of `Primitives.h`), calls `readlist` enough times to gather up the required input, calls the desired function, and finally prints out the answer. There is nothing tricky about it at all. New functions are added by including them in the menu and including their declarations and bodies in `Functions.h` and `Functions.p`. Well, there is one little detail that needs explaining. Since variables are not supposed to be allowed, why is the call that tests `append` written as

A Simple Driver Program

```
10: begin InitIO; p := readlist; q := readlist;
         writelist(append(p,q)) end;
```

and not

```
10: begin InitIO; writelist(append(readlist,readlist)) end;
```

A limited use of variables

The difficulty is that the Pascal standard does not state in which order the arguments to a function are to be evaluated. Some systems evaluate them left-to-right and others evaluate them right-to-left. When the latter order is used, the net effect is to perform append(q,p) instead of append(p,q). By assigning the results of the calls to readlist to variables, this problem is circumvented. Because calls to all our high-level functions and to the other primitive functions have no side effects, the order of evaluation is irrelevant, so we do not need to sequence the calls using variables.

To gain a little more experience before doing something significant with lists, we examine the function reverse, which takes a list as an argument and returns a list with the elements in reverse order, with each sublist recursively reversed as well. That is,

$$\text{reverse(} (l_1 \ l_2 \ \dots \ l_n) \text{)}$$
$$= (\text{ reverse}(l_n) \ \text{reverse}(l_{n-1}) \ \dots \ \text{reverse}(l_1) \text{)}$$

The original lists can be found on p. 166.

For the complex lists used as examples where the definition of a list was given, reverse yields

```
(b a)
(c)
( ((e))  ((d c) b)  a  () )
( (b c)  (b (a)) )
(())
```

One detail that might not be clear from the definition is what to do about reversing an atom. Because atoms are indivisible, reverse(AnAtom) is the atom AnAtom, and not the atom motAnA, which we have no way of constructing anyway. This makes our base cases clear.

$$\text{reverse(( )) = ( ) and reverse(}\langle\text{atom}\rangle) = \langle\text{atom}\rangle$$

The coding of reverse begins with

```
1  function reverse(p: list): list;
2    begin
3      if null(p)
4        then  reverse := NILL
5      else if atom(p)
6        then reverse := p          reverse := p would work just as well.
7      else ...
```

Handling the recursive step is more difficult. reverse(car(p)), if we trust in recursion and our ability to correctly code reverse, produces reverse(l_1). Here, if l_1 is itself a complex list, all its sublists and their sublists, and so on, are reversed as well. In addition

$$\text{reverse(cdr(p))}$$
$$= \text{reverse(} (l_2 \ l_3 \ \dots \ l_n) \text{)}$$
$$= (\text{ reverse}(l_n) \ \text{reverse}(l_{n-1}) \ \dots \ \text{reverse}(l_2) \text{)}$$

This gives us all the pieces. *Isn't recursion wonderful! Just a few simple function calls and almost all the work is done for us.* All we need to do is insert reverse(car(p)) at the *right* end of reverse(cdr(p)). Unfortunately, cons puts it first, not last. While it might look like we are stuck, or at the very least what we have left to do is very hard, a little bit of trickery saves the day. Notice that

reverse (left margin)

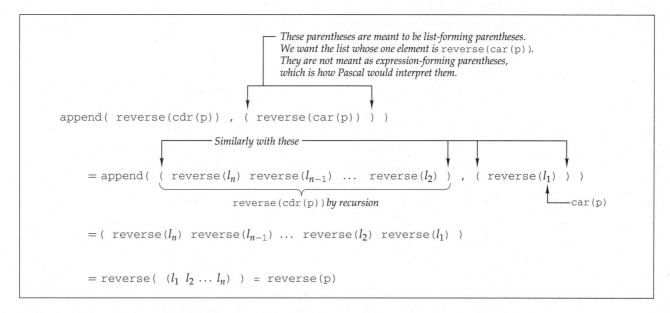

We are almost there! We just need a way of making a list whose only sublist is `reverse(car(p))`. Too bad the line formed by just placing parentheses around `reverse(car(p))`

```
reverse := append( reverse(cdr(p)) , ( reverse(car(p)) ) )
```

won't work—Pascal, quite correctly, will interpret them as "Pascal expression-forming parentheses" and not as "LISP list-forming parentheses." But if `r` is a list, we can form the list `(r)` in the following simple way:

$$\text{cons(r,NILL)}$$

`NILL` returns the list `( )`, whose parentheses have nothing to do with the parentheses of the Pascal programming language, and applying `cons` to `r` and this list inserts `r` as the first element, giving us `(r)`. Thus, the entire program for `reverse` is

```
1  function reverse(p: list): list;
2    begin
3      if null(p)
4        then reverse := NILL
5      else if atom(p)
6        then reverse := p
7      else    reverse := append(reverse(cdr(p)),cons(reverse(car(p)),NILL))
8    end; (* reverse *)
```

reverse($(l_2\ l_3\ \dots\ l_n)$)   reverse(l_1)   ( )

by recursion, this

becomes this

cons inserts this object

as the first element of this list,

yielding

(reverse(l_n) reverse(l_{n-1}) $\dots$ reverse(l_2))   (reverse(l_1))

applying append *to these two pieces gives*
(reverse(l_n) reverse(l_{n-1}) $\dots$ reverse(l_2) reverse(l_1))

A Small Set Manipulation Package

Can we do anything useful with lists? To show how easy it is to develop sophisticated applications using lists, we will develop a small set manipulation package. While in mathematics sets are delimited by braces, {...}, we will delimit sets by parentheses, (...). A set will be represented as a list, except that we will not include the commas that traditionally separate the elements of the set. So the set

$$\{house, car, TV, stereo\}$$

will be represented in our package as

$$(house\ car\ TV\ stereo)$$

Of course, we will be limited to finite sets, since we are planning on just listing their elements and lists do not have any form of ellipsis or permit use of "which have the property" notation. We will not consider sets specified as $\{1, 3, 5, ...\}$ or $\{x \mid x\ odd\}$. For that matter, we do not have numbers either. But, and this is an important point since it is what makes writing a set manipulation package from scratch difficult, we are *not* limited to sets of atoms. In mathematics, sets can contain other sets. The most obvious example is the power set of a set S, denoted by 2^S. If S is any set, then the power set of S is the set of all subsets of S. By way of example, if $S = \{a, b, c\}$, then the power set of S has eight elements, each one a set. It is

$$\{\varnothing, \{a\}, \{b\}, \{c\}, \{a, b\}, \{a, c\}, \{b, c\}, \{a, b, c\}\}$$

We represent this set as

$$(\ (\ )\ (a)\ (b)\ (c)\ (a\ b)\ (a\ c)\ (b\ c)\ (a\ b\ c)\ )$$

The notation 2^S serves as a reminder that for a set of size n, 2^S has 2^n elements. Notice that the empty set, while often written $\varnothing$, is really { }, and we represent it by ( ).

One small problem is that sets, by their very definition, do not allow elements to be repeated, whereas nothing prevents the user from typing (a b a) in response to a request to type in a set. As is our style in this chapter, we will ignore this: if the user provides invalid input, the behavior of the program cannot be guaranteed. On the other hand, it will be our responsibility to make sure that union(p,q) does not include repeated elements where neither p nor q has repeated elements in the first place. union(p,q) is not just append(p,q). append makes one list out of two lists, but append does nothing about eliminating repeats.

$$append(\ (a\ b)\ ,\ (b\ c)\ ) = (a\ b\ b\ c)$$

whereas

$$union(\ (a\ b)\ ,\ (b\ c)\ ) = (a\ b\ c)$$

Something else we need to keep in mind is that testing for equality of sets is not accomplished by the call equal(p,q). equal checks to see if two lists are equal, which means that they contain the same elements, *in the same order*, whereas two sets are mathematically equal if they contain the same elements, without regard to the order of their elements. And yet one last problem. The basic set operation of complement, $\overline{S}$, does not make sense in our context. $\overline{S}$ implies an understood universe of discourse with respect to which the complement is to be taken. We have no such predefined universe. Our package does implement set difference, so that if the universe, U, is understood, the user can obtain the complement by forming $U - S$.

The most fundamental operation on sets is membership: is $x \in B$? This is because answering the question of whether $A \subseteq B$ can be reduced to answering the question: is $x \in B$, for all $x \in A$? member is also crucial in preventing repetitions in forming the union and for determining the elements of the intersection.

member is not nearly as difficult to code as append or reverse. To see if $x \in B$ we first ask, "is B the empty set?" If it is, then x is certainly not a member of B. If B is not the empty set, then we ask "by chance, is x the same as some element of B?" By "some element," we don't mean *any element*, in the mathematical sense, we mean "any element of B that we can get our hands on." And the element of B we can most readily get our hands on is the first one, since car(q) will give it to us. If x is the same as this element, then x is a member of B. If it is not, then we can recursively ask the question "is $x \in B'$?" where B' is B with the element x wasn't equal to removed. Since B' is smaller than B, the recursion is heading toward the base case of $B = \varnothing$.

Refer to the code in Sets.p *while reading this.*

subset is just another eight lines of code: using car and recursion, we just successively check to see if each element of A is a member of B. And checking for the equality of sets is just the pair of checks $A \subseteq B$ and $B \subseteq A$, although we will have to do this without the Boolean connective and.

union, intersection, and setdifference also use member. Its use in union is especially instructive, since this is how we prevent duplicates from occurring in the answer. $A \cup B$ can be viewed as B, with those elements of A that are not already in B tossed in for good measure. That is precisely what the code for union does. First it asks the question "is A empty?" If it is, there is nothing to toss into B, and the result is just B. If A is not empty, then we can ask "is some element of A already in B?" Again we don't mean this in the mathematical sense of "does there exist an element of A that is in B," we mean it in the sense "is any element of A that we can get our hands on in B?" If it is, then there is no need to toss it into the union; it is already there by virtue of its being in B. If not, then we will need to toss it into the union. Again, it is easy to get our hands on the first element of A using car. Whether or not we need to toss this element into the union, we will need to form the union of cdr(p) and q, since this is either the union of A and B, or it is the union of A and B, except for the one element we need to toss in. If car(p) is not a member of B, then we will need to incorporate it into the union—the call to cons on line 32 does this.

EXERCISE 4—5 Without running the program to find out the answer, determine which of the expressions

```
(a b e d c)
(b a e d c)
(a b c e d)
(c b a e d)
```

is equal to

```
union( (a b c) , (e d c) )
```

EXERCISE 4–6 Does the following function correctly perform
`union(p,q)`?

```
function union(p, q: list): list;
  begin
    if null(p)
      then union := q
      else if member(car(p),q)  (* will capture element via  q  *)
             then union := union(cdr(p),q)
             else union := union(cdr(p),cons(car(p),q))
  end; (* union *)
```

What will the function call

$$union(\ (a\ b\ c)\ ,\ (e\ d\ c)\ )$$

produce? Is this version of `union` better or worse than the one found in
`Sets.p`? Why?

powerset

The function in our package that is the most difficult to code is `powerset`. It
requires a bit of mathematical ingenuity to see how to do it recursively and then
a bit of programming trickery to get it to work. First we should decide on the
base case of the recursion. While the power set of $\{a\}$ is $\{\emptyset, \{a\}\}$, because the
only two subsets of $\{a\}$ are the empty set and the set itself, what is the powerset
of $\emptyset$? Is it $\emptyset$ or is it $\{\emptyset\}$? If you consider carefully the definition of the power
set, you will see that the correct answer is $\{\emptyset\}$. This is because the power set
is the set of subsets of the given set. While $\emptyset$ has no *elements*, it does have one
subset. That subset is the empty set. In fact, with one exception, every set, A,
has two extremal subsets: the empty set and the set itself. The exception occurs
when $A = \emptyset$, in which case the two extremal subsets merge into one. So our
base case is

$$powerset(\ (\ )\ ) = (\ (\ )\ )$$

which is what line 67 returns.

See **Above and Beyond: Sets in
Pascal** *in Chapter 1.*

Now we consider the case where A is not empty. The iterative view of forming
the power set of a set of size n is to form all the bit patterns of n bits. There are
2^n such patterns, with each corresponding to a distinct subset. This is just how
Pascal represents sets: each bit position represents one particular element of A
and the zero/one status of the bit determines whether the element is or is not
in the current subset. The bit patterns vary from all zeros, which represents the
empty set, to all ones, which is A itself. We can cycle through all the bit patterns
by starting an integer variable at zero and repeatedly adding one, until we get
to $2^n - 1$. For each bit pattern, we will have to form a list of those elements
of A where the corresponding bit is one, and then gather these subsets together
into a set. The iterative view of forming the power set does not seem helpful—
remember, we are not permitted any variables or loops. We need to learn to
think recursively. If we recursively take

$$powerset(cdr(p))$$

Too bad

we will form a set whose elements are all the subsets of A that do not contain the
first element of A as a member. Returning to our three element example, where
$A = \{a, b, c\}$, so that p = (a b c), `powerset(cdr(p))` is $\{\emptyset, \{b\}, \{c\}, \{b, c\}\}$.
A few moments' thought will reveal that this is half the answer, and that the
missing subsets are identical to these four subsets, only with a added to each of
them. The missing subsets are $\{a\}$, $\{a, b\}$, $\{a, c\}$, and $\{a, b, c\}$. Getting a second
copy of `powerset(cdr(p))` to modify is easy; we just call `powerset` again.

The programming trickery mentioned earlier is the use of an auxiliary function.

■ The function `insert(p,q)` on lines 53–62 inserts its first argument into every sublist found at the top level of its second argument.

While there are no restrictions on `p`, the form of the second argument is very special. It is

$$(\ (\ldots) \ (\ldots) \ \ldots \ (\ldots) \ )$$

a list of nonatomic lists. But this is just the type of list returned by `powerset`. `insert` called with a first argument of `a` and a second argument of

$$(\ (\ ) \ (b) \ (c) \ (b \ c) \ )$$

returns

$$(\ (a) \ (a \ b) \ (a \ c) \ (a \ b \ c) \ )$$

The crucial line of `powerset` is line 68

```
powerset := union(powerset(cdr(p)),insert(car(p),powerset(cdr(p))))
```

Our entire set manipulation package is less than 70 lines! Not bad—you can hardly do anything interesting from scratch in so few lines.

EXERCISE 4–7   The ordering of the subsets produced by `powerset` isn't the natural ordering one might produce by hand. It is not the empty set, followed by all the one-element sets, followed by all the two-element sets, with *A* at the very end. What is the ordering produced by `powerset`?

EXERCISE 4–8   The function `powerset` is not efficient. What changes to `powerset` can you make that will make it more efficient?

Programming Exercises

It is now high time for you to write a large number of list-handling functions on your own. Try your hand at these. None of this first group of exercises requires the use of an auxiliary function other than `append`.

EXERCISE 4–9   Code the function `islat`, which takes as input a list that is not an atom and returns true if the list is a (potentially empty) list of atoms. For example

```
islat( (a b c) ) = true
islat( (a (b) c) ) = false
islat( ( ) ) = true
```

Remember: No `while` loops, variables, Boolean connectives, `begin ... end` blocks, or `goto` statements are allowed.

EXERCISE 4–10   Code the function `last`, which takes a complex list and returns the last element of the list.

A Small Problem in `member`

If you look carefully at line 5 of `member`, you will discover a problem. Why isn't that line

```
else if eq(x,car(q))
```

If we restrict ourselves to sets of atoms, the above line would be correct, but one of the benefits claimed for our set manipulation package is its ability to form sets whose elements are themselves sets. We would, for example, expect

```
equalsets(powerset( (a b c) , (a b c) ))
```

to return true. However, if the `equal` on line 5 is replaced by `eq`, the program produces the runtime error message

```
ERROR -- error in  eq
```

This happens because the argument indirectly passed to `x` by `equalsets` is a set and not an atom. This is why `member` calls `equal`. But `equal` isn't quite right either. The expression

```
equalsets(powerset( (a b c) , (b c a) ))
```

should also return true, but if you run it, it returns false. Why? The problem is that the power set of (a b c) contains (a b), whereas the powerset of (b c a) contains (b a). When `member` tries to find (a b) in the power set of (b c a) it won't find it. Because the comparison is made with `equal`, `member` compares (a b) and (b a) *as lists, not as sets.*

This is a symptom of a very general problem. Consider an ADT, like STACK, which has to be customized to deal with "atoms" of another ADT—a STACK is really a "STACK of ⟨type⟩." In order to do PUSH and POP, the ADT STACK needs to know how to copy data values of type ⟨type⟩ and this may vary from type to type. ADTs like STACK, SET, and TREE, which hold atoms of another ADT in a data structure, are often called ***container types***; they are very common and they always must be customized because they rely on the ADT ⟨type⟩ for primitive operations like assignment and comparison.

Here we really have "SET of ⟨type⟩" and the equality check on line 5 should be the equality check of type ⟨type⟩. The use of `equal` says that our ADT SET is really SET of LIST, whereas using `eq` makes it SET of ATOM. Defining the ADT as SET of ⟨type⟩ semantically eliminates the problem with `powerset`; the power set of *A* is not a SET of ⟨type⟩, it is a SET of SET of ⟨type⟩ and this ADT should have its own `member` function, different from the one in SET of ⟨type⟩.

This solution is not entirely satisfactory, however. We will also need two `union` functions, as `union` calls `member`, and if we allow SET of SET of SET of ⟨type⟩, we would need three versions of each function, all because the meaning of `equal` keeps changing. What we hoped to achieve was a set manipulation package that allows "SET of ...," where ... indicates a collection of elements drawn from the "ground ADT" and sets-of or sets-of-sets-of and *ad infinitum* -sets-of-sets-of-sets-of ground elements. For us, the natural choice for the "ground ADT," and what we intended, is "atom." Can we define an equality check to replace the call on line 5 that will work? Strangely enough, replacing `equal` by `equalsets` almost works, despite the indirect recursive call to

(continued)

ABOVE
AND BEYOND

(concluded)

member. It will work fine if x is a set and q is a set of sets, but it makes no sense if x is an atom. What we want on line 5 is a call to the function

```
 1   function GeneralizedSetEqual(p, q: list): boolean;
 2     begin
 3       if atom(p)
 4         then if atom(q)
 5                then GeneralizedSetEqual := eq(p,q)
 6                else GeneralizedSetEqual := false
 7       else if atom(q)
 8         then GeneralizedSetEqual := false
 9       else   GeneralizedSetEqual := equalsets(p,q) (* p  and  q  aren't atoms
10                                                    so they are sets *)
11     end; (* GeneralizedSetEqual *)
```

That member indirectly calls equalsets and equalsets indirectly calls member is not a problem. At each recursive call, the lists get shorter and the objects lose one level of nesting. Now

        equalsets(powerset((a b c) , (b c a)))

returns true.

EXERCISE 4—11   Code the function flat, which takes a list that is not an atom and returns a list that is the original list with all the parentheses removed, except for the outer set. For the complex lists used as examples where the definition of a list was given, flat returns

The lists can be found on p. 166

                (a b)
                (c)
                (a b c d e)
                (a b c b)
                ( )

EXERCISE 4—12   Code the function shape, which takes a list that is not an atom and returns a list that is the original list with all the atoms removed. For the complex lists referred to in the previous exercise, shape returns

                ( )
                ( )
                (() (( )) (( )))
                ((( )) ( ))
                (())

EXERCISE 4—13   Code the function `pair`, which takes two lists of the same length, $(k_1 \ k_2 \ \ldots \ k_n)$ and $(l_1 \ l_2 \ \ldots \ l_n)$, and returns the list $(\ (k_1 \ l_1) \ (k_2 \ l_2) \ \ldots \ (k_n \ l_n)\ )$.

EXERCISE 4—14   Code the function `firsts`, which takes a (possibly empty) list whose sublists are complex lists and returns a list consisting of the first element of each of the sublists, as shown in the example

```
firsts( ( (a b c) (d e f) (c d b a) ) ) = (a d c)
```

EXERCISE 4—15   Code the function `substitute`, which takes three arguments. The second argument is an atom, while the first and third are arbitrary lists. The function substitutes its first argument for every occurrence of the specified atom in the third list, as shown in the example

```
substitute( (a b) , a , ((b a) a) ) = ((b (a b)) (a b))
```

The logician's view of arithmetic   Numbers can be represented, albeit rather awkwardly, using lists. The idea is to represent numbers in unary. This is how small children represent numbers and how we represent them when we keep track of how much money we owe the office coffee pool. Every time we drink a cup, we place a mark by our name, and on the day of reckoning we count up the number of marks. (To make the final accounting a bit easier, we usually group the marks into blocks of five, like so: ＼＼＼.) This suggests two ways to represent nonnegative integers. One way is to represent the number n as $(\ (\ (\ \ldots \ )\ )\ )$, where there are $n+1$ nested pairs of parentheses. The extra pair of parentheses arises because zero is represented as $(\ )$. The other approach is to represent n as

$$(\ ()\ ()\ \ldots \ ()\ )$$

a list containing n empty sublists. More by accident than by design, the representations of zero and one are the same in both systems, being $(\ )$ and $((\ ))$. Actually, logicians use neither representation. They define the nonnegative integers using sets, which are a more fundamental structure than numbers. Numbers are defined recursively by the formula

$$n = \begin{cases} \{\ \} & \text{if } n = 0 \\ \{\{\ \}, n-1\} & \text{otherwise} \end{cases}$$

The first few integers are

$$
\begin{array}{ll}
0 & \{\ \} \\
1 & \{\{\ \},\{\ \}\} \\
2 & \{\{\ \},\{\{\ \},\{\ \}\}\} \\
3 & \{\{\ \},\{\{\ \},\{\{\ \},\{\ \}\}\}\} \\
& \vdots
\end{array}
$$

Using sets to represent numbers eliminates the $(\ ()\ ()\ \ldots \ ()\ )$ representation, since $\{\{\ \},\{\ \}, \ldots, \{\ \}\}$ is just $\{\{\ \}\}$. And while the $((\ (\ \ldots \ )\ ))$ representation makes sense, it isn't the form generally used.

EXERCISE 4–16 Develop a simple arithmetic package based upon the logician's representation of nonnegative integers. Include the functions

```
function greater(p, q: list): boolean;
function add(p, q: list): list;
function sub(p, q: list): list;
function mul(p, q: list): list;
function divv(p, q: list): list;
function modd(p, q: list): list;
```

The standard function `equal` can be used to determine if two numbers are equal, provided that we maintain the convention that n is represented as (( ) $n-1$) and not the equivalent, from the point of view of sets, ($n-1$ ( )). There is also a need for the `boolean` function `iszero(p)`, which determines whether its argument is zero, though this is just `null(p)`, which has a nice ring to it, since an old-fashioned word for zero is *null*. Also, while `readlist` and `writelist` read and write integers in the logician's form, it is helpful to include

```
function readint: list;
procedure writeint(p: list);
```

which convert back and forth between the internal form and the normal human-readable form. These functions rely on two internal recursive functions

```
function IntToList(n: integer): list;
function ListToInt(p: list): integer;
```

to perform the actual conversion. Your package should make no attempt to be efficient.

Lists are a very general data structure. They represent stacks very easily: a stack is just a variable of type `list` (because a stack must retain its contents between operations, we violate our convention of not allowing variables). ISEMPTY is just `null`, POP returns the `car` and resets the stack to the `cdr`, and PUSH is just `cons`.

EXERCISE 4–17 Binary search trees can also be represented as lists, if we define a `lessthan` operator on atoms. A binary tree is either ( ) or a list of the form (⟨atom⟩ ⟨tree⟩ ⟨tree⟩). Develop a binary search tree package using lists. (Because lists are immutable, it is not possible to insert or delete a node into the tree directly. The tree created by INSERT and DELETE will have to build a new tree from the parts of the old one. This problem arises whenever we model an inherently mutable data structure with an immutable one. How bad is the loss of efficiency?)

EXERCISE 4–18 This exercise is more difficult. You will need to use auxiliary functions. Code the function `permute`, which takes a list of atoms and returns a complex list in which each sublist is a different permutation of the original list, as shown in the example

```
permute( (a b c) ) = ( (a b c) (a c b) (b a c) (b c a)
                       (c a b) (c b a) )
```

It is not necessary that the order of the permutations produced by your solution be the same as the order shown here.

> **EXERCISE 4–19**   Improve the set manipulation package by defining the function `readset`. `readset` calls `readlist`, but then eliminates any duplicates by calling the function `elimdups`
>
> ```
> function readset: list;
>    begin
>       readset := elimdups(readlist)
>    end; (* readset *)
> ```
>
> `elimdups` takes as input a list that is not an atom and returns a list in which the duplicates have been eliminated. Code `elimdups`.

4.3   IMPLEMENTING THE ADT List

Once you have the correct mental picture of the data structure used to represent lists, the code for all the primitive functions, except `readlist` and `writelist`, is straightforward, with no one procedure taking more than a few lines. The difficulty, and why the correct internal representation of a list isn't obvious, is that lists can be nested to an arbitrary depth. Just as the functions that process lists are recursive, the lists themselves are recursive. Figure 4–3 shows the internal representation of (() a (b (c d)) ((e))). While the process of comprehending a recursive data structure or algorithm normally involves first specifying and understanding the base cases, here it is easier to begin by examining the representation of complex lists, worrying about the base cases later. A high-level view of the list

$$(l_1 \ l_2 \ \dots \ l_n)$$

is

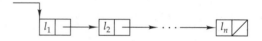

It is just a linked list with one node for each of the l_i.

Because the l_i are themselves potentially complex lists, the above picture is misleading. Even if we wanted to do so, we could not store l_i in the first component of a `cell`; in general, there just won't be enough room. What is really stored there is a pointer to the linked structure that represents the list l_i. A more accurate picture is

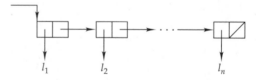

The top level of a list is a linked list of cells, where the first component of each cell points to a sublist.

The parentheses that enclose a list, and which indicate the nesting, are not explicitly kept in the internal representation; the nesting of the lists is captured in the nesting of the linked structures. Not representing the parentheses explicitly does raise a question: how will we represent the empty list? Looking at the

FIGURE 4–3   Representing Lists

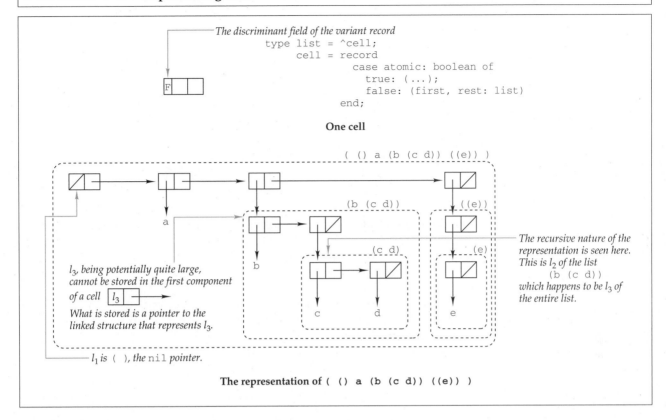

The discriminant field of the variant record

```
type list = ^cell;
     cell = record
               case atomic: boolean of
                  true: (...);
                  false: (first, rest: list)
            end;
```

One cell

(() a (b (c d)) ((e)))

(b (c d))   ((e))

l_3, being potentially quite large, cannot be stored in the first component of a cell

What is stored is a pointer to the linked structure that represents l_3.

a

b

(c d)   (e)

c   d   e

The recursive nature of the representation is seen here. This is l_2 of the list
(b (c d))
which happens to be l_3 of the entire list.

l_1 is ( ), *the* nil *pointer.*

The representation of (() a (b (c d)) ((e)))

limiting case, if (l_1) is represented as

l_1

then ( ) *shouldn't* be a pointer to a cell. It should be a pointer to a linked list of no cells. But a pointer has to point someplace. The natural choice is to make the representation of the empty list the Pascal nil—a pointer to nowhere.

Imagine taking the car of the complex list $(l_1 \ l_2 \ \dots \ l_n)$. Except for the error checks, car(p) is just one line of code (line 83)

$$car := p\hat{}.first$$

which pictorially is

Implementing car *and* cdr

Refer to lines 72–98 of Primitives.p *while reading this.*

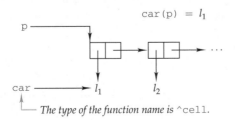

p

car(p) = l_1

car ⟶ l_1 l_2

The type of the function name is ^cell.

Similarly, cdr(p), which should return a pointer to $(l_2\ l_3\ \ldots\ l_n)$, is also just one line of code (line 97)

$$\texttt{cdr := p\^{}.rest}$$

with the corresponding picture being

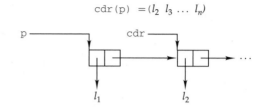

$\texttt{cdr(p)} = (l_2\ l_3\ \ldots\ l_n)$

We must be wary of one situation: if we take the cdr of any complex list enough times, which is what we do when we deal with lists recursively in functions like equal and append, we should eventually return ( ). Looking carefully at our representation of lists, if we perform

$$\texttt{cdr := p\^{}.rest}$$

n times on a list of length n, we will return nil, the contents of the rest field of the last cell of the linked list pointed to by p. This confirms the decision to represent the empty list as the Pascal nil.

Implementing cons

See lines 100–121.

Implementing cons(p,q) is no harder, requiring only five lines of code

```
new(r);
r^.atomic := false;
r^.first := p;
r^.rest := q;
cons := r
```

The effect on memory is shown in Figure 4–4.

Things are not what they seem to be. Do this exercise now!

> **EXERCISE 4–20**   In the definition of cons, it was stated that if p is a complex list
>
> $$\texttt{cons(car(p),cdr(p)) = p}$$
>
> and, if q is not at atom, then
>
> $$\texttt{car(cons(p,q)) = p} \quad \text{and} \quad \texttt{cdr(cons(p,q)) = q}$$
>
> Are these three equations true if "equal" means the equal operator of Pascal, as opposed to having the same logical structure?

If you were to go through the unrewarding task of determining exactly what memory looks like after performing

$$\texttt{append((a) , (b))} \quad \text{or} \quad \texttt{reverse((a (b c)))}$$

you would discover that it looks like what you see in Figure 4–5. Certain bits and pieces of memory are pointed to many times, like the atoms a, b, and c in reverse((a (b c))) and the list (b) in append((a) , (b)), which is pointed to by both the q of the main program and the rest field of the cell to which append returned a pointer. There is also a lot of "dead" memory. Executing reverse((a (b c))) leaves six unreachable cells lying around. The root cause of all this can be seen in the implementation of car, cdr, and cons. Unlike in the infinite precision arithmetic package of Chapter 3, where

---

FIGURE 4–4   Implementing cons

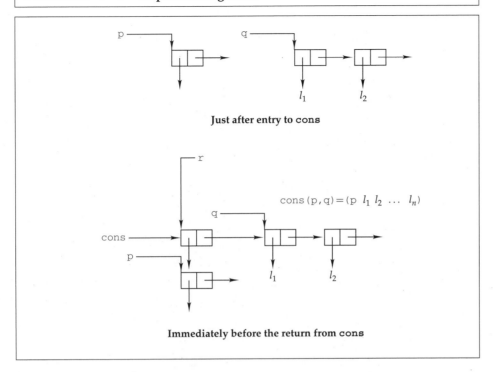

Just after entry to cons

$$\texttt{cons}(\texttt{p},\texttt{q}) = (\texttt{p}\ l_1\ l_2\ \cdots\ l_n)$$

Immediately before the return from cons

`Assign(n,m)` made a copy of the data structure pointed to by `m`, and didn't just execute `n := m`, here `car(p)` and `cdr(p)` return pointers to structures that are physically substructures of the original structure. Similarly, `cons(p,q)` does not make a copy of what `p` and `q` point to. It just grabs a new `cell` with `new(r)` and makes the `first` and `rest` fields point directly to what `p` and `q` point to, so these cells are pointed to more than once. But where does the dead memory in `reverse( (a (b c)) )` come from? All of it results from the fact that there are no variables in our programs. Everything is just function calls, with the call-by-value parameters of one function call being just the results returned by other function calls. In fact after executing

$$\texttt{writelist(reverse(readlist))}$$

all ten cells and the three atoms are dead—no named variable points to any of them.

This discussion points out two potential problems with the approach taken to the implementation of lists. First, when two pointers point to the same place in memory and one of them changes what it points to, memory is changed from the perspective of the other pointer as well. *This cannot happen here.* In our high-level programs that manipulate lists, as well as in the functions that implement the primitive operations, once a cell is created, the contents of the cell is *never* modified. The functions `null`, `atom`, and `eq` treat their input in a read-only manner, and while `car` and `cdr` return pointers to existing cells, the contents of the cells themselves are not modified. The only place that cells are created is in `cons`, but even it does not modify other cells. Since the primitive functions don't modify cells and the high-level functions are just composed of calls to the six primitive functions, *nothing* is ever modified after it is created. So while copying the data structures within `car`, `cdr`, and `cons` might make for a less confusing picture, it isn't any safer, and it would waste considerable storage and

Immutability revisited

FIGURE 4–5   A Look Inside Memory

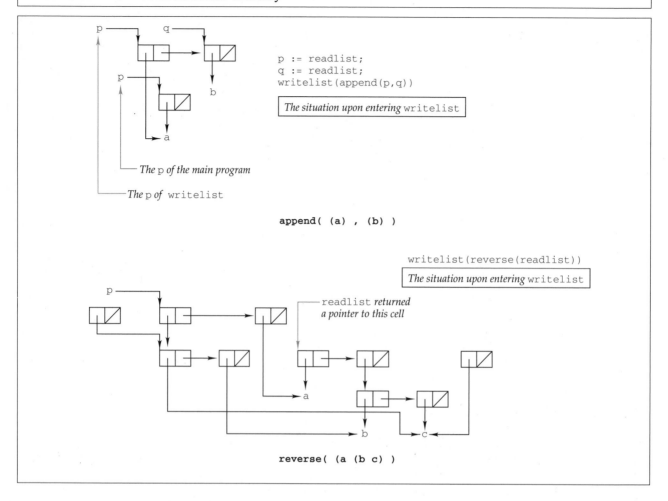

```
p := readlist;
q := readlist;
writelist(append(p,q))
```

The situation upon entering `writelist`

The p of the main program

The p of `writelist`

append((a) , (b))

`writelist(reverse(readlist))`

The situation upon entering `writelist`

`readlist` *returned a pointer to this cell*

reverse((a (b c))

cause the programs to run much more slowly. As written, `car(p)`, `cdr(p)`, and `cons(p,q)` take constant time no matter how large the lists p and q are, whereas if what they pointed to had to be copied, their execution times would be proportional to the size of the lists being manipulated.

Memory management in LISP   The other problem is that the amount of dead memory increases over time and eventually we might run out of storage. Real LISP systems tackle this problem in a totally different manner from the way we attacked it in the infinite precision arithmetic package. There, because every `LongInteger` was pointed to by only one Pascal variable, we could manage memory ourselves, knowing that when we reclaimed storage (by calling `DisposeNum`), we were not inadvertently destroying a data structure pointed to by another pointer variable. That premise is not true here—one substructure may be pointed to many times. Real LISP systems include a ***garbage collector***. When LISP runs out of memory, it invokes the garbage collector, which sweeps through memory, searching for cells that are no longer pointed to, either directly or indirectly, by any named variable (including the call-by-value parameters and function names). The garbage collector is part of the runtime support system of the language processor—it must be able to access all the named variables tucked away in the stack segment. The details of garbage collection are beyond the scope of this book. Our interest in lists isn't so much to do something useful, but to gain practice thinking recursively. We don't intend to execute programs that consume vast amounts of memory, so if, by accident, we run out of memory, then so be it.

All we have left to resolve is the representation of atoms. The `first` field of a `cell` usually needs to point to some other `cell` and so its type needs to be `^cell`. It needs to do this whenever the `car` of a list is a complex list. But when the `car` of a list is an atom, having `first` point to a `cell` is inappropriate. It needs to point to a different type of structure; if we were willing to limit the length of an atom, it could point to a `packed array of char`. Pascal's variant record provides just the right mechanism. It allows us to have two kinds of cells with the same type name; the normal one for representing cells that make up the list structure, and a special one for representing the base case of an atom. The `first` field can point to either kind. The discriminant field, `atomic: boolean`, distinguishes which type of `cell` we are dealing with. Within this framework, we are now free to represent an atom in any way that seems convenient. The method chosen in this chapter is easy to implement, though a bit wasteful of memory: it is just a linked list of the characters that make up the atom. It is convenient to have the length of an atom included as part of its description; it makes it easier to check for line overflow in `writelist`, and since it is there, we can also use it in `eq` to speed up the check for equality—two atoms of different lengths cannot possibly be the same. The code for `atom` and `eq` now falls neatly into place. We will see a better way of representing atoms in Chapter 6, where we encounter essentially the same problem: efficiently storing strings of characters whose lengths we cannot predict in advance.

Representing atoms

Refer to the type declarations and the code for `atom` *and* `eq` *while reading this.*

The procedure `writelist`, despite its 90-line length, is really quite simple. It is nothing more than the following recursive routine.

Implementing `writelist`

```
1 procedure writelist(p: list);
2   begin
3     if atom(p)
4       then writeatom(p)
5       else begin
6             write('(');              (* write opening parenthesis *)
7             while p <> nil do        (* while not all l_i printed do *)
8               begin
9                 writelist(car(p));   (* recursively write l_i *)
10                p := p^.rest         (* move on to l_{i+1} *)
11              end;
12            write(')')               (* write closing parenthesis *)
13          end
14  end; (* writelist *)
```

If `writelist` is so conceptually simple, then why is the real version so long? The answer is that the above solution overlooks issues of aesthetics. For example, if `writeatom(p)` is implemented in the obvious way, as a simple loop that runs down the linked list of letters, writing them out along the way, then the list `(a b)` will print as `(ab)`. This is easily remedied by having `writeatom` print a space before and after the atom, but this causes `(a b)` to print as `( a b )`, which, while technically correct, is not very pleasing. A better solution is to have `writelist` print a blank between l_i and l_{i+1}. This adds a few lines of code. Another small problem is that no carriage return is printed at the end of a list. This cannot be handled inside the recursive routine, since we don't want to have a carriage return printed after each sublist. The standard approach to

Recursion and Stack Frames

In the discussion of stack frames in Section 1.4, the reason given for keeping local variables on a stack, instead of associating them with the code of the procedure, was that the stack discipline supports recursion. To see why recursion and stacks are so deeply interwoven, we examine a program for solving the Towers of Hanoi problem—this quintessential recursive program is given in Figure 4–6. The task is to move n disks from spike 1 to spike 2, one disk at a time, so that at no time does any disk rest on top of one with smaller diameter. The beauty of this problem is that it is almost impossible to solve iteratively—is the correct first step to move the top disk to spike 2 or spike 3?—yet the recursive solution is only 15 lines long. The approach can be summarized in a few sentences:

> *To move n disks from spike 1 to spike 2, we need to first move $n - 1$ disks to spike 3, where they are out of the way. Then we can move the largest disk, which is still sitting on spike 1, to spike 2. Finally we need to move the $n - 1$ disks now sitting on spike 3 to spike 2.*

The first and third steps are essentially the Towers of Hanoi problem with n replaced by $n - 1$. The only difference is that in the first step, the starting and ending spikes are spikes 1 and 3, and in the third step they are spikes 3 and 2. This suggests a recursive procedure that solves a slight generalization of the Towers of Hanoi problem, one with declaration

```
procedure Towers(n: integer; a, b: spike);
```

a is the spike on which the disks start out and b is the spike on which they are supposed to end up. The base case, $n = 1$, is trivial, we just move the disk, while lines 12–15 implement the strategy outlined above.

Figure 4–7 says it all. In fact, it says far too much. Nobody can keep all these details in mind, and shouldn't even try. When thinking recursively, attempting to see what is going on in such great depth is paralyzing. Actually, the figure displays even more than the goings-on inside the computer: the arrangement of the disks on the three spikes and the number of moves made is not known to the program. This information was reconstructed from the output. Only the stack of stack frames is present in the memory of the computer.

The point of the figure is to see the relationship between stack frames and recursion. Look at the stack on the tenth entry to Towers. How did it get to be this way? First, the main program, after querying the user for input, called Towers to solve the entire problem, and became inactive. This first call to Towers, after testing n and discovering it to be greater than one, called Towers recursively (with $n = 4$), and so became inactive as well. This second call to Towers called Towers yet again (with n equal 3, a equal 1 and b equal 2), and so also became inactive. At some later time, after disks were moved seven times, this third call returned, and the call to Towers with n equal 4 was reactivated. At that very moment, the situation looked like

(continued)

FIGURE 4–6   The Towers of Hanoi

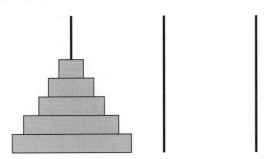

Initial configuration when *n* = 5

```
 1 program TowersOfHanoi(input,output);
 2   type spike = 1..3;
 3   var N: integer;
 4   procedure Towers(n: integer; a, b: spike);
 5     (* Solve the Towers of Hanoi problem for  n  disks, moving them from
 6         spike  a  to spike  b .
 7     *)
 8     var c: spike; (* the "work" spike *)
 9     begin
10       if n > 1
11         then begin
12                   c := 6 - a - b;   (* determine the third spike *)
```

Because 1 + 2 + 3 = 6, the third spike, the one used to temporarily hold the n−1 disks that are initially on top of the largest disk, can be determined by this simple calculation. Though trickier than the more obvious
```
          if (a = 1) and (b = 2)
            then c := 3
            else if (a = 1) and (b = 3)
              then ...
```
once understood it is clearly much better.

```
13                 Towers(n-1,a,c); (* move  n-1  disks out of the way *)
14                 writeln('Move a disk from spike ',a:1,' to spike ',b:1);  (1)
15                 Towers(n-1,c,b)  (* move  n-1  disks to where they belong *)
16              end  (2)
17         else writeln('Move a disk from spike ',a:1,' to spike ',b:1)
18     end; (* Towers *)
19   begin
20     write('Number of disks: '); readln(N);
21     Towers(N,1,2)
22 end. (* TowersOfHanoi *)  (3)
```

The program for solving the problem

(concluded)

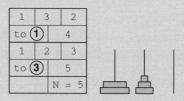

The reactivated second call to `Towers` then executed the `writeln` on line 14, which printed

```
Move a disk from spike 1 to spike 3
```

changing the situation to

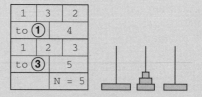

and then it made the call `Tower(3,2,3)`, which, when it completes, will also complete the overall task of the call `Towers(4,1,3)`. Just after making the call to `Towers` on line 15, memory will look as shown in the part of Figure 4–7 labeled "on the 10th entry to `Towers`."

For calls to `Towers` where `n` is greater than one, the procedure is active three times:

- When it is first entered, where it tests `n` and makes the first of its recursive calls.
- When it moves the largest disk for its subproblem from one spike to another and then makes its second recursive call.
- Just for a moment, where it appears to do nothing, but actually does a return on reaching the `end` of the procedure.

Each time an invocation of `Towers` is active, the stack frame that contains that invocation's local variables is on the top of the stack. When the procedure is inactive, its stack frame will be covered by other, similar, stack frames. It will sit there, dormant and protected by the stack frames above it. When the procedure is reactivated, its variables will be there, just as it left them. Only when an invocation finally returns, will its stack frame be destroyed.

EXERCISE 4–21   The information required to draw Figure 4–7 was obtained from an enhanced version of the `TowersOfHanoi` program. Add code to the program to print out enough information to verify that the figure is correct.

FIGURE 4–7   **Memory as the Towers of Hanoi Program is Running**

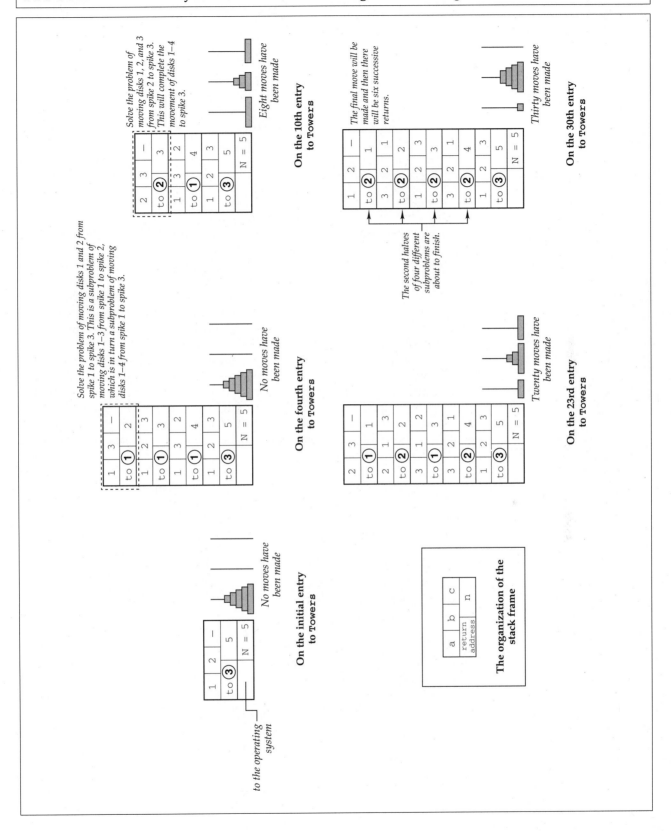

this sort of difficulty is to use a ***nonrecursive shell***. The strategy is very simple. `writelist` is coded as

```
procedure writelist(p: list);
  procedure RecWriteList(p: list);
    ... The recursive code given earlier for writelist, modified to
        put spaces between the sublists and with the recursive calls
        made to RecWriteList instead of to writelist ...
  begin (* writelist *)
    RecWriteList(p); (* write out the complete list *)
    writeln          (* write out the carriage return *)
  end; (* writelist *)
```

`writelist` first calls `RecWriteList`, which writes out the list recursively. Then it writes out the carriage return. Almost all the work is done in the subprocedure, which is hidden from public view by a "shell" placed around it.

While we are fixing small problems, there is one other that deserves attention. Some of the functions we have developed, like `powerset`, can produce lists that are too long to be written on one line. The formatting of these long lists should not be left to the vagaries of the operating system or the physical output device—the best we can hope for is that an atom will be split over line boundaries, while, at worst, the rightmost character of the line might be overprinted with all the remaining characters or the line might be truncated. Thus, before printing a left or right parenthesis or an atom, `writelist` makes sure that it will fit on the line. If it won't, then it issues a carriage return and indents the subsequent line slightly. If the break happens to fall between two sublists, the intersublist blank is suppressed, since the carriage return serves the same function. And while we are at it, we prevent the empty list from being split across a line boundary. This is accomplished by treating the empty list as a single object. This makes it equally easy to print the empty list as ( ) or (), depending on which we think more aesthetically pleasing.

The most difficult of the primitive routines to code, both conceptually and because of quirks and potential errors when dealing with input, is `readlist`. It is 140 lines long; more than one-third of the program. `readlist` is like a little recursive compiler that converts the linear input of opening parentheses, closing parentheses, and atoms into its corresponding list structure. In this respect, it is the inverse of `writelist`, but it seems easier to walk the data structure recursively linearizing it, than it does to convert the linear representation into a collection of interconnected cells. Actually, if looked at from a high-level perspective, `readlist` is not all that hard to understand. It consists of two mutually recursive procedures, `readlist` and `GetRest`. `readlist` looks at the next character in the input stream (after skipping over white space) to determine if it is processing a list that begins with a left parenthesis or if it is processing a list that is simply an atom. Although it takes almost 50 lines of code to deal with them, conceptually, atoms pose no difficulties. If, however, the list begins with a left parenthesis, `readlist` throws this character away, since parentheses aren't part of the internal representation, and calls `GetRest`, whose job it is to convert

$$l_1\ l_2\ \dots\ l_n\ )$$

without a leading opening parenthesis, into the internal representation of the list $(l_1\ l_2\ \dots\ l_n)$.

Ignoring possible errors in the input, there are two cases for `GetRest` to consider. Either the next character (again ignoring white space) is a right parenthesis or it is either a left parenthesis or a letter. In the first case, there are no sublists, so the original list is the empty list, and `GetRest` returns the internal representation of ( ). On the other hand, if the next character is a left parenthesis or a letter, then there is at least one sublist, so `GetRest` calls `readlist` recursively to turn this sublist into its internal representation. Since `readlist` consumes the input for l_1, after the recursive call to `readlist` returns, `GetRest` is faced with $l_2\ l_3\ \dots\ l_n$) or, if n equals 1, a right parenthesis. While we can proceed iteratively, like we did in `writelist`, it is more clever to continue recursively. In fact, the essence of `GetRest` can be summarized in just a few lines as

```
if  the next character is a right parenthesis (* base case *)
    then GetRest := NILL and throw away the right parenthesis
    else GetRest := cons(readlist (* process l₁ *),
                         GetRest (* process l₂ l₃ ... lₙ) *))
```

Look carefully at the `else` clause. The call to `readlist` should return the internal representation of l_1 and the call to `GetRest` should return the internal representation of $(l_2\ l_3\ \dots\ l_n)$, because it should be facing $l_2\ l_3\ \dots\ l_n)$ when called recursively . The `cons` of l_1 onto $(l_2\ l_3\ \dots\ l_n)$ gives us $(l_1\ l_2\ \dots\ l_n)$. Not only that, the recursive call to `GetRest` will ultimately consume the trailing right parenthesis of $l_2\ l_3\ \dots\ l_n)$. This is good, since it is also the trailing right parenthesis of $l_1\ l_2\ \dots\ l_n)$, and the call to `readlist` that initiated the calls to `GetRest` should consume the entire list, including the closing parenthesis. The right parenthesis is actually consumed when `GetRest` executes the clause "and throw away the right parenthesis" in the handling of the base case. Thus, taken together, `readlist` is just

```
function GetRest: list;
  begin
    if the next character is a right parenthesis (* base case *)
       then GetRest := NILL and throw away the right parenthesis
       else GetRest := cons(readlist,GetRest)
  end; (* GetRest *)

function readlist: list;
  begin
    if the next character is a letter
       then readlist := ReadAtom
       else begin
              throw away the left parenthesis;
              readlist := GetRest
            end
  end; (* readlist *)
```

The rest is all details of dealing with the quirks of the input stream and possible errors, not that these difficulties should be minimized. The unintuitive nature of `eoln` and `eof`, and the fact that Turbo Pascal is nonstandard in its handling of text files, makes writing a bug-free and portable program more difficult. We accomplish this by having a procedure, `ReadClean`, which defines for the rest of the program what the character set looks like. If we encounter another Pascal compiler, with different nonstandard behavior, only this one routine will need to be changed. We are doing nothing other than putting into practice a good general principle:

See the section `eoln` *and* `eof` *in Chapter 1.*

Isolate the interface to the real input in a single routine.

From the perspective of `readlist`, the input consists of six types of characters: `(`, `)`, letters and digits, white space, end-of-file, and illegal characters. The procedure `ReadClean` on lines 132–156 basically performs the following actions:

- If `eof` is true, it returns the end-of-file character. This is done even if, as in UNIX, there is no end-of-file character.
- If `eoln` is true, it returns blank and does whatever is necessary to throw away the end-of-line character or characters, as the case may be.
- It translates the tab character into a blank.
- It returns all other characters, the true blank, letters, digits, `(`, `)`, and illegal characters, untouched.

The decision to translate the end-of-line character(s) into a blank means that a list can span more than one line without `readlist`, `GetRest`, and `ReadAtom` having to worry about it separately. Also, the decision to translate tabs into blanks is isolated in one place. If making this translation is undesirable, we need to delete only one line of code; we don't have to go searching for the translation in three different places.

The idea of translating `eof`-is-true into an end-of-file character is fraught with difficulty. The problem is that there is no free character into which to translate it. MS-DOS uses `^Z` (control-Z) for this purpose, but in the UNIX world, `^Z` is a perfectly valid input character, though an illegal one in the context of this program. The solution is to define a "supercharacter" type. The declaration on lines 4–7 of `Primitives.p`

```
type FullChar = record
                endfile: boolean; (*  ch  field set to ^ Z *)
                ch: char (* the character, if  endfile  is false *)
            end;
```

accomplishes this. A `^Z` in the input and the true end-of-file are distinguished by the value in the field `endfile`.

This situation occurs as well in the Nero project of Chapter 5, where it creates significantly greater difficulties.

A problem that arises when reading atoms is the driving force for exactly where in `readlist` the calls to `ReadClean` are performed. The procedure `ReadAtom` cannot tell when it has finished reading an atom until it has read one character too many. Only when `CurrentChar` contains a character that is not a letter or digit can the procedure know that the atom has terminated. This character is one we cannot afford to ignore, since it might be a right parenthesis. For this reason we establish and maintain the following invariant:

> *On entry to* `readlist`, `GetRest`, *and* `ReadAtom`, *the first character of unconsumed input is already in* `CurrentChar`.

This affects, in a number of small and subtle ways, many lines of code. For example, procedure `SkipBlanks`, which is called when we enter `GetRest` and `readlist`, is written as a `while` loop and not as

```
repeat
   ReadClean(CurrentChar)
until CurrentChar.ch <> ' '
```

When `SkipBlanks` is called, the character stored in `CurrentChar` is an unprocessed character, so we should not blindly perform a read. With this invariant in mind, the details of the code in `readlist` and its subsidiary procedures should be easy to follow. There is one last detail. While the unavoidable reading of an extra character in `ReadAtom` and the reading of a character on line 234 in `GetRest` (a read that effectively throws away the right parenthesis) ensures that the invariant is satisfied on recursive calls to `readlist`; the invariant should be satisfied on the initial entry to `readlist` as well. We need to preread the first character. This problem is similar to printing the carriage return after writing a list, except that here our problem is needing to read a character on the front end rather than a writing a carriage return on the back end. Why then do we not have a nonrecursive shell, but instead have the annoying presence of a call to procedure `InitIO` on every line of the driver program? The answer is that, after reading the list (either an atom or a list that ends with a right parenthesis), `readlist` will actually have read the character that follows the list as well. This would not be a problem, except that on the second call to `readlist`, in lines like

```
10: begin InitIO; p := readlist; q := readlist;
        writelist(append(p,q)) end;
```

the preread of the first character will already have been done as a consequence of the extra character read by the first call to `readlist`. If we do a preread as part of `readlist`, we will probably not notice the problem, since the user is likely to type

```
(a) (b)
```

when responding to a request for two lists. But, on some dark night, when the user types

```
(a)(b)
```

if the preread is part of `readlist`, this will be interpreted as

```
(a) b)
```

because the opening parenthesis of `(b)`, read by the first call to `readlist`, will be thrown away by the preread of the second call. We need one preread before a *sequence* of calls to `readlist`, not one for each call. The reason that there is a call to `InitIO` in each alternative of the `case` statement in the driver, instead of just one such call at the very start of the program, is that the driver program does not obey our conventions—it does regular Pascal reads to input the user's selection and to prevent the screen from scrolling.

There are only a few remarks that need to be made about spotting errors in the input. Detection of illegal characters is no problem, but what happens if the user types in

Error detection in `readlist`

```
(a (b c)
```

or

```
(a (b c)))
```

where a single list is required? The answer in the first case depends on whether the input is coming from a file or from the terminal. If the input is coming from a file, the end-of-file character will be returned and `GetRest`, because it didn't see the desired right parenthesis, will assume that there is an l_3 at the outermost level, and so will call `readlist`. `readlist` then generates the error message

```
ERROR -- error in readlist (unexpected end-of-file)
```

If the input is coming from a terminal, `SkipBlanks`, in attempting to skip over the blank that is the converted carriage return at the end of the line, will have nothing to read. The user will sit there waiting for an answer while `ReadClean` will be waiting to do a read, hoping that the closing right parenthesis will be typed on the next line. Eventually, the user will realize something is wrong and upon examining the input should realize that the final closing parenthesis is missing and that the program is waiting for it to be typed in. An alternate approach would have been to insist that a list must all be typed on one line and to treat the missing right parenthesis as an error. This requires translating eoln-is-true into a special extended character, just like we did with the end-of-file character.

In the case of the second error, where there is an extra right parenthesis at the end of the line, the error might not even be detected! The program correctly interprets (a (b c)) as a list. After reading this list, CurrentChar contains the extra right parenthesis, but this will never be noticed. There is really very little we can do about this as long as we do not want to insist that every list occupy a line by itself.

EXERCISE 4–22   Rewrite RecWriteList so that it, like readlist, is less dependent on knowledge of the internal representation of lists.

EXERCISE 4–23   Some LISP systems use] as a "super right parenthesis." It means "assume enough right parentheses to close the top-level list." Add this feature to readlist.

EXERCISE 4–24   Make the ADT LIST package more robust by modifying readlist so that lists must be input one per line.

PROJECT 4–1   Add to the ADT LIST package the primitive function quote, which takes a list represented as a string of characters and returns the internal representation of the list. This allows a programmer using our package to place constants in a program, something which is currently lacking. The body of quote is essentially the same as the body of readlist, only the data comes from a string and not the file input.

PROJECT 4–2   Extend the type declaration cell and the functions readlist and quote to include the Pascal type integer as a third base case. Define primitives such as

```
function add(p, q: list): list;
```

a function that takes two lists that are integers and returns the list that is their sum. If either p or q is not an integer, then report an error and halt. (Don't confuse what is asked for in this project with the discussion of how logicians view integers. There an integer was represented as a list. Here we mean to include integers, as we normally think of them, as a base case of list. It is because of this project that atoms were defined as beginning with a letter.)

PROJECT 4–3   After doing Project 4–2, develop a package for symbolically manipulating polynomials in up to three variables. Represent a polynomial as a list, with each monomial represented by a sublist. These sublists should themselves be complex lists consisting of up to four sublists, the lead coefficient and up to three lists of the form (x 2), which represents x^2. For example, the polynomial

$$3x^2y + xyz^3 - 5y + 4$$

is to be represented as

```
( (3 (x 2) (y 1)) (1 (x 1) (y 1) (z 3)) (-5 (y 1)) (4) )
```

Notice that variables that are missing are not represented at all, but coefficients and exponents of 1 are explicitly included, even though this does not conform to standard mathematical notation. (Internally, it might be convenient to include (z 0) if z is missing from a monomial.) Also notice that $\ldots xyz^3 - 5y \ldots$ becomes $\ldots xyz^3 + (-5y) \ldots$. Define functions to add, subtract, and multiply polynomials, to evaluate polynomials when values for x, y, and z are specified, and to take their partial derivatives with respect to each of the three variables. You may wish to include an auxiliary function in your package

```
function normalize(p: list): list;
```

which returns a polynomial in "normal form." The normal form for a polynomial has the monomials sorted into decreasing order by the exponent of x, looking successively at the exponents of y and z in the event of a tie.

ABOVE
AND BEYOND   **A Look at Real LISP**

If your programming experience has been limited to imperative languages like Pascal and C, the merest glance at Figure 4–8 shows that LISP does not look even remotely like any programming language you have seen before. After recovering from the shock of seeing all the right parentheses that gang up every so often, you might notice that LISP doesn't have any familiar keywords, like `if` or `begin`, and doesn't even appear to have an assignment operator. These differences are not just syntactical, they reflect a radically different underlying philosophy.

A major difference between LISP and imperative languages is that the distinction between the program and the data is one of context and not one of form. In Pascal, programs and data are neatly segregated. We write and compile a program and then we execute it on the data. In LISP, *everything*, both the program and the data, is just a sequence of lists. At the most fundamental level, it is best to think of everything as if it were data, with there being no program at all. The lists in the sequence are simply "processed" one after the other until they are all consumed, at which time the LISP system halts. Internally, all lists are processed by the LISP system in exactly the same way. However, in certain contexts, "processing" a list has the effect of "defining a function," while in other contexts it means "executing a line of code."

In LISP, there are only three types of symbols: opening parentheses, closing parentheses, and atoms. The main difference between the ADT LIST, which is only a data structure, and LISP, which is a programming language, is that atoms are always constants in our package, whereas an atom in real LISP can be a constant, a variable, or a function name. Which role an atom takes on at any moment depends on the context in which it is used. Suppose, after immediately starting up the LISP system, you bravely type

```
(atom q)
```

or, more interestingly,

```
(atom atom)
```

What will happen? LISP will see the opening left parenthesis and say to itself "this is a function call and the next item should be a function object." Since the next item is `atom` and `atom` is a primitive function, all is well. Then, just as in imperative languages, the arguments to the function must be *evaluated* before the function can be *applied*. `q` and `atom` are therefore interpreted as variables whose values should be passed to the function `atom`, but since neither `q` nor `atom` have a value (are *bound* to anything), the LISP system prints out the error message

```
Error: Attempt to take the value of the unbound symbol q
```

If we were a bit braver still and typed

```
(atom (quote atom))
```

the LISP system would print `t`, which means "true." Why is this? Upon seeing the opening parenthesis, LISP says to itself "this is a function call and the next item should be a function object," which `atom` indeed is. Then it says, "okay,

(continued)

ABOVE
AND BEYOND

(continued)
See the discussion of quote
on pages 170 and 200.

I should evaluate the argument to atom." The argument is (quote atom).
Since this expression begins with a left parenthesis, it is also a function call.
The function in (quote atom) is quote. quote is a primitive function of
LISP. Its argument is special in that, unlike all other functions, its argument
is not evaluated but treated literally. It serves the same purpose as the quote
function mentioned in the main body of the text and in Project 4–1. Atoms
within the expression are not variables or functions, but stand for themselves.
They are constants. So the function call (quote atom) returns the constant
atom. Since atom applied to the constant atom is true, the entire function call

$$(atom \ (quote \ atom))$$

returns true. If we next try

$$(atom \ (quote \ (atom)))$$

LISP returns (and prints) nil, which means "false." This is because the function call (quote(atom)) returns the list (atom), and while here atom is a
constant, (atom) is not an atom, but is, instead, a complex list.

To summarize, when the LISP interpreter encounters a list, it views it as

$$(\langle function\_name \rangle \ \langle argument_1 \rangle \ \langle argument_2 \rangle \ ... \ \langle argument_n \rangle)$$

and it attempts to *apply* the function to its arguments after first *evaluating*
them. If an argument is a variable, that is, just an atom, then its associated
value is used. If an argument is a function call, which LISP detects because the
argument begins with a left parenthesis, then LISP evaluates the function and
uses what it returns for the argument. As in all other programming languages,
it is an error to use a variable that has no associated value. Like a variable, a
function name can also have no associated function body to execute. If you
intend to type

$$(append \ (quote \ (a)) \ (quote \ (b)))$$

expecting to get back (a b), but instead type

$$(apend \ (quote \ (a)) \ (quote \ (b)))$$

misspelling append, you will be told

Error: attempt to call 'apend' which is an undefined function.

There are very few exceptions to this general rule about how to process a
list. We have already seen one—if the function name is quote, its argument
is not evaluated but is returned unchanged with all its atoms interpreted as
constants.

EXERCISE 4–25   What does the LISP interpreter return when
evaluating the following two expressions:

   (append (cons (quote a) nil) (cons (quote b) nil))

   (append (quote (cons a nil)) (quote (cons b nil)))

Neither of these produces an error message.

(continued)

ABOVE
AND BEYOND

(continued)

Armed with the understanding that LISP just processes list after list after list, and that it interprets a list as

$$(\langle \text{function\_name} \rangle \; \langle \text{argument}_1 \rangle \; \langle \text{argument}_2 \rangle \; \ldots \; \langle \text{argument}_n \rangle)$$

we are ready to look more carefully at the program in Figure 4–8. Lines 12 and 14 of the program we understand. Line 12 is nothing other than the call

```
equal( (a (b)) , (a (b)) )
```

and line 14 is nothing other than the call

```
append( (a) , (b) )
```

Lines 1–7 define the function `equal` and lines 9–10 define the function `append`. To understand these lines, we need to understand the function `def` and the function `lambda`. It takes a while to find the matching parentheses, but we see that calls to the function `def` have the form

```
(def (atom) (lambda ... ))
```

We also see the function `cond` buried in the `lambda` portion.

cond

`cond` is the easiest of the three to understand. It is the primitive function of LISP that corresponds to the `if ... then ... else ...` construction of Pascal, though being a function, and not a statement, it has to return something. Its general form is

$$(\text{cond} \; (\langle \text{fn}_1 \rangle \; \langle \text{fn}_2 \rangle) \; (\langle \text{fn}_3 \rangle \; \langle \text{fn}_4 \rangle) \; \ldots \; (\langle \text{fn}_{2n-1} \rangle \; \langle \text{fn}_{2n} \rangle))$$

The first pair of the `cond` *in* `equal` *is* `((null p) (null q))`. $\langle \text{fn}_1 \rangle$ *is* `(null p)` *and* $\langle \text{fn}_2 \rangle$ *is* `(null q)`.

`cond` takes an indefinite number of arguments, each of which is a list with two entries. When processing `cond`, the LISP interpreter proceeds through the list of pairs. It first evaluates the function $\langle \text{fn}_1 \rangle$. If the function evaluates to true, which means that its value is anything other than `nil`, then $\langle \text{fn}_2 \rangle$ is evaluated and the result of this evaluation is returned as the value of the entire `cond`.

(continued)

FIGURE 4–8   `equal` and `append` as They Really Are in LISP

```
 1  (def equal (lambda (p q) (cond ((null p) (null q))
 2                                 ((null q) nil)
 3                                 ((atom p) (cond ((atom q) (eq p q))
 4                                                 (t nil) ))
 5                                 ((atom q) nil)
 6                                 ((equal (car p) (car q)) (equal (cdr p) (cdr q)))
 7                                 (t nil) ) ))
 8
 9  (def append (lambda (p q) (cond ((null p) q)
10                                  (t (cons (car p) (append (cdr p) q))) ) ))
11
12  (equal (quote (a (b))) (quote (a (b))))
13
14  (append (quote (a)) (quote (b)))
```

This program was run on the popular Common LISP system. All real LISP systems provide a convenient mechanism, like the nonprimitive function `def`, *for defining functions.*

If $\langle fn_1 \rangle$ evaluates to false, that is, $\langle fn_1 \rangle$ returns nil, then $\langle fn_2 \rangle$ is not evaluated and the LISP interpreter goes on to the pair ($\langle fn_3 \rangle$ $\langle fn_4 \rangle$). It continues in this manner until the first component of one of the pairs returns true, in which case the value returned by the second component of the pair is the value returned for the entire cond. Since one of the options should always be true (it is an error to fall off the list without finding a pair whose first element evaluates to true), the last pair is invariably

$$(\text{t}\ \langle fn_{2n} \rangle)$$

since t always evaluates to true. If this convention is observed, a cond is nothing other than an arbitrarily long series of nested if statements

```
if ...        (* ⟨fn₁⟩ *)
   then ...    (* ⟨fn₂⟩ *)
else if ...   (* ⟨fn₃⟩ *)
   then ...    (* ⟨fn₄⟩ *)
      ⋮
else   ...   (* ⟨fn₂ₙ⟩ -- ⟨fn₂ₙ₋₁⟩ is forced to be true *)
```

cond was not needed in our Pascal-based implementation of the ADT LIST, since the procedures, written in Pascal, were kept completely separate from the data. The function def is not a primitive LISP function. It, or a function similar to it, is included in real LISP systems to make defining functions more like what we are used to. Because def can be expressed using the primitive LISP functions, its presence adds nothing to the language except convenience. The first argument to def is an atom. def builds an association between an atom and the body of a function. When this atom subsequently appears in the position where a function object is required, there is a corresponding function body to execute. The def on lines 1–7 defines the function equal, so that when the equal on line 12 is encountered, there is a function to execute. The (lambda ...) is the function that def associates with the $\langle$atom$\rangle$. This primitive function, used to define nonprimitive functions, is what most separates the ADT LIST from the LISP language. The first of its two arguments is a list of variables, the call-by-value parameters of the function, and the second is the function body, the begin ... end of Pascal. Thus

def

lambda

```
(def equal (lambda (p q) ... ))
```

corresponds to

```
function equal(p, q: list): boolean; ...
```

and

```
(cond ((null p) (null q)) ... (t nil))
```

(continued)

**ABOVE
AND BEYOND**

(concluded)

corresponds to

```
begin
  if null(p)
    then equal := null(q)
         ⋮
    else   equal := false
end; (* equal *)
```

```
 1 (* ADT List Private Type Declarations *)
 2 type PtrToLetter = ^letter; (* Store an atom as a linked list of characters. *)
 3     letter = record
 4                 ch: char; (* letter/digit (first character must be a letter) *)
 5                 next: PtrToLetter
 6             end;
 7     word =  record
 8                 length: integer; (* for convenience in  eq  and  writelist  *)
 9                 identifier: PtrToLetter
10             end;
11
12     list = ^cell;
13     cell = record
14                 case atomic: boolean of
15                 true:  (name: word);
16                 false: (first, rest: list)
17            end;
18
19
20 (* The behavior of those functions that take arguments is undefined
21    if the actual parameters have not been initialized.
22 *)
23 (* Primitive ADT List Functions *)
24 function null(p: list): boolean; external;
25   (*  null  returns true if  p  is the empty list, otherwise it
26       returns false.
27   *)
28
29 function atom(p: list): boolean; external;
30   (*  atom  returns true if  p  is an atom, otherwise it returns false. *)
31
32 function eq(p, q: list): boolean; external;
33   (*  eq  returns true if  p  and  q  are the same atom, returns false
34       if  p  and  q  are different atoms, and halts the program
35       if either  p  or  q  is not an atom.
36   *)
37
38 function car(p: list): list; external;
39   (*  car  returns the first element of a complex list -- it halts the
40       program if  p  is the empty list or an atom.
41   *)
42
43 function cdr(p: list): list; external;
44   (*  cdr  returns the remainder of a complex list -- it halts the
45       program if  p  is the empty list or an atom.
46   *)
47
48 function cons(p, q: list): list; external;
49   (*  cons  returns the result of inserting  p  as the first element of
50       nonatomic list  q  --  q  is not altered.   cons  halts the program
51       if  q  is an atom.
52   *)
53
54
```

It would be better if, like in Ada and C++, the details of these types could be placed in the private implementation section instead of in the public specification section.

In Pascal, we cannot guard against this user error.

```
55 (* ADT List Format Conversion Routines *)
56 function NILL: list; external;
57   (*  NILL  returns the empty list, that is,  NILL  returns  () . *)
58
59 function readlist: list; external;
60   (*  readlist  reads a list, which can span several lines, building up its
61       internal representation and returning the list.  readlist  halts the
62       program if the input is not a valid list.
63   *)
64
65 procedure writelist(p: list); external;
66   (*  writelist  writes the external representation of  p . *)
67
68
69 (* Service Routines *)
70 procedure InitIO; external;
71   (* This procedure initializes the input stream for a sequence of calls
72       to  readlist .
73   *)
```

```
 1  #include "Primitives.h"
 2  #include "Functions.h"
 3
 4  program RecursiveLists(input,output);
 5    (* Driver program to test recursive list functions. *)
 6
 7    label 99;
 8    const QUIT = 11; (* Increase as more functions are added to  Functions.h . *)
 9    var p, q: list;  (* This should not be necessary, but there is an ambiguity
10                         in Pascal regarding the order of evaluation of function
11                         arguments.  This is relevant when the arguments are
12                         themselves function calls that have side effects, as in
13                            writelist(append(readlist,readlist));
14                      *)
15        i: integer;
16
17    procedure WriteMenu;
18      begin
19        writeln('< 1> null');
20        writeln('< 2> atom');
21        writeln('< 3> eq');
22        writeln('< 4> car');
23        writeln('< 5> cdr');
24        writeln('< 6> cons');
25        writeln('< 7> NILL');
26        writeln('< 8> writelist');
27        writeln('< 9> equal');
28        writeln('<10> append');
29        writeln('<',QUIT:1,'> QUIT');
30        writeln;
31        write('---> ')
32      end; (* WriteMenu *)
33
34    procedure writebool(b: boolean);
35      begin
36        if b
37          then writeln('TRUE')
38          else writeln('FALSE')
39      end; (* writebool *)
40
41  begin
42    while true do
43      begin
44        WriteMenu;
45        readln(i);
46        case i of
47          1: begin InitIO; writebool(null(readlist)) end;
48          2: begin InitIO; writebool(atom(readlist)) end;
49          3: begin InitIO; p := readlist; q := readlist;
50                   writebool(eq(p,q)) end;
51          4: begin InitIO; writelist(car(readlist)) end;
52          5: begin InitIO; writelist(cdr(readlist)) end;
53          6: begin InitIO; p := readlist; q := readlist;
54                   writelist(cons(p,q)) end;
```

The declarations of equal *and* append *are in this file.*
Their bodies are in Functions.p.

The order of evaluation of these two arguments is unspecified in Pascal. The side effect is that readlist *consumes input. If the second argument is evaluated first—some compilers do this—then the input* (a) (b) *will be interpreted as* append((b),(a)), *which is not what the user expects.*

FILE   `Driver.p` Page 2

```
55              7: writelist(NILL);
56              8: begin InitIO; writelist(readlist) end;
57              9: begin InitIO; p := readlist; q := readlist;
58                    writebool(equal(p,q)) end;
59             10: begin InitIO; p := readlist; q := readlist;
60                    writelist(append(p,q)) end;
61          QUIT: goto 99 (* halt *)
62          end;
63          (* Prevent the screen from scrolling.  This works only if there are
64             no trailing blanks on the last line read by  readlist . *)
65          write('Type carriage return to continue'); readln;
66          writeln; writeln
67       end;
68 99:
69   end. (* RecursiveLists *)
```

This is not a good solution to the problem of having the answer scroll off the screen before it can be read, but since the driver is for our own use during testing, and is not a polished program, the solution is acceptable.

```
                  ┌─── See Above and Beyond: A Small Problem in member
                  │       for why this isn't eq, but why equal isn't quite right either.
 1 │function member(x, q: list): boolean;
 2 │  begin
 3 │    if null(q)                      ⎫
 4 │    then member := false            ⎬ ──────────────── If B = Ø, then x ∉ B.
 5 │        else if equal(x,car(q))     ⎭
 6 │                then member := true ⎫──────────────── Since x equals car(q), x ∈ B.
 7 │                else member := member(x,cdr(q)) ⎬──── Since x is not equal to car(q), x's
 8 │  end; (* member *)                                  membership in B depends on whether or not
 9 │                                                      x is in the rest of B.
10 function subset(p, q: list): boolean;
11   begin
12     if null(p)                       ⎫
13     then subset := true              ⎬──────────────── Ø is a subset of every set.
14     else if member(car(p),q)
15            then subset := subset(cdr(p),q)
16            else subset := false ⎬──────────────── The presence of even a single element of A
17   end; (* subset *)                                that is not in B means A ⊄ B.
18
19 function equalsets(p, q: list): boolean;
20   begin
21     if subset(p,q)
22     then equalsets := subset(q,p)
23     else equalsets := false
24   end; (* equalsets *)
25
26 function union(p, q: list): list;
27   begin
28     if null(p)                       ⎫
29     then union := q                  ⎬ Ø ∪ A = A
30     else if member(car(p),q) (* will capture element via  q  *)
31            then union := union(cdr(p),q)
32            else union := cons(car(p),union(cdr(p),q))
33   end; (* union *)
34
35 function intersection(p, q: list): list;
36   begin
37     if null(p)                       ⎫
38     then intersection := NILL        ⎬ Ø ∩ A = Ø
39     else if member(car(p),q)
40            then intersection := cons(car(p),intersection(cdr(p),q))
41            else intersection := intersection(cdr(p),q)
42   end; (* intersection *)
43
44 function setdifference(p, q: list): list;
45   begin
46     if null(p)
47     then setdifference := NILL
48     else if member(car(p),q) (* element is not in the set difference *)
49            then setdifference := setdifference(cdr(p),q)
50            else setdifference := cons(car(p),setdifference(cdr(p),q))
51   end; (* setdifference *)
52
```

FILE   Sets.p   **Page 2**

```
53 function insert(p, q: list): list;
54   (*  p  is any list,  q  is a list of lists, each one of which is either
55       an empty list or a complex list.  Insert  p  as the first element of
56       every list of  q .
57   *)
58   begin
59     if null(q)
60       then insert := NILL
61       else insert := cons(cons(p,car(q)),insert(p,cdr(q)))
62   end; (* insert *)
63
64 function powerset(p: list): list;
65   begin
66     if null(p) (* The power set of ( ) is ( ( ) ), not ( ). *)
67       then powerset := cons(NILL,NILL)
68       else powerset := union(powerset(cdr(p)),insert(car(p),powerset(cdr(p))))
69   end; (* powerset *)
```

FILE   Primitives.p   Page 1

> In the routines of `Primitives.p` *we are not bound by the requirements*
> *of no local variables, no iteration constructs, no Boolean connectives,*
> *no* begin ... end *blocks, and no* goto *statements.*

```
 1 #include "Primitives.h"
 2
 3 (* Translate the next "character" in the input in a system independent way. *)
 4 type FullChar = record
 5                     endfile: boolean; (*  ch  field set to ^Z *)
 6                     ch: char (* the character, if  endfile  is false *)
 7                 end;
 8 var CurrentChar: FullChar; (* private static variable for lexical analysis *)
 9
10
11 (* The behavior of the publicly visible functions that take arguments is
12    undefined if the actual parameters have not been initialized.
13 *)
14 (* Primitive ADT List Functions *)
15 (* function null(p: list): boolean; *)
16 function null;
17   (*  null  returns true if  p  is the empty list, otherwise it
18       returns false.
19   *)
20   begin
21     null := (p = nil)
22   end; (* null *)
23
24 (* function atom(p: list): boolean; *)
25 function atom;
26   (*  atom  returns true if  p  is an atom, otherwise it returns false. *)
27   begin
28     if null(p)
29       then atom := false
30       else atom := p^.atomic
31   end; (* atom *)
32
33 (* function eq(p, q: list): boolean; *)
34 function eq;
35   (*  eq  returns true if  p  and  q  are the same atom, returns false
36      if  p  and  q  are different atoms, and halts the program
37      if either  p  or  q  is not an atom.
38   *)
39   label 99;
40   var r, s: PtrToLetter;
41   begin
42     if not atom(p) or not atom(q)
43       then begin
44             writeln('ERROR -- error in  eq ');
45             halt
46           end
47     else if p^.name.length <> q^.name.length
48       then eq := false (* If they don't have the same length, they can't be
49                           the same. *)
```

— *This is more professional than*
```
if p = nil
  then null := true
  else null := false
```

— *This is better than* if p = nil, *because it makes the*
code less dependent on the internal representation of lists.

```
50      else    begin
51              r := p^.name.identifier;
52              s := q^.name.identifier;
53
54              (* while both atoms still have characters to compare do *)
55              while r <> nil (* and s <> nil *) do
56                if r^.ch <> s^.ch
57                  then begin
58                          eq := false;
59                          goto 99 (* return *)
60                       end
61                  else begin
62                          r := r^.next;
63                          s := s^.next
64                       end;
65              (* Because they have the same length and they never disagree,
66                 the two atoms are equal. *)
67              eq := true
68            end;
69 99:
70   end; (* eq *)
71
72 (* function car(p: list): list; *)
73 function car;
74   (*  car  returns the first element of a complex list -- it halts the
75       program if  p  is the empty list or an atom.
76   *)
77   begin
78     if null(p) or atom(p)
79       then begin
80               writeln('ERROR -- error in  car ');
81               halt
82            end
83       else car := p^.first
84   end; (* car *)
85
86 (* function cdr(p: list): list; *)
87 function cdr;
88   (*  cdr  returns the remainder of a complex list -- it halts the
89       program if  p  is the empty list or an atom.
90   *)
91   begin
92     if null(p) or atom(p)
93       then begin
94               writeln('ERROR -- error in  cdr ');
95               halt
96            end
97       else cdr := p^.rest
98   end; (* cdr *)
99
```

Because the two lists have the same length, we need to check only one of the lists to see if there are any more characters to examine.

```
100 (* function cons(p, q: list): list; *)
101 function cons;
102  (*  cons  returns the result of inserting  p  as the first element of
103      nonatomic list  q  --  q  is not altered.   cons  halts the program
104      if  q  is an atom.
105  *)
106  var r: list;
107  begin
108    if atom(q)
109      then begin
110             writeln('ERROR -- error in  cons ');
111             halt
112           end
113      else begin
114             new(r);  (* A system generated error will occur if the heap
115                         is totally exhausted. *)
116             r^.atomic := false;
117             r^.first := p;
118             r^.rest := q;
119             cons := r
120           end
121  end; (* cons *)
122
123
124 (* ADT List Format Conversion Routines *)
125 (* function NILL: list; *)
126 function NILL;
127  (*  NILL  returns the empty list, that is,  NILL  returns  () . *)
128  begin
129    NILL := nil
130  end; (* NILL *)
131
132 procedure ReadClean(var ch: FullChar);
133  (* Read a character, dealing with tabs, end-of-file, and end-of-line. *)
134  const TAB = 9; (* tab = ^I = ASCII 9 *)
135        ENDOFFILE = 26; (* ^Z -- just not blank, (, ), a letter, or a digit *)
136  begin
137    with ch do
138      if eof
139        then begin
140               (*  endfile = false  and  ch = ^Z  is NOT end-of-file *)
141               endfile := true;
142               ch := chr(ENDOFFILE)
143             end
```

This is less likely to occur in real LISP systems, which include garbage collection routines to reclaim storage that is no longer reachable.

Although most systems use ASCII, the use of const *ties the program to ASCII as little as possible.*

Because a "supercharacter" is a record, *with a special field used to distinguish end-of-file, this choice is arbitrary. It can be any value other than a legal character. That the program even bothers to set the* ch *field when* eof *is true, is only a matter of convenience. It simplifies the loop control in* SkipBlanks *(line 170) and the tests on lines 201 and 232.*

```
144              else begin                    Even in Turbo Pascal, which processes
145                    endfile := false;       end-of-line in a nonstandard way.
146                    if eoln
147                      then begin (* Convert logical end-of-line to blank. *)
148                               readln; (* throw away the end-of-line character(s) *)
149                               ch := ' '
150                           end
151                      else begin (* read(ch), but convert tab to blank. *)
152                               read(ch);
153                               if ch = chr(TAB) then ch := ' '
154                           end
155              end
156     end; (* ReadClean *)                  See Error detection in readlist (p. 199)
157                                            for why certain errors are not detected.
158 (* function readlist: list; *)
159 function readlist;
160  (*  readlist  reads a list, which can span several lines, building up its
161      internal representation and returning the list.   readlist  halts the
162      program if an illegal character or premature end-of-file is detected.
163      Certain errors, such as an extra right parenthesis (when another list
164      is not immediately read) are not detected.
165  *)
166
167  procedure SkipBlanks;
168     (* Read, if necessary, until a nonblank character is found. *)
169     begin
170       while CurrentChar.ch = ' ' (* or tab or carriage return *) do
171          ReadClean(CurrentChar)
172     end; (* SkipBlanks *)              That end-of-file is not translated into a blank permits a simple
173                                        and efficient loop termination condition.
174  function ReadAtom: list;
175     (* Read the atom starting with  CurrentChar , which has already been read.
176        Read one character too many -- on exit this extra character is returned
177        in  CurrentChar .
178     *)                            This unavoidable read is the reason for the invariant that on calls to readlist
179     var p: list;                   and GetRest the first character has already been read into CurrentChar.
180         q: PtrToLetter;
181         i: integer; (* number of characters in atom *)
182         done: boolean;
183     begin
184       new(p); (* A system generated error will occur if the heap
185                   is totally exhausted. *)
186       p^.atomic := true;
187
188       (* One character (a letter) has already been read.  The one character
189          is in  CurrentChar . *)
190       new(q);
191       i := 1;
192       p^.name.identifier := q;
193       q^.ch := CurrentChar.ch;
194
```

```
195        (* Read any remaining characters. *)
196        done := false;
197        repeat
198          ReadClean(CurrentChar);
199          (* Atoms are composed of letters and digits (after the first character),
200             case distinguished. *)
```

Place the most likely case first. The second case is true only once per loop entry, while the third is, hopefully, never true. The first case, on the other hand, is true as many times as there are letters in the atom (minus one).

```
201          if CurrentChar.ch in ['a'..'z','A'..'Z','0'..'9'] (* ASCII ASSUMED *)
202             then begin
```

This may need to be changed if the character set is non-ASCII. In EBCDIC, for example, the letters are not consecutive in the collating sequence, though they are in alphabetical order. This can be made totally portable by listing each character individually, writing ... in ['a','b','c',...].

```
203                  (* The atom contains at least one more character. *)
204                  new(q^.next);
205                  q := q^.next;
206                  q^.ch := CurrentChar.ch;
207                  i := i + 1
208                end
209          else if CurrentChar.endfile or (CurrentChar.ch in ['(',' ',')'])
210             then done := true
211          else  begin
212                  writeln('ERROR -- error in  readlist  (illegal character)');
213                  halt
214                end
215        until done;
216        (* One character too many has been read into  CurrentChar . *)
217
218        q^.next := nil;
219        p^.name.length := i;      A small efficiency: only the next field of the last letter is assigned nil.
220        ReadAtom := p
221     end; (* ReadAtom *)
222
223   function GetRest: list;
224      (* Process  l_1 l_2 ... l_n )  of an empty or complex list. *)
225      (* If there is no  l_1 l_2 ... l_n  then the list is  ( ) .  Otherwise
226         form the list recursively as
227            cons( l_1 , list formed by  GetRest  of  l_2 l_3 ... l_n ) )
228      *)
229      var p, q: list;
```

```
230        begin
231          SkipBlanks;
232          if CurrentChar.ch = ')'
233            then begin
```

This maintains the invariant for the next call to GetRest *(and* readlist*). This happens in situations where the input is* (... (...) ...)

The final recursive call to GetRest *when processing this list consumes this parentheses.*

There will be another call to GetRest *(and possibly* readlist*) to consume the input starting from here.*

```
234               ReadClean(CurrentChar); (* advance over  )  . *)
```

```
235               GetRest := NILL
```
This is better than GetRest := nil *since it makes the code less dependent on the internal representation of lists.*

```
236            end
237          else begin
238                (* cons( readlist, GetRest );
239                   but we cannot use  cons  directly since arguments
240                   are not necessarily evaluated left to right and
241                    readlist  and  GetRest  have side effects. *)
242                p := readlist;
243                q := GetRest;
244                GetRest := cons(p,q)
245             end
246        end; (* GetRest *)
247
248    begin (* readlist *)
249      SkipBlanks;
250      (* We expect either an atom or opening  ( . *)
251      if CurrentChar.endfile
252        then begin
253                writeln('ERROR -- error in  readlist  (unexpected end-of-file)');
254                halt
255             end
```
See the annotation at line 201.
```
256      else if CurrentChar.ch in ['a'..'z','A'..'Z'] (* ASCII ASSUMED *)
257        then readlist := ReadAtom (* atoms start with a letter *)
```
On entry to ReadAtom *the invariant holds.* CurrentChar *contains the first character of the atom.*
```
258      else if CurrentChar.ch = '('
259        then begin
260                (* The opening and closing parentheses, while necessary for
261                   determining the start and end of the list, do not form
262                   part of the internal representation of the list.
263                *)
264                ReadClean(CurrentChar); (* advance over  (  . *)
265                readlist := GetRest
266             end
```
This makes the invariant hold for GetRest*.*
```
267      else    begin
268                writeln('ERROR -- error in  readlist  (letter or "(" expected)');
269                halt
270             end
271    end; (* readlist *)
272
```

```
273  (* procedure writelist(p: list); *)
274  procedure writelist;
275    (*  writelist  writes the external representation of  p . *)
276    const LINELEN    = 79;   (* safe screen width *)
277          LEADER     = '  '; (* for indentation of lines after the first *)
278          LENofLEADER = 2;
279          NILSYMBOL  = '()'; (* or possibly  '( )'  *)
280          LENofNIL   = 2;
281
282    var count: integer;     (* The number of characters printed on the current
283                               output line. *)
284        CRIssued: boolean; (* Was a carriage return issued by  CheckRoom . *)
285
286    procedure CheckRoom(numchars: integer; var ReturnIssued: boolean);
287      (* Determine if the object to print will fit on the current line.
288         If not, issue a carriage return (and indent the next line).  Don't
289         actually print the object, since it might be an intersublist blank.
290      *)
291      begin
292        if count + numchars > LINELEN (* does it fit *)
293          then begin
294                  writeln;        (* no *)
295                  ReturnIssued := true;
296                  write(LEADER); (* indent subsequent lines *)
297                  count := LENofLEADER
298               end
299          else ReturnIssued := false
300      end; (* CheckRoom *)
301
302    procedure RecWriteList(p: list);
303      (* Write out a list recursively. *)
304      var q: list; (* really ^cell *)
305          r: PtrToLetter;
306      begin
307        if null(p)
308          then begin
309                  CheckRoom(LENofNIL,CRIssued);
310                  write(NILSYMBOL);
311                  count := count + LENofNIL
312               end
313          else if atom(p)
314            then begin
315                    (* In the case of a very long atom, even starting it on a new
316                       line might not prevent line overflow, but the atom will
317                       overflow as little as possible.
318                    *)
319                    CheckRoom(p^.name.length,CRIssued);
```

79 is safer than 80 because some terminals issue their own carriage return as soon as the 80th space is written into. The carriage return generated by the program would then cause occasional double spacing.

While not absolutely necessary, this prevents () from being split over a line boundary and allows the empty list to be printed as ( ), instead of (), if we so desire.

Comments like this one indicate that the programmer has thought of all the contingencies.

```
320                    r := p^.name.identifier;
321                    while r <> nil do
322                      begin
323                        write(r^.ch);
324                        r := r^.next
325                      end;
326                    count := count + p^.name.length
327                end
328        else   begin
329                    (* A complex list is... *)
330                    CheckRoom(1,CRIssued); (* ...a left parenthesis... *)
331                    write('(');
332                    count := count + 1;
333
334                    (* ...followed by a listing of its sublists... *)
335                    q := p;
336                    RecWriteList(q^.first);
```

Since p *is a call-by-value parameter, we don't really need* q. *We could just as readily use and modify* p, *but to do so seems aesthetically unpleasing.*

There is definitely an l_1. *It is printed without a preceding blank.*

```
337                    q := q^.rest;
338                    while q <> nil do
339                      begin
340                        (* l_2 through l_n are each preceded by a blank.  This code
341                           might leave a harmless intersublist blank at the end of
342                           a line, that is, the blank might be written, only to
343                           discover afterwards that the next object doesn't fit
344                           on the line.
345                        *)
346                        CheckRoom(1,CRIssued);
```

This comment also shows that the programmer has carefully analyzed the workings of the program.

```
347                        if not CRIssued
348                          then begin write(' '); count := count + 1 end;
349                        RecWriteList(q^.first);
350                        q := q^.rest
351                      end;
```

The intersublist blank is not written at the beginning of a line.

```
352
353                    CheckRoom(1,CRIssued); (* ...followed by a right parenthesis. *)
354                    write(')');
355                    count := count + 1
356                end
357    end; (* RecWriteList *)
358
359  begin (* writelist *)
360    count := 0;         (* Nothing has been written so far. *)
361    RecWriteList(p); (* Recursively write out the entire list... *)
362    writeln              (* ...and place a carriage return at its end. *)
363  end; (* writelist *)
364
365
```

```
366 (* Service Routines *)
367 (* procedure InitIO; *)
368 procedure InitIO;
369    (* This procedure initializes the input stream for a sequence of calls
370       to  readlist .
371    *)
372    begin
373      ReadClean(CurrentChar)
374    end; (* InitIO *)
```

CHAPTER 5

NERO—THE ROMAN CALCULATOR

The following memorandum was recently sent to the president of Archimedes Computing by the head of research.

```
From:     Pythagoras, Head of Research
To:       Archimedes, President
Subject:  The Model 19 hand calculator
```

Sales of our new Model 19 hand calculator have been much slower than expected. To ascertain why, the marketing staff undertook an extensive survey which revealed that adding open and close parenthesis keys, so that complex expressions like

```
    IX * (XXI - XVIII) * (VIII*(III + VII) + XIV)
```

can be evaluated without writing down intermediate results, is an unqualified success. However, another of our innovations, the introduction of the Arabic digital interface for input and output, has met with significant consumer resistance. Our customers just don't like typing

```
    9 * (21 - 18) * (8*(3 + 7) + 14)
```

and getting an answer of 2538, instead of the more familiar MMDXXXVIII. There appears to be no problem with our use of binary arithmetic internally, as this is not visible to the user. Since the adoption of binary arithmetic has enhanced our performance significantly, I propose we retain it, but that we accede to the wishes of potential customers and market an Enhanced Model XIX with traditional Roman interface.

From this was born Nero—The Roman Calculator. ◘

5.1 LANGUAGES

In approaching the problem of simulating a hand calculator that uses Roman numerals, two overwhelming difficulties come immediately to mind: how are we going to make the computer "understand" a complex arithmetic expression, and how are we going to convert back and forth between Roman numerals and the computer's internal representation of integers. Although the number of lines of code needed to perform these two tasks is about the same, the first is by far the more difficult. How computers "understand" arithmetic expressions is something that just might have piqued your curiosity since your first exposure to programming. After all, the ordering of the steps in a computation doesn't always follow a left-to-right scan of the expression. As an example, the evaluation of the expression in Pythagoras' letter takes six steps:

- First, we subtract 18 from 21.
- Then we multiply the result by 9, getting 27.
- Next we evaluate the internal parenthetical expression, $3 + 7$.
- We then multiply the result by the 8 to its left, getting 80.
- We then add the 14, getting 94.
- Finally, we multiply the 27 obtained four steps ago by 94, getting the final answer of 2538.

As humans, we solve this problem by scanning back and forth, keeping track of where parenthetical groups start and end, accumulating partial results along the way. We also expect that real-life expressions will be so simple that we can keep the whole process in our heads. While such a heuristic approach may work for humans, it isn't a very good starting point from which to write a computer program that evaluates expressions. Finding a systematic way to deal with this problem was the main task faced by the first compiler writers—we will benefit from their years of struggle.

Before we concern ourselves with how to write a program that understands arithmetic expressions, we need to make a long, but necessary, digression. First, we will study a mechanism for describing legitimate arithmetic expression. Only then will we consider how to incorporate the ideas into a program. The descriptive method, known as ***context-free grammars***, was developed independently in the late 1950s by Noam Chomsky, who was studying natural language comprehension, and by John Backus and Peter Naur, who were involved in the specification of ALGOL, a precursor of Pascal. Normally we begin by having in mind a particular ***language***.

> *A language is a set of strings over some alphabet.*

Examples of languages

Some examples are

$$\{ 0^n 1^m 0^{n+m} \mid n, m > 0 \}$$

Example 1

Here 0 and 1 are not numbers. They are just symbols (they could just as well have been *a* and *b*). The notation 0^n does not mean to exponentiate, but to write down n zeros in a row, so $0^n 1^m 0^{n+m}$ means

$$\underbrace{000\cdots00}_{n \text{ times}}\underbrace{111\cdots11}_{m \text{ times}}\underbrace{000\cdots00}_{n+m \text{ times}}$$

This language has infinitely many strings, and could have been written, less clearly, as

$$\{0100, 001000, 011000, 00010000, 00110000, 01110000, \ldots\}$$

The fourth string in the above enumeration has $n = 3$ and $m = 1$.

$$\boxed{\{\, ww^R \mid w \in (0+1)^+ \,\}}$$ *Example 2*

This is the set of all even-length strings, in which the second half (the w^R) is a mirror image (the R stands for *reverse*) of the first half (the w). w itself is any string of 0's and 1's of length one or more (the $w \in (0+1)^+$). In "$w \in (0+1)^+$" the plus sign in the exponent means *one or more times* (that is, $w \in \{\, (0+1)^n \mid n > 0 \,\}$), and the plus sign of "$(0+1)$" means *or*, (that is, for each character of w there is complete freedom to choose either a 0 or a 1). Typical strings in this language are 010010 ($w = 010$), 01111110 ($w = 0111$) and 0000 ($w = 00$).

$$\boxed{\text{The set of strings of balanced parentheses.}}$$ *Example 3*

This set consists of those strings of "(" and ")" in which the total number of each are the same and in a left-to-right scan the number of left parentheses never falls behind the number of right parentheses. This language can be viewed as a simplification of the input to the Model XIX calculator, because the strings in this language are what remain if we systematically delete all the operators and operands from the strings in the language of arithmetic expressions. Typical strings in the language are (( ) (( ))) and (( )) ( ) (( ) ( )), but (( ) (and (( ))) ( ) (are not. The first of these does not have an equal number of left and right parentheses, whereas in the second, the right parentheses "get ahead" of the left parentheses.

$$\boxed{\begin{array}{l} \text{The set of arithmetic expressions involving parentheses,} \\ \text{(positive) integers, and the four arithmetic operators,} \\ \text{plus, minus, times, and divide.} \end{array}}$$ *Example 4*

This is the language we face in the Nero Project.

$$\boxed{\text{All the syntactically legal Pascal programs.}}$$ *Example 5*

The restriction *syntactically legal* means that semantic considerations such as "is i declared twice in the same block?" or "is a variable of type `real` passed by reference to a formal parameter of type `integer`?" are not being considered.

Being a bit more formal, we begin by defining an ***alphabet***.   *Alphabets*

> *An alphabet is a finite set of symbols, to which no meaning is attached.*

An alphabet is usually denoted by the symbol Σ or by the letter T. T is an abbreviation for the word ***terminals***. In our first two examples, $\Sigma = \{0, 1\}$ and in our third, $\Sigma = \{(,)\}$.

Our fourth example raises a fine point: an alphabet is supposed to be finite, and while the parentheses and the operators contribute six symbols to the alphabet, there are infinitely many numbers. When describing valid arithmetic expressions we are not concerned with the values of the numbers—we can consider the concept of "number" a single symbol. So our alphabet has seven symbols. The same situation arises in our last example: in terms of the syntax, one variable is just as good as any other. Together, "variables" comprise one symbol.

This example illustrates another fine point: a symbol does not have to correspond to a single printed character. In Pascal, the keyword `while` is thought of as a single, unbreakable symbol, not as the five symbols w, h, i, l, and e. Of course, we have to type five characters into our Pascal programs, but we think of `while` as a single concept. The conversion of the stream of characters, symbols in the ASCII alphabet, into a string of symbols in Σ is known as *lexical analysis*. It can be viewed as a preprocessing step imposed by the real-world nature of the input. Our program for the Nero Project will require a lexical analyzer—while most of the translations are immediate (the characters for parentheses and the arithmetic operators translate into themselves), lexical analysis is where we will convert Roman numerals into integers that the computer can manipulate.

Strings and languages

One step up from alphabets are **strings**. A string, like a line in geometry, is one of those primitive, undefinable concepts that we all know. It is just a sequence of symbols from the alphabet, written back to back. Because we are English speakers, we implicitly understand that the symbols are written from left to right. If our alphabet is $\Sigma = \{a, b\}$, then some typical strings are *aab*, *bbabb*, and *abababa*. One important aspect of a string is that it must be of finite length.

There is one pesky detail concerning "finite length." Strings of length 4 or 5, or even 100, pose no problems. If a string has length one, then it is just a single alphabet symbol. But can a string have length zero? And if so, what does it look like and how do we write it on paper? The answer is "yes," but writing down the **empty string** is a bit of a problem. Since it is composed of no symbols it doesn't take up any space or use any ink, so it is hard to see. By convention, we give the empty string a name, ϵ, though some authors use λ. ϵ is *not* a symbol of the alphabet. It is just a visual placeholder for the empty string. One question you might ask is: why allow the empty string anyway? Part of the answer is that it is the identity element for the basic operation on strings, **concatenation**. If s_1 and s_2 are strings, then the string $s = s_1 s_2$, formed by first writing down the symbols of s_1 and then writing down the symbols of s_2 without any break, is their concatenation. If $s_1 = 011$ and $s_2 = 00$, then $s_1 s_2 = 01100$. As this example shows, normally $s_1 s_2 \neq s_2 s_1$. We say that the concatenation operation is not commutative. It is associative, however, in that for any three strings $(s_1 s_2)s_3 = s_1(s_2 s_3)$. The empty string acts as the identity element for concatenation, just like zero is the identity element for addition: for any string, s, we have $s\epsilon = \epsilon s = s$.

A **language**, or more properly, **a language over an alphabet** Σ, is any set of strings composed of symbols from Σ. Unlike the alphabet, which must be a finite set of symbols, or strings, each of which must be of finite length, a language can be infinite. All five of our examples are infinite. While there is no restriction on the set of strings that taken together form a language—any mishmash of strings, with no underlying rhyme or reason, will do—we usually have a language in mind before we begin. This is certainly the case in the Nero Project, where the language we have in mind is the set of all arithmetic expressions. Because a language is just a set, it can be specified in any way a set can be specified: by listing all its members, by giving a rule that determines whether any particular string is or isn't in the set, or in some other manner. What we will be pursuing in the next pages is a systematic way to describe languages, one that will lead us to a method for "understanding" them and for mechanically determining if a string is or isn't in a particular language.

We end this section by looking at one more detail. Since any set of strings drawn from the alphabet Σ is a language, does that make the empty set a language? And is this the same language as $\{\epsilon\}$? The answer to the first question is "yes." Since any set of strings defines a language, the empty set is, by definition, a language, the language containing no strings at all. But it is not the same language as $\{\epsilon\}$. This is a language that contains one string. The string it contains just happens to be the empty string. This is another reason for having a symbol to denote the empty string. Without it, { } would be ambiguous. It could either mean the empty set, or the set containing the invisible-to-the-eye empty string.

5.2 CONTEXT-FREE GRAMMARS

We are ready to get to the heart of our definitional system. We will do this mostly by example, starting with the first of the five languages given earlier, $\{0^n1^m0^{n+m} \mid n, m > 0\}$. The *productions* of the context free grammar that generate this language are

Nonterminals and productions

$$S \rightarrow 0S0$$
$$S \rightarrow 0T0$$
$$T \rightarrow 1T0$$
$$T \rightarrow 10$$

The presence of the 0's and 1's makes sense, since they are the terminals of the language we wish to describe. The S and T are *nonterminals*. The "$\rightarrow$" is a symbol that is used in defining productions. Though we don't yet know how they come about, or how to use them, you should think of each nonterminal as responsible for defining a portion of a string. To make this a bit more concrete, English has a very large terminal vocabulary, something on the order of a million words, but the words are divided into a limited number of classes, like *nouns*, *verbs*, and *adjectives*. At a higher level, sentences consist of *subjects*, *direct objects*, *indirect objects*, *prepositional phrases*, *subordinate clauses*, and the like. These class concepts are the nonterminals of English. In our small example, S is responsible for generating the entire string, and in particular, the n zeros on the left and the rightmost n of the $n + m$ zeros on the right, while the T is responsible for generating the m ones and the m remaining zeros on the right. All of this may seem like a jumble of words—it all will become clear when you see how productions are used to derive strings.

Every language has its grammar, or several competing grammars, each with its own set of nonterminals and productions, but the rules for applying the productions remain the same. The strategy is to start with one special nonterminal, called the *sentence* or *start symbol*, usually denoted by S, and to write it down on a line by itself, so:

$$S$$

We then repeatedly apply this rule:

- If the current line contains only terminals, stop.
- Otherwise, choose any nonterminal on the line and then choose any production for which the nonterminal on the left of the arrow matches the chosen nonterminal.
- Write a new line beneath the old one by copying the old one, but replace the chosen nonterminal by what is on the right-hand side of the chosen production.

Although the second step seems to imply free choice, this rule is not applied blindly. We need to look at where we want to go. For example, if our goal is to derive 0011100000, then in the first application of the rule we have no choice. The first and second productions appear to apply, but if we choose the second we get

| (0) | S |
| (1) | $0T0$ |

and on the next application, no matter which production we use to replace the T, we will get a string that starts 01..., and we will never be able to arrive at

0011100000. Therefore, given our goal of deriving 0011100000, we see we need to choose the first production, replacing the S by $0S0$.

We repeat this process, only now our starting point is $0S0$. Looking at where we are trying to go, we see that again there is no choice: to derive a string that begins 001... we must apply the second production, getting

(0)	S
(1)	$0S0$
(2)	$00T00$

The only other applicable choice was $S \rightarrow 0S0$, but then we would have wound up with $00S00$ and on the next application of the rule we would be forced to construct the string 000..., which cannot lead us to 0011100000, since there is no mechanism for erasing symbols. From $00T00$, we see that in order to get to 0011100000 we need to apply the third production twice, and then we need to apply the fourth production. This will give us 0011100000. Since it is a string of terminals, we stop. The complete derivation is shown in Figure 5–1.

It should not be hard to see that (*i*) for every string in $\{0^n1^m0^{n+m} \mid n, m > 0\}$ we can come up with a derivation, and (*ii*) anything we can derive, no matter how we go about it, will be a string of the form $0^n1^m0^{n+m}$. We say that we have a context-free grammar for the language.

EXERCISE 5–1   Give the derivations for 0001100000 and 0100. Why can you not derive 001100, a string not in the language?

Of course, developing a context-free grammar that describes a prespecified language is a bit of an art, one that develops only with practice. It helps to look at more examples. The grammar for our second language is even simpler than our previous grammar. It is

$$S \rightarrow 0S0$$
$$S \rightarrow 1S1$$
$$S \rightarrow 00$$
$$S \rightarrow 11$$

FIGURE 5–1   The Derivation of 0011100000

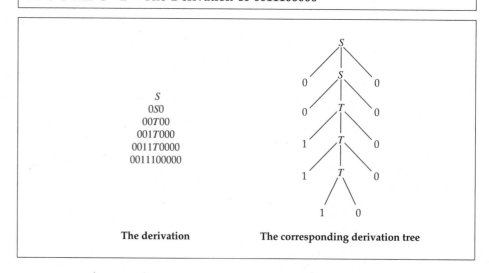

| The derivation | The corresponding derivation tree |

The derivation of 00100100 is four steps long.

(0)	S	(apply production 1)
(1)	$0S0$	(apply production 1)
(2)	$00S00$	(apply production 2)
(3)	$001S100$	(apply production 3)
(4)	00100100	

Again, it is easy to see that any string in $\{\, ww^R \mid w \in (0+1)^+ \,\}$ can be derived. But just as important, no string not in $\{\, ww^R \mid w \in (0+1)^+ \,\}$ can be derived by any sequence of steps, no matter how long or how twisted. This is very important.

> *Just because all the desired strings can be derived if we choose carefully which productions to apply when does not mean we have found a grammar for the language. It must also be the case that any enemy, bent on foiling our efforts, cannot derive even a single string not in the language.*

Sometimes little things make a big difference in the grammars we produce. Suppose in the first example we had allowed n and m to equal zero, instead of requiring them to be one or more. A grammar for this new language, which includes additional strings like 111000 ($n = 0$), 0000 ($m = 0$), and even ϵ (both n and m equal zero), is

$$S \rightarrow 0S0$$
$$S \rightarrow T$$
$$T \rightarrow 1T0$$
$$T \rightarrow \epsilon$$

To derive $0^n1^m0^{n+m}$ we start with S, apply the first production n times, then the second production, then the third production m times, and finally the fourth production, which makes the T disappear—the ϵ is swallowed in the final string, unless the entire string is ϵ, producing, for example, 0011100000 and not $00111\epsilon00000$.

Similarly, in the second example, if we had allowed w to be chosen from $(0 + 1)^*$, the set of all strings of length zero or greater, with each element of the string chosen independently from 0 and 1, the grammar corresponding would be

$$S \rightarrow 0S0$$
$$S \rightarrow 1S1$$
$$S \rightarrow \epsilon$$

These two examples might appear a bit silly. After all, $\{\, 0^n1^m0^{n+m} \mid n, m > 0 \,\}$ describes the language very precisely and writing a computer program to determine if an input string is of this form seems a simple matter, even if we are required to detect illegalities like invalid characters and strings that do not consist of three groups, such as the string 00110000110. Can we do something more interesting with grammars? Can we describe the language of arithmetic expressions or the syntax of Pascal? One of several possible grammars for arithmetic expressions is

The standard expression grammar

$$E \rightarrow E + T \mid E - T \mid T$$
$$T \rightarrow T * F \mid T / F \mid F$$
$$F \rightarrow \texttt{num} \mid (E)$$

We have introduced a new symbol, the vertical bar, "|". This really adds nothing. It is just a shorthand for saying that there are three productions all of whose left-hand sides are E and whose right-hand sides, respectively, are $E + T$, $E - T$, and T. It allows us to write the productions on three lines, instead of eight.

But this grammar, known as the **standard expression grammar**, does introduce a host of new concepts. We see that the sentence symbol does not have to be S. Here it is E, which stands for *expression*. T stands for *term* and F stands for *factor*. Also notice that while our previous grammars were recursive, meaning that S on the left was defined in terms of S on the right, here the recursion can be a bit more indirect. E is defined in terms of T, which is, in turn, defined in terms of F, which then refers back to E. And most important of all, in derivations using this grammar we now have more choices to make. In all our previous examples we had to decide on which production to apply, but there was only one nonterminal on the current line, so the choice of which nonterminal to replace was taken away. Consider the derivation of

$$\text{num} * (\text{num} - \text{num}) * (\text{num} * (\text{num} + \text{num}) + \text{num})$$

the expression in Pythagoras' letter. One possible derivation is

(0)	E
(1)	T
(2)	$T * F$
(3)	$T * F * F$
(4)	$F * F * F$
(5)	$\text{num} * F * F$
(6)	$\text{num} * (E) * F$
(7)	$\text{num} * (E - T) * F$
(8)	$\text{num} * (T - T) * F$
(9)	$\text{num} * (F - T) * F$
(10)	$\text{num} * (\text{num} - T) * F$

$$\vdots$$

This will end after 27 steps. In this derivation we have systematically chosen the leftmost nonterminal as the one to replace. This is known as a **leftmost derivation**. We could just as well have chosen the rightmost nonterminal every time or we could have jumped around in a haphazard manner. Despite having multiple derivations for most strings, where in our previous examples every string in the language had exactly one derivation, this grammar has the two properties that every grammar for the language of arithmetic expressions must have:

> *Every arithmetic expression can be derived and, conversely, any string of terminals that can be derived is a valid arithmetic expression.*

The power of context-free grammars should now be clear. To someone who understands the rules of the game, we have described arithmetic expressions in just three short lines! Try to do that in English, without falling back on the intuitive understanding of arithmetic expressions that we have built up over many years. You would need to explain balanced parentheses, that an expression cannot start or end with an operator, or have two adjacent operators, or two adjacent operands.

Because of the freedom we have in choosing the nonterminal to replace next, *Derivation trees* there is no longer a unique derivation of most expressions. The expression

num ∗ (num − num) ∗ (num ∗ (num + num) + num)

has thousands of derivations. But in some sense they are all the same. For any arithmetic expression you derive using this grammar, once you choose a particular nonterminal to replace, no matter when you get around to choosing it, there is only one production that can be applied. In deriving the expression in Pythagoras' letter, at some point the *sentential form*, the name given to strings of terminals and nonterminals that can appear during a derivation, must end in $\cdots \ast F$ and the production that must be applied is $F \rightarrow (E)$. And at some point this E will have to be replaced by $E + T$.

To capture this broadened sense of uniqueness we need the concept of a *derivation tree*. Using the grammar of our first example, the derivation tree for 0011100000 is shown on the right of Figure 5–1; using the standard expression grammar, the derivation tree for Pythagoras' expression is shown in Figure 5–2.

The derivation tree captures, in a single picture, which productions were applied to which nonterminals, but it throws away the extraneous information regarding the order of their application.

FIGURE 5–2   The Derivation of the Arithmetic Expression in Pythagoras' Letter

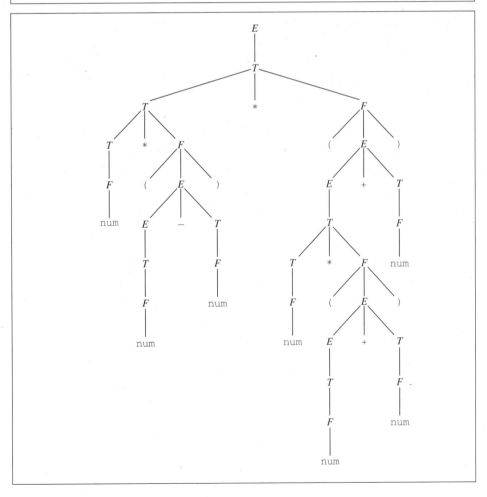

It does not have to be the case that a grammar implicitly defines a unique derivation tree for each string in the language. Consider the following perfectly legal grammar that describes the set of strings of balanced parentheses:

$$S \to SS \mid (\, S\,) \mid \epsilon$$

Clearly, every string that can be derived from this grammar has balanced parentheses, since the only way to get any at all is to use the second production. It is also not hard to see that any string of balanced parentheses can be derived. Take, for example, the string

$$(\,(\,)\,(\,)\,)\,(\,)\,(\,(\,(\,)\,)\,)$$

It can be viewed as

$$\underbrace{(\,(\,)\,(\,)\,)}_{S} \quad \underbrace{(\,)}_{S} \quad \underbrace{(\,(\,(\,)\,)\,)}_{S}$$

and a sequence of three S's can be derived using the first production. Then each S can be expanded using $S \to (\,S\,)$ and we can proceed to tackle each part recursively in its own time—there is very little to do for the middle part, just apply $S \to \epsilon$.

But $(\,(\,)\,(\,)\,)\,(\,)\,(\,(\,(\,)\,)\,)$ and some other strings have more than one possible derivation tree. The essence of the problem is shown in Figure 5–3, where we see that there are two ways to derive the sentential form SSS. If every string in the language has only one derivation tree we say the grammar is *unambiguous*. Our standard expression grammar is unambiguous. Conversely, if even one string has two or more derivation trees we say the grammar is *ambiguous*. Ambiguity is a property of grammars, not languages. Some other grammar may describe the same language and be unambiguous. For example,

$$\begin{aligned} S &\to ST \mid \epsilon \\ T &\to (\,S\,) \end{aligned}$$

is an unambiguous grammar for the set of strings of balanced parentheses.

EXERCISE 5–2   What is the unique derivation tree for $(\,)\,(\,)\,)\,(\,)\,(\,(\,(\,)\,)\,)$ using the above grammar?

FIGURE 5–3   Why There Are Two Derivation Trees for $(\,(\,)\,(\,)\,)\,(\,)\,(\,(\,(\,)\,)\,)$

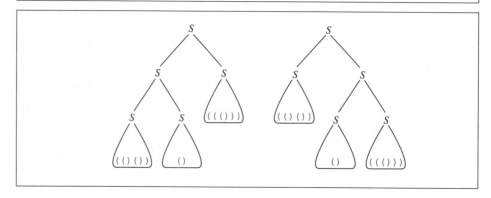

EXERCISE 5–3 Though possibly what was intended, it is a bit annoying that the language of strings of balanced parentheses contains the empty string. We have seen two grammars for this language. Modify both so the empty string is no longer derivable.

As powerful as context-free grammars are, they incapable of describing every language. Some simple languages for which it is impossible to give a context-free grammar are

Not all languages have context-free grammars

- $\{0^n1^n0^n \mid n \geq 1\}$ and
- $\{1^n \mid n$ is a prime number$\}$

Attempting to devise grammars that describe these languages might convince you that it is not possible to do so, but that is not a proof—it might just mean you are too inexperienced to see the trick. While we are in no position to prove that these languages cannot be described by context-free grammars, this claim can be proven.

One last remark before we leave this long digression into context-free grammars and return to the programming of the Nero Project: why are they called *context-free* grammars? There are other grammatical systems, which allow complex expressions to appear on the left-hand side of the arrow. The general form of our productions is $A \to \beta$, where A is some nonterminal and β is the replacement string. When the productions have the general form $\alpha A \gamma \to \alpha \beta \gamma$, which means the nonterminal A can be replaced by β, but only when surrounded by the strings α and γ, then we call the grammar a *phrase-structure grammar*. In the grammars we have been considering, the ability to replace a nonterminal by what is on the right-hand side is not affected by the "context" surrounding the nonterminal. Hence the name: context-free grammars. A language for which it is possible to give a context-free grammar is called a *context-free language*.

EXERCISE 5–4 Give context-free grammars for each of the following languages. Wherever possible, your grammar should be unambiguous.

1. $\{0^n1^n \mid n \geq 1\}$
2. $\{1^n0^m1^m \mid n, m \geq 1\}$
3. $\{0^n1^m \mid n \geq m \geq 0\}$
4. $\{0^n1^n0^m1^m \mid n, m \geq 1\}$
5. $\{0^n1^m0^m1^n \mid n, m \geq 1\}$
6. $\{0^n1^n \mid n \geq 1\} \cup \{0^n1^{2n} \mid n \geq 1\}$
7. { all sequences of zeros and ones with an equal number of each }
8. $\{0^n1^m \mid 0 < n \leq m \leq 2n\}$
9. $\{0^n1^n0^m1^m \mid n, m \geq 1\} \cup \{0^n1^m0^m1^n \mid n, m \geq 1\}$

5.3 RECURSIVE DESCENT PARSING

The standard expression grammar is not the only grammar for arithmetic expressions. It is not even the only unambiguous grammar describing them. Another is

Mimicking semantic content

$$E \to E + F \mid E - F \mid E * F \mid E / F \mid F$$
$$F \to \texttt{num} \mid (E)$$

Somehow, the standard expression grammar feels "right," whereas this grammar doesn't feel right at all. The standard expression grammar seems to capture our understanding of what an expression means, while this grammar does not. Why is this? A look at Figure 5–4 shows us why. It is very easy to evaluate an expression given its derivation tree—ignoring details of internal representation, the recursive pseudocode given in Figure 5–5 is only a few lines long. *But this works only because the derivation tree models our understanding of the precedence and associativity of operators!* The same procedure applied to the derivation tree produced by

$$E \rightarrow E + F \mid E - F \mid E * F \mid E / F \mid F$$
$$F \rightarrow \text{num} \mid (\ E\ )$$

doesn't give the correct answer, not because the procedure is wrong, but because the derivation tree is "wrong." While uniquely deriving $4 + 5*8$, this grammar places the multiplication near the root of the tree, which does not correspond to the semantics of arithmetic expressions.

Another unambiguous grammar for expressions is

$$E \rightarrow T + E \mid T - E \mid T$$
$$T \rightarrow F * T \mid F / T \mid F$$
$$F \rightarrow \text{num} \mid (\ E\ )$$

This grammar looks almost the same as the standard expression grammar, and it respects the precedence of the operators, but like our second grammar for arithmetic expressions it also is not "correct." The expression $17 - 8 - 6$ is supposed to be interpreted as $(17 - 8) - 6$ and not $17 - (8 - 6)$ which, as Figure 5–6 shows, is how this third grammar interprets it.

It is important to keep in mind that this discussion of "correctness" is motivated by semantic considerations. These concerns lie outside the grammatical framework of the previous section. All three grammars for arithmetic expressions are equally good from a formal perspective: they all generate the desired language and they are all unambiguous. This doesn't mean they are equally good for developing a program to evaluate expressions.

FIGURE 5–4   Derivation Trees for 4 + 5∗8

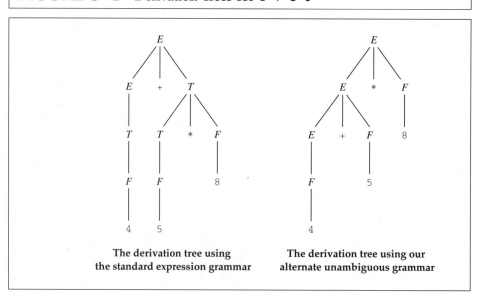

The derivation tree using
the standard expression grammar

The derivation tree using our
alternate unambiguous grammar

FIGURE 5–5 Evaluating Expressions from Their Derivation Trees

```
function EvalExpr(p: ^Node): integer;
  (* Evaluate the expression pointed to by p *)
  begin
    if p  points to a num
      then return ( the number p  points to)
    else if p  points to a single-child node
                  (*  E → T, T → F
                        or F →  num*)
      then return (EvalExpr(p^.child))
    else if p  points to F → (E)
      then return (EvalExpr(p^.second_child))
    else    begin (* E → E + T, E → E − T, T → T * F or  T → T/F*)
            left_operand    := EvalExpr(p^.first_child);
            right_operand   := EvalExpr(p^.third_child);
            return ( the result of applying p^.second_child to
                     left_operand and right_operand)
          end
  end; (* EvalExpr *)
```

The main task, which we are about to tackle now that we have built up the necessary background, is known as *parsing*. A *parser* for a language specified by a grammar is a program that determines whether or not an input string is in the language. Additionally, if the string is in the language, it outputs a derivation tree. As a practical matter, we don't always want the output of the parser to be a derivation tree. In the case of a Pascal compiler we want it to be an object file that can be directly executed on the hardware, and in the Nero Project, which simulates a calculator where expressions are evaluated and then discarded, we might prefer to integrate the building of the derivation tree with the recursive walk that evaluates it, so that the tree need never be present explicitly.

Recursive descent parsing, invented in the early 1960s, is popular because it is easy to understand and implement. The method does have its drawbacks, however. The most serious is that not every grammar can form the basis for a recursive descent parser, even when the grammar captures the semantics of the language and generates it unambiguously. Unfortunately for us, the standard expression grammar is one of these unusable grammars—we will need to develop some tricks for massaging unusable grammars into usable ones.

In our initial examination of recursive descent parsing our goal will be to determine if the input string is part of the language described by the grammar. Adding code to output the derivation tree or some other useful representation will turn out to be a simple matter, taking just a few more lines. So that we can have a concrete example to parallel our abstract discussion we will first develop a recursive descent parser for the language of strings of balanced parentheses. This is a good choice because it is related to arithmetic expressions and is complicated enough to be interesting, but has no semantics to muddy the waters. In a recursive descent parser there is one function corresponding to each nonterminal of the grammar. The pseudocode for a typical nonterminal, A, is given in Figure 5–7. The entire parsing process is initiated by calling the function corresponding to the sentence symbol with `l` set to `1` and `r` set to the length of the string being examined.

Converting a Context-Free Grammar into a Recursive Descent Parser

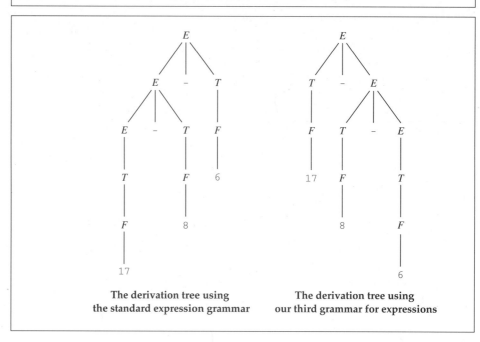

FIGURE 5–6   Derivation Trees for 17 – 8 – 6

The derivation tree using
the standard expression grammar

The derivation tree using
our third grammar for expressions

This bit of pseudocode isn't terribly useful. The problem is: in the first and second steps, how are we to determine which, if any, production with A on the left-hand side can be applied and how are we to determine the partitioning of $s_l . . s_r$? For the standard expression grammar, we would need to determine if there was a + or – at the outermost level (to see if we should apply $E \rightarrow E + T$ or $E \rightarrow E - T$, instead of $E \rightarrow T$) and would then have to find the rightmost one to perform the partitioning. *We don't want to have to do this.* We don't want to have to scan the entire substring to determine what to do. We prefer to proceed in an orderly manner, *looking at just the next unprocessed symbol of the string*, that is, just at s_l. To be able to do this we need just the right grammar. For the language of strings of balanced parentheses, the right grammar is

$$S \rightarrow T S \mid \epsilon$$
$$T \rightarrow (S)$$

The function corresponding to S can determine which production to apply by looking at just the next character:

- If there is no next character (which occurs when `l = r + 1`), it is $S \rightarrow \epsilon$.
- If the next character is a (, it is $S \rightarrow T S$.
- If the next character is a), no production applies and the string is not in the language.

It is even easier for the function corresponding to T to determine which production to apply—there is only one choice.

There is still the issue of partitioning the substring $s_l . . s_r$. It is not particularly difficult for the function for T to make its decision. To match $T \rightarrow (S)$, s_l has be a (and s_r had better be a). The interior portion of $s_l . . s_r$ must be derivable from an S. The function for T handles this by calling `S(l+1,r-1)`, letting S decide if this is possible. The function for S has a harder job. The problem occurs when it selects the production $S \rightarrow T S$. It must then decide

---

FIGURE 5–7   **An Overly Optimistic View of Recursive Descent Parsing**

```
function A(l, r: integer): ^derivation_tree;
  (* A is supposed to derive substring s_l..s_r of input string s. *)
  begin
    Determine which production, A → ···, to apply. Suppose the production
      is A → A₁A₂···A_m. If no production applies the entire string is not
      in the language.
    Partition s_l..s_r into pieces. A₁ is supposed to derive the first piece,
      A₂ is supposed to derive the second piece, etc. If A_i is a terminal
      then its corresponding piece must consist of one symbol and that
      symbol must match A_i, that is, terminals must match themselves.
    For each nonterminal, A_i, recursively call A_i with the bounds for
      its subpiece.
    Build an m-child node from the m trees and return a pointer to it.
  end; (* A *)
```

---

what portion corresponds to T and what portion corresponds to S. T ends with the matching right parenthesis. But finding this parenthesis suggests a scan of the string starting at s_l—what we said we wished to avoid.

The solution to the dilemma is to do something your mother told you never to do:

> *Put off until tomorrow what you don't absolutely have to do today.*

A more refined view of recursive descent parsing is given in Figure 5–8. While this version of `function A` determines which production to apply, it doesn't decide on the partitioning of $s_l..s_r$. Via a recursive call, it lets `A_1` consume as much input as it needs. When `A_1` returns, `l` has been advanced to the start of the subpiece that `A_2` is supposed to derive. Similarly, when `A_2` returns, more input has been consumed and `l` has been advanced to the start of the subpiece that `A_3` is supposed to derive. At the very end, when `A_m` returns, not only will `l` have been advanced to just past the end of the subpiece corresponding to A_m, it will also have been advanced to just past the end of everything A derives. In other words, `l` will have been advanced to `r+1`.

The requirement that we be able to decide solely on the basis of s_l what production to apply *severely* restricts the grammars we can use. With the standard expression grammar, when staring at the first symbol of an expression we cannot tell whether to apply $E \rightarrow E + T$, $E \rightarrow E - T$, or $E \rightarrow T$ and we cannot use this grammar to build a recursive descent parser. But we can build a recursive descent parser for strings of balanced parentheses using

$$S \rightarrow TS \mid \epsilon$$
$$T \rightarrow (S)$$

The code is given in Figure 5–9. To keep the program as simple as possible, certain error checks, such as a check for invalid characters in the input, have been omitted.

FIGURE 5–8   A More Refined View of Recursive Descent Parsing

---

```
function A(var l: integer): ^derivation_tree;
  (* A is supposed to derive s_l..s_r, even without knowing  r .
     Besides returning the derivation tree,  l  is advanced to  r+1 .
  *)
  begin
      Based only on s_l determine the production that derives s_l..s_r.
        If no production applies, the string is not in the language.
      for i := 1 to m do  (*  A → A_1A_2···A_m  *)
        if  A_i is a terminal
          then if  A_i = s_l  (* current value of  l  *)
                  then l := l + 1 (* the terminal matches the next
                                      symbol in the string *)
                  else  the string is not in the language
          else A_i(l);  (*  l  gets advanced *)
      Build an m-child node from the m trees and return a pointer to it.
  end; (* A *)
```

When presenting recursive descent parsing abstractly, it is customary to pad the string with a $ and to add the production

$$S' \rightarrow S\$$$

to the grammar, making S' the new sentence symbol. The $ corresponds to end-of-file in real input. This allows the parser to make sure that the entire input string doesn't consist of a string in the language followed by some extraneous characters. When the call to S on line 52 returns to Sprime there should be no characters left to process except the $.

One minor difference between the code of Figure 5–9 and the pseudocode of Figure 5–8 is the elimination of the parameter l. Instead of first reading the entire input string into an array and then processing the string, there is a global variable, ch, which always contains s_l. In the earlier program l is advanced when a terminal is matched; here the program just reads the next character.

There is a fundamental difference between what was presented earlier and the code of Figures 5–8 and 5–9. In Figure 5–7 where we had both l and r as parameters, if s_l was a) we had an error. Now, since r isn't specified, we are not sure when to apply $S \rightarrow \epsilon$ and when to report an error. In some circumstances it is appropriate to apply $S \rightarrow \epsilon$ when ch = ')', but in other circumstances it is not. Examining lines 41–44 of the program, we see that if the next character of the string is a (the parser applies $S \rightarrow TS$ and if it is a) or the string is completely consumed it applies $S \rightarrow \epsilon$, *whether this is appropriate or not*. Will this cause the program to reject a valid string or accept one that is not in the language? The answer is "no." First, the parser never chooses incorrectly in the sense of selecting the wrong production to apply. If it sees a (, the only choice that will allow it to generate $s_l..s_r$ is $S \rightarrow TS$. It will also apply $S \rightarrow \epsilon$ when it needs to, such as when facing the third, fifth, sixth, or seventh characters of

$$(\; (\;) \; (\;) \;) \; \$$$

FIGURE 5–9   A Recursive Descent Parser for the Language of Strings of Balanced Parentheses

```
 1  program BalancedParentheses(input,output);
 2  (* Determine if a string of left and right parentheses, terminated by
 3     a dollar sign, is a balanced string of parentheses.
 4
 5     There are no checks for illegal characters (including spaces), the dollar
 6     sign in the wrong place, or the absence of a dollar sign.
 7  *)
 8  label 99; (* error exit *)
 9  type ErrorType = (LeftParenExpected, RightParenExpected, TooManyRights);
10  var ch: char; (* one character lookahead *)
11
12  procedure ReportError(Error: ErrorType);
13    begin
14      ... (* write an appropriate message *)
15      goto 99
16    end; (* ReportError *)
17
18  procedure scan;
19    begin
20      read(ch)
21    end; (* scan *)
22
23  procedure S; forward;
24
25  procedure T;
26    (* This routine corresponds to the production
27        T --> ( S )
28    *)
29    begin
30      if ch = '(' then scan else ReportError(LeftParenExpected);
31      S;
32      if ch = ')' then scan else ReportError(RightParenExpected)
33    end; (* T *)
34
35  procedure S;
36    (* This routine corresponds to the productions
37        S --> T S
38        S --> epsilon
39    *)
40    begin
41      case ch of
42        '(':        begin T; S end; (* S --> T S *)
43        ')', '$':                   (* S --> epsilon *)
44      end
45    end; (* S *)
46
47  procedure Sprime;
48    (* This routine corresponds to the production
49        S' --> S $
50    *)
51    begin
52      S;
53      if ch <> '$' then ReportError(TooManyRights)
54    end; (* Sprime *)
55
56  begin
57    scan; (* load  ch  with  s_1  *)
58    SPrime;
59    writeln('The string was legal.');
60 99:
61  end. (* BalancedParentheses *)
```

But can it apply $S \to \epsilon$ when it shouldn't? Yes it can! It will when facing the $ in (( ) $ or the right parenthesis in position 7 of

$$(( ) ( ))) ( ) \$$$

But these errors will be caught. Consider (( )) $. The sequence of calls made by the program on this input is depicted in Figure 5–10.

The error is detected when T, expecting to find a), instead finds the $. The right parenthesis that is out of place in

$$(( ) ( ) `)) ( ) \$$$

will also be caught. The program will eventually return to Sprime, which expects to see a $. When it sees the) that is the first character of the remaining input, which is) ( ) $, it knows that the right parentheses have gotten ahead of the left ones.

EXERCISE 5–5   Add code to the program of Figure 5–9 to return the derivation tree.

EXERCISE 5–6   Why must a recursive descent parser choose the correct production based on s_l? Why can't it just successively try them all until one succeeds?

There is another view of recursive descent parsing that should be mentioned. Recursive descent parsers are sometimes called *predictive parsers*. This is because, in the for loop of Figure 5–8, when A is about to call A_i it has consumed enough of the string starting at s_l to match what is derived from $A_1 A_2 \cdots A_{i-1}$ and is "predicting" that $A_i A_{i+1} \cdots A_m$ will derive the remainder of $s_l . . s_r$. Carrying this one step further, we see that the parser is producing a leftmost derivation. The left half of the sentential form corresponds to what the parser has derived and confirmed by matching its derivation against the input. The right half of the sentential form, which "predicts" the remainder of the string, is tucked away in the partially completed for loops of the suspended recursive calls. This is illustrated in Figure 5–11 for the language of strings of balanced parentheses.

Tricks for Manipulating Grammars

To form the basis of a recursive descent parser, a grammar must satisfy the not-always-easy-to-satisfy requirement:

> *For any nonterminal-lookahead pair, there should be at most one production whose left-hand side matches the nonterminal and whose right-hand side has the potential to match the next piece of the string.*

When this requirement is satisfied the recursive descent parser can unerringly derive the string s or at some point in the derivation can declare that s is not in the language. The one production that applies, if any do at all, is the parser's only hope of deriving the next piece of s.

When a grammar is not usable we can resort to a number of tricks to make it usable. One simple trick is to change the parser. Sometimes a little more lookahead will resolve the matter. While we don't want to return to the situation created by the productions $E \to E + T$, $E \to E - T$, or $E \to T$, where the amount of lookahead required is essentially unbounded and variable, a fixed amount of

FIGURE 5–10   Locating the Error in (( ) $

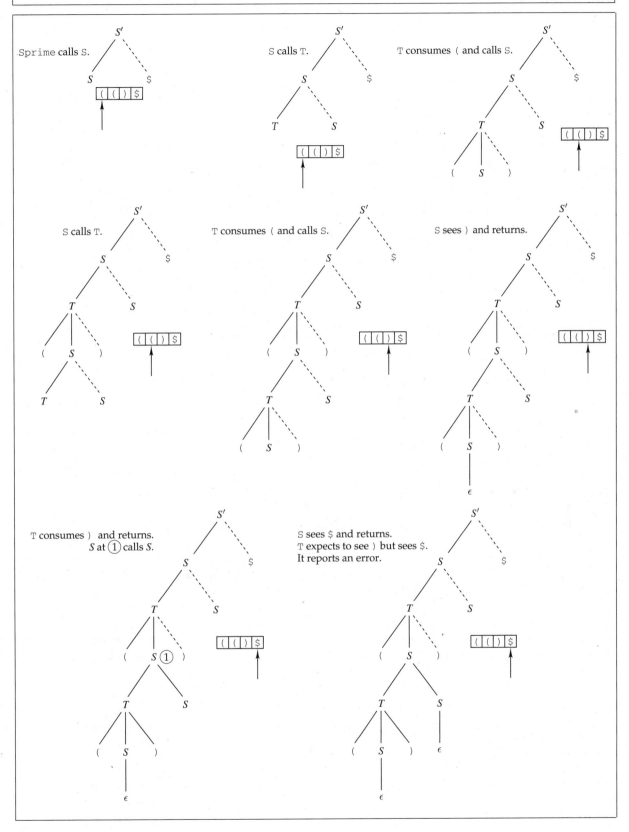

FIGURE 5–11   A Recursive Descent Parser in Operation

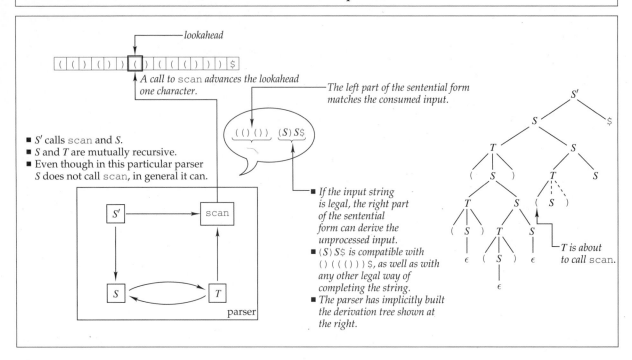

extra lookahead isn't a problem. For example, in many programming languages a statement is defined by the productions

$$\langle Stmt \rangle \rightarrow \langle label \rangle : \langle Stmt \rangle \mid \langle Unlabeled\_Stmt \rangle$$

where ⟨label⟩ is, unlike in Pascal, an identifier. One of the options for an ⟨Unlabeled_Stmt⟩ is invariably

$$\langle Unlabeled\_Stmt \rangle \rightarrow \langle variable \rangle := \langle Expr \rangle$$

where a ⟨variable⟩ is also an identifier. This makes the grammar unusable, since, when faced with ⟨Stmt⟩ and an identifier, the parser doesn't know whether to replace ⟨Stmt⟩ with ⟨label⟩ : ⟨Stmt⟩ or ⟨Unlabeled_Stmt⟩. By using two symbols of lookahead it can resolve the matter. If the next symbol is : then the correct choice is ⟨label⟩ : ⟨Stmt⟩, but if it is := (the multicharacter assignment operator symbol) then the correct choice is ⟨Unlabeled_Stmt⟩.

Left factoring   A generalization of this technique is known as ***left factoring***. To see why left factoring is needed and to see how it works, we consider a programming language construct found in BASIC, FORTRAN, and ALGOL, the `for` loop with optional variable step size. Essentially the same problem exists in Pascal, except the keywords are `to` and `downto` and the implied step sizes are 1 and −1. The relevant portion of the grammar is

$$\langle Stmt \rangle \rightarrow \text{for } \langle variable \rangle := \langle Expr \rangle \text{ to } \langle Expr \rangle \text{ step } \langle Expr \rangle \text{ do } \langle Stmt \rangle \mid$$
$$\text{for } \langle variable \rangle := \langle Expr \rangle \text{ to } \langle Expr \rangle \text{ do } \langle Stmt \rangle$$

When faced with a ⟨Stmt⟩ and a `for` the parser does not know which production to apply. Furthermore, because of the intervening expressions, no fixed amount of lookahead will suffice. This can be handled by rewriting the grammar as

$$\langle Stmt \rangle \quad \rightarrow \text{for } \langle variable \rangle := \langle Expr \rangle \text{ to } \langle Expr \rangle \langle for\_rest \rangle$$
$$\langle for\_rest \rangle \rightarrow \text{step } \langle Expr \rangle \text{ do } \langle Stmt \rangle \mid \text{do } \langle Stmt \rangle$$

Now for the combination ⟨Stmt⟩ and for there is only one choice. The code for the procedure for ⟨Stmt⟩ will contain, in the spirit of lines 41–44 of Figure 5–9, the lines

```
case symbol of
   ⋮
  for: begin
          if (symbol = for) then scan else error; (* or just  scan  *)
          variable;
          if (symbol = :=) then scan else error;
          Expr;
          if (symbol = to) then scan else error;
          Expr;
          for_rest
       end;
   ⋮
```

The procedure for ⟨for_rest⟩ will include

```
case symbol of
  step:  begin
            if (symbol = step) then scan else error; (* or just  scan  *)
            Expr;
            if (symbol = do) then scan else error;
            Stmt
         end;
  do:    begin
            if (symbol = do) then scan else error; (* or just  scan  *)
            Stmt
         end;
  else  error (* any symbol besides  step
                    and  do  are illegal *)
end
```

This grammar fragment is sometimes written as

⟨Stmt⟩ → for ⟨variable⟩ := ⟨Expr⟩ to ⟨Expr⟩ [step ⟨Expr⟩ do ⟨Stmt⟩
            | do ⟨Stmt⟩]

The symbols "[" and "]" are a convenience, just like the vertical bar. They are grouping symbols, performing the same function parentheses perform in algebraic expressions. The phrase

… ⟨Expr⟩ [step ⟨Expr⟩ do ⟨Stmt⟩ | do ⟨Stmt⟩]

means … ⟨Expr⟩, followed by one of step ⟨Expr⟩ do ⟨Stmt⟩ or do ⟨Stmt⟩. The notation suggests why the technique is called left factoring: in algebra when we write $xy + xz$ as $x(y + z)$ we say we are *factoring*. Another way to achieve the same effect is to write this grammar fragment as

⟨Stmt⟩   → for ⟨variable⟩ := ⟨Expr⟩ to ⟨Expr⟩ ⟨for_step⟩ do ⟨Stmt⟩
⟨for_step⟩ → step ⟨Expr⟩ | ε

or

⟨Stmt⟩ → for ⟨variable⟩ := ⟨Expr⟩ to ⟨Expr⟩ [step ⟨Expr⟩ | ε] do ⟨Stmt⟩

Left factoring solves many problems that arise in grammars for programming languages, but the technique is not strong enough to handle arithmetic expressions. Left factoring the productions

$$E \rightarrow E + T \mid E - T \mid T$$

yields

$$E \rightarrow E\ X \mid T$$
$$X \rightarrow +T \mid -T$$

but this still leaves the procedure E with two choices when the next symbol of the string is either a (or a num. It is just this sort of difficulty that forced us to choose the grammar

$$S \rightarrow T S \mid \epsilon$$
$$T \rightarrow (\ S\ )$$

for the language of strings of balanced parentheses, instead of

$$S \rightarrow S T \mid \epsilon$$
$$T \rightarrow (\ S\ )$$

Grammars that contain productions of the form $A \rightarrow A\alpha \mid \beta$ are called **left-recursive**. If you stare at this pair of productions for a few moments you will see that what they, taken together, really generate is

$$\beta \underbrace{\alpha\ \alpha \ldots \alpha}_{0 \text{ or more times}}$$

This same set of possibilities can be generated by replacing the productions

$$A \rightarrow A\alpha$$
$$A \rightarrow \beta$$

by

$$A \rightarrow \beta A'$$
$$A' \rightarrow \alpha A'$$
$$A' \rightarrow \epsilon$$

This substitution is known as **left recursion elimination**, and is what we did, somewhat less formally, when we selected the grammar

$$S \rightarrow T S \mid \epsilon$$
$$T \rightarrow (\ S\ )$$

over the grammar

$$S \rightarrow S T \mid \epsilon$$
$$T \rightarrow (\ S\ )$$

It also motivated the design of the grammar

$$E \rightarrow T + E \mid T - E \mid T$$
$$T \rightarrow F * T \mid F / T \mid F$$
$$F \rightarrow \text{num} \mid (\ E\ )$$

This modification works fine for the language of strings of balanced parentheses, where there are no implied semantics, but we have already seen that this alternative won't do for expressions.

The solution to our dilemma is to combine left factoring and left recursion elimination in an ad hoc manner. We can think of the three productions $E \rightarrow E + T$, $E \rightarrow E - T$, and $E \rightarrow T$ as generating

$$T \; [+|-] \; T \; [+|-] \; \cdots \; [+|-] \; T$$

that is, as many terms as desired (but at least one) separated by additive operators. Similarly, $T \rightarrow T*F$, $T \rightarrow T/F$, and $T \rightarrow F$ can be thought of as generating

$$F \; [*|/] \; F \; [*|/] \; \cdots \; [*|/] \; F$$

The productions $F \rightarrow (\;E\;)$ and $F \rightarrow$ num don't need any modification, as the one-symbol lookahead can separate a num from an $(\;E\;)$. These modified productions respect the precedence of the arithmetic operators and the left-to-right associativity of equal-strength operators, as long as we process

$$T \; [+|-] \; T \; [+|-] \; \cdots \; [+|-] \; T$$

left to right. But how do we incorporate these modified productions into our recursive descent parser? The code for the procedure corresponding to E effectively becomes the code shown in Figure 5–12. In the else clause where we return, the lookahead should be either) or $, depending on whether the E is part of an $F \rightarrow (\;E\;)$ or part of the $S' \rightarrow E\;$. We don't check this in the procedure for E. The invariant for the procedure is

> *On entry the lookahead should be the leftmost symbol derived from the E, and on exit the lookahead should be the first symbol following the entire string derived from the E.*

The actual symbol that appears in the input just past what E derives may be illegal, but that is not the concern of E. In some circumstances E cannot even tell with certainty if the next symbol is illegal. A right parenthesis, for example, isn't always legal; its legality depends on whether E was called from Sprime or F. It is better to let the caller decide whether there is an error. E just returns.

FIGURE 5–12   Parsing Expressions with a Recursive Descent Parser

```
procedure E;
  begin
    T; (* The expression must begin with a term. *)
    loop (* indefinitely -- until executing return *)
      case symbol of
        +,-: scan;
        else return (* We have seen the last term, so
                       the expression is complete. *)
      end;
      T (* Look for the term after the + or - and
           then iterate again. *)
    endloop
  end; (* E *)
```

Parsing is an excellent example of the power of invariants. The maintenance of the following invariant is essential to the correct functioning of the parser:

> *On entry to a procedure corresponding to a nonterminal the lookahead should be the leftmost symbol that the nonterminal derives, and on exit the lookahead should be the first symbol following the entire string derived by the nonterminal.*[1]

The code of Figure 5–12 is essentially what is done by the procedure `Expr` in the file `parser.p`. Except for the issue of embedding the semantics, or more precisely, actually evaluating the expression, we are ready to build a parser for expressions.

Embedding the semantics

We have converted the standard expression grammar into

$$E \rightarrow T \ [+|-] \ T \ [+|-] \ \cdots \ [+|-] \ T$$
$$T \rightarrow F \ [*|/] \ F \ [*|/] \ \cdots \ [*|/] \ F$$
$$F \rightarrow \text{num} \mid (\ E\ )$$

and the derivation tree for

$$\text{num} * (\text{num} - \text{num}) * (\text{num} * (\text{num} + \text{num}) + \text{num})$$

into the tree shown in Figure 5–13. Embedding the evaluation of the expression into the parsing process is not difficult. The procedure of Figure 5–5 needs to be modified slightly to account for the new shape of the tree, where nodes labeled E and T can have a variable number of children. If we imagine the children of E and T stored in a variable-length array, the crucial lines become

```
else begin  (*  E → T [+|-] T [+|-] ··· [+|-] T or
                T → F [*|/] F [*|/] ··· [*|/] F  *)
        result := EvalExpr(p^.child[1]);
        i := 2;
        while p^.child[i] exists do
          begin
            next := EvalExpr(p^.child[i+1]);
            result := the result of applying p^.child[i] to
                        result and next;
            i := i + 2
          end;
        return (result)
     end
```

Even better, we can integrate the evaluation of the expression with the parsing. All we need to do is add the `var` parameter `result` to each of the procedures for E, T, and F. The modifications to Figure 5–12 are highlighted in Figure 5–14; variables `next` and `operator` are *local* variables of procedure E.

There is only one detail left to examine, and it is not an issue of parsing, but what we want the Model XIX calculator to do. If we have several calculations to make, we would like to be able to make them one after another, without having to rerun the Nero program: we would like to have multiline input. Along with this requirement, we make the design decision that calculations should be specified

---

[1] For nonterminals for which an option is $A \rightarrow \epsilon$, on entry to A the lookahead can contain the symbol after the string derived from A. The parser must still be able to unerringly decide which production to apply from the nonterminal-lookahead pair.

FIGURE 5–13   **The Derivation Tree after Eliminating Left Recursion**

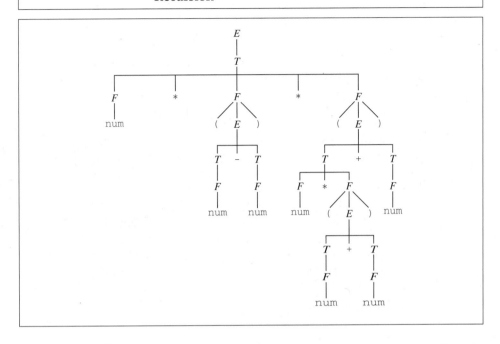

FIGURE 5–14   **Embedding the Semantics**

```
procedure E(var result: integer);
   var operator: ...(* same type as  symbol  *)
      next: integer;
   begin
      T(result); (* The expression must begin with a term. *)
      loop (* indefinitely -- until executing return *)
         case symbol of
            +,-: begin operator := symbol; scan end;
            else return (* We have seen the last term, so
                            the expression is complete. *)
         end;
         T(next); (* Look for the term after the + or - and
                     then iterate again. *)
         case operator of
            +: result := result + next;
            -: result := result - next
         end
      endloop
   end; (* E *)
```

one per line. This makes for a natural style of input. Thus, we arrive at our final grammar for the Nero Project

$$C \rightarrow S\,S \cdots S\,\text{end-of-file}$$
$$S \rightarrow E\,\text{end-of-line}$$
$$E \rightarrow T\;[+|-]\;T\;[+|-]\cdots[+|-]\;T$$
$$T \rightarrow F\;[*|/]\;F\;[*|/]\cdots[*|/]\;F$$
$$F \rightarrow \text{num}\;|\;(\,E\,)$$

ABOVE
AND BEYOND   **Ambiguous Grammars and Nonparsable Languages**

An ambiguous grammar cannot form the basis of a recursive descent parser. This is a consequence of the fundamental requirement that there be at most one applicable production for every nonterminal-lookahead pair—at every moment the parser must be able to decide with certainty what to do next. Since a recursive descent parser is guessing a leftmost derivation and since there is at least one string for which there are two derivation trees, or what amounts to the same thing, two leftmost derivations, when faced with this string there will come a point when two productions apply. Having more than one character of lookahead will not help. In fact, since either choice is consistent with the entire remainder of the input, no matter how long or how short, no amount of lookahead can resolve the matter.

The dangling else *problem*

Fortunately, the unusability of ambiguous grammars is of little consequence in practice, because the grammars that specify programming languages are not normally ambiguous. There is, however, one common programming language construct for which the corresponding portion of the grammar is an exception to this rule. The exception is so famous that it even has a name: *the dangling* **else** *problem*. The offending language construct arises in both Pascal and C and, in condensed form, is given by the grammar

$$SL \to SL \; ; \; S \; | \; S$$
$$S \; \to \text{begin } SL \text{ end } |$$
$$\text{if } BE \text{ then } S \; |$$
$$\text{if } BE \text{ then } S \text{ else } S \; |$$
$$\vdots$$

This grammar is ambiguous because

```
if ...
    then if ...
            then ...
            else ...
```

has the two parse trees shown in Figure 5–15: the one suggested by the indentation above and the one suggested by

```
if ...
    then if ...
            then ...
    else ...
```

Pascal and C disambiguate the situation by adding the rule that "the **else** should be paired with the closest unmatched **then**," which means that the language favors the first interpretation over the second. That this additional rule is not captured by the grammar makes parsing more difficult. Simply performing left factoring, so that the offending productions become

$$S \; \to \text{if } BE \text{ then } S \; X$$
$$X \to \text{else } S \; | \; \epsilon$$

is not enough, as the grammar is still ambiguous. In procedure X, if the

(continued)

ABOVE
AND BEYOND

(concluded)

Nonparsable languages

lookahead is not else, then the production to apply is definitely $X \rightarrow \epsilon$. But based solely on grammatical considerations, if the lookahead is else, we do not know whether to replace X by else S or ϵ. If we adopt the strategy of always choosing else S when the lookahead is else, we are effectively enforcing the rule that the else should be matched with the closest unmatched then—we are back to having only one applicable production for each nonterminal-lookahead pair. What is more, the recursive descent parser built from this grammar respects the semantics.

Not all grammars can be made usable by the tricks we have outlined. Nothing can save the grammars

$$S \rightarrow 0S0 \mid 1S1 \mid \epsilon$$

and

$$S \rightarrow T \mid U$$
$$T \rightarrow 0T1 \mid 01$$
$$U \rightarrow 0U11 \mid 011$$

which generate the languages $\{ww^R \mid w \in (0+1)^*\}$ and $\{0^n1^n \mid n > 0\}$ $\cup \{0^n1^{2n} \mid n > 0\}$. No fixed amount of lookahead and no massaging of the grammars seems to work, even though both grammars are unambiguous. Though we are in no position to prove it, it can be shown that there do not exist grammars that allow these languages to be parsed in a single left-to-right scan with any fixed amount of lookahead. This is true irrespective of the parsing method used—even techniques more sophisticated than recursive descent parsing are doomed to failure.

FIGURE 5–15   The Dangling else Problem

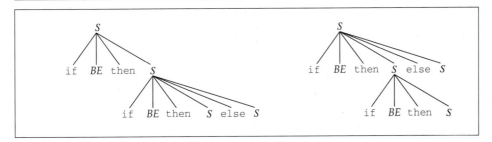

---

end-of-file is our endmarker (the $\$$), whereas end-of-line, though it is intended to indicate the termination of expressions, is a normal character. It can occur in the wrong place (an expression can end prematurely) or be left out (the user can inadvertently type two expressions on the same line). An example of the latter is

```
VIII + IV*V     II*(XIII - VI)
```

This error will be reported as a "missing operator." The parser will not realize that two expressions have been typed on the same line. When faced with the II, procedure Term (on line 103 of parser.p) will decide there is not another $[*|/]F$ and so will return. Then Expr (on line 134) will decide there is not another $[+|-]T$ and will also return. Since Expr was called by Stmt (as opposed to Factor) control returns to line 153, where the error is detected.

5.4   THE STRUCTURE OF THE MODEL XIX CALCULATOR

Lexical Analysis

Parsers for real programming languages never deal with the actual input. Forcing the parser to deal with such things as blanks and comments would muddy the code of the parser or the grammar from which it is built. It is better to provide the parser with a clean interface and take care of the messy details elsewhere. The process of converting the stream of actual characters into the stream of logical symbols expected by the parser is called ***lexical analysis***, which is why in the program for the Nero Project `scan` is actually called `Lex`. Because they interface with the real world, lexical analyzers are much harder to write and make bug-free than parsers, which are grounded in theory and have clean interfaces.

Refer to the code of `lex.h` *while reading this.*

The type `InputTokens` defines the alphabet the parser actually deals with. Some of the names are obvious, like `lparen` and `times`, and have a direct correlation with characters of the physical input. `endofline` corresponds to a logical end-of-line character and `endoffile` is the $ of our abstract treatment. Other symbols, like `number`, are abstract concepts and have associated semantic information. This semantic information is recorded in the variant part of the variant record type `FullToken`, whose discriminant field is of type `InputTokens`. There is one mysterious symbol in our alphabet, `errtok`. This symbol appears nowhere in our grammar, but reflects the reality that the user can type any ASCII character, no matter how inappropriate, or can type something that looks more or less like a Roman numeral, but isn't legal—something like `IC` or `IIIII`. In such cases `Lex` will tell the parser that the next symbol is `errtok`. When the parser uses the lookahead there will either be a terminal-terminal mismatch or no production will apply, and an error will be reported. The variant part for `errtok` provides additional information, which is used to generate an informative error message. The variable `Token` is the one-symbol lookahead.

Refer to the code of `charfilter.h` *and* `charfilter.p` *while reading this.*

To keep the lexical analyzer well structured, we don't have it read the input directly either; the program does some minor cleaning up of the actual characters even before the lexical analyzer gets them. This is done by procedure `GetChar`, which is just a glorified version of `read(ch)`. From the perspective of the lexical analyzer, the characters in the input fall into the six categories specified in the type `CharClass`. Just as `number` needs to carry along the number's value, characters in the classes `roman` and `algebraic` need to carry along their semantic information. That we also save the actual input character for the classes `blank` and `illegal` is more a matter of programming convenience than anything else, since this information is not used elsewhere in the program. While it is convenient to group together logically related characters, the real motivation for having `GetChar` is to provide a clean interface. This is made necessary by the way Pascal handles the logical end-of-line and logical end-of-file. Because we have decided that an expression to be evaluated should stand on a line by itself, we must deal with standard Pascal's automatic conversion of end-of-line into a blank when performing `read(ch)`. Not having an end-of-file character, so that we always have to call `eof`, is also unpleasant. Isolating the reading of the actual input in one, 50-line procedure makes it easy to port the program to systems that have non-ASCII character sets or handle end-of-line or end-of-file in nonstandard ways—in the entire program only a few lines of this one routine may need adjustment.

See the section `eoln` *and* `eof` *in* **Chapter 1.**

Putting the Pieces Together

The structure of our calculator is shown in Figure 5–16. Abstractly, we can think of the Model XIX calculator as having three independent parts:

- `GetChar`, which reads the input, producing a stream of `FullChar`.

FIGURE 5–16   The Overall Design of the Model XIX Calculator

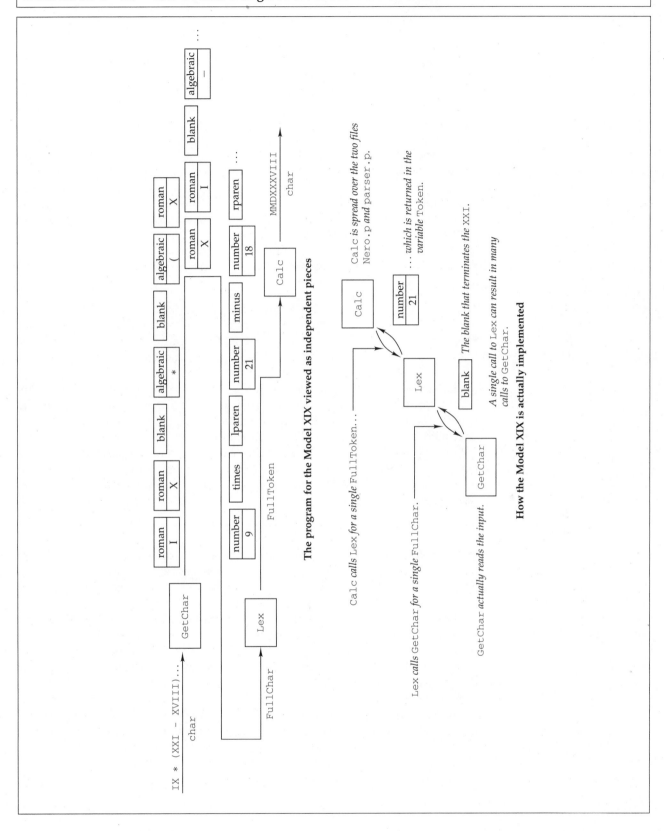

The program for the Model XIX viewed as independent pieces

Calc calls Lex *for a single* FullToken...

Lex calls GetChar *for a single* FullChar.

GetChar *actually reads the input.*

How the Model XIX is actually implemented

Calc *is spread over the two files* Nero.p *and* parser.p.

...*which is returned in the variable* Token.

The blank that terminates the XXI.

A single call to Lex *can result in many calls to* GetChar.

■ Lex, which reads this stream and converts it into a stream of `FullToken`.

■ The parser, which processes the stream of `FullToken`, analyzing and evaluating the expressions.

This is a useful way of thinking because it clarifies the program structure and aids the coding of the individual pieces. It is not, however, what is implemented. The three pieces of the program are more closely linked than the independent-piece model of computation suggests, with Lex being subordinate to the parser and GetChar being subordinate to Lex. The parser does not need to have the entire expression sitting available as a list of `FullToken`. Because we have designed our parser to function with only one symbol of lookahead, all it needs is the one logical symbol in Token. When it is done with this symbol, after making a terminal-terminal match, it calls Lex, which consumes actual input to build the next logical symbol. If there were a stream of `FullToken` to read, the calls to Lex would all be replaced by read(Token). To the parser it makes no difference if the symbols it processes are all out there in advance or if they are produced on the fly. Lex stands in the same relationship to GetChar as the parser stands to Lex—the lexical analyzer doesn't care if all the `FullChar` are available in advance or whether they are produced on demand.

Error Reporting and Recovery

That a calculator is used interactively affects the code in a number of significant ways. Take, for example, the question of whether the input should be echoed? Since the operating system typically echoes the input as it is typed, we do not have to do this, as we would if the input were read from a file. The natural place to echo the input, if this were necessary, would be in GetChar, as it is read. Not only is the input echoed by the operating system, it is typically line buffered as well; a whole line is delivered to the Pascal subsystem at once. This is both good and bad: we will take advantage of the good aspects, and have to deal with the bad ones. Not all programs have their input line buffered—visual editors and the worm program of Chapter 2 need to respond immediately to each key as it is struck. One good aspect of line buffering is that we don't have to deal with certain kinds of typing errors. In a line-buffered environment, the user who types

```
                    VIII + IV**
```

by inadvertently hitting the asterisk key a second time can back up with the backspace key, correct the mistake, and finish typing the entire line. The erroneous asterisk and the backspace won't be delivered to our program, and GetChar and Lex won't have to deal with them.

We also can take advantage of line buffering to provide nicer looking error messages in the event of an uncorrected user error. When an error occurs it is better to give some indication of where the error is, instead of forcing the user to search for it. While the detection of an error is primarily the job of the parser, the program relies on GetChar to aid in pinpointing its location. The parser cannot really do this by itself, since it lacks any information about spaces the user might have inserted to increase readability. For this reason GetChar performs an additional chore as it reads the input: it maintains a private static variable, CharsProcessed, which indicates how many characters from the current line have been read. This way, when an error occurs, the procedure ReportError can print under the input line the location of the error, as in

```
    VIII + IV**II - X
    -----------^
    At or near the indicated point a number or left ...
```

See procedure `ReportError` *in* `error.p` *and the manipulation of the variable* `CharsProcessed` *in* `charfilter.p`.

Marking the location of the error isn't perfect—the parser does not know that an error has occurred until the token after the point of the error has been examined. This token can be preceded by blanks and, in the case of Roman numerals, doesn't end until after the last character of the number.

EXERCISE 5–7 Predict the location and nature of the error reported by the Model XIX calculator when processing the line

```
IV + II XVIII + VI
```

Still, the error reporting is adequate. Notice that in producing

```
VIII + IV**II - X
-----------^
At or near the indicated point a number or left ...
```

the program has not yet read the `II - X`, although these characters appear on the line above the error indicator. These characters appear only because of the line-buffered nature of the input.

EXERCISE 5–8 Though it isn't intended, nothing prevents us from running the Model XIX calculator with `input` redirected to come from a file, as in

```
ModelXIX < FileOfExpressions
```

What will the output look like if one of the expressions has an error? Assume that `GetChar` has been modified to echo the input as it is read. Modify the program so that if the Model XIX calculator is run in this mode, the output is the same as it is now.

Error recovery

Error reporting brings up the issue of error recovery. It would be unreasonable to have the Model XIX simply report an error and quit. Real calculators don't shut themselves off when an error occurs. The user usually has to take some simple action to reset the calculator, like pressing a button labeled `clr`. We would like the Model XIX to have similar behavior. In fact, we can arrange it so that the user doesn't have to do anything—we simply flush the remainder of the input line. The user, who has already typed the whole line, won't really be aware that the program has read just to the point of the error. It appears as if the whole line has been readand that only afterwards was the error detected. Thus, by throwing away the remainder of the line, the program.actually conforms to the user's expectations. After examining the error message, the user can just retype the line.

Unfortunately, flushing the input line is not as simple as just doing a `readln`. `Stmt` is deeply buried in recursion, being somewhere in the middle of parsing an S, and the main program, in the midst of processing the production

$$C \rightarrow S\,S\, \cdots\, S\, \text{end-of-file}$$

is executing the loop on lines 23–25 of `Nero.p`:

```
while Token.LexicalObject <> endoffile do
   Stmt (* Process a statement -- on return the first token of the
            next statement has been read into the global variable  Token .  *)
```

Somehow we need to fool the parser into thinking the input line is correct so that `Stmt` will return normally. We are fortunate that the grammar is so simple. There is only one production with S on the left-hand side,

$$S \rightarrow E \text{ end-of-line}$$

and due to the line buffering, the problem cannot be that the `end-of-line` is missing. If `Stmt` advances the input, by repeated calls to `Lex`, until the `endofline` symbol is found and consumed, it can continue as if nothing had gone wrong. Within procedure `ErrorOccurred` the lines (lines 40–43 of `parser.p`)

```
(* Flush the remainder of the input line. *)
while (Token.LexicalObject <> endofline) and
      (Token.LexicalObject <> endoffile) do Lex;
if Token.LexicalObject = endofline then Lex;
```

advance `Token` past `endofline`, and the `goto 99` on line 44 makes it appear to procedure `Stmt` that it has successfully processed an expression.[2] `Stmt` returns to the main program, which is totally unaware that something went wrong along the way. The main program checks the next token to see if it is `endoffile`, and if it isn't it calls `Stmt`—the program is back on track, having recovered from the user's error.

There is one disadvantage to having line-buffered input, though it is not immediately obvious. The problem occurs in `Lex` and involves reading Roman numerals. With the exception of Roman numerals, all the tokens are one character long. Because they all have fixed length we can tell in advance where in the input a token ends. But with Roman numerals, which have indefinite length, we cannot tell when one has ended until we have read one character too many, that is, until we have read the character *after* the last character of the Roman numeral. This is a nuisance, since this means that sometimes we have one character to save and process on the next entry to `Lex`, while at other times we do not have this extra character. To increase the regularity of our program, which tends to make for bug-free code, we adopt the invariant

> On entry to `Lex` the static variable `CurrentChar` should contain the character immediately following the last character of the previous token.

Lexical analysis: dealing with the interaction of Roman numerals and line buffering

For a different way of handling this problem see **For Your Information: An Alternate Approach—UnGetChar.**

This is reflected in the call to `GetChar` on line 111 of `lex.p`, after the processing of the one-character tokens +, -, *, /, (, and). Unfortunately, if we adopt this strategy with respect to the one-character token `endofline`, we cannot return this token until we read the first character of the next line, even though we are not planning on processing this character now and read it only for the purpose of maintaining our invariant. This is totally contrary to the user's expectations: the user expects the answer to appear immediately after typing the carriage return. We are likely to end with an unfriendly stalemate: `GetChar` will be sitting at line 41 of `charfilter.p` waiting for the first character of the next line to be typed and the user will be waiting for the answer to appear. This would not be a problem in a noninteractive environment, where the input comes from a file, since then the next line is already available. But ours is an interactive environment, so we must deal with this difficulty. We have a design dilemma: the need to read one character beyond the end of a Roman numeral, so that we know it is really over, conflicts with the need to deliver and process the `endofline` token before

---

[2] This `goto` isn't legal in Turbo Pascal. As discussed in For Your Information: Turbo Pascal and the `goto` Statement in Chapter 1, getting around this deficiency clutters the Turbo Pascal version of the program with needless parameters and `if` statements.

reading the first character of the next line. Thus, despite our good intentions, we need code in Lex to handle this special case. This is the purpose of the static private variable ReadDelayed declared on line 16 of lex.p.

Dealing with Roman Numerals
Refer to the code of roman.p *while reading this.*

This leaves us with one topic: converting back and forth between Roman numerals and the computer's internal representation of integers. The rules governing what is and what is not a legal Roman numeral are arcane and complex. Most of us know them, at least roughly, though there is some question as to how to write the number four; IV and IIII both being popular. The "standard" way is IV, with IIII being generally reserved for clock faces. Our program will accept only IV. Another issue, which the Romans never really resolved, was the representation of the numbers 5000 and above. Since none of the alternatives correspond to any symbols on the standard keyboard, we will limit ourselves to the characters I, V, X, L, C, D, and M, which makes the maximum representable Roman numeral 3999. Traditionally, a Roman numeral can be written all in lowercase or all in uppercase (both iv and IV are allowed), but the two cases cannot be mixed. For the sake of simplicity, we will restrict ourselves to uppercase letters. Even with all these restrictions it is hard to describe what is and what is not a legal Roman numeral.

> **EXERCISE 5–9**   Try to write a clear English description of what is and what is not a legal Roman numeral. Describe how to convert a legal Roman numeral into a base 10 integer.

Do this exercise before reading further.

Of the two tasks, converting a number stored in a variable of type integer into a Roman numeral and converting a Roman numeral into an integer as the computer represents them, the first isn't too difficult. It is basically a table lookup. This is more efficient and clearer than trying to be clever. The case statement on lines 25–53 of procedure ConvertDigit does just this. If you ask it to convert a 4, it says "hey, it is just a IV." If you ask it to convert a number in the range 5 through 8, it says, "this is just a V, followed by the correct number of I's." To have a table with 3999 entries is a bit much, but we can take advantage of what little regularity there is in Roman numerals to keep things much shorter. When converting a number like 872, we first convert the 8, but instead of getting VIII we get DCCC, because the 8 appears in the hundreds place. When converting the 7, the result is LXX instead of VII. The conversion is just the same, except the particular letters used to represent 10, 5, and 1 are different. All that procedure ConvertToRoman does is call ConvertDigit, first with the thousands digit, then with the hundreds digit, then with the tens digit, and finally with the ones digit, building up the Roman numeral piece by piece. Table lookup is a very general principle—it appears often in computer programs, especially when translating from one alphabet to another. We will use it as well in performing the opposite conversion: the program determines that the value of V is 5 by just looking it up.

Because the rules for describing Roman numerals are so complex, writing a program to enforce them appears to be a nightmare. And it would be, except for one trick that makes the entire process incredibly simple. The trick is rather clever, and you would be very unlikely to figure it out for yourself. The author of this book didn't either—someone suggested it to him. It is based on the fact that every integer has exactly one representation as a Roman numeral. What we propose to do is write a procedure that takes something that looks more or less like a Roman numeral and converts it into an integer. "More or

An Alternate Approach—UnGetChar

The lexical analyzer was difficult to make bug-free because of two conflicting factors: (*i*) the lexical analyzer cannot tell that a Roman numeral has ended until it has read one character too many, and (*ii*) in an interactive, line-buffered environment it cannot advance past the end-of-line token, because this requires the user to input the first character of the next line (actually, the entire line) before seeing the result of the previous computation. Except for complications caused by these competing factors, the lexical analyzer was pretty simple. It was just

- Skip over blanks.
- Based on the nonblank character read, determine which token is next—one character is sufficient to separate all the cases.
- In the case of Roman numerals, keep reading until the entire Roman numeral has been consumed. After it has been read, check it for legality.

Since we cannot avoid having to read past the end of a Roman numeral, we opted to enforce the invariant that on entry to `Lex` the static variable `CurrentChar` should contain the character immediately following the last character of the last token returned, while making an exception for `endofline`. For all the other one-character tokens, enforcing this invariant simply meant calling `GetChar` after the token was recognized. The exception for `endofline` was handled by setting the `boolean` flag `ReadDelayed` to true when `endofline` is returned. When reentered, `Lex` checks this flag, and if it is set, the postponed read is performed.

This conflict could have been resolved in the opposite way. We could have made the invariant "on entry to `Lex`, `CurrentChar` contains the last character of the last token returned," making Roman numerals the exception. The `boolean` flag would now be named `ReadAlreadyDone`. This is the approach we explore in this For Your Information box, only we do it in a more sophisticated manner. If we could "unread" a character, then after processing a Roman numeral, we would simply unread the one character we should not have read in the first place. Now, there would be no need for an exception to the invariant that on entry to `Lex` the last character read was the last character of the previous token. `CurrentChar` would become a local variable of procedure `Lex`, `Lex` would begin by skipping blanks (only now this would be done with a `repeat` loop instead of a `while` loop, since at least one character would need to be read), and the code that handles the one-character tokens wouldn't need to end with a call to `GetChar`. The code for Roman numerals would be the same as it is now, only it would be followed by an "unread."

The idea, illustrated in Figure 5–17, is to define a procedure

```
procedure UnGetChar(LogicalCh: FullChar);
```

and to include in `charfilter.p` a static variable that acts as a one-character buffer. `UnGetChar` simply stores its argument in the buffer. In the modified version of `charfilter.p`, `GetChar` first checks the buffer: if it is full, then

(continued)

GetChar returns what is in the buffer, emptying it. Otherwise it actually reads a character from the input. Because the buffer is only one character long, we cannot have two calls to UnGetChar without an intervening call to GetChar, but since Lex never needs to push two characters back into the input, this is not a problem. This technique has become so popular that it is part of the standard C library, which includes two functions, getc and ungetc, for reading and unreading characters. If you study this strategy for a moment, you will see that it is really no different than having a flag within Lex stating whether the last token returned was a Roman numeral, and if so, avoiding the call to GetChar at the start of Lex. We have just shifted the burden from lexical analysis to the preprocessing of characters. Still, this is a better approach. It provides a useful, universal tool, since there are many other applications where an extra character of input sometimes needs to be buffered—the programs of Chapters 4 and 6 are examples.

PROJECT 5–1 Modify the program for the Model XIX calculator to implement this approach.

FIGURE 5–17   charfilter.p with UnGetChar

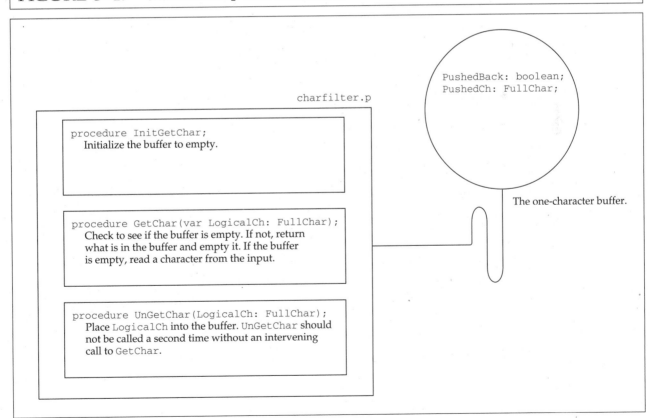

less like a Roman numeral" means any string of I's, V's, X's, L's, C's, D's, and M's of up to length 15—this being the length of the longest Roman numeral, MMMDCCCLXXXVIII. The only requirement we place on this procedure is that if the string being converted is a valid Roman numeral, then it should return the correct value. If the string is invalid, the procedure can return any integer whatsoever. If we had such a procedure, turning it into a procedure that converts Roman numerals into integers, *and detects illegal input*, is easy. The algorithm is

- Convert the supposed Roman numeral into an integer.
- If the integer is less than 1 or greater than 3999, then the input is invalid.
- Convert the integer back into a Roman numeral, using the procedure ConvertToRoman we have already described.
- Compare the input string and the result of this second conversion. If they agree character for character, the original string is a valid Roman numeral. If they disagree, it is invalid.

This algorithm works because a valid Roman numeral, when converted to an integer and then converted back to a string, should give us what we started with. Conversely, if the original input is invalid, then no matter what integer is returned in the first step, when it is converted back to a string, it won't be what we started with, since the output of ConvertToRoman is always *some* valid Roman numeral. The strategy behind this algorithm is pictured diagrammatically in Figure 5–18.

We have simplified our problem. Now all we need is an algorithm that converts valid Roman numerals correctly and we can ignore what it does on invalid strings. This is much simpler. In a Roman numeral the last character and those followed by a character of equal or lesser value make a positive contribution,

FIGURE 5–18   Checking Roman Numerals for Legality

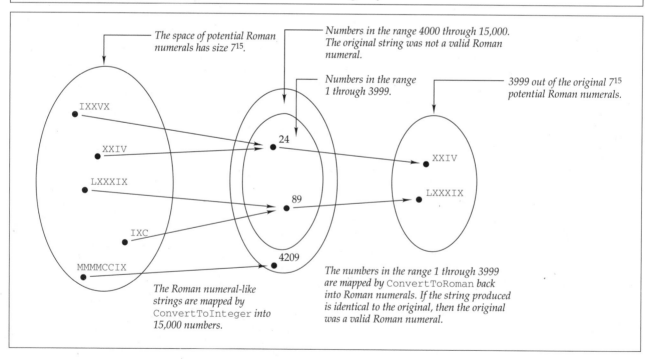

whereas the contribution of characters followed by characters of greater value is negative. For example, the number CDLXXIX is interpreted as

$$(-100) + 500 + 50 + 10 + 10 + (-1) + 10$$

The C is followed by a D, which has greater value, so it is treated as a −100. The I, which is followed by a X, is treated the same way. The D, L, and the first two X's are followed by characters of equal or lesser value, so they make a positive contribution, as does the final X. The conversion of nonsense strings such as IC and IVXLCDM to 99 and 334 is of no consequence, because the error will be caught when these numbers are converted back to strings. This algorithm is easy to code. It consists of a table lookup, to convert single characters into values, and a simple loop. The remainder of procedure ConvertToInteger is just a straightforward implementation of the second through fourth steps of the general algorithm described above.

EXERCISE 5–10   The procedure ConvertToInteger explicitly checks (on line 140) that the result of a conversion is not less than 1. Prove that this test can never be true and that the line could just as well have been written

```
if result > MAXROMAN
```

In tricky situations like this one, it is often better to program defensively than to be too clever. The amount of wasted computer time is negligible.

PROJECT 5–2   Modify the Model XIX calculator to accept Roman numerals in all lowercase as well.

FILE   Nero.p

```
 1  #include "charfilter.h"
 2  #include "roman.h" (* needed by lex.h *)
 3  #include "error.h" (* needed by lex.h *)
 4  #include "lex.h"
 5  #include "parser.h"
 6
 7  program NeroTheRomanCalculator(input,output);
 8    (* Process a series of lines that specify calculations in infix form,
 9       but with the integers written as Roman numerals.
10    *)
11    begin
12      InitGetChar;
13      InitLex;
14      Lex; (* Initialize the lookahead for the parser. *)
15
16      (* This routine corresponds to the productions
17          Calc --> Stmt—List endoffile
18          Stmt—List --> Stmt—List Stmt
19          Stmt—List --> epsilon
20        with the recursion replaced by iteration, that is,
21          Stmt—List --> Stmt Stmt ... Stmt
22      *)
23      while Token.LexicalObject <> endoffile do
24        Stmt (* Process a statement -- on return the first token of the
25              next statement has been read into the global variable  Token . *)
26    end.
```

Because DEC Pascal for RISC allows initialization of static variables, these calls can be eliminated. The even greater flexibility provided by the initialization part of a Turbo Pascal unit also makes them unnecessary.

This is a consequence of the invariant:
On entry to a procedure corresponding to a nonterminal the lookahead should be the leftmost symbol that the nonterminal derives, and on exit the lookahead should be the first symbol following the entire string derived by the nonterminal.

The sentence symbol of the grammar.

FILE	roman.h

```
const MAXROMAN = 3999; (* MMMCMXCIX *)
      LONGESTROMAN = 15; (* 3888 = MMMDCCCLXXXVIII *)

type RomanRange = 1..MAXROMAN;
     RomanNumeral = record
                      numdigits: integer;
                      number: array [1..LONGESTROMAN] of char
                    end;

procedure ConvertToRoman(n: RomanRange; var RN: RomanNumeral); external;
  (* Convert an integer into a Roman numeral. *)

procedure ConvertToInteger(    RN: RomanNumeral;
                           var n: RomanRange; var error: boolean); external;
  (* Convert a supposed Roman numeral into an integer.  If the input is
     not a valid Roman numeral then  error  is set to true and  n  has
     no defined value.  Otherwise  error  is set to false and  n  is the
     value of  RN .
  *)
```

```
 1  #include "roman.h"
 2
 3  (* procedure ConvertToRoman(n: RomanRange; var RN: RomanNumeral); *)
 4  procedure ConvertToRoman;
 5    (* Convert an integer into a Roman numeral. *)
 6    var m: integer;
 7
 8    procedure ConvertDigit(      digit: integer;
 9                                 tens, fives, ones: char;
10                          var  (* in out *) RN: RomanNumeral);
11
12    (* Convert the next digit (thousands, hundreds, tens, ones), tacking
13       the result of the conversion onto the end of the Roman numeral
14       being developed.
15
16       The method of conversion is independent of whether the digit is
17       in the thousands, hundreds, tens, or ones place -- the only
18       difference is which letters are used in forming the piece of the
19       answer.  For example: 7 in the hundreds place (700) is DCC, while 7
20       in the tens place (70) is LXX, while 7 in the ones place is VII.
21    *)
22    var i: integer;
23    begin
24      with RN do
25        (*  digit  is in the range 0 .. 9. *)
26        case digit of
27          0: (* do nothing *) ;
28          1, 2, 3: (* I, II, III *)
29            for i := 1 to digit do
30              begin
31                numdigits := numdigits + 1;
32                number[numdigits] := ones
33              end;
34          4: begin (* IV *)
35               number[numdigits+1] := ones;
36               number[numdigits+2] := fives;
37               numdigits := numdigits + 2
38             end;
39          5, 6, 7, 8: (* V, VI, VII, VIII *)
40            begin
41              numdigits := numdigits + 1;
42              number[numdigits] := fives;
43              for i := 6 to digit do (* loop skipped if  digit = 5  *)
44                begin
45                  numdigits := numdigits + 1;
46                  number[numdigits] := ones
47                end
                 end;
```

Even though n is a call-by-value parameter, we need to use a temporary variable because repeated application of the mod *operator can reduce* m *to zero.*

This bit of Ada syntax reminds the reader that RN *is modified, as opposed to just set.*

Because Digit *can equal zero, we must have the case label* 0: *in the* case *statement, even though there is nothing to do. The comment informs the reader that the programmer didn't accidentally leave out some code.*

```
48              9: begin (* IX *)
49                    number[numdigits+1] := ones;
50                    number[numdigits+2] := tens;
51                    numdigits := numdigits + 2
52                  end
53            end
54      end; (* ConvertDigit *)
55
56    begin
57      m := n;
58      RN.numdigits := 0;
59
60      (* Convert each successive digit, removing what we convert from
61         the value of the number. *)
62      (* Thousands *)
63      ConvertDigit(m div 1000,' ',' ','M',RN); (* no 5,000 or 10,000 character *)
64      m := m mod 1000;
65
66      (* Hundreds *)
67      ConvertDigit(m div 100,'M','D','C',RN);
68      m := m mod 100;
69
70      (* Tens *)
71      ConvertDigit(m div 10,'C','L','X',RN);
72      m := m mod 10;
73
74      (* Ones *)
75      ConvertDigit(m,'X','V','I',RN)
76    end; (* ConvertToRoman *)
77
78  (* procedure ConvertToInteger(    RN: RomanNumeral;
79                            var n: RomanRange; var error: boolean); *)
80  procedure ConvertToInteger;
81    (* Convert a supposed Roman numeral into an integer.  If the input is
82       not a valid Roman numeral then  error  is set to true and  n  has
83       no defined value.  Otherwise  error  is set to false and  n  is the
84       value of  RN .
85    *)
86    (* The general algorithm is:
87        Go through the supposed Roman numeral converting it to an integer,
88          even if the string of characters is not a legal Roman numeral.
89          Use an algorithm that does the conversion correctly if the supposed
90          Roman numeral is legal.  If the string of characters is not a
91          Roman numeral, the result of the conversion can be anything.
92          The string is assumed to be "plausible," that is, it consists only
93          of the characters I, V, X, L, C, D, and M.
94        Convert the integer back into a Roman numeral.
95        Compare the two strings of characters.  If they agree, the input
96          was a valid Roman numeral and we have converted it correctly.  If
97          they disagree, the input was not a Roman numeral.  This works because
98          each integer has only one valid representation as a Roman numeral.
99          (Four, which is correctly written as IV, is sometimes written as
100         IIII.  This exception, which we ignore, is used mostly on clock
101         faces.)
102   *)
```

Something must be passed in, though it doesn't matter what.

```
103    label 99; (* return *)
104    var result: integer;                          ── The maximum plausible result is 15,000, which is fifteen M's.
105        ResultAsRoman: RomanNumeral; (* for the conversion back *)
106        i: integer;
107
108    function Value(ch: char): integer;
109      (* Return the integer equivalent of a one-letter Roman numeral. *)
110      begin
111        case ch of
112          'I': Value := 1;
113          'V': Value := 5;
114          'X': Value := 10;
115          'L': Value := 50;
116          'C': Value := 100;
117          'D': Value := 500;
118          'M': Value := 1000
119        end
120      end; (* Value *)
121
122    begin
123      (* Convert the supposed Roman numeral to an integer.  Process the letters
124         one at a time.  If a letter is followed by a letter of higher value,
125         such as the  I  in  IX , then treat the letter as if it were negative.
126         Otherwise, treat it as positive.  The last letter always makes a
127         positive contribution.
128      *)
129      with RN do
130        begin
131          result := 0;
132          for i := 1 to numdigits - 1 do
133            if Value(number[i]) < Value(number[i+1])
134              then result := result - Value(number[i])
135              else result := result + Value(number[i]);
136          result := result + Value(number[numdigits])
137        end;
138
139      (* Check it for legality. *)
140      if (result < 1) or (result > MAXROMAN)      ── This check is done explicitly, because if this
141        then error := true                           condition is met, result cannot legally be
142        else begin                                    passed to ConvertToRoman.
143              ConvertToRoman(result,ResultAsRoman);
144              if RN.numdigits <> ResultAsRoman.numdigits
145                then error := true
146                else begin
147                      for i := 1 to RN.numdigits do
148                        if RN.number[i] <> ResultAsRoman.number[i]
149                          then begin
150                                error := true;
151                                goto 99 (* return *)
152                              end;
153                      error := false;
154                      n := result
155                    end
156            end;
157  99:
158    end; (* ConvertToInteger *)
```

FILE `charfilter.h`

```
 1 type CharClass = ( blank,        (* blank or tab *)
 2                    endline,      (* logical carriage return *)
 3                    endfile,      (* logical end-of-file character *)
 4                    roman,        (* I, V, X, L, C, D, M *)
 5                    algebraic,    (* (, ), +, -, *, / *)
 6                    illegal       (* anything else *)
 7                  );
 8       FullChar = record
 9                    case CharObject: CharClass of
10                      endfile, endline: ();
11                      blank, roman, algebraic, illegal: (ch: char)
12                 end;
13
14 procedure InitGetChar; external;
15   (* This procedure should be called once, before  GetChar  is called for
16       the first time.
17   *)
18
19 procedure GetChar(var LogicalCh: FullChar); external;
20   (* Acts as  read(ch)  to the rest of the program.  This procedure allows the
21       lexical subsystem to think of the input as a file of  FullChar  terminated
22       by an end-of-file character, instead of as a file of ASCII characters.
23   *)
24
25 procedure HowFarOnLine(var HowFar: integer); external;
26   (* Return the position within the line of the last character read.  This
27       is used by  ReportError  to pinpoint the location of the error.
28   *)
```

That we record the actual character in the case of blank *and* illegal *is just a programming convenience—see lines 53–70 of* charfilter.p. *In the case of* illegal, *this extra information would be useful if we had a more elaborate error processor.*

```
 1  #include "charfilter.h"
 2
 3  var CharsProcessed: integer; (* The number of characters read from the
 4                                 current input line -- maintained internally
 5                                 and returned by  HowFarOnLine . *)
 6      LastWasCR: boolean; (* Was the last character read a logical carriage
 7                           return?  This needed so that  CharsProcessed  can
 8                           be reset. *)
 9
10  (* procedure InitGetChar; *)
11  procedure InitGetChar;
12    (* This procedure should be called once, before  GetChar  is called for
13       the first time.
14    *)
```

> Notice that the input is not echoed. The program is designed under the assumption that the input is coming from a terminal, so that characters are echoed by the operating system as they are typed, and under the assumption that the input is line buffered by the operating system. These assumptions affect this routine, the pinpointing of the error by ReportError, and the special treatment given the token endofline by the lexical analyzer.

```
15    begin
16      (* Initialize static variables. *)
17      CharsProcessed := 0;
18      LastWasCR := false (* not that it really matters *)
19    end; (* InitGetChar *)
20
21  (* procedure GetChar(var LogicalCh: FullChar); *)
22  procedure GetChar;
23    (* Acts as  read(ch)  to the rest of the program.  This procedure allows the
24       lexical subsystem to think of the input as a file of  FullChar  terminated
25       by an end-of-file character, instead of as a file of ASCII characters.
26    *)
27    const TAB = 9; (* ASCII control-I *)
28          TABWIDTH = 8; (* Some systems allow "soft tabs" -- adjust this
29                           constant accordingly. *)
30    var ch: char;
31    begin
32      (* The input is logically viewed as ending with an infinite string of
33         end-of-file characters, which are not on any line.
34      *)
35
36      (* If we are about to read the first character on a line, then
37         reset  CharsProcessed . *)
38      if LastWasCR then CharsProcessed := 0;
39
40      (* Read the next character. *)
41      if eof
42        then begin
43              LogicalCh.CharObject := endfile;
44              LastWasCR := false
45            end
```

```
46      else if eoln
47        then begin
48               LogicalCh.CharObject := endline;
49               readln;
50               CharsProcessed := CharsProcessed + 1;
51               LastWasCR := true
52             end
53      else begin
54               read(ch);
55               CharsProcessed := CharsProcessed + 1;
56               LastWasCR := false;
57               if ch in [' ', chr(TAB)]
58                 then begin
59                        LogicalCh.CharObject := blank;
60                        if ch = chr(TAB) (* round up to nearest  TABWIDTH  *)
61                          then CharsProcessed :=
62                                 ((CharsProcessed - 1) div TABWIDTH + 1) * TABWIDTH
63                      end
```

The entire purpose of maintaining CharsProcessed *is to be able to indicate the approximate location of an error by a line like*

```
--------------^
```

written directly beneath the input when an error occurs. Since the effect of a tab is to advance the cursor to the next column that is a multiple of eight plus one, we adjust CharsProcessed *accordingly.*

```
64               else if ch in ['I','V','X','L','C','D','M']
65                 then LogicalCh.CharObject := roman
66               else if ch in ['(',')','+','-','*','/']
67                 then LogicalCh.CharObject := algebraic
68               else   LogicalCh.CharObject := illegal;
69               LogicalCh.ch := ch
70             end
71   end; (* GetChar *)
72
73 (* procedure HowFarOnLine(var HowFar: integer); *)
74 procedure HowFarOnLine;
75   (* Return the position within the line of the last character read.  This
76      is used by  ReportError  to pinpoint the location of the error.
77   *)
78   begin
79     HowFar := CharsProcessed
80   end; (* HowFarOnLine *)
```

FILE   error.h

```
1 type ErrorType = ( (* Lexical *)   IllegalCharacter, IllegalRoman,
2                     (* Syntactic *) NumOrLParenExpected, RightParenExpected,
3                                     MissingOperator, ExcessRightParen,
4                     (* Runtime *)   Overflow
5                   );
6
7 procedure ReportError(Error: ErrorType); external;
8   (* Report an error.  The remainder of the line is flushed by the parser. *)
```

FILE   error.p

```
1  #include "charfilter.h"
2  #include "error.h"
3
4  (* procedure ReportError(Error: ErrorType); *)
5  procedure ReportError;
6    (* Report an error.  The remainder of the line is flushed by the parser. *)
7    var i, j: integer;
8    begin
9      (* Indicate approximately where the error occurred. *)
10     HowFarOnLine(j);
11     for i := 1 to j-1 do write('-'); writeln('^');
12
```
The presumption is that input is line buffered, which makes the output of this loop appear directly beneath the input line.

```
13     (* Print an informative message. *)
14     write('At or near the indicated point ');
15     case Error of
16       IllegalCharacter:
17         writeln('an illegal character was detected.');
18       IllegalRoman:
19         writeln('an improperly formed Roman numeral was detected.');
20       NumOrLParenExpected:
21         writeln('a number or left parenthesis was expected.');
22       RightParenExpected:
23         writeln('a right parenthesis was expected.');
24       MissingOperator:
25         writeln('an operator was expected.');
26       ExcessRightParen:
27         writeln('an excess right parenthesis was detected.');
28       Overflow:
29         writeln('the computation overflowed/underflowed.')
30     end
31   end; (* ReportError *)
```

FILE parser.h

```
 1 procedure Stmt; external;)
 2    (* Parse and evaluate an expression at the outermost level, printing
 3       its value.
 4
 5       This routine corresponds to the production
 6         Stmt --> E endofline
 7
 8       Invariant: The global variable  Token  contains the first logical
 9                  token of the statement.  This invariant applies to all
10                  the other nonterminals as well.  That is, upon entering the
11                  procedure corresponding to a nonterminal,  Token  contains
12                  the first token derived from that nonterminal, and upon
13                  exiting  Token  contains the token that immediately
14                  follows the tokens derived from the nonterminal.  (The user
15                  cannot avoid typing the  endofline  token at the end of a line,
16                  nor the  endoffile  token at the end of the entire input.)
17
18       Side effects:   If no errors occur, then the value of the expression is
19                       printed.
20
21       Error handling: A simple error message is printed and the input line
22                       is flushed.
23    *)
```

```
 1 #include "roman.h"
 2 #include "error.h"
 3 #include "lex.h"
 4 #include "parser.h"
 5
 6 (* procedure Stmt; *)
 7 procedure Stmt;
 8   (* Parse and evaluate an expression at the outermost level, printing
 9      its value.
10
11     This routine corresponds to the production
12       Stmt --> E endofline
13
14     Invariant: The global variable  Token  contains the first logical
15                token of the statement.  This invariant applies to all
16                the other nonterminals as well.  That is, upon entering the
17                procedure corresponding to a nonterminal,  Token  contains
18                the first token derived from that nonterminal, and upon
19                exiting  Token  contains the token that immediately
20                follows the tokens derived from the nonterminal.  (The user
21                cannot avoid typing the  endofline  token at the end of a line,
22                nor the  endoffile  token at the end of the entire input.)
23
24     Side effects:  If no errors occur, then the value of the expression is
25                    printed.
26
27     Error handling: A simple error message is printed and the input line
28                     is flushed.
29   *)
30   label 99; (* return after error reported, including in subprocedures *)
31   var EVal: integer;
32       RN: RomanNumeral;
33       i: integer;
34
35   (* Service Procedures *)
36   procedure ErrorOccurred(Error: ErrorType);
37     (* Report a syntax error, flush the remainder of the line, and return. *)
38     begin
39       ReportError(Error);
40       (* Flush the remainder of the input line. *)
41       while (Token.LexicalObject <> endofline) and
42             (Token.LexicalObject <> endoffile) do Lex;
```

— *This really must be true in a line-oriented environment.*

```
43       if Token.LexicalObject = endofline then Lex;
44       goto 99 (* return from  Stmt  *)
45     end; (* ErrorOccurred  *)
46
```

The error might not be detectable until the carriage return is read, as with an input line like
        II*(IX - IV
where there is a missing right parenthesis. For this reason there may be nothing to flush—the while *loop will simply be skipped.*

FILE   parser.p   Page 2

```
47    procedure CheckRange(i: integer);
48      (* Check for and report an overflow/underflow error during a computation. *)
49      begin
50        if (i < 1) or (i > MAXROMAN)
51          then ErrorOccurred(Overflow)
52      end; (* CheckRange *)
53
54
55    (* Procedures Relating To The Parsing *)
56
57    procedure Expr(var EVal: integer); forward;
58
59    procedure Factor(var FVal: integer);
60      (* Parse and evaluate a factor.
61
62         This routine corresponds to the productions
63           F --> number
64           F --> ( E )
65      *)
66      begin
67        case Token.LexicalObject of
68          number: (* F --> number *)
69            begin
70              FVal := Token.value;
71              Lex (* maintain invariant *)
72            end;
73          lparen: (* F --> ( E ) *)
74            begin
75              Lex; (* scan over the  ( , preparing for the  E . *)
76              Expr(FVal);
77              if Token.LexicalObject <> rparen
78                then ErrorOccurred(RightParenExpected);
79              Lex (* maintain invariant -- we have scanned past entire factor *)
80            end;
81          rparen, plus, minus, times, divide, endofline, endoffile:
82            ErrorOccurred(NumOrLParenExpected);
83          errtok: (* a lexical error occurred *)
84            ErrorOccurred(Token.message)




85        end
86        (* Hopefully:  Token.LexicalObject in
87                       [plus,minus,times,divide,rparen,endofline] *)
88    end; (* Factor *)
89
```

Since Factor *can call* Expr.

It would also be reasonable to make Expr, Term, *and* Factor *functions. The main reason for not doing so is that they have a side effect: they cause the input to be read. Many programmers feel that, by convention, functions should never have side effects.*

This can be easily modified to distinguish errtok *from other tokens that are not right parentheses.*

It is better to let the parser handle the errors discovered by the lexical analyzer, since it has a better understanding of the "big picture." At this point, and others like it, a more sophisticated recursive descent parser would attempt serious error recovery. Because our environment is interactive, the crude approach of simply flushing the input line is adequate. This case could have been combined with the previous one—it depends on what error message we feel is the most appropriate.

The situation is the same as the one described at the end of Term.

```
 90    procedure Term(var TVal: integer);
 91      (* Parse and evaluate a term.
 92
 93        This routine corresponds to the productions
 94          T --> T * F
 95          T --> T / F
 96          T --> F
 97        with the recursion replaced by iteration, that is,
 98          T --> F [*|/] F [*|/] ... [*|/] F
 99      *)
100      var FVal: integer;
101      begin
102        Factor(TVal);
103        while Token.LexicalObject in [times,divide] do
104            if Token.LexicalObject = times
105              then begin
106                    Lex;
107                    Factor(FVal);
108                    TVal := TVal * FVal;
109                    CheckRange(TVal)
110                end
111              else begin
112                    Lex;
113                    Factor(FVal);
114                    TVal := TVal div FVal;
115                    CheckRange(TVal)
116                end
117        (* Hopefully:  Token.LexicalObject in [plus,minus,rparen,endofline] *)
118      end; (* Term *)
119
```

*We are using our invariant here. After parsing a factor, Token, contains the first token following the factor. It might be a * or /, in which case the term is not yet complete, or it might not be a * or /, in which case it is.*

Notice that when the term finally ends, Factor, has read the first token following the factor. Implicitly, because a term always ends with a factor, this means that Token contains the first token following the term, preserving the invariant from the perspective of Term as well.

These calls reflect a decision to require intermediate, as well as final, results to remain in range.

*While straightforward-looking, these lines are really quite subtle. They are the basis for the entire recursive descent parsing method. We are using the stack mechanism implicit in recursion to remember what to do when. The time between reading the * or / and the execution of the multiplication or division can be quite long, as the factor to the right of the * or / can be an (E). This E will cause Term to be called again, and that term can contain its own multiplies and divides, but whether to multiply or divide for this term-factor pair will not be forgotten—it will be remembered when the recursion unwinds. Effectively, our recursive descent parser converts an infix expression into a postorder evaluation of the implicit parse tree.*

Instead of explicitly checking for an error, Term passes the potential problem off to Expr, since we hope there is no error. This is different than on entry to Factor, where we must see either a number or a (, or in Stmt, where, after parsing an expression we must see an endofline. Failure to see a number, (, or endofline indicates an error in the factor or statement, whereas Term has seen a valid term, even if the next token, the one following the term, is inappropriate.

```
120    (* procedure Expr(var EVal: integer); *)
121    procedure Expr;
122      (* Parse and evaluate an expression.
123
124        This routine corresponds to the productions
125          E --> E + T
126          E --> E - T
127          E --> T
128        with the recursion replaced by iteration, that is,
129          E --> T [+|-] T [+|-] ... [+|-] T
130      *)
131      var TVal: integer;
132      begin
133        Term(EVal);
134        while Token.LexicalObject in [plus,minus] do
135          if Token.LexicalObject = plus
136          then begin
137                 Lex;
138                 Term(TVal);
139                 EVal := EVal + TVal;
140                 CheckRange(EVal)
141               end
142          else begin
143                 Lex;
144                 Term(TVal);
145                 EVal := EVal - TVal;
146                 CheckRange(EVal)
147               end
148        (* Hopefully:  Token.LexicalObject in [rparen,endofline] *)
149    end; (* Expr *)
150
151    begin (* Stmt *)
152      Expr(EVal);
153      case Token.LexicalObject of
154        number, lparen:
155          ErrorOccurred(MissingOperator);
156        rparen:
157          ErrorOccurred(ExcessRightParen);
158        endofline, (* what is desired *)
159        endoffile: (* accept it *)
160          begin
161            write('Evaluates to ');
162            ConvertToRoman(EVal,RN);
163            for i := 1 to RN.numdigits do write(RN.number[i]);
164            writeln;
165            if Token.LexicalObject = endofline then Lex
166          end;
167        errtok: (* a lexical error occurred *)
168          ErrorOccurred(Token.message);
169        plus, minus, times, divide: (* not possible *)
170      end;
171
172  99:
173    end; (* Stmt *)
```

— *The caller, either* Factor *or* Stmt, *will sort out which of these is appropriate in the current situation.* Stmt *expects to see an* endofline *and rejects a*), *whereas* Factor *expects to see a*) *and rejects an* endofline.

This really can't occur in a line-oriented environment.

```
 1 type InputTokens = (number, lparen, rparen, plus, minus, times,
 2                       (* integer *) divide, endofline, endoffile, errtok);
 3
 4     FullToken = record
 5                   case LexicalObject: InputTokens of
 6                     lparen, rparen, plus, minus,
 7                       times, divide, endofline,
 8                         endoffile: (); (* no semantic information *)
 9                     number: (value: RomanRange);
10                     errtok: (message: ErrorType)
11                       (* let the parser handle errors discovered by the
12                          lexical analyzer *)
13                   end;
14
15 var Token: FullToken; (* current logical token *)
16
17 procedure InitLex; external;
18   (* This procedure should be called once, before  Lex  is called for
19      the first time.
20   *)
21
22 procedure Lex; external;
23   (* Get and return, in the global variable  Token , the next logical token
24      from the input stream.
25   *)
```

The lexical analyzer behaves as a filter for tokens in much the same way that GetChar *acts as a filter for characters. Each views the input as a stream in one alphabet, translating it into a stream in another alphabet.*

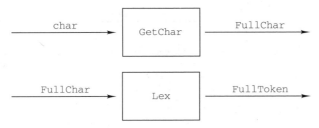

The translation performed by Lex *is more complex than the one performed by* GetChar, *because Roman numerals destroy the one-to-one correspondence between the input and the output.*

The approach used here is used in compiling languages like Pascal, only in Pascal Lex *must deal with many multicharacter tokens. Some have fixed length, like the keywords (*while, begin, *etc.) and* :=, *whereas others vary in length, like variables and numbers.*

```
 1 #include "roman.h"
 2 #include "charfilter.h"
 3 #include "error.h"
 4 #include "lex.h"
 5
 6 (* Invariant: On entry to  Lex  the static variable  CurrentChar  contains
 7                the character immediately following the last token processed.
 8                This happens naturally when the token is a Roman numeral.
 9                For consistency, we force it to happen in all cases.  The
10                token  endofline  is a special case.  We cannot force the read
11                in this one case, because the user expects the answer to appear
12                immediately after typing a line specifying a computation
13                (immediately after typing the carriage return).
14 *)
15 var CurrentChar: FullChar;
16     ReadDelayed: boolean; (* True on entry to  Lex  when the previous token
17                             returned was  endofline . *)
18
19 (* procedure InitLex; *)
20 procedure InitLex;
21   (* This procedure should be called once, before  Lex  is called for
22      the first time.
23   *)
24   begin
25     ReadDelayed := true (* Force a read on the first call to  Lex . *)
26   end; (* InitLex *)
27
28 (* procedure Lex; *)
29 procedure Lex;
30   (* Get and return, in the global variable  Token , the next logical token
31      from the input stream.
32   *)
33   label 99; (* return after error detected *)
34   var RN: RomanNumeral;
35       RNval: RomanRange; (* value of Roman numeral *)
36       error: boolean;
37   begin
38     (* If reading the character after the token was delayed, do the read now. *)
39     if ReadDelayed then GetChar(CurrentChar);
40
41     (* Skip to start of token --  we may already be there. *)
42     while CurrentChar.CharObject = blank do GetChar(CurrentChar);
43
44     case CurrentChar.CharObject of
45       blank:    (* not possible *) ;
46       endfile: begin
47                  (* Don't read past end of file. *)
48                  Token.LexicalObject := endoffile; (* No forced read, now... *)
49                  ReadDelayed := false (* ...and forevermore. *)
50                end;
51       endline: begin
52                  Token.LexicalObject := endofline; (* no forced read *)
53                  ReadDelayed := true
54                end;
```

See the discussion at Lexical analysis: dealing with the interaction of Roman numerals and line buffering, *p. 254.*

```
55      roman:
56        begin
57          (* The hard case -- a Roman numeral. *)
58          ReadDelayed := false; (* It won't be, even if the Roman numeral
59                                      is illegal because it is too long. *)
60        with RN do
61          begin
62            numdigits := 0;
63            (* Read characters that comprise a Roman numeral into  RN  until
64                we have read them all or the array is full, in which case,
65                if there is yet another character, the supposed Roman numeral
66                cannot be legal.
67            *)
68            repeat
69              numdigits := numdigits + 1;
70              number[numdigits] := CurrentChar.ch;
71              GetChar(CurrentChar)
72            until (numdigits = LONGESTROMAN)
73                  or (CurrentChar.CharObject <> roman)
74            (* If the Roman numeral wasn't illegal by being too long, then
75                we have maintained the invariant that after processing a
76                token we have read the logical character following the token.
77            *)
78          end;
79        if CurrentChar.CharObject = roman
80          then begin
81                Token.LexicalObject := errtok;
82                Token.message := IllegalRoman;
83                (* maintain invariant *)
84                repeat
85                  GetChar(CurrentChar)
86                until CurrentChar.CharObject <> roman;
87                goto 99 (* return *)
88              end;
89        ConvertToInteger(RN,RNval,error);
90        if error
91          then begin
92                Token.LexicalObject := errtok;
93                Token.message := IllegalRoman;
94                goto 99 (* return *)
95              end;
96        Token.LexicalObject := number;
97        Token.value := RNval
98      end;
99    algebraic:
100      begin
101        case CurrentChar.ch of
102          '+': Token.LexicalObject := plus;
103          '-': Token.LexicalObject := minus;
104          '*': Token.LexicalObject := times;
105          '/': Token.LexicalObject := divide;
106          '(': Token.LexicalObject := lparen;
107          ')': Token.LexicalObject := rparen
108        end;
```

This, as opposed to
    if RN.numdigits = LONGESTROMAN
is the correct test.

```
109              (* Force the read -- maintain the invariant that  CurrentChar  should
110                 be advanced past the token. *)
111              GetChar(CurrentChar);
112              ReadDelayed := false
113            end;
114        illegal:
115          begin
116            Token.LexicalObject := errtok;
117            Token.message := IllegalCharacter;
118            GetChar(CurrentChar); (* maintain invariant *)
119            ReadDelayed := false
120          end
121        end;
122 99: (* an error has been detected *)
123    end; (* Lex *)
```

CHAPTER 6

A SIMPLE MAKE
UTILITY

make (māk) *vb* **1** to bring into being by an action or process, manufacture **2** to enact or establish <*make* laws> *n* **1** a brand <send in the *make* and model number> **2** a UNIX utility for managing large programming projects (usu. written `make`)

In our discussion of the UNIX approach to independent compilation we saw how a hard-to-find bug can creep into a large program. The problem occurs when the programmer changes a procedure declaration in one of the `.h` files, but forgets to modify one of the `.p` files containing a call to the changed procedure. Even worse, the programmer might correctly modify all the affected `.p` files, but then accidentally fail to recompile one of them—finding the bug is now next to impossible, as no amount of staring at the source code will locate it.

The underlying cause of this problem is the inability of humans to remember masses of detail and to flawlessly perform simple, but repetitive, tasks; we shouldn't forget which `.p` files `include` which `.h` files and we shouldn't forget to recompile them, but we do. Turbo Pascal eliminates the need to worry about these details by providing a program management tool, the `Compile|Make` option. The compiler tracks down all the pieces of a program that need to be recompiled, does the compilation, and then links all the pieces together to form a single, executable program. In the absence of a built-in facility, it would be helpful if we could at least record the structure of a program once and for all and then just issue a single command that compiles those files that need recompiling. Actually, the UNIX operating system does provide such a tool. It is called `make` and it is a general, language-independent utility for managing large projects. While `make` has many bells and whistles that improve the user interface, understanding the essential ideas behind `make` and the Turbo Pascal `Compile|Make` option is not difficult—in this final chapter we develop a simple, but usable, `make` utility. ▫

6.1   OVERVIEW OF THE make UTILITY

So that we can begin our discussion of make with a concrete example, we return to the program where independent compilation was first used—the program for the game of worm. Here, the details of the code and even the overall purpose of the program are unimportant; all we care about is the program's structure, which is diagrammed in Figure 6–1. The upper portion of the figure reflects the structure of the source code—it indicates which .p and .c files physically incorporate which .h files; there are arrows from worm.p to pscr.h and random.h because lines 7 and 8 of worm.p are

```
#include "pscr.h"
#include "random.h"
```

The lower portion of the figure contains the same information, but it subtly shifts our thinking away from considering the worm program as source code text to viewing it as a collection of source (.h, .p, and .c), object (.o), and executable (worm) files. In the upper portion, a change to a file at the head of an arrow implies that the file at the tail of the arrow should be modified and then recompiled. In the lower portion, a change to a file at the head of an arrow implies that the file at the tail of the arrow needs to be recreated. The shift in emphasis is away from "who it is done to" to "who it is done for." This change of perspective is important to understanding how make works and what it can do for us.

The information displayed graphically in the lower portion of Figure 6–1 is recorded by the programmer in an ordinary text file (usually named makefile) as the program is developed. make reads this file and, based on its contents and

---

FIGURE 6–1   The Dependency Graph for the Files of worm

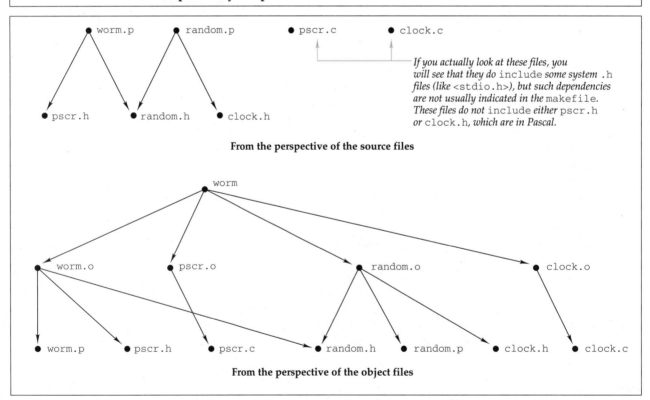

If you actually look at these files, you will see that they do include some system .h files (like <stdio.h>), but such dependencies are not usually indicated in the makefile. These files do not include either pscr.h or clock.h, which are in Pascal.

From the perspective of the source files

From the perspective of the object files

on information it obtains from the file system, determines which files need to be rebuilt. It then issues the appropriate rebuilding commands. The `makefile` for the `worm` program is shown in Figure 6–2. Each pair of lines, like lines 11 and 12

```
random.o:       random.h random.p clock.h
                pc -c -casesense random.p
```

defines a set of ***dependencies*** and a ***rebuilding command***. The file to be rebuilt is referred to as the ***target***, while the files from which it is created are called its ***sources***. A target in one context can be a source in another; for example, on line 1,

```
worm:           worm.o pscr.o random.o clock.o
```

`random.o` is a source for `worm`. In the `makefile` of Figure 6–2 every target but one is used as the source of some other target; the single exception is `worm`. It is the ultimate target, the executable program we really want to build. At the

---

FIGURE 6–2   The `makefile` for the `worm` Program

*The UNIX `make` utility automatically takes its input from a file named `makefile`. Our `make` utility takes its input from a file redirected to standard input (`make < `**filename**`). The UNIX `make` utility has an option, the `-f` option (`make -f `**filename**`), which instructs `make` to take its input from a user-specified file.*

The UNIX `make` utility has a number of annoying rules. The first character of a line containing a rebuilding command must be a tab and cannot be the visually identical sequence of blanks.

```
1 worm:           worm.o pscr.o random.o clock.o
2                 pc worm.o pscr.o random.o clock.o -ltermlib -o worm
3
4 worm.o:         worm.p pscr.h random.h
5                 pc -c -C -casesense worm.p
6
```

Options to the DEC Pascal for RISC compiler.

In violation of the Pascal standard, treat upper and lowercase letters as different, that is, be case sensitive.

Perform various runtime checks, such as checking for array subscripts out of bounds.

Compile this file with the understanding that independent compilation is being used.

```
7 pscr.o:         pscr.c
8                 cc -c pscr.c
9
10 # runtime checks off as  random.p  relies on integer overflow being undetected
11 random.o:       random.h random.p clock.h
12                 pc -c -casesense random.p
13
14 clock.o:        clock.c
15                 cc -c clock.c
```

The order in which the source files are listed is irrelevant. It need not be the same as the order of the `#include` statements.

The UNIX `make` utility allows exploration to be limited to a subportion of the dependency graph. The command

```
                make worm.o
```

rebuilds only `worm.o` and any files on which it depends, directly or indirectly.

other end of the spectrum, the .h, .p, and .c files never appear as targets. This is because they cannot be rebuilt automatically—their creation and maintenance are the responsibility of the programmer.

Studying the makefile reinforces the language-independent, file-oriented nature of make. make does not look inside files. It does not examine worm.p, searching for the lines #include "pscr.h" and #include "random.h"; this information must be explicitly stated on the dependency line. And make does not know that worm.o should be rebuilt by compiling worm.p; it has to be told this as well.

make is also not a tool for determining when source files require modification. Its purpose is to ensure that any necessary compilations are performed, without resorting to simply recompiling everything. The arrow from random.p to random.h in the upper portion of Figure 6–1 acts as a reminder that changes made to random.h necessitate changes to random.p. The diagram in the lower portion of the figure and the contents of the makefile don't convey this information. If the programmer fails to modify random.p to reflect changes made to random.h, this will be caught, but not directly by make. make will see that random.o is older than the modified random.h, and so will issue the command

```
pc -c -casesense random.p
```

It is the Pascal compiler that will discover the error.

Before we look more carefully at make, we pause to compare it to the Turbo Pascal Compile|Make option. Deep down, the two programs are the same. They both build an internal representation of the relationships between the source files (.p or .PAS), the object files (.o or .TPU), and the executable file (.EXE in MS-DOS) and they both rebuild any out-of-date files. The two programs differ in where they get their information. make expects the programmer to provide it in the form of a makefile; the Compile|Make option has built-in knowledge about the structure of Turbo Pascal programs—it searches for uses clauses and knows that the way to build a .TPU file is to compile the corresponding .PAS file. The UNIX approach is more flexible—it isn't tied to Pascal or even compilation, and the rebuilding commands can be anything—but it requires effort on the part of the programmer. It is also error prone: the humanly constructed makefile might not reflect the structure of the program accurately, a problem that cannot arise with the Turbo Pascal Compile|Make option. They both have their place and are really just different interfaces to the same fundamental process.[1]

How does make actually work? When make is invoked it first reads the makefile and analyzes it. Next, for each dependency line, make queries the operating system to determine if the target file exists, and if it does, at what time it was last created. It also determines the last-modified time for all the source files on which the target depends. make's basic rule of operation is

> *If the target does not exist, or if any source is newer than the target, rebuild the target by invoking the rebuilding command.*

make applies this rule recursively, *in an intelligent order*. For example, suppose that worm is newer than all the .o files on which it depends, but random.o

---

[1] In addition to the Compile|Make option, Turbo Pascal also comes with a make utility, but because the Compile|Make option is so handy, it is hardly ever used. The real UNIX make utility, unlike ours, does have some built-in knowledge and includes a mechanism for teaching it more—see Project 6–4.

is out of date with respect to `random.p`—perhaps there was a small bug in the coding of the algorithm that has just been corrected. Using its basic rule of operation, `make` first rebuilds `random.o` and then notices that `worm` is out of date with respect to its sources so it rebuilds `worm` as well. As the lower portion of Figure 6–1 suggests, `make` works more or less from the bottom to the top, and does not just proceed linearly through the `makefile`—the reason for the "more or less" is that an understanding of the exact order will have to wait until we develop a little more of the theory underlying `make`. This bottom-up approach guarantees that when `make` considers rebuilding a target it won't get caught in the position of deciding that the target is up to date, only to have its understanding invalidated by a subsequent action.

6.2 MODELING THE `make` PROCESS ABSTRACTLY

Of course, `make` does not have the representation of Figure 6–1 at its disposal. It has to build it up from the contents of the `makefile`, and since the layout and the notions of "up" and "down" are peculiarly human, some more abstract representation is necessary. The fundamental mathematical structure needed is the *graph* (not to be confused with the graphs you drew in high school or with those that chart the rise and fall of the stock market). Graphs come in two kinds, *directed* and *undirected*. An undirected graph, $G = (V, E)$, is a collection of *vertices* and *edges*. A small graph is shown in Figure 6–3. The physical layout may aid our comprehension, but it is just for our convenience. The real graph is just the formal description of V and E. That edges cross in the layout is of no special significance; possibly a different arrangement would have no crossings, though it is not always possible to produce such a layout.

A directed graph, $G = (V, A)$, is similar, except the edges (now called *arcs*) have a direction. Pictorially, we draw them as arrows, as shown in Figure 6–4, which suggest a direction of travel. Graphs, both undirected and directed, have a myriad of applications. Undirected graphs with weights associated with the edges model networks of highways. Each vertex is a city, each edge a highway, and the weight of an edge is the distance between the two cities. The results of a summer's worth of friendly games of tennis can be represented as a directed graph. There is an arc from Fred to Charlie if Fred beat Charlie. If Fred and

---

FIGURE 6–3   An Undirected Graph

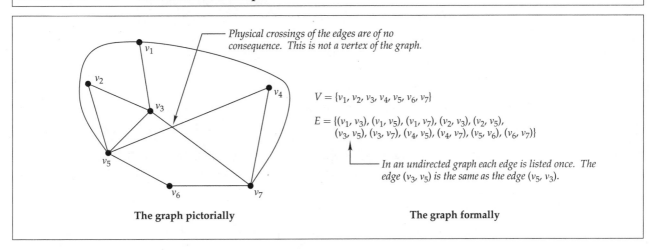

Physical crossings of the edges are of no consequence. This is not a vertex of the graph.

$V = \{v_1, v_2, v_3, v_4, v_5, v_6, v_7\}$

$E = \{(v_1, v_3), (v_1, v_5), (v_1, v_7), (v_2, v_3), (v_2, v_5),$
$\quad (v_3, v_5), (v_3, v_7), (v_4, v_5), (v_4, v_7), (v_5, v_6), (v_6, v_7)\}$

In an undirected graph each edge is listed once. The edge (v_3, v_5) is the same as the edge (v_5, v_3).

The graph pictorially   **The graph formally**

FIGURE 6–4   A Directed Graph

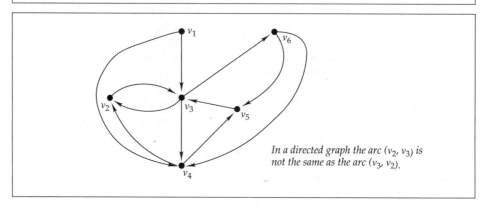

In a directed graph the arc (v_2, v_3) is not the same as the arc (v_3, v_2).

Representing graphs inside a computer

Charlie played a second time and this time Charlie won, then there will be an arc from Charlie to Fred as well—the arcs connecting v_2 and v_3 in Figure 6–4 illustrate this possibility. We can use weights to indicate that Mary has clobbered Bob, beating him five times in the course of the summer. If a player never lost, then all the arcs incident to the vertex representing that player will be directed away from the vertex. Such a vertex is called a *source*. If some poor soul lost every game, all the arcs incident to the vertex representing that player will be directed inward. Such a vertex is called a *sink*. Because people have good days and bad days, the results of a summer of tennis might not leave any players undefeated nor leave any unvictorious—a directed graph need not have any sources or sinks. From Figure 6–1 we see that the dependencies between program modules are best modeled as a directed graph.[2]

The diagrammatic representations of Figures 6–3 and 6–4 may be convenient for humans, but they aren't very practical for use inside a computer. There are two standard representations of graphs well-suited to computer applications: *adjacency matrices* and *adjacency lists*. Figure 6–5 gives both for the graph of Figure 6–4. The two representations are rather obvious. In the adjacency matrix representation there is a 1 in M_{ij} if there is an arc from v_i to v_j and a 0 otherwise. The adjacency list representation uses an array of linked lists. For each vertex there is a linked list indicating those vertices to which the vertex is connected by an outward-directed arc. Those vertices to which it isn't connected by an outward-directed arc are defined implicitly: they are just absent from the list. For sparse graphs, those without many edges, the adjacency list representation takes up less space. Adjacency lists are also often easier to use in the framework of a computer program because we often wish to execute the line

                for all neighbors of v do ...

and with the adjacency list representation there is no need to include program logic to skip over nonneighbors. For undirected graphs, each edge is represented twice: the value of M_{ij} is the same as that of M_{ji} and j is on the adjacency list of vertex i if and only if i is on the adjacency list of vertex j. It is as if we replaced each undirected edge with two directed arcs, one in each direction.

---

[2] The terminology with respect to make is a bit confusing. The ultimate target is a source in the graph theory sense, and the sources on the dependency lines are never sources to the graph theorist, since they always have a least one incoming arc. In fact, some of the sources in make terminology, the .h, .p, and .c files, are really sinks.

FIGURE 6–5 The Internal Representation of the Directed Graph of Figure 6–4

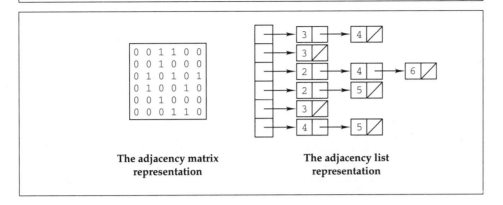

$$\begin{bmatrix} 0 & 0 & 1 & 1 & 0 & 0 \\ 0 & 0 & 1 & 0 & 0 & 0 \\ 0 & 1 & 0 & 1 & 0 & 1 \\ 0 & 1 & 0 & 0 & 1 & 0 \\ 0 & 0 & 1 & 0 & 0 & 0 \\ 0 & 0 & 0 & 1 & 1 & 0 \end{bmatrix}$$

The adjacency matrix
representation

The adjacency list
representation

In representing the dependency graph of a collection of program modules, there is one problem with the standard representations: the names of the vertices are character strings instead of numbers. In a `makefile` there is no v_3. There are only names like `random.o` and `clock.h`. This makes it hard to have an array of adjacency lists, since we cannot index into an array with character strings. We can get around this difficulty by being a little more fluid in our thinking. Figure 6–6 shows how we can achieve much the same effect using only dynamically allocated storage. The main difference is that, unlike with an array of linked lists, this representation won't let us jump to the start of an adjacency list out of the blue. This is a capability we will not need when we check the graph implicitly defined by the `makefile` for legality or when we use the graph to rebuild the ultimate target, though we will need to be able to find the `Node` associated with a file name when building the internal representation of the graph from the `makefile`. In the representation of Figure 6–6, the only vertex we will be able to reach directly will be the one for the ultimate target, which we get to via the variable `Root`. `Node` has other fields not shown in the figure—we will need to record the name of a vertex, when the corresponding file was last modified, and how to rebuild the file if it is out of date—but these fields need not concern us for now.

The complete declaration for a `Node` *is given in* `Basic_Defs.h`.

The graph that describes the dependencies among a collection of program modules has some special properties. For one thing, it should have only one source, though it can have many sinks. More importantly, and unlike the graph of Figure 6–4, it cannot have any cycles. A *cycle* is a sequence of arcs that to the eye form a circle. Formally, it is a sequence of vertices where there is an arc from each vertex to the next vertex in the sequence, with a final arc connecting the last vertex to the first vertex. In Figure 6–4 the vertices v_3, v_4, and v_5 form a cycle. Some cycles are harder to see: the vertices v_6, v_4, v_2, and v_3 also form a cycle. The structure of a program dictates that the graph defined by the `makefile` should have no cycles. If there were a cycle, then one of the files would always have to be out of date with respect to some other file, since we cannot travel all the way around the cycle saying "the file at the head of the arrow is older," "the file at the head of the arrow is older," "the file at the head of the arrow is older." If we could, eventually we would come back to where we started and have to conclude that the file from which we started is older than itself—a ridiculous situation. The dependency graph of a program is a *directed acyclic graph*— *acyclic* means "without cycles." The requirement that a program dependency graph not have cycles doesn't prevent a user from typing in a `makefile` that

Directed acyclic graphs

FIGURE 6–6   Representing the Dependency Graph for worm inside the Computer

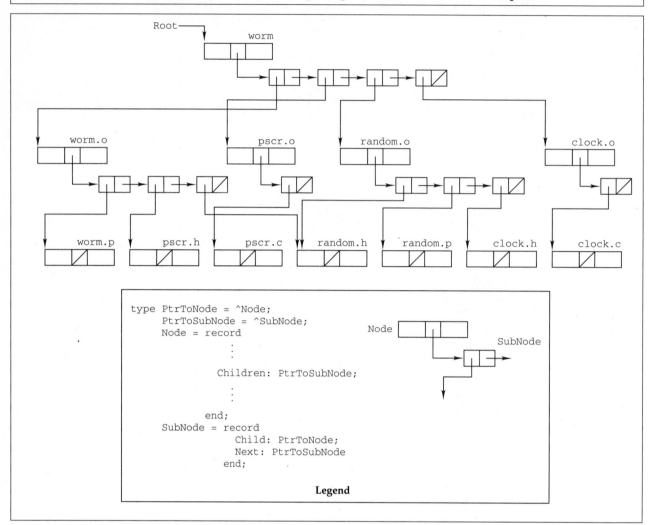

Legend

does—it just means that our program will have to detect the presence of cycles, and print out an error message if it finds any. A finite, directed acyclic graph always has at least one source, though it can have many. One of the ground rules of the simple `make` processor we are going to write is that the very first target it encounters should be the ultimate target, and consequently must be a source (in the graph theory sense) and must be the only source. The program will have to check for this condition as well.

EXERCISE 6–1   Prove that a finite, directed acyclic graph must have at least one source.

Depth-First Search

The main program of our `make` utility, found in the file `Make.p`, is essentially three lines long:

```
BuildGraph(Root); (* convert the input file into a directed graph *)
CheckGraph(Root); (* check the graph for errors *)
Rebuild(Root)     (* do the  make  *)
```

BuildGraph reads the makefile and builds the graph. CheckGraph checks that the graph is a single-source, acyclic graph and that the ultimate target is the single source. If the graph is free of errors, Rebuild processes the graph, issuing commands to the operating system to perform any necessary rebuilding. The most interesting steps from an algorithmic stand point are the second and the third, and we will begin there, assuming that CheckGraph is passed a pointer to a graph represented as pictured in Figure 6–6. The underlying algorithm used in both CheckGraph and Rebuild is known as ***depth-first search***. This algorithm is a generalization of a recursive tree walk. Because the different subtrees of a tree do not share nodes, recursively walking a tree is very easy—the code is given in Figure 6–7. The call to Visit is an abstraction of "process the data associated with the node pointed to by p." The two natural locations for this call are either immediately before or immediately after recursively processing the subtrees. If the call to Visit is performed first, the walk is called a ***preorder traversal***; if done afterwards, it is called a ***postorder traversal***. Whether preorder or postorder traversal is more appropriate depends on the application. Referring back to Figure 6–1, we see that make needs to work from the bottom up: the question of whether worm needs to be rebuilt cannot be answered until each of worm.o, pscr.o, random.o, and clock.o has either been rebuilt or certified as up to date. Since the children of a node must be processed before the node itself, a postorder traversal is what we need.

FIGURE 6–7   Recursively Walking a Tree

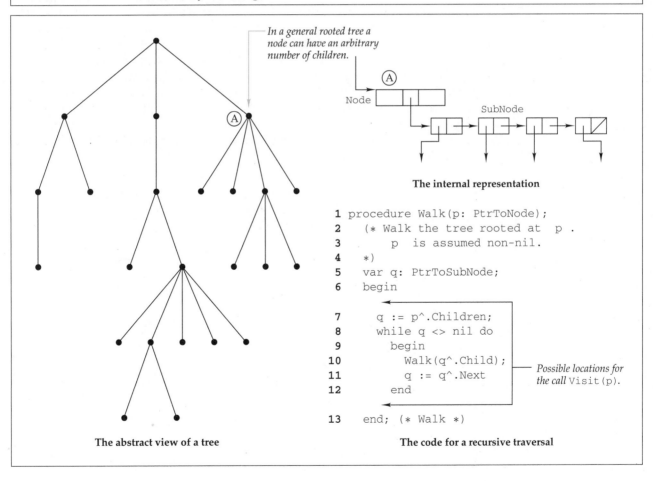

In a general rooted tree a node can have an arbitrary number of children.

The internal representation

```
1  procedure Walk(p: PtrToNode);
2    (* Walk the tree rooted at  p .
3        p  is assumed non-nil.
4    *)
5    var q: PtrToSubNode;
6    begin

7      q := p^.Children;
8      while q <> nil do
9        begin
10         Walk(q^.Child);
11         q := q^.Next
12       end

13   end; (* Walk *)
```

— *Possible locations for the call* Visit(p).

The abstract view of a tree   **The code for a recursive traversal**

The procedure of Figure 6–7 is a too simplistic for traversing graphs. As an extreme example, consider what the procedure does if passed the root of the graph of Figure 6–8. If you trace the execution of the program by hand you will see that the procedure will enter the subgraph at Ⓐ time after time, and will explore it completely over and over again. If there are n vertices on the second level of this graph and n vertices in the subgraph rooted at Ⓐ, then there will be $n^2 + n + 1$ calls to Visit, even though the graph has only $2n + 1$ vertices and $3n - 1$ edges. As extreme as this example is, there are worse.

EXERCISE 6–2   Construct an example where the number of calls to Visit grows exponentially with the number of vertices and edges.

Worst of all, if the graph contains a cycle, the recursive procedure of Figure 6–7 will go into an infinite loop.

This repetitious visitation of previously visited subgraphs can be prevented by including a flag with each vertex, an extra field that indicates whether this vertex has been encountered before. The code for recursively walking a graph so that no vertex is visited twice is given in Figure 6–9. In the representation of the graph used in Figure 6–6, it isn't clear how we will set all the Encountered fields to false before making the initial call to Walk, but for problems where it is possible to use the standard adjacency list representation of Figure 6–5 this step is simple: the Encountered field is stored as part of the list header, and the initialization is accomplished by just running down the array, setting the field to false. This flag prevents both repetitive visits to subgraphs and infinite looping. In the case of the graph of Figure 6–8, the first time the subgraph at Ⓐ is entered all the Encountered fields in the subgraph will still be false. As the algorithm explores this portion of the graph it will set them all to true. Later, when the algorithm attempts to reenter this subgraph it will discover that the Encountered field of the vertex at Ⓐ is true, and it will back out immediately. In the case of a graph with cycles, when the algorithm is about to return to the vertex that begins the cycle, it will likewise discover that the vertex has been encountered previously, and will just back out.

FIGURE 6–8   A Potential Source of Difficulty for a Recursive Graph Search algorithm

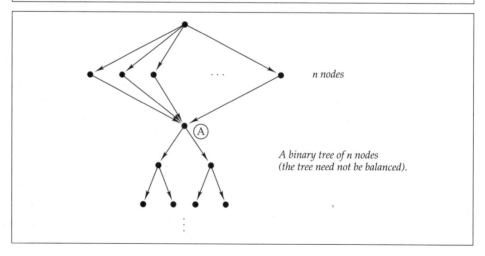

n nodes

A binary tree of n nodes
(the tree need not be balanced).

FIGURE 6–9   Depth-First Search of a Graph

```
 1 procedure DFS(Root: PtrToNode);
 2   procedure Walk(p: PtrToNode);
 3     var q: PtrToSubNode;
 4     begin
 5       if not p^.Encountered
 6         then begin
 7                 p^.Encountered := true;
 8                 q := p^.Children;
 9                 while q <> nil do
10                   begin
11                     Walk(q^.Child);
12                       q := q^.Next
13                   end
14             end
15     end; (* Walk *)
16   begin (* DFS *)
17     ... initialize all the Encountered fields to false ...
18     Walk(Root)
19   end; (* DFS *)
```

Note very carefully the placement of the line

```
p^.Encountered := true
```

This *must* be done before the recursive calls are made. For a directed acyclic graph (like the one in Figure 6–8) this line can safely be placed either before or after the recursive calls, but for a graph with cycles it is essential that the Encountered field be set to true when the algorithm first reaches the vertex and not when it backs out of the vertex. The location of the call to Visit is a separate matter, and it can still come either before or after the recursive calls. As we have seen, for the make program it must come afterward.

On *any* directed graph, depth-first search will call Visit for each node at most once and traverse (that is, make a recursive call for) each arc at most once as well. Whether it backs out of the traversal immediately or only after visiting the vertex at the far end of the arc (and visiting all that vertex's unvisited descendants as well) will depend on whether the Encountered field of the vertex is true or false. A graph traversal algorithm cannot do less work than to just visit each vertex and traverse each arc at most once; depth-first search is as efficient as possible!

EXERCISE 6–3   To see how the depth-first search algorithm avoids infinite looping when run on a graph with cycles, execute the algorithm by hand on the graph of Figure 6–4, starting from v_1. Use the ordering as it is stored in the adjacency lists of Figure 6–5, not as it appears to the eye in Figure 6–4. As you encounter the vertices for the first time, number them consecutively—this numbering is known as the *dfs numbering*.

EXERCISE 6–4   If depth-first search is performed on an undirected graph, how efficient is it?

6.3   THE LOGIC BEHIND `Rebuild`

When the depth-first search algorithm finds a vertex with the `Encountered` field set to `true`, it does not know if the field is `true` because it has rediscovered a completely explored subgraph, or because it has just walked the last arc that proves the graph has a cycle. We will need to add a bit more to the code of Figure 6–9 to separate these two cases, but we have already learned enough about depth-first search to understand how `Rebuild` works. By the time `Make` calls `Rebuild` the graph has already passed the checks performed by `CheckGraph`, so we are assured that the graph is a single-source, acyclic graph, and that `Root` points to that source. This implies that when the depth-first search performed by `Rebuild` finds a vertex where `Encountered` is `true`, it must be because the algorithm is reentering a previously explored subgraph, which means the file at the head of the arrow has either already been rebuilt or has been certified as up to date; `Rebuild` can safely back out without doing additional work. All that remains to be discussed are a lot of system details involved with determining the time that a file was last modified and the issuing of commands that have been stored away someplace as strings. In high-level pseudocode, `Rebuild` is given in Figure 6–10.

Details of the data structures

Refer to `Basic_Defs.h` *and* `String.h` *while reading this.*

To fully understand the code in `Rebuild.p` we need to learn more about the fine details of the data structures used in this case study. Figure 6–11 displays pictorially what is contained in the files `Basic_Defs.h` and `String.h`. We have already studied the field `Children` and the type `SubNode`, and should have a sense that `Touched` and `Rebuilt` are somehow tied up with the depth-first

---

FIGURE 6–10   The Overall Logic of `Rebuild`

```
procedure Rebuild(Root: PtrToNode);
  (* Rebuild the ultimate target and any descendants that need rebuilding. *)
  procedure RecRebuild(p: PtrToNode);
    begin
      if not p^.Encountered
        then begin
              p^.Encountered := true;

              Recursively rebuild the descendants of p, if it has any. None, some, or all of the
              descendants may have already been rebuilt. After any rebuilding, determine the
              time at which the most recently modified child was created.

              Query the system to determine whether the file described by p exists, and if it does,
              when it was last modified.

              if the file does not exist or is out of date
                then begin
                      if there is no rebuilding command, as would be the case with a .h, .p, or .c file,
                      then report an error.

                      Call on the system to execute the rebuilding command that will rebuild the file.
                  end
          end

      (* else the node pointed to by p has already been either rebuilt or certified as up to date. *)
    end; (* RecRebuild *)
  begin (* Rebuild *)
    ... initialize all the Encountered fields to false ...
    RecRebuild(Root)
  end; (* Rebuild *)
```

FIGURE 6–11　The Data Structures Used in the make Case Study

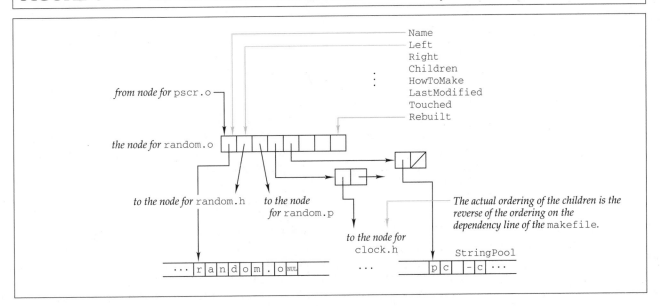

search, taking the place of Encountered in the abstract treatment. HowToMake and the type MakeNode parallel Children and SubNode, so there aren't any surprises lurking there, except that based on the makefile for the worm program you might wonder why we need a list of rebuilding commands, instead of space for just one. We are just giving ourselves some flexibility: it is sometimes necessary to execute a sequence of commands to rebuild a file—remember that make is a general tool, not tied to Pascal.

You might have noticed, by looking at either the figure or the fields Name in Node and Command in MakeNode, that the file names and the rebuilding commands are stored in what appears to be a funny way. They are not stored as linked lists, one character per cell, which is what most Pascal programmers expect. They are all jammed into one long array of characters, StringPool, one right after the other, filling up the left-hand portion of the array, while the right-hand portion is vacant. The variable NextFree (declared on line 15 of BuildGraph.p) marks the transition between these two portions. There are advantages and disadvantages to this general approach. Provided that strings are never deleted or modified, storing strings in a long array of characters is both time and space efficient. If there are no deletions or modifications, there will never be fragments of unused storage lying around in the left-hand portion of StringPool nor will a string need to grow but find that it does not have the room to do so. With this no-deletion/no-modification regimen there is no need for complicated storage management algorithms, like those found in BASIC interpreters where strings are free to grow and shrink. When a new string needs to be added, it is just placed in StringPool starting at NextFree and this pointer is then bumped up. This regimen of additions, but no deletions or modifications, describes our situation exactly: when BuildGraph reads the makefile, building up the graph, it adds to the collection of strings that occur in the file. During this graph-building phase nothing is ever deleted or changed; the collection of strings just grows and grows. During the checking and file-rebuilding phases the strings stored in StringPool are used, but not modified or deleted. When the entire program terminates, the storage used by the program is returned to the operating system all at once.

Storing file names and command lines

There are just a few small details to clarify. If `Name` and `Command` are indices into `StringPool`, each pointing to the start of a file name or command, how do we know where each string ends and the next string begins? There are two standard approaches. Either the first byte can contain the number of characters in the string (the approach used by Turbo Pascal to support the built-in type `string`) or a flag can be placed at the end of the string (the approach taken by C, which uses the ASCII NUL character as the flag). Both variations are storage efficient because a string of length n occupies $n+1$ bytes, whereas a linked list of single characters can require up to eight bytes per character, depending on the hardware. This savings of space is a bit artificial, however. The entire array must be allocated when the program begins execution, even if only a tiny fraction of it gets used, and if we need more space than we have allocated to `StringPool` we are simply out of luck.

The real motivation for storing strings in this manner is not, however, a concern for efficiency—the approach used in the `make` program matches the interface to UNIX exactly and the interface to MS-DOS very closely. In the same vein, while the need for `LastModified` is fairly obvious in the context of a `make` utility, its type is `integer` and not some record containing the year, month, day, and time of day to conform to the operating system's notion of how time is represented internally. If time were represented by the operating system as a record `LastModified` would be stored as a record and we would need to write a small routine to compare two times. Our interest in time is not absolute; the program for `make` needs to know only if one file is older than another. How to query the operating system to determine if a file exists and how to issue a command like

```
pc worm.o pscr.o random.o clock.o -ltermlib -o worm
```

from inside a program are details that vary from operating system to operating system. To enable our `make` utility to be as portable as possible, this portion of the code is isolated in the file `System_Interface.p` in the UNIX version of the program and in the implementation section of `unit SystemInterface` in the Turbo Pascal version. This is the only portion of the program that will require modification if we decide to port the program to a new system. UNIX provides access to procedures with the same functionality as `TimeStamp` and `ExecuteCommand` through one of its standard library files; Turbo Pascal does this through the `Dos` library unit.

The only unresolved issue in translating the pseudocode of Figure 6–10 into the code found in `Rebuild.p` is how to initialize all the `Encountered` fields to `false`. Because `Rebuild` is the last of the three main procedures to execute, the issue is moot: a side effect of `CheckGraph` is that it leaves all the `Rebuilt` fields set to `false`. By letting `Rebuilt` take on the role of `Encountered` the difficulty goes away—though not for long, since `CheckGraph` also does a depth-first search, and it does it under less ideal circumstances, since it cannot assume the graph is cycle free and single source.

This is as good a place as any for an admission: there is a bug in the program for `make`. More precisely, there are certain abuses that it does not detect. The program we are developing is meant to be a useful tool, not a bulletproof monstrosity. While it deals successfully with the kinds of errors users will almost certainly make (for example, spelling the name of a file incorrectly or creating a Pascal file that contains syntax errors), our program assumes that the user isn't malicious. In particular, it assumes that the rebuilding commands for one file will not delete some other file that has already been certified as up to date or otherwise cause earlier work done by `make` to be invalidated. Since our program doesn't analyze the commands, it has no way of telling whether something un-

FIGURE 6–12   A Maliciously Designed makefile

```
1 pgm:        a.o b.o
2             pc a.o b.o -o pgm
3
4 a.o:        b.h a.p
5             pc -c a.p
6
7 b.o:        b.h b.p           If neither a.o nor b.o exist, make first builds a.o and
8             rm a.o            then builds b.o. When it goes to build pgm, pc discovers
9             pc -c b.p         that a.o does not exist and issues an error message.
```

FIGURE 6–13   The Essence of BuildGraph

```
 1 read(N);
 2 for i := 1 to N do G[i] := nil; (* set adjacency list headers to  nil  *)
 3 for i := 1 to N do
 4   begin
 5     read(j); (* read vertex name at head of arrow *)
 6     while j <> -1 do
 7       begin
 8         (* insert edge into graph *)
 9         new(p);
10         p^ .data := j;
11         p^ .next := G[i];
12         G[i] := p;
13
14         read(j)
15       end
16   end
```

derhanded, like the situation depicted in Figure 6–12, is occurring. The program does, on lines 77–83 of `Rebuild.p`, attempt to detect obvious problems: after supposedly rebuilding a file it checks to see that it exists and is up to date.

6.4   BuildGraph AND CheckGraph

The principles underlying `BuildGraph` are straightforward. Returning to the simplified situation of Figure 6–4, where the names of the vertices are just integers, if the data file describing the graph in human-readable form looks like

```
        ┌─── number of vertices in graph
        ▼
6
3   4  -1 ◄─── adjacency list for v_1 (-1 is a flag)
3  -1
2   4   6  -1
2   5  -1
3  -1
4   5  -1
```

then the body of the code for `BuildGraph` is the code fragment in Figure 6–13. When run on the above data, this code will produce the adjacency list representation of Figure 6–5, except that the lists will be stored in reverse order because the procedure places each new edge on the front of the list instead of at the back. Since the edges incident to a vertex have no implied order, this reversal is of no consequence.

In the context of `make`, `BuildGraph` is logically no more complex; the line

```
random.o:        random.h random.p clock.h
```

is the same as

```
2    4    6  -1
```

except that the end-of-list flag is implicit, the vertex associated with this adjacency list (`random.o`) is explicitly stated, the number of vertices the graph has is unknown in advance, and *the names of the vertices are strings.*

Binary Search Trees

The need to do the logical equivalent of indexing an array with a string occurs so frequently that many efficient solutions have been developed for this operation. The conceptually simplest is the ***binary search tree***. A binary search tree is a binary tree in which each node contains a key, and the nodes of the tree satisfy the following property, known as the Binary Search Tree Property:

For every node in the tree, the keys of all the nodes in its left subtree must be less than the key of the node and the keys of all the nodes in its right subtree must be greater than the key of the node.

Keys can be integers or strings—they just must have an implied ordering. The binary search tree constructed by `BuildGraph` for the file names that occur in the `makefile` for the `worm` program is shown in Figure 6–14. Finding a node

FIGURE 6–14   A Binary Search Tree Containing the Names of the Files in the `makefile` for the `worm` Program

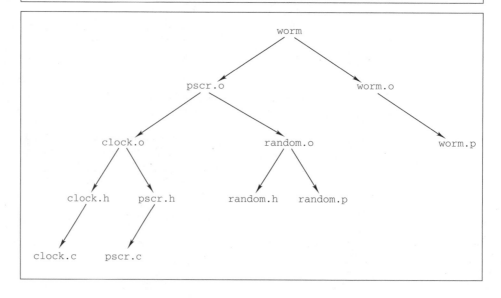

in a binary search tree given its key is simple:

- Begin at the root.
- If we have fallen off the tree, a node with this key is not present.
- Based on the relationship between the key of the node we are at and the key of the node we are searching for, either quit, because we have found the desired node, or continue the search in either the left or the right subtree.

The binary search tree property allows us to continue the search in just one of the subtrees without fear that the node we are searching for lies down the unexplored branch.

EXERCISE 6–5   Can we change the binary search tree property to the weaker rule?

> *For every node in the tree, the key of the left subchild (if it has one) must be less than the key of the node and the key of the right subchild (if it has one) must be greater than the key of the node.*

Insertion of a new node is a slight extension of searching for a node: the search proceeds until it falls off the tree—the new node is then inserted as a leaf at that point. At the time when `random.h` was inserted into the tree of Figure 6–14 the tree looked like

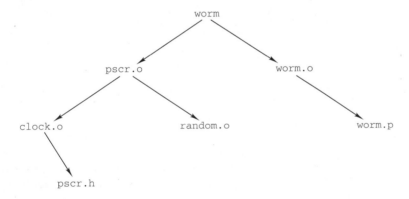

The search for `random.h` started at `worm`, went to the left and, after a comparison with `pscr.o`, went to the right. A comparison to `random.o` caused the search to go to the left; since the algorithm fell off the tree at this point, `random.h` was inserted as the left child of `random.o`.

Deletion of a node in a binary search tree is more complicated, but in the `make` project we do not have deletions. Binary search trees exhibit good average-case performance: on a tree constructed by inserting n randomly ordered keys into an initially empty tree, the average time to perform a FIND is $O(\log n)$. Unfortunately, if the data used to build the tree is in alphabetical order, the tree degenerates into a list and the search time becomes $O(n)$. This is a problem when n is large, and sophisticated rebalancing strategies have been developed to guarantee $O(\log n)$ worst-case performance. But using such algorithms here would be overkill. Even a large `makefile` has less than 100 file names and the names are unlikely to be inserted in alphabetical order anyway. This $O(\log n)$ performance is worse than

**FOR YOUR
INFORMATION**

When Not to Use Recursion

Recursion is a wonderfully elegant tool, but its use isn't always appropriate. An example of the inappropriate use of recursion is the ever popular program of Figure 6–15. The code is a recursive implementation of the binary search tree operations FIND and INSERT. It is so easy to express these operations recursively that we often overlook the fact that the iterative version used in `FindAndInsert` is better. (That FIND and INSERT are combined into one routine in `FindAndInsert` is immaterial; it is the principle that is at issue.)

There are several minor flaws with the recursive code given in the figure, but even after fixing these we will see that a devastating criticism remains. Among the minor flaws, first there is the ugliness of the repeated passing in of x on lines 7 and 9 of `Find` and lines 13 and 15 of `Insert`, even though x never changes. This can be remedied by defining a nonrecursive shell, containing a recursive subprocedure. Using this approach `Find` becomes

```
1   function Find(x: integer; Root: PtrToNode): PtrToNode;
2     (* Find the node containing  x  in the binary search tree rooted at  Root . *)
3     function RecFind(p: PtrToNode): PtrToNode;
4       begin
5         if p = nil
6           then RecFind := nil
7         else if x < p^.Data
8           then RecFind := RecFind(p^.Left)
9         else if x > p^.Data
10          then RecFind := RecFind(p^.Right)
11        else (* x = p^.Data *) RecFind := p
12      end; (* RecFind *)
13    begin (* Find *)
14      Find := RecFind(Root)
15    end; (* Find *)
```

A second complaint that can be levied against both the code of Figure 6–15 and the modification just discussed is that after recursively working its way down the tree to the node containing x, the code does nothing while it unwinds the recursion through repeated returns, except to keep handing the answer back. This is particularly annoying in `Insert`, which passes nothing back at all, but still must execute the sequence of returns. Use of a nonrecursive shell and a `goto` allows us to eliminate this inefficiency as is shown for `Find` in Figure 6–15. This is an example of "catastrophic success," a situation mentioned in the section The Great `goto` Controversy of Chapter 1.

(continued)

FIGURE 6–15   Recursive Versions of FIND and INSERT

```
1  type PtrToNode = ^Node;
2       Node = record
3                   Data: integer;
4                   Left, Right: PtrToNode
5            end;
```

```
1  function Find(x: integer; p: PtrToNode): PtrToNode;
2   (* Find the node containing  x  in the binary search tree rooted at  p . *)
3   begin
4     if p = nil
5       then Find := nil
6       else if x < p^.Data
7         then Find := Find(x,p^.Left)
8       else if x > p^.Data
9         then Find := Find(x,p^.Right)
10      else (* x = p^.Data *) Find := p
11   end; (* Find *)
```

```
1  procedure Insert(x: integer; var p: PtrToNode);
2   (* Insert a node containing  x  into the binary search tree rooted
3      at  p  if it is not already present. *)
4   begin
5     if p = nil
6       then begin
7               new(p);
8               p^.Data := x;
9               p^.Left := nil;
10              p^.Right := nil
11          end
12      else if x < p^.Data
13        then Insert(x,p^.Left)
14      else if x > p^.Data
15        then Insert(x,p^.Right)
16  (* else  x  is already in the tree -- do nothing *)
17   end; (* Insert *)
```

> *How to deal with repeated keys is an important software engineering question. As the header comment indicates, the procedure ignores the request. An alternative is to return an error flag. In Ada we could raise an* **exception**.

FOR YOUR INFORMATION

(concluded)

A third criticism is that there is a subtlety in `Insert` that is easily overlooked. While the lines

```
12     else if x < p^.Data
13        then Insert(x,p^.Left)
14     else if x > p^.Data
15        then Insert(x,p^.Right)
```

seem simple enough, it is critical that `p^.Left` and `p^.Right` be passed by reference to `p`. To understand the subtlety, we need to consider the location in memory to which the parameter `p` really refers. `p` is not just some local variable. As shown in Figure 6–17, `p` is effectively either the `Root`, the `Left` field of some node, or the `Right` field of some node. The call on line 7, `new(p)`, thus not only allocates a `Node`, it attaches the `Node` to the tree. If `p^.Left` and `p^.Right` are passed to `p` by value, the whole procedure falls apart. This is fundamentally different from passing `Root` by reference to `BSTRoot` on line 20 of `Build_Graph.p`. In the iterative version of `Insert` the only reason `BSTRoot` is a call-by-reference parameter is the algorithm must correctly handle the once-in-a-lifetime situation where `x` is being inserted into the empty tree—in the absence of deletions, line 96 of `Build_Graph.p` will execute exactly once. In the recursive version, `var` parameters create a coupling of the caller and the callee that is hard to understand.

But none of these considerations is the real reason that the recursive versions of these routines are inferior. *It is because they use extra space.* This space is the storage used by the stack frames that support the recursion. In the case of FIND and INSERT, the amount of extra space is equal to the depth of `x` in the tree. The iterative versions use only constant extra space, no matter how deep `x` is in the tree. To the theoretician, this use of extra space is a fundamental flaw.

You should not come away from this discussion with the impression that recursion is always bad. It most situations where it is used, it is necessary. While technically this last statement isn't true—recursion can *always* be simulated by a stack—in situations where recursion is vital, the recursive version of a procedure is invariably much clearer than the nonrecursive version and there is essentially no loss of efficiency and no significant use of extra storage. Depth-first search, many of the functions in the recursive lists chapter (`readlist`, `writelist`, and the nonprimitive functions), and the recursive descent parsing of expressions in the Nero project are all examples of where recursion is both necessary and greatly adds to the clarity.

FIGURE 6–16   Using a goto to Escape from Recursion

```
1  function Find(x: integer; Root: PtrToNode): PtrToNode;
2   (* Find the node containing  x  in the binary search tree rooted at  Root . *)
3   label 99;
4   procedure RecFind(p: PtrToNode);
5     begin
6       if p = nil
7         then begin
8                Find := nil;
9                goto 99 (* return from  Find  *)
10              end
11        else if x < p^.Data
12          then RecFind(p^.Left)
13        else if x > p^.Data
14          then RecFind(p^.Right)
15        else   begin (* x = p^.Data *)
16                 Find := p;
17                 goto 99 (* return from  Find  *)
18               end
19    end; (* RecFind *)
20    begin (* Find *)
21      RecFind(Root);
22  99:
23    end; (* Find *)
```

As discussed in For Your Information: Turbo Pascal and the goto Statement, *this approach cannot be used in Turbo Pascal because the compiler does not allow* goto *statements to branch from a procedure into a containing procedure.*

FIGURE 6–17   The Effect of Passing p by Reference in Insert

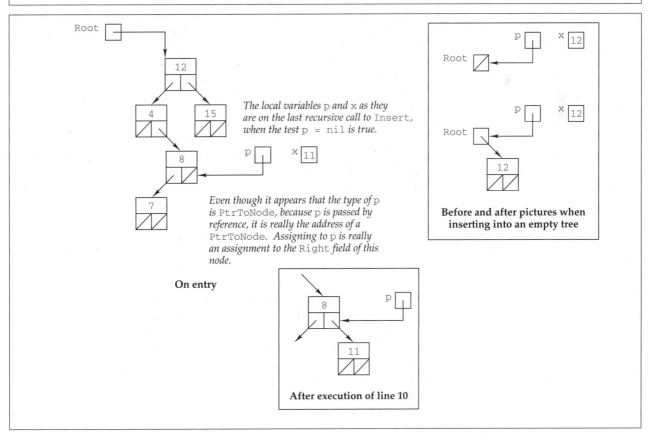

The local variables p and x as they are on the last recursive call to Insert, when the test p = nil is true.

Even though it appears that the type of p is PtrToNode, because p is passed by reference, it is really the address of a PtrToNode. Assigning to p is really an assignment to the Right field of this node.

On entry

After execution of line 10

Before and after pictures when inserting into an empty tree

the constant-time lookup we get with arrays, but we get the freedom to label the vertices with user-friendly names instead of numbers.

In the declaration of `Node`, the fields `Left` and `Right` are used to construct a binary search tree containing all the vertices. The complete data structure is an intertwining of the data structures of Figures 6–6 and 6–14. When `BuildGraph` needs to create an edge from ⟨name1⟩ to ⟨name2⟩ in the internal representation of the graph, it uses the binary search tree to find the vertices corresponding to ⟨name1⟩ and ⟨name2⟩; then it switches perspective and uses the `Children` field of ⟨name1⟩ to insert a `SubNode` linking the `Node` for ⟨name1⟩ to the `Node` for ⟨name2⟩. This is done in lines 123–132 of `BuildGraph`. The lines are a direct translation of lines 8–12 of Figure 6–13.

In `BuildGraph`, the logically separate tasks of FIND and INSERT are combined into one. Before making the call to `FindAndInsert`, the file name of the vertex we are searching for will have been stored in `StringPool` just to the right of `NextFree`, at the left edge of the unused portion of the array. `FindAndInsert` is passed a pointer to the root of the tree and the index of the start of the file name. If the name has been encountered before, `FindAndInsert` returns a pointer to the previously created `Node` associated with that file name. If the name is new, a `Node` is created and initialized and `NextFree` is advanced over the name. A pointer to this new `Node` is returned—the remainder of the `BuildGraph` procedure is oblivious to the fact that a new name has been encountered in the `makefile` and entered into the `StringPool`. Notice that a name can be encountered for the first time as either a target or a source.

Cycle Detection

Incorporating every file name into the binary search tree during the graph-building process, no matter how disconnected or otherwise invalid the graph specified by the `makefile` may be, solves the problem of initializing all the `Encountered` fields before beginning a depth-first search: the depth-first search algorithm need only walk the binary search tree recursively, setting all these fields to `false`. This is the equivalent of running down the array of list headers. Also, since the first name in the `makefile` will necessarily become the root of the binary search tree and is, by definition, supposed to be the ultimate target, we have easy access to the presumed single source.

We are ready to return to a more abstract level and consider how to detect cycles during depth-first search. To understand the algorithm it is best to return to our childhood and pretend we are Hänsel and Gretel. When the two children ventured into the forest, Hänsel dropped a trail of bread crumbs behind them, so that they could find their way home. Unfortunately for the two children, birds ate the bread crumbs and they became lost, which made for an entertaining story. We will do the same, but we will not get lost. Imagine the depth-first search algorithm starting out with a can of paint and a ball of string. Every time it reaches a vertex for the first time, it splashes it with paint. This corresponds to setting the `Encountered` field to `true` when the vertex is encountered for the first time. But also imagine that as the algorithm walks an arc it lets out the string. Furthermore, as it backs out of an arc, which the code of Figure 6–9 does when it returns from a recursive call, pretend that it rewinds the string. Suppose we stop the algorithm in the middle. What will we see? Some nodes in the graph, those that we have encountered during the search, will be stained with paint. The string, on the other hand, will trace out a direct path from the vertex where we initially entered the graph to the vertex we are at now. This crucial property depends not only on letting the string out as we advance, but on rewinding the string as we retreat. Inside the computer, the sequence of stack frames mimics the string. Stated differently, each vertex along the path except the last one corresponds to a suspended recursive call. The algorithm for

FIGURE 6–18   Detecting Cycles in a Directed Graph

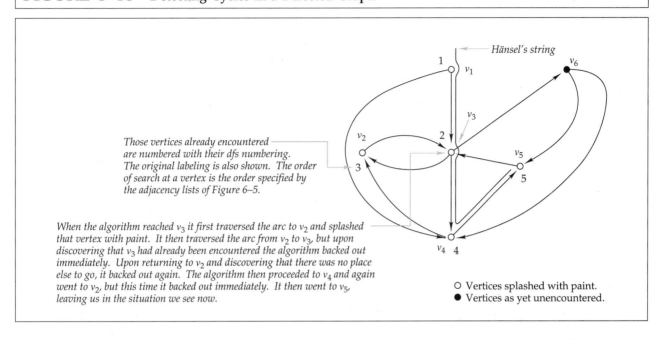

Those vertices already encountered are numbered with their dfs numbering. The original labeling is also shown. The order of search at a vertex is the order specified by the adjacency lists of Figure 6–5.

When the algorithm reached v_3 it first traversed the arc to v_2 and splashed that vertex with paint. It then traversed the arc from v_2 to v_3, but upon discovering that v_3 had already been encountered the algorithm backed out immediately. Upon returning to v_2 and discovering that there was no place else to go, it backed out again. The algorithm then proceeded to v_4 and again went to v_2, but this time it backed out immediately. It then went to v_5, leaving us in the situation we see now.

○ Vertices splashed with paint.
● Vertices as yet unencountered.

distinguishing a previously visited subgraph from a vertex that closes a cycle is just

> *If the depth-first search algorithm encounters a previously encountered vertex that is not on the current exploration path, then the search is reentering a previously explored subgraph, whereas if the vertex is on the current exploration path, the algorithm has detected a cycle.*

While it is easy to see that if the algorithm finds a cycle, there really is one, it isn't so easy to see that if the graph has a cycle the algorithm will find it. Actually it won't. What it will do is determine if the subgraph defined by the set of vertices reachable from the vertex initially passed to the cycle-finding routine has a cycle. But this will suffice for our purposes, since we know which vertex ought to be the ultimate target. The code for cycle detection is given in Figure 6–19.

`CheckGraph` now falls nicely into place. It is essentially three lines long (lines 71–73)

```
SetTouchedFalse(Root);
CycleCheck(Root);
CheckTouched(Root)
```

The procedure first sets all the `Touched` (that is, `Encountered`) fields to `false` by recursively walking the binary search tree. It then executes the cycle-finding algorithm of Figure 6–19, calling `Error`, from which it never returns, if it finds a cycle. Finally, it checks to see if the ultimate target is the single source of the graph. If it is, then `CycleCheck`, which always encounters every vertex reachable from `Root`, should have visited all the vertices of the graph and all the `Touched` fields should now be `true`. If the ultimate target is either not a source or not the only source, some vertex will not be reachable from `Root` and its `Touched` field will still be `false`. A second walk of the binary tree checks

FIGURE 6–19   The Code for Detecting Cycles in a Directed Graph

```
1    function CyclePresent(Root: PtrToNode): boolean;
2      (* Determine if the subgraph of a directed graph rooted at  Root  contains
3         a cycle.
4      *)
5      label 99;
6      procedure Walk(p: PtrToNode);
7        var q: PtrToSubNode;
8        begin
9          if not p^.Encountered (* If we have never been here, the vertex
10                                        cannot complete a cycle. *)
11           then begin
12                  p^.Encountered := true;
13                  p^.OnCurrentPath := true;
14                  q := p^.Children;
15                  while q <> nil do
16                    begin
17                      Walk(q^.Child);
18                      q := q^.Next
19                    end;
20                  p^.OnCurrentPath := false (* Back out of this vertex. *)
21                end
22           else if p^.OnCurrentPath
23              then begin
24                     CyclePresent := true;
25                     goto 99
26                   end
27      (* else    just back out *)
28        end; (* Walk *)
29    begin (* CyclePresent *)
30      ... initialize all the Encountered fields to false ...
31      Walk(Root);
32      CyclePresent := false; (* didn't find a cycle *)
33 99:
34    end; (* CyclePresent *)
```

This test is safe because p^.OnCurrentPath *cannot be uninitialized if* p^.Encountered *is* true.

p^.Encountered *is* true *and* p^.OnCurrentPath *is* false. *We have encountered an already processed subgraph.*

This line executes only if we do not branch to 99.

for this. As a side effect, if the graph passes the tests of CheckGraph, all the OnCurrentPath fields will have been set first to true and then to false. They are all false now. If we use the Rebuilt field of Node in two ways, here to mean OnCurrentPath and in Rebuild as its name implies, we can save one field per Node and avoid the initialization step in Rebuild. (It is structurally better, but less efficient, to have Rebuild make no assumptions about the status of the Rebuilt field. By walking the binary search tree itself, it can set the Rebuilt fields of all the vertices to false, but since they are false already, this will be wasted work.)

EXERCISE 6–6   The cycle-finding algorithm given in Figure 6–19 does not work for undirected graphs. Why? How can it be fixed?

Hashing—An Alternative to Binary Search Trees

The make utility is one example of a program where the abstract statement of the problem uses numbers for names, but where the real-world version uses strings for names instead. There are many others. Because strings cannot be used as array indices, the real-world versions of such programs have an extra layer of code whose function is to convert names to locations. In the make program this extra layer is the procedure FindAndInsert, which finds the Node corresponding to a file name. Using a binary search tree for this task is a good general approach, but we can do better. Although the average-case behavior of a binary search tree is $O(\log n)$, its worst-case behavior is $O(n)$ and it is the relatively common case of the names being presented in alphabetical order during the construction phase that causes the tree to degenerate into a linear linked list. The search for effective algorithms for finding an object given its name has been a major concern of theoretical computer scientists over the last 30 years and the study of these algorithms consumes a good portion of a semester-long class devoted to data structures and algorithms. Here we can only hope to scratch the surface of this very important topic.

The nature of the input to the make utility makes it unlikely that the binary search tree will degenerate into a linear list, and even if we are very unlucky, we are not likely to notice, since n is typically not very large: make itself has only 20 files, the most of any of our case studies. Be that as it may, there are two approaches to improving on the performance of binary search trees: we can insist that the worst-case behavior be no worse than $O(\log n)$, or we can insist on improved average-case performance, while limiting the appearance of the worst-case behavior to input sequences that are not common. The first approach leads to **balanced search trees** like 2-3 trees, AVL trees, and red-black trees. The second leads to a technique known as **hashing**. It is a very old technique, but it is still popular, and it works very well if names are never deleted.

The basic idea is that the graph will be stored more or less as depicted in Figure 6–5: it will be an array of type Node. Each vertex will have all the fields that it had before, except Left and Right, which are no longer needed. The only other difference is that the declaration of type SubNode must be changed to conform to the standard adjacency list representation: the type of the Child field becomes integer. The secret behind all of this is that somehow we will convert a string of characters into an integer. We don't really care if random.o is v_3, v_{12}, or v_1, as long as whenever we encounter the name random.o we can convert it into the same integer. To get into the spirit of hashing you will need to recognize and banish from your thoughts two deep-seated prejudices:

- The first file name encountered should correspond to v_1 and the fifteenth distinct file name should correspond to v_{15}.
- The array, known as a **hash table**, should be just the right length and shouldn't have any holes in the middle.

The graph underlying the makefile of the worm project, stored in a hash table of length 20, looks like what you see in Figure 6–20. That the ultimate target isn't v_1 is not a problem; the variable Root just stores the integer into which the name of the ultimate target is converted.

(continued)

**ABOVE
AND BEYOND**

(continued)

Crucial to this entire discussion is the development of a function that converts strings into integers:

```
function hash(s: string): integer;
```

It doesn't matter, except at the lowest level of coding, if a `string` is stored as a linked list of characters or in consecutive bytes of memory. The `hash` function, as in corned beef hash, is just some crazy-looking function that treats the characters as small integers (by applying the built-in Pascal function `ord`) and then performs some strange arithmetic operations on them, ending up with a single integer. The simplest of all hash functions, though not a very good one, is

> *Add up all the characters in the name and at the last minute take the sum* `mod` *the size of the array.*

This hash function presents us with two small problems: the range of indices produced is `0..TableSize-1`, and the maximum number of distinct keys must be known in advance. The former problem is easily handled in Pascal, which allows the bounds of an array to be arbitrary, and the latter isn't a new restriction—the same restriction applies to the `StringPool`. If some

(continued)

FIGURE 6–20   A Hash Table Representation of the Dependency Graph for the `worm` Program

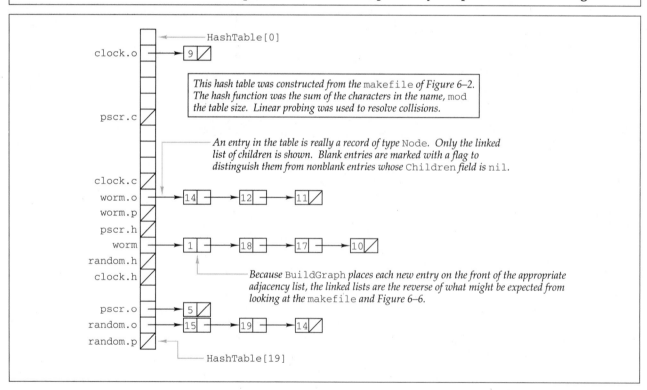

This hash table was constructed from the `makefile` *of Figure 6–2. The hash function was the sum of the characters in the name, mod the table size. Linear probing was used to resolve collisions.*

An entry in the table is really a record of type `Node`. *Only the linked list of children is shown. Blank entries are marked with a flag to distinguish them from nonblank entries whose* `Children` *field is* `nil`.

Because `BuildGraph` *places each new entry on the front of the appropriate adjacency list, the linked lists are the reverse of what might be expected from looking at the* `makefile` *and Figure 6–6.*

`makefile` contains so many file names that the hash table is too small, we just need to change a constant and recompile `make`.

The real problem with all hash functions is that two totally unrelated strings can have the same hash. If the number of distinct names is almost as large as the size of the hash table, there will almost certainly be a *collision*—in a room containing 300 people, it is almost certain that two of them will have the same birthday. Even if the array is fairly large, it doesn't take very many names to cause a collision—it takes only 23 people before the probability that two of them have the same birthday rises to above one-half. Since each location in the array is capable of holding only one vertex, we need to have some way of resolving collisions. The simplest, known as *linear probing*, is to apply the following algorithm to convert a name to an integer:

- Determine an initial guess at the translation by applying the hash function. Call the resulting integer i.
- Begin searching the hash table, starting at position i (wrapping around to the beginning of the array if necessary), comparing the name for which we are searching to the name stored in the `Node`, until one of the following conditions is met:
  - We find the item in the hash table.
  - We find an empty place in the hash table.
  - We cycle back to location i. (The table is full and we have an error.)

When the second condition causes termination, the name has never been seen before, and the index of the free location becomes the translation of this name. Linear probing is diagrammed in Figure 6–21. This termination condition needs to be studied with great care. The primary consequence is that a name doesn't have an absolute translation; the slot where it winds up depends on what other names have already been inserted into the data structure. *As long as there are no deletions*, the algorithm will not run into any difficulties. When the name `random.h` is encountered a second time, the hash function will return the same initial guess as before, and the search for `random.h` will begin at the same place. The names that were skipped over when `random.h` was inserted will still be there, and they will be skipped over again. The algorithm will arrive safely at the entry for `random.h`.

The basic principles of hashing have been laid out. The issues that need to be considered are:

- What are good hash functions?
- What other methods besides linear probing can be used to resolve collisions?
- How well does hashing perform?

These questions have been studied in great detail, and a considerable body of analysis related to hashing has been developed. Choosing good hash functions, ones that hash similar names to different locations and that have no more collisions than hash functions that appear truly random, is as much an art as a science. It depends in part on knowledge of the habits of the people who create the names that will be hashed. In a `makefile`, for example, we would expect to see the same name followed by different extensions (`.h`, `.p`, and `.o`). Summing the characters in a name is considered a poor choice because it maps names that are permutations of each other to the same place.

Linear probing is also not a very good collision resolution mechanism. It tends to create runs that intermingle, making them longer than necessary.

ABOVE
AND BEYOND

(continued)

A popular collision resolution method that is better is **double hashing**. Double hashing is just like linear probing, but the increment is not 1. The algorithm successively checks locations i, $i + k$, $i + 2k$, ..., wrapping around the end of the table when necessary. k is a function of the name—a second hash, calculated using a different hash function. Since two names that agree on the first hash will probably disagree on the second, runs are avoided. The only requirement is that k and the size of the table be **relatively prime**, meaning they have a greatest common divisor of 1. This guarantees that the algorithm will not cycle back to the location from which it started until every location of the array has been investigated. If the size of the hash table is chosen arbitrarily, designing a hash function that guarantees that k and the size of the table are relatively prime is not easy. For this reason, the size of the table is often chosen as a prime number.

Another technique for resolving collisions doesn't involve looking through the table at all. Instead of an array of type `Node`, the hash table is declared as an array of pointers to linked lists of nodes. The linked list for the ith hash table entry contains a node for each name that hashes to i. Simply put, all the ties are stored in a linear linked list. Since we expect that there aren't very many ties, none of the lists should be very long.

The question of average-case performance is very interesting. If we use linear probing or double hashing to resolve collisions instead of using linked lists of ties, there is always the possibility of running out of space. What is more, as the array becomes almost full, the time to search for a free location becomes $O(n)$. The solution is to declare the array to be somewhat larger than

(continued)

FIGURE 6–21   Linear Probing to Resolve Collisions

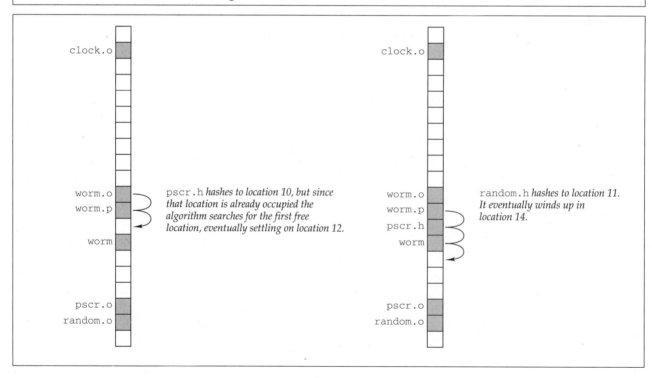

the number of names we really expect to encounter. But how much larger? The mathematics used to derive the answer is complex, but the results are easy to understand and interpret. The average number of probes to find a free location into which to insert a new entry is

$$I_{av} = \frac{1}{1 - \alpha}$$

and the average number of probes to find a name that has already been inserted into the table is

$$F_{av} = \frac{1}{\alpha} \ln(\frac{1}{1 - \alpha})$$

where α is the *loading factor*. (These formulas are only close approximations.) The loading factor is the number of in-use entries divided by the size of the hash table. If the table is half full, α is 0.50 and if it is 90 percent full, it is 0.90. These results are startling! If the table is half full, then the average number of probes to insert a new entry is 2, only twice the absolute minimum; if it is three-fourths full the average number of probes is only 4; and even if the table is 90 percent full, which is regarded as a very full table, the average number of probes is only 10. Notice that this is independent of n. When using a binary search tree, the average number of iterations is $O(\log n)$. If n is around 1000, we can expect the search to take about 10 iterations (actually it will be bit more, because the coefficient of the $\log n$ term is not 1). When n approaches 1,000,000, the average number of iterations rises to 20. But even if n is 1,000,000, if the hash table is only half full, the expected number of probes is still 2. Of course, these wonderful numbers depend on a reasonable loading factor, which means that we must have both a good estimate of the number of names we will ultimately be inserting and must be prepared to waste a lot of space. The main drawback of hashing is that the size of the hash table cannot grow dynamically as it fills up. Once it is full, it is full, whereas a dynamic data structure like a binary search tree can grow until the computer's memory capacity is exceeded. When hash tables are used it is wise to declare them full slightly before they actually get full.

EXERCISE 6–7   Why can't a random number generator be used to determine the initial hash value?

EXERCISE 6–8   (Requires some knowledge of discrete probability.) Why is it that in a room containing 23 people, the probability that two of them will have the same birthday is greater than one-half? Generalize your solution so that you can answer the question: if a hash table is m entries long, how many distinct names, on average, will have to be hashed before two of them will hash to the same location?

PROJECT 6–1   Recode the `make` processor so that it uses hashing, with double hashing as the collision resolution method. Experiment with different hash and rehash functions.

6.5   `BuildGraph`—INTERFACING WITH THE `makefile`

So far the discussion has centered on the algorithmically interesting half of the `make` processor: checking the graph for legitimacy and using the graph to rebuild the ultimate target and any other files that need rebuilding. This is roughly 75 percent of the intellectual work, but only 25 percent of the code. The great majority of the code deals with reading and interpreting the `makefile`. This code is itself divided into two parts, `BuildGraph`, which takes an abstract view of the `makefile`, and `Lex`, which deals with the actual input. `BuildGraph` views the input as a long sequence of tokens

⟨target⟩ ⟨source⟩ ⟨source⟩ ... ⟨source⟩ ⟨rebuilding_rule⟩
⟨rebuilding_rule⟩ ... ⟨rebuilding_rule⟩ ⟨target⟩ ⟨source⟩ ...
⟨rebuilding_rule⟩ ⟨end_of_file⟩

Refer to `Lex.h` *and lines 102–151 of* `Build_Graph.p` *while reading this.*

Each call to `Lex` returns what it found (in `What`) and in all cases, except `EndOfFile`, places the file name or rebuilding command at the beginning of the unused portion of `StringPool`. To aid `Lex`, which is written so that it has lots of knowledge about the peculiarities of the input file but doesn't have a lot of knowledge about the structure of a `makefile`, `BuildGraph` tells `Lex` what it could hope to find next (the parameter `Possible`). We have already discussed the first 100 lines of `BuildGraph`. Our discussion now centers on the last 50 lines of that procedure.

Just to summarize what we know about `BuildGraph`, it contains the routine `FindAndInsert`, which when given a pointer to the start of a file name, be it a target or be it a source, will search the graph being built (using a binary search tree containing all the file names) and will return a pointer to the `Node` for this file. If this is the first time the file name has been encountered, `FindAndInsert` creates a record for the file, initializes it (on lines 83–99), and returns a pointer to it. During the construction phase, the graph is in bits and pieces, mostly disconnected and incomplete. But `FindAndInsert` has no trouble finding the record for a file name, since all the records are always linked together in a single binary search tree. Even after the `makefile` is processed the graph might be disconnected or ill-formed, but checking for this is the job of `CheckGraph`.

`BuildGraph` begins (on line 107) by asking for a target, since the `makefile` must begin with the ultimate target. We impose a natural requirement on the `makefile`: any file specified as a target should be specified as a target only once. Whenever `BuildGraph` is told by `Lex` that it has a target, it checks (line 115) to see if this file has appeared as a target previously. After determining that all is well, `BuildGraph` says to itself, and to `Lex`, that it should find a sequence of sources on which this target depends, followed by a sequence of rebuilding commands. At first, it seems a bit odd that line 120 should be

```
Wanted := [Source,Command]
```

and not just

```
Wanted := [Source]
```

How can a target not depend on anything? Though certainly uncommon, it isn't impossible. A target with no dependencies can't be out of date with respect to its sources, but it can fail to exist. The target file might be some file that is generated automatically. It might, for example, contain the current time and date in the form of a Pascal comment. On UNIX systems the lines

```
date.h:
        date +"(* %c *)" > date.h
```

will create such a file if `date.h` does not exist. The file will contain a single line similar to

```
(* Fri Jan 22 13:10:40 1993 *)
```

This provides a crude means of revision control.

Our `make` utility does insist, however, that every target file have at least one rebuilding command, and, as noted earlier, `Rebuild` checks, after the fact, that the commands actually did rebuild the file.

> **EXERCISE 6–9** The above bit of trickery to create a comment that records the date and time of the most recent revision isn't foolproof. If the programmer forgets to delete `date.h` before invoking `make`, it will exist from the last time `make` was executed and will not be rebuilt. Can you think of a way of forcing `date.h` to be rebuilt every time `make` is invoked?

Every time `Lex` finds a source, `BuildGraph` adds an arc to the graph. Because of the way `Possible` is set, the only place sources can appear is immediately after targets. Once `Lex` finds a command, `BuildGraph` instructs `Lex` that it can find nothing other than more commands for this target, a new target, or the end-of-file. The operation of `BuildGraph` is summarized in Figure 6–22. It is always in one of three states. The action it takes and the state it transitions into after processing what `Lex` finds depends on the object returned by `Lex`. For example, when `BuildGraph` is in the state `[Source,Command]`, if `Lex` reports back that the next object is a source, `BuildGraph` stays in this state and adds an arc to the graph.

The Form of a `makefile`

This brings us to the discussion of `Lex`, whose job it is to process the input file and return whatever it finds. Up until now, we have been working at an abstract enough level that we didn't need to consider the details of what a `makefile` should look like at the character level. We now must descend into the nitty-gritty. The syntax of a `makefile`, as our `make` utility expects it, is not quite the same as the syntax of either a UNIX `makefile` or a Turbo Pascal `makefile`, which themselves differ slightly, though a "neatly typed" `makefile` in the formats

FIGURE 6–22   The Possible States in Which `BuildGraph` Can Be

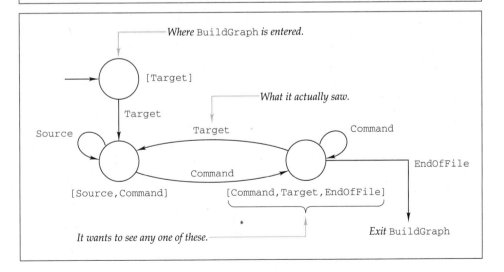

required by either of these system utilities can be used with our utility. The `make` utility is line oriented. Because a target can have many dependencies and because a command can be very long, sometimes things don't fit on one line. To handle these situations, our `make` utility, like those of UNIX and Turbo Pascal, recognizes two different end-of-line characters. The first is the normal end-of-line character that the editor puts in at the end of every line. However, if a line ends with a \⟨cr⟩ then this two-character combination is treated as the equivalent of a space and the two physical lines of the `makefile` are treated as one logical line. The backslash must be *immediately* followed by the carriage return. There cannot even be an intervening space. If a backslash is followed by some character other than a carriage return, the backslash is just treated as a normal character. It can even be part of a file name or command.

The target and the list of sources on which it depends must all be on one logical line. The line looks like

⟨target⟩: ⟨source⟩ ⟨source⟩ ... ⟨source⟩

The colon must abut the target file name. In the context of a file name, the colon is a special character whereas in a command, it is treated as an ordinary character. Each rebuilding command must also be on a single logical line. `Lex`, and the `make` utility in general, doesn't know anything about the content of a rebuilding command. It just treats it as a string of characters to be passed off to the operating system. If they don't make any sense to the operating system or if the command fails during execution, `make` relies on the operating system to inform it of this fact. The only processing of commands done by `Lex` is to interpolate the \⟨cr⟩ to a space and to squeeze out excess white space, since there is no reason to fill up `StringPool` with lots of blank characters. Besides a true blank and the \⟨cr⟩, tabs and comments are also considered white space. A comment begins with a # and continues up to, but not including, the end of the line. Thus # cannot not be part of either a file name or a rebuilding command. Blank lines, either with or without blanks on them, are allowed. No special provision need be made for them. A blank line will either be interpreted by `Lex` as nothing but a carriage return or as, after compressing blanks, a single blank followed by a carriage return. A line containing just a comment will also be interpreted as a single blank followed by a carriage return. While it is traditional to separate each target-source-command trio from the next by a blank line, there is no requirement to do so and blank lines can be scattered anywhere. Lastly, targets must begin in column 1, whereas commands are not allowed to begin in column 1. This is how the two are distinguished from each other.

Refer to `GetChar.h` *while reading this.*

This long list of rules makes it clear that `Lex` is going to be an ugly routine to write! Much of what we will do here we have done before in the case studies for recursive lists and the Nero Project, so if you read those chapters, you will not find what is said here new or difficult. Even if you skipped those chapters, processing the input isn't hard, just messy. In fact, dealing with the input is sufficiently difficult that this task is itself divided into two parts, the routine `Lex` and the routine `GetChar`. `GetChar` is the routine that really deals with the input. It returns a "character" to `Lex`. A `Character` is a record whose first field classifies the character as one of an end-of-file character, an end-of-line character (a real one, not the \⟨cr⟩, which is returned to `Lex` as a blank), a blank (really any "white space"), a colon (which is given special treatment by `Lex`), an ordinary character, or an illegal character (a nonprinting control character other than a tab). For the last three categories the actual character in the input is returned as well. This provides a clean interface for `Lex`, which doesn't have to worry any longer about the difficulties associated with processing end-of-line and end-of-file in Pascal, dealing with \⟨cr⟩, and removing comments. `GetChar` is also

See the Section `eoln` *and* `eof` *in Chapter 1.*

where we compress a sequence of blanks, in all its myriad forms, into a single blank.

Besides the general technique of filtering the input so that the next routine down the line has a clean interface, the most interesting aspect of `GetChar` is the one-character buffer it maintains, `CharBuf`. The problem, as always, is that we cannot tell when an indefinite length object has ended until we have read one character too many. In `GetChar` that object is white space. Since `GetChar` compresses a sequence of blanks into a single blank, how is it to know that the sequence has ended? It cannot, until it has read one character too many. And while it can compress a lot of white space down to a single blank, it cannot simply throw the white space away and return the character after the white space, because `Lex` uses a blank to detect that a file name has ended and to distinguish a target, which must begin in column 1, from a command, which starts in column 2 or beyond. So what should `GetChar` do with the extra character it has read? What it does do is store it away in a one-character buffer. When `GetChar` is next called it first checks the buffer to see if it contains a character. If it does, `GetChar` begins its processing with that character. If the buffer is empty, `GetChar` reads a character from the input instead. It then proceeds, at line 56, without knowledge of where the character came from.

In the background, `GetChar` also keeps track of the physical line of the `makefile` from which it is reading. This is to aid `Error` in the printing of helpful error messages. The input to `make` is assumed to come from a file. The program is meant to be used by typing

Error Processing
Refer to `Error.p` *while reading this.*

`make < makefile`

at an operating system prompt. (In MS-DOS the executable program is named `MAKE.EXE`.) Our error processing needs to reflect the noninteractive nature of the program. Error messages for errors caught during the construction of the graph are prefaced by

`Error: Line ⟨line number⟩ -- ...`

This helps the user rapidly locate the source of the problem. `Error` also terminates the execution of the `make` utility. In a noninteractive environment, there is not much else that it can do.

With all the preprocessing done by `GetChar`, `Lex` isn't that complicated anymore. On entry, `Lex` it is either searching for a (*i*) target, (*ii*) a source or a command, or (*iii*) a command, a target, or the end of the input. The first of these options can occur only on the very first entry. `Lex` is faced with the second option whenever `BuildGraph` has seen a target and, possibly, some sources for the target. In this situation `BuildGraph` is expecting either more sources or the first rebuilding command. Considering the structure of a `makefile`, `Lex` should give preference to sources, which it does. Basically `Lex` skips to the next interesting character, which will either be the first character of a file name or the end-of-line character. In the former case `Lex` stores the file name in `StringPool` and returns, whereas in the latter case it switches gears and admits that it will have to find a command. The remainder of the routine sorts out whether the next object is a target or a command. The determining factor is whether or not it begins in column 1. After making this distinction, `Lex` copies the object into the `StringPool`.

The Structure of `Lex`

`Lex` faces, in its own way, exactly the same problem that `GetChar` faces: sometimes it has to read one character too many to know that what it is processing has ended. In the case of `GetChar` an indefinitely long sequence of blanks was the cause of this difficulty, whereas here it is a file name. `Lex` cannot know that a file name has ended until it has read the character that follows the file name. While `BuildGraph` doesn't want to know about this extra character, `Lex` cannot just throw it away. It might be the carriage return abutting the last source on a line or it might be a blank, or in the case of the target, it should be the colon. `Lex` uses exactly the same technique as `GetChar`. When it reads one character too many, it saves it in the buffer `LexBuf`, which it reads the next time it is called.

EXERCISE 6—10   As a user of `make`, but knowing how it operates internally, can you rig the `makefile` so that a warning is generated when it appears likely that a `.h` file has been modified, but one of the `.p` files that includes it has not been modified to reflect the changes.

EXERCISE 6—11   Because the ordering of the vertices on the adjacency lists built by `BuildGraph` is the reverse of the ordering of the sources on the target-source dependency lines of the `makefile`, the order in which rebuilding occurs can seem strange to the user. Fix this.

EXERCISE 6—12   Some users might find `make` more natural if they could place the target-source-command trio that defines the ultimate target last. This is more in the bottom-up spirit—working from the small to the large, instead of from the large to the small. Modify the `make` utility so that the single source in the graph is discovered by the program.

EXERCISE 6—13   As noted in the comment on lines 14–17 of `GetChar.p`, `Line` is off by one when `GetChar` processes a carriage return. This makes some error messages refer to the wrong line. Correct this deficiency.

EXERCISE 6—14   Compressing consecutive blanks into a single blank isn't always appropriate. In some commands, like `grep`, which searches files for lines containing a specified string, the replacement of a sequence of blanks by one blank effectively changes the command. For example

```
grep ":    " ⟨filename⟩
```

isn't the same as

```
grep ": " ⟨filename⟩
```

Modify the `make` utility so that it doesn't compress blanks when reading a rebuilding command from the `makefile`.

PROJECT 6—2   Modify the code for the recursive lists case study so that the names of the atoms are kept in a string pool, instead of in linked lists, one character per cell. Each atom should appear in the string pool only once. In addition, use the technique discussed in Above and Beyond: Hashing—An Alternative to Binary Search Trees to search for an atom.

PROJECT 6—3   Depth-first search is not the only way to detect cycles and process the graph so that the rebuilding of files proceeds in an orderly manner. A ***topological sort*** of a directed graph is a listing of its vertices, so that for each arc, (*v,w*), in the graph, *v* appears before *w* in the listing. In plain English, for each vertex, its successors appear after it and its predecessors appear before it. Every directed acyclic graph can be topologically sorted, usually in many ways, whereas directed graphs with cycles cannot be placed in topologically sorted order. If we have a topological sort for the graph described by the `makefile` we can do the rebuilding by processing the vertices in reverse topologically sorted order, that is, last to first. Develop a nonrecursive algorithm for topologically sorting a directed acyclic graph. Your algorithm should detect the presence of cycles. How much extra storage does your algorithm use? How efficient is it? Use this algorithm as the basis of the `make` utility.

PROJECT 6—4   Always having to specify that a `.o` file depends on the `.p` file of the same name is a nuisance. Both the UNIX and Turbo Pascal versions of `make` have ways of "teaching" `make` about standard dependencies. The syntax, using the UNIX `make` utility as an example, is

```
.p.o:
     pc -c -C $<
```

Define your own syntax for specifying standard dependencies and incorporate it into the `make` utility.

```
 1  (* Basic Type Definitions *)
 2
 3  type PtrToNode = ^Node;
 4       PtrToSubNode = ^SubNode;
 5       PtrToMakeNode = ^MakeNode;
 6       Node = record
 7                  (* Facts About Target Or Source Files *)
 8                  Name: integer; (* Pointer to the "name" of this node in the
 9                                    string pool. *)
10                  Left, Right: PtrToNode; (* Fields for the binary search tree
11                        that links all the names together so that a node can
12                        be found quickly (on average). *)
13                  Children: PtrToSubNode; (* Pointer to the linked list of
14                        immediate successors in the directed graph (can be nil). *)
15                  HowToMake: PtrToMakeNode; (* Pointer to the linked list of
16                        commands saying how to rebuild this file. *)
17                  LastModified: integer; (* Gotten by a call to  TimeStamp  -- in
18                        system-determined, packed form. *)
19
20                  (* Flags For Graph Search Algorithms *)
21                  Touched: boolean; (* Used in the cycle-finding depth-first search
22                        to determine if the graph is cycle free -- set to true as
23                        soon as the node is touched for the first time [crucial]. *)
24                  Rebuilt: boolean (* Set true during the rebuilding phase
25                        when the node is rebuilt or certified as up to date.
26                        Also used during the cycle-finding depth-first search
27                        to determine if an edge closes a cycle, where a more
28                        appropriate name would be  OnCurrentPath . *)
```

Normally, each variable or field should be used for only one purpose. The two uses to which this field is put do not overlap in time. While not a good practice, using this field for two unrelated purposes saves one field per node and a small amount of time.

```
29             end;
30
31      SubNode = record
32                  Child: PtrToNode; (* Pointer to a node for a file on which
33                                       this file depends. *)
34                  Next: PtrToSubNode
35               end;
36
37      MakeNode = record
38                  Command: integer; (* Pointer to the command in the
39                                       string pool. *)
40                  Next: PtrToMakeNode
41               end;
```

FILE   Make.p

```
1  #include "Basic_Defs.h"
2  #include "Build_Graph.h"
3  #include "Check_Graph.h"
4  #include "Rebuild.h"
5
6  program Make(input,output);
7    (* A simple, but usable, make utility. *)
8
9    var Root: PtrToNode;
10
11   begin
12     BuildGraph(Root); (* convert the input file into a directed graph *)
13     CheckGraph(Root); (* check the graph for errors *)
14     Rebuild(Root)     (* do the  make  *)
15   end. (* Make *)
```

FILE   Build_Graph.h

```
1  procedure BuildGraph(var (* out *) Root: PtrToNode); external;
2    (* Build up the graph implied by the  makefile , filling in the
3       string pool along the way.  Also build the binary search tree
4       of file names.
5    *)
```

FILE   Check_Graph.h

```
1  procedure CheckGraph(Root: PtrToNode); external;
2    (* Determine if the graph is cycle free and if the ultimate target is
3       the single source.
4    *)
```

FILE   Rebuild.h

```
1  procedure Rebuild(Root: PtrToNode); external;
2    (* Rebuild the ultimate target and any descendants that need rebuilding. *)
```

```
 1  #include "Basic—Defs.h"
 2  #include "Error.h"
 3  #include "String.h"
 4  #include "Lex.h"
 5  #include "Build—Graph.h"
 6
 7  (* procedure BuildGraph(var /* out */ Root: PtrToNode); *)
 8  procedure BuildGraph;
 9    (* Build up the graph implied by the  makefile , filling in the
10       string pool along the way.  Also build the binary search tree
11       of file names.
12    *)
13    var Wanted: Modes;       (* what  BuildGraph  wants *)                    ── See Lex.h.
14        Found: ObjectType;  (* what it got (from what it wanted) *)
15        NextFree: integer;  (* starting location of where it was put *)
16        p, p1: PtrToNode;
17        q: PtrToSubNode;
18        r, r1: PtrToMakeNode;
19
20    function FindAndInsert(var BSTRoot: PtrToNode; var Start: integer): PtrToNode;
21      (* Find the node corresponding to the file name starting in the string
22         pool at  Start  and return a pointer to it, creating the node and
23         adding it to the binary search tree if it is new.  If it is new
24          Start  is advanced over the file name or command.  Otherwise  Start
25         is not changed and the storage to the right of  Start  is automatically
26         recovered.
27      *)
28      label 99;
29      type RelOps = (Less, Equal, Greater);
30      var p, q: PtrToNode;
31          Condition: RelOps;
32
33      function Compare(Start1, Start2: integer): RelOps;
34        (* Determine the relationship between the file names starting
35           at  Start1  and  Start2 .
36        *)
37        label 99;
38        begin
39          while true do
40            if StringPool[Start1] < StringPool[Start2]
41              then begin
42                     Compare := Less;
43                     goto 99 (* return *)
44                   end
45            else if StringPool[Start1] > StringPool[Start2]
46              then begin
47                     Compare := Greater;
48                     goto 99 (* return *)
49                   end
50            else if StringPool[Start1] = chr(NUL)                          ── since the two characters
51              then begin (* they both equal chr(NUL), in fact *)              are equal.
52                     Compare := Equal;
53                     goto 99 (* return *)
54                   end
```

FILE   Build_Graph.p   Page 2

```
55              else    begin
56                          Start1 := Start1 + 1;
57                          Start2 := Start2 + 1
58                      end;
59      99: end;  (* Compare *)
60
61        begin  (* FindAndInsert *)
62          p := BSTRoot;
63          q := nil;
64          while p <> nil do
65            begin
66              Condition := Compare(Start,p^.Name);
67              case Condition of
68                Less:     begin
69                              q := p;
70                              p := p^.Left
71                          end;
72                Equal:    begin
73                              FindAndInsert := p;
74                              goto 99 (* return and don't change  Start  *)
75                          end;
76                Greater: begin
77                              q := p;
78                              p := p^.Right
79                          end
80            end
81          end;
82
83        (* We have a new file name. *)
84        new(p);
85        FindAndInsert := p;
86        p^.Name := Start;
87        ScanString(Start); (* Skip over characters added to the string pool. *)
88        p^.Left := nil;
89        p^.Right := nil;
90        p^.Children := nil;  (* None yet, and there may never be any. *)
91        p^.HowToMake := nil; (* We don't know how to make it yet and, in
92                                 fact, it might appear as a source before it
93                                 appears as a target or it might never
94                                 appear as a target. *)
95        if q = nil
96          then BSTRoot := p (* root of tree and supposed single source of graph *)
97        else if Condition = Less (*  q <> nil  implies  Condition  is set *)
98          then q^.Left := p
99        else   q^.Right := p;
100   99: end; (* FindAndInsert *)
101
102     begin (* BuildGraph *)
103        InitLex;
104        NextFree := 1;
105        Root := nil;
106
```

q is always one behind p, that is, it points to the parent of p, except initially, when p has no parent.

Searching a binary search tree recursively is elegant, but the iterative approach used here is better—see For Your Information: When Not to Use Recursion.

```
107      Wanted := [Target];  (* must see a target first *)
108      repeat
109        Lex(Wanted,Found,NextFree);
110        (* We don't return from  Lex  if we did not find something acceptable. *)
111        case Found of
112          Target:
113            begin
114              p := FindAndInsert(Root,NextFree);
115              if p^.HowToMake <> nil
116                then Error(DuplicateSpecification,p^.Name);
117              (* Get all the children on which this file name depends -- it can
118                  depend on nobody at all, but there must be at least one
119                  rebuilding command. *)
120              Wanted := [Source,Command]
121              (*  p  is preserved while all the sources are found. *)
122            end;
123          Source:
124            begin
125              p1 := FindAndInsert(Root,NextFree);
126              new(q);
127              q^.Child := p1;
128              (* The ordering of the children is irrelevant, so put it first. *)
129              q^.Next := p^.Children;
130              p^.Children := q
131              (* ...and continue to search for a source or a command. *)
132            end;
133          Command:
134            begin
135              new(r);
136              (* Rebuilding commands must be kept in order. *)
137              if p^.HowToMake = nil
138                then p^.HowToMake := r
139                else r1^.Next := r;
140              r^.Command := NextFree;
141              ScanString(NextFree);
142              r^.Next := nil;
143              r1 := r; (* keep track of the end of the list *)
144              Wanted := [Command,Target,EndOfFile] (* Either we should find
145                          another rebuilding command for this target, we
146                          should find a new target, or we are done. *)
147            end;
148          EndOfFile: (* quit *)
149        end
150      until Found = EndOfFile
151    end; (* BuildGraph *)
```

This prevents acceptance of an empty makefile.

It is slightly inefficient to set the Next *field to* nil, *correcting it if we find another command. However, the complexity introduced into the code to set the* Next *field of each* MakeNode *only once is not worth the slight gain. Besides, there is usually only one rebuilding command.*

```
1  #include "Basic_Defs.h"
2  #include "Error.h"
3  #include "Check_Graph.h"
4
5  (* procedure CheckGraph(Root: PtrToNode); *)
6  procedure CheckGraph;
7    (* Determine if the graph is cycle free and if the ultimate target is
8       the single source.
9    *)
10   (* The strategy is:
11      Set the  Touched  field of all nodes to false (done by walking the
12        binary search tree which contains all the nodes).
13      From the supposed single source do a depth-first search looking for cycles.
14        (Use the  Rebuilt  field along with the  Touched  field. This is
15        rigged so that, if there are no cycles, the  Rebuilt  field winds up
16        false for all nodes, which is what it should be initialized to for
17        the rebuilding phase.)
18      Make sure the graph is a single-source graph, with the ultimate target the
19        single source, by checking for nodes with a  Touched  field still false
20        (using the binary search tree).
21   *)
22
23   procedure SetTouchedFalse(p: PtrToNode);
24     begin
25       if p <> nil
26         then begin
27                 p^.Touched := false;
28                 SetTouchedFalse(p^.Left);
29                 SetTouchedFalse(p^.Right)
30              end
31     end; (* SetTouchedFalse *)
32
33   procedure CycleCheck(p: PtrToNode);
34     (* Perform a depth-first search looking for cycles. *)
35     var q: PtrToSubNode;
36     begin
37       if not p^.Touched (* If we have never been here, the vertex
38                            cannot complete a cycle. *)
39         then begin
40                 p^.Touched := true;
41                 p^.Rebuilt := true; (* p^.OnCurrentPath := true *)
42
43                 (* Recursively explore its descendants. *)
44                 q := p^.Children;
45                 while q <> nil do
46                   begin
47                     CycleCheck(q^.Child);
48                     q := q^.Next
49                   end;
50
51                 p^.Rebuilt := false (* p^.OnCurrentPath := false -- back out
52                                        of this vertex. *)
53              end
```

Interprocedural dependencies like this one generally should be avoided, but the alternative of having Rebuild walk the binary search tree setting this field to false involves needless work. The cross-referenced comment in procedure Rebuild is adequate warning that we are indulging in an unsafe practice.

```
54          else if p^.Rebuilt (* else if p^.OnCurrentPath *)
55            then Error(Cycle,0 (* irrelevant *))
56       (* else    p^.Touched and not p^.OnCurrentPath -- a previously explored
57                     subgraph *)
58       end; (* CycleCheck *)
59
60    procedure CheckTouched(p: PtrToNode);
61      begin
62        if p <> nil
63          then begin
64                 if not p^.Touched then Error(NotSingleSource, Root^.Name);
65                 CheckTouched(p^.Left);
66                 CheckTouched(p^.Right)
67               end
68       end; (* CheckTouched *)
69
70    begin (* CheckGraph *)
71      SetTouchedFalse(Root);
72      CycleCheck(Root);
73      CheckTouched(Root)
74    end; (* CheckGraph *)
```

— *Note the reference to the global variable* Root *from potentially deep inside the recursion.*

FILE   Rebuild.p   Page 1

```
 1 #include "Basic-Defs.h"
 2 #include "System-Interface.h"
 3 #include "Error.h"
 4 #include "String.h"
 5 #include "Rebuild.h"
 6
 7 (* procedure Rebuild(Root: PtrToNode); *)
 8 procedure Rebuild;
 9   (* Rebuild the ultimate target and any descendants that need rebuilding. *)
10   (* The strategy is:
11     Make essentially the same recursive walk through the graph that we
12       did when looking for cycles, but this time rebuild each node.
13     Actually go to the trouble of building/rebuilding a node only if it
14       does not exist or any of its children have a more recent time stamp
15       than the node itself.  Otherwise declare it rebuilt without executing
16       the commands that rebuild it.  It is crucial that this be done
17       in postorder.
18   *)
19         ──── See the related annotation in Check-Graph.p
20   (* On entry all the nodes in the graph have their  Rebuilt  field set to
21     false.  When  Rebuild  exits, all the  Rebuilt  fields will have been
22     set to true.
23   *)
24   var NoChanges: boolean; (* so that we can print something even when no work
25                             needs to be done *)
26   procedure RecRebuild(p: PtrToNode);
27     var q: PtrToSubNode;
28         r: PtrToMakeNode;
29         oops: boolean; (* if something goes wrong when we inquire about
30                           time stamps or attempt to issue a command *)
31         MaxTimeStamp: integer; (* maximum time stamp of children, after any
32                                   necessary rebuilding *)
33     begin                       ──── If p^.Rebuilt is true then this node and all its descendants have been rebuilt or
34       if not p^.Rebuilt              certified as up to date. There is no need to do the work again.
35         then begin
36               MaxTimeStamp := -maxint; (* all times are newer than this *)
37
38               (* Recursively rebuild its descendants, none, some, or all of
39                  which may have already been rebuilt.  Also, determine
40                  the time stamp for the most recently constructed child. *)
41               q := p^.Children;
42               while q <> nil do
43                 begin
44                   RecRebuild(q^.Child); (* Rebuild this child, if necessary. *)
45                   if q^.Child^.LastModified > MaxTimeStamp
46                     then MaxTimeStamp := q^.Child^.LastModified;
47                   q := q^.Next
48                 end;
49               (* MaximumTimeStamp is either -maxint (no children) or the
50                  time of the latest modification of the most recently modified
51                  child. *)
52
```

```
53              (* Determine if this node needs to be rebuilt. *)
54              TimeStamp(p^.Name,oops,p^.LastModified);
55              if oops then Error(TimeStampError,p^.Name);
56              if (p^.LastModified = DOESNOTEXIST) or
57                 (p^.LastModified < MaxTimeStamp)
58                then begin
59                    (* Rebuild it explicitly. *)
60                    r := p^.HowToMake;
61                    if r = nil then Error(FileDoesNotExist,p^.Name);
62                    write('Rebuilding `');
63                    WriteString(p^.Name);
64                    writeln('''');
65                    while r <> nil do
66                      begin
67                        write('   ');
68                        WriteString(r^.Command);
69                        writeln;
70                        ExecuteCommand(r^.Command,oops);
71                        if oops then Error(CommandBombed,0);
72                          (* command already written out *)
73                        r := r^.Next
74                    end;

75                    NoChanges := false; (* since this one was rebuilt *)
76

77                    (* Set the time stamp to "now". *)
78                    TimeStamp(p^.Name,oops,p^.LastModified);
79                    if oops (* this really shouldn't happen *)
80                      then Error(TimeStampError,p^.Name);
81                    if (p^.LastModified = DOESNOTEXIST) or
82                       (p^.LastModified < MaxTimeStamp)
83                      then Error(StillDoesNotExist,p^.Name)
84                end;
85              p^.Rebuilt := true (* whether or not it was actually rebuilt *)
86            end
87      end; (* RecRebuild *)
88

89  begin (* Rebuild *)
90    NoChanges := true; (* until proven otherwise *)
91    RecRebuild(Root);
92    if NoChanges
93      then begin
94          write('`'); WriteString(Root^.Name); writeln(''' is up to date')
95        end
96  end; (* Rebuild *)
```

If a node has no children, then MaxTimeStamp *is* -maxint, *so this test is false and the entire condition reduces to "does the file exist?"*

Note the reference to the global variable NoChanges *from potentially deep inside the recursion. This is an example of where "set and change" is appropriate.*

While the program performs some obvious checks, it assumes that the rebuilding commands don't do anything devious. See **Undetected errors—we have a bug in our program!**

When viewed from the perspective of depth-first search, this assignment statement should be placed at the beginning of RecRebuild, *instead of at the end. Because the graph is acyclic, it can be placed at the end, after the file has really been rebuilt.*

FILE String.h

```
1  (* Constant, type, and variable declarations relating to the string pool. *)
2
3  const NUL = 0; (* ASCII NUL is zero (but stored in a byte). *)
4        STRINGPOOLLEN = 5000; (* extend if overflow occurs. *)
5
```

In the rare event that the make file *is so large that the strings that define the file names (with repetitions removed) and commands exceed* STRINGPOOLLEN *characters in length, increase this value, remake the* make *utility, and try again.*

```
6  type Pool = array [1..STRINGPOOLLEN] of char;
7
8  var StringPool: Pool;
9
10 (* Some Useful Service Procedures *)
11 procedure ScanString(var (* in out *) i: integer); external;
12   (* Scan over the string starting at location  i . *)
13
14 procedure WriteString(i: integer); external;
15   (* Write out the string starting at location  i . *)
```

FILE String.p

```
1  #include "String.h"
2
3  (* procedure ScanString(var /* in out */ i: integer); *)
4  procedure ScanString;
5    (* Scan over the string starting at location  i . *)
6    begin
7      while StringPool[i] <> chr(NUL) do i := i + 1;
8      i := i + 1 (* scan over terminating NUL *)
9    end; (* ScanString *)
10
11 (* procedure WriteString(i: integer); *)
12 procedure WriteString;
13   (* Write out the string starting at location  i . *)
14   begin
15     while StringPool[i] <> chr(NUL) do
16       begin
17         write(StringPool[i]);
18         i := i + 1
19       end
20   end; (* WriteString *)
```

```
 1 type ErrorCodes = ((* Errors From  Lex  *)
 2                     IllegalChar, (* Only visible characters, blanks, tabs, and
 3                        carriage returns allowed (except in comments). *)
 4                     UnexpectedColon,
 5                     ColonMissing,
 6                     TargetNotInCol1,
 7                     CommandInCol1,
 8                     PrematureEOF,
 9                     StringPoolFull,
10
11                     (* Errors From  BuildGraph  *)
12                     DuplicateSpecification,
13
14                     (* Errors From  CheckGraph  *)
15                     NotSingleSource,
16                     Cycle,
17
18                     (* Errors From  Rebuild  *)
19                     FileDoesNotExist, (* A file that is not a target, and so
20                                       cannot be automatically rebuilt,
21                                       does not exist. *)
22                     TimeStampError,   (* Error on call to  TimeStamp .  If the
23                                       file does not exist, but the path name
24                                       is such that we can get to where the
25                                       file ought to be, then it is not an
26                                       error. *)
27                     CommandBombed,
28                     StillDoesNotExist (* A file which should have been created
29                                       or updated is still out of date. *));
30
31 procedure Error(Message: ErrorCodes;
32                 FileName: integer (* location of file name in string
33                                    pool, if applicable *)); external;
34    (* Print Error Message And Quit *)
```

FILE

```
 1 #include "GetChar.h" (* for  GetLineNumber  *)
 2 #include "String.h"  (* for  WriteString    *)
 3 #include "Error.h"
 4
 5 (* procedure Error(Message: ErrorCodes;
 6                    FileName: integer /* location of file name in string
 7                                      pool, if applicable */); *)
 8 procedure Error;
 9   (* Print Error Message And Quit *)
10   (* Line number and file name are not always relevant. *)
11   begin
12     case Message of
13       IllegalChar:
14         writeln('ERROR: Line ',GetLineNumber:1,
15                 ' -- Illegal character found in  makefile');
16       UnexpectedColon:
17         writeln('ERROR: Line ',GetLineNumber:1,' -- Unexpected colon');
18       ColonMissing:
19         writeln('ERROR: Line ',GetLineNumber:1,
20                 ' -- Colon missing after target');
21       TargetNotInCol1:
22         writeln('ERROR: Line ',GetLineNumber:1,
23                 ' -- Targets must begin in column 1');
24       CommandInCol1:
25         writeln('ERROR: Line ',GetLineNumber:1,
26                 ' -- Commands may not begin in column 1');
27       PrematureEOF:
28         writeln('ERROR: Premature end-of-file');
29       StringPoolFull:
30         writeln(
31           'ERROR: String pool full -- increase dimension and remake  make');
32
33       DuplicateSpecification:
34         begin
35           write('ERROR: Line ',GetLineNumber:1,' ''');
36           WriteString(FileName); writeln('''');
37           writeln('  has a duplicate rebuilding specification')
38         end;
39
40       NotSingleSource:
41         begin
42           write('ERROR:  makefile  invalid -- ''');
43           WriteString(FileName); writeln('''');
44           writeln(
45             '  is not a source or not the only source in the dependency graph')
46         end;
47       Cycle:
48         writeln(
49           'ERROR:  makefile  invalid -- dependency graph not cycle free');
50
```

```
51        FileDoesNotExist:
52          begin
53            write('ERROR: Do not know how to make '');
54            WriteString(FileName); writeln('''')
55          end;
56        TimeStampError:
57          begin
58            write('ERROR: While attempting to ascertain the status of '');
59            WriteString(FileName); writeln('''');
60            writeln('  an unclassifiable error occurred')
61          end;
62        CommandBombed:
63          (* Command to be executed printed by  Rebuild . *)
64          writeln('  ... appears to have bombed out');
65        StillDoesNotExist:
66          begin
67            write('ERROR: Even after attempting to rebuild file '');
68            WriteString(FileName); writeln('''');
69            writeln('  the file is out of date')
70          end
71      end;
72      halt (* nonstandard exit call *)
73    end; (* Error *)
```

FILE	GetChar.h

```
 1  type CharacterClasses = (eofchar, logicalCR, blank, colon, ordinary, illegal);
 2    (* Filter the input so that the rest of  Lex  has a clean interface.
 3        GetChar  returns one of the following logical characters:
 4            eof is true  --> eofchar
 5            eoln is true --> logicalCR (and eats the carriage return)
 6            a sequence of blanks, tabs, comments, and \<carriage return>s --> blank
 7                (compression of a sequence of logical blanks into one blank saves
 8                    space in the string pool)
```

— Lex *is written without knowledge of this.* Lex *would work just as well if each blank were returned separately (as long as tabs, comments, and* \ ⟨cr⟩*'s are returned as blanks). Decoupling the two routines makes for a more robust program.*

```
 9            : --> colon (which is sometimes interpreted by  Lex  as an
10                        ordinary character)
11            other visible characters --> ordinary (but not #)
12            nonvisible characters --> illegal (other than tab)
13    *)
14
15        Character = record
16                        Class: CharacterClasses;
17                        Actual: char (* The actual character for  colon ,  ordinary ,
18                                        and  illegal .  Blank for all others. *)
19                    end;
20
21  procedure InitGetChar; external;
22    (* Call this routine once, before calling  GetChar  for the first time. *)
23
24  procedure GetChar(var ch: Character); external;
25    (* Read the next logical character from the input. *)
26
27  function GetLineNumber: integer; external;
28    (* Return the line number of the line we are processing -- for helpful
29        error messages.
30    *)
```

— *This is better than making* Line (*in* GetChar.p) *public, since effectively it makes* Line *read-only.*

This character filter is not as innately complex as the one in the Nero Project—the code is more ad hoc.

```
 1  #include "GetChar.h"
 2
 3  const (* for easy reconfiguration *)
 4      TAB = 9; (* ASCII DEPENDENT: TAB is ^I = 9 (but stored in a byte). *)
 5      logicalSharp     = '#';
 6      logicalBackslash = '\';
 7      logicalColon     = ':';
 8
```

— *In case we encounter a system where these characters are common in file names.*

—*Because of a bug in some UNIX Pascal dialects, these static, private variables must have names that are different from those of the functionally similar variables in* Lex.p.

```
 9  var CharBuf: char; (* One-character buffer -- sometimes we need to read one
10                        character too many when compressing white space.
11                        The stored character is never a carriage return or
12                        end-of-file marker. *)
13      CharBufFull: boolean; (* Is it full or is it empty? *)
14      Line: integer; (* What line number we are processing -- for helpful error
15                        messages.  This can be off by one on occasion, since
16                        we advance it after reading a carriage return, but
17                        before reading the next character. *)
18
19  (* procedure InitGetChar; *)
20  procedure InitGetChar;
21    (* Call this routine once, before calling  GetChar  for the first time. *)
22      begin
23        CharBufFull := false;
24        Line := 1
25      end; (* InitGetChar *)
26
27  (* procedure GetChar(var ch: Character); *)
28  procedure GetChar;
29    (* Read the next logical character from the input. *)
30    label 1, 99;
31    var c: char;
32        WhiteSpace: boolean;
33    begin
34      (* Get the next character from the "input". *)
35      if CharBufFull
36        then begin
37              c := CharBuf; (* just as if we had read it from the input *)
38              CharBufFull := false
39            end
40      else if eof (* nothing to read *)
41        then begin
42              ch.Class := eofchar;
43              ch.Actual := ' ';
44              goto 99 (* return *)
45            end
```

If the character that would be read, if we could read it by normal means, is an end-of-file or end-of-line character, then read and process it.

```
46      else if eoln
47        then begin
48              ch.Class := logicalCR;
49              ch.Actual := ' ';
50              readln; (* read the carriage return character(s) *)
51              Line := Line + 1;
52              goto 99 (* return *)
53            end
54      else   read(c);
55
56      (*  c  is not end-of-file or end-of-line.  Essentially, classify and
57         return  c , but identify (# and \<carriage return>) and compress white
58         space -- it comes in many varieties. *)
59      WhiteSpace := false; (* so far *)
60
61      (* Really white white space. *)
62      if c in [' ',chr(TAB)] then WhiteSpace := true;
```

> *It is difficult to see that this statement can be placed outside both the gross loop (that starts at* `1:`*) and the tight loop (the* `while (c in ...)`*), but doing so makes for a slightly more efficient program. The high density of comments is a reflection of the complexity of the code.*

```
63  1: (* Determine if  c  is a "white space character".   c  can be a converted
64         comment or \<cr>. *)
65     while (c in [' ',chr(TAB)]) and
66           not eof and not eoln do read(c);
```

> *eof can be true at this point if the last line erroneously ends with a \⟨cr⟩.*

```
67      (* We have read a nonwhite space character or are stuck at end-of-file or
68         end-of-line. *)
69
70      (*  c  can be a blank (real or artificial) or tab backed up against a
71         carriage return or end-of-file, a #, a \, or some other character. *)
72      (* Do we have comment style white space? *)
73      if c = logicalSharp
74        then begin
75              (* illegal characters allowed in comments *)
76              while not eof (* should not be possible *) and not eoln do read(c);
```

> *The Pascal standard says that* eoln *should become true just before* eof *becomes true, but just in case . . .*

> *Logically, a comment starts with # and ends with the character just before the ⟨cr⟩ or \⟨cr⟩, but in the latter case it is easier to treat the comment as including the \⟨cr⟩, which is okay, since it is all just white space anyway.*

```
77              if (c = logicalBackslash) and eoln
78                then begin readln; Line := Line + 1 end;
79              (* Turn entire comment (and possibly end-of-line character) into
80                 a blank and try again. *)
81              WhiteSpace := true;
82              c := ' ';
83              goto 1
84            end;
85
```

```
 86          (* Do we have \<carriage return> white space? *)
 87          if (c = logicalBackslash) and (eof (* not really possible *) or eoln)
 88            then begin
 89                   if eoln then begin readln; Line := Line + 1 end;
 90                   WhiteSpace := true;
 91                   c := ' '; (* force it to be a blank *)
 92                   goto 1
 93                 end;
 94
 95          (*  c  can be a blank (real or artificial) or tab backed up against a
 96             carriage return or end-of-file, a \ not backed up against a carriage
 97             return, or some other character. *)
 98          if WhiteSpace
 99            then begin
100                   ch.Class := blank;
101                   ch.Actual := ' ';
102                   if not (c in [' ',chr(TAB)])
103                     then begin
104                            (* push back unwanted character *)
105                            CharBuf := c;
106                            CharBufFull := true
107                          end
108                 end
109            else begin
110                   if c = logicalColon
111                     then ch.Class := colon
112                     else if c in ['!'..'~'] (* ASCII DEPENDENT -- test must be
113                                             preceded by special case *)
114                     then ch.Class := ordinary
115                     else   ch.Class := illegal;
116                   ch.Actual := c
117                 end;
118 99:
119    end; (* GetChar *)
120
121 (* function GetLineNumber: integer; *)
122 function GetLineNumber;
123    (* Return the line number of the line we are processing -- for helpful
124       error messages.
125    *)
126    begin
127      GetLineNumber := Line
128    end; (* GetLineNumber *)
```

FILE   `Lex.h`

```
 1 (* Get the next "object" from the input. *)
 2
 3 type ObjectType = (Target,   (* file being described *)
 4                    Source,   (* one of the files it depends on *)
 5                    Command,  (* how it is rebuilt *)
 6                    EndOfFile);
 7      Modes = set of ObjectType;
 8
 9 procedure InitLex; external;
10    (* Call this routine once, before calling  Lex  for the first time. *)
11
12 procedure Lex(    Possible: Modes;   (* what  BuildGraph  thinks  Lex  can
13                                         legally see next *)
14               var What: ObjectType; (* what  Lex  found *)
15                   NextFree: integer (* where in the string pool  Lex  should
16                                         put it *)); external;
17    (* Place the next object into the string pool starting at position  NextFree ,
18       returning its type.
19    *)
```

```
 1 (* Get the next "object" from the input. *)
 2
 3 #include "GetChar.h"
 4 #include "String.h"
 5 #include "Error.h"
 6 #include "Lex.h"
 7
```

— *Because of a bug in some UNIX Pascal dialects, these static, private variables must have names that are different from those of the functionally similar variables in* GetChar.p.

```
 8 var LexBuf: Character; (* One-character buffer of type  Character  -- Lex
 9                           cannot know that a file name has ended until it
10                           has read one character too many. *)
11     LexBufFull: boolean; (* Is it full or is it empty? *)
12
13 (* procedure InitLex; *)
14 procedure InitLex;
15   (* Call this routine once, before calling  Lex  for the first time. *)
16   begin
17     (* Initialize character handling package on which  Lex  depends. *)
18     InitGetChar;
19
20     LexBufFull := false
21   end; (* InitLex *)
22
23 (* procedure Lex(    Possible: Modes;  /* what  BuildGraph  thinks  Lex  can
24                                        legally see next */
25                  var What: ObjectType; /* what  Lex  found */
26                      NextFree: integer /* where in the string pool  Lex  should
27                                        put it */); *)
28 procedure Lex;
29   (* Place the next object into the string pool starting at position  NextFree ,
30      returning its type.
31   *)
32   (* Possibilities are: [Target] (first entry only), [Source,Command], and
33                         [Command,Target,EndOfFile]. *)
34   label 99;
35   var ch: Character;
36       LastWasCR, (* so we can determine if the current character is the first
37                     character on a line *)
38       FoundFirstChar: (* have we found the first character of a target
39                         or command *)
40         boolean;
41
```

```
42    procedure Assign(ch: char);
43      (* Assign  ch  to the next free place in the string pool, checking for
44         overflow.
45      *)
46      begin
47        if NextFree > STRINGPOOLLEN
48          then Error(StringPoolFull,0 (* irrelevant *))
49          else begin
50                   StringPool[NextFree] := ch;
51                   NextFree := NextFree + 1
52               end
53      end; (* Assign *)
54
55    begin
56      (* "Read" the next character. *)
57      if LexBufFull
58        then begin
59                 ch := LexBuf;
60                 LexBufFull := false
61             end
62        else GetChar(ch);
63
64      (* If it is possible to find a  Source  make that the top priority.
65         As long as we don't leave the current line, there is still hope. *)
66      if Possible = [Source,Command]
67        then begin
68                 (* Skip over white space. *)
69                 while ch.Class = blank do GetChar(ch);
70                 case ch.Class of
71                   illegal: Error(IllegalChar,0 (* irrelevant *));
72                   blank: (* not possible *);
73                   eofchar: Error(PrematureEOF,0 (* irrelevant *));
74                   logicalCR: (* didn't find a  Source , maybe we will find a
75                                 Command *)
76                     begin
77                       Possible := [Command];
78                       GetChar(ch)
79                     end;
80                   colon: Error(UnexpectedColon,0 (* irrelevant *));
81                   ordinary: (* found a  Source  -- first character of file name *)
82                     begin
83                       repeat
84                         Assign(ch.Actual); (* process previous character *)
85                         GetChar(ch)          (* get next character *)
86                       until ch.Class <> ordinary;
87                       Assign(chr(NUL)); (* terminate string *)
```

This is just
```
      StringPool[NextFree] := ch;
      NextFree := NextFree + 1
```
with an overflow check.

White space is compressed into a single blank character by GetChar. *Lex acts like this does not happen, which is why there is a* while *and not an* if. *When dealing with something as complex as the input it is wise to have each routine distrust the other. The loss of efficiency is so minor, and the difficulty in writing bug-free code so great, that this extra level of protection is worthwhile. With an* if *there is always the nagging doubt that the comment at line 72 is not true. With a* while *we are certain it is.*

FILE   Lex.p   Page 3

```
88                What := Source;
89                   (* push back unwanted character *)
90                LexBuf := ch;
91                LexBufFull := true;
92                goto 99 (* return *)
93              end
94            end
95          end;
96
97      (* Possibilities are: [Command], [Target] (first entry only), and
98                            [Command,Target,EndOfFile] *)
99      (* Targets start in column 1 and commands don't.  If either is acceptable,
100        then sort out which we have. *)
```

— *The truth of this assertion can be verified only by considering the interaction of* Lex *and* BuildGraph.

```
101     (* No matter how we arrive here  ch  contains the first character of
102         a line. *)
103     LastWasCR := true;
104     FoundFirstChar := false; (* of target or command *)
105     repeat
106       case ch.Class of
```

Colons are permitted in commands.

```
107         illegal:   Error(IllegalChar,0 (* irrelevant *));
108         colon:     if LastWasCR (* Either it is a target, at which time
109                                   it cannot begin with a colon, or it is
110                                   a command, at which time it cannot begin
111                                   in column 1. *)
112                    then Error(UnexpectedColon,0 (* irrelevant *))
113                    else ch.Class := ordinary; (* convert to ordinary character
114                               and treat as first character of command *)
115         eofchar:   if EndOfFile in Possible
116                    then begin
117                        What := EndOfFile;
118                        goto 99 (* return *)
119                      end
120                    else Error(PrematureEOF,0 (* irrelevant *));
121         logicalCR: begin
122                       (* A blank line is present in the makefile.  A blank
123                          line isn't necessarily just a carriage return (it
124                          could contain a comment). *)
125                    LastWasCR := true;
126                    GetChar(ch)
127                    end;
128         blank:     begin
129                    LastWasCR := false;
130                    GetChar(ch)
131                    end;
```

Lex will not be called again.

Either there was nothing in the makefile *except blank lines and comments, or the last target has no rebuilding command.*

```
132          ordinary:  begin
133                         (* We have found the first character of either a target
134                            or a command.  Based on whether we are in column 1
135                            decide if we are trying for a target or a command. *)
136                         if Possible = [Command,Target,EndOfFile]
137                           then if LastWasCR
138                                   then Possible := [Target]
139                                   else Possible := [Command];
140                         FoundFirstChar := true
141                       end
142       end
143    until FoundFirstChar;
144
145    if Possible = [Target] (* because of above, or on first entry *)
146      then begin
147            if not LastWasCR then Error(TargetNotInCol1,0 (* irrelevant *));
148            repeat
149               Assign(ch.Actual); (* process previous character *)
150               GetChar(ch)        (* get next character *)
151            until ch.Class <> ordinary;
152            Assign(chr(NUL)); (* terminate string *)
153            if ch.Class <> colon
154               then Error(ColonMissing,0 (* irrelevant *));
155            (* else colon present -- it is noise, throw it away -- buffer
156                    remains empty *)
157            What := Target
158          end
159      else (* Possible = [Command] *)
160            begin
161               if LastWasCR then Error(CommandInCol1,0 (* irrelevant *));
162               repeat
163                  Assign(ch.Actual); (* process previous character *)
164                  GetChar(ch);       (* get next character *)
165                  (* colons are ordinary characters while processing commands *)
166                  if ch.Class = colon then ch.Class := ordinary
167               until ch.Class in [eofchar,logicalCR,illegal];
168               Assign(chr(NUL)); (* terminate string *)
169               What := Command;
170               (* Unlike sources, commands eat the carriage return. *)
171               if ch.Class = illegal then Error(IllegalChar, 0 (* irrelevant *));
172               if ch.Class = eofchar then Error(PrematureEOF,0 (* irrelevant *))
173            end;
174 99:
175   end; (* Lex *)
```

This can occur only on the first entry. Other dependency lines that are accidentally indented will be interpreted as commands. In all likelihood, the graph will not be well formed.

By a small addition here we could permit white space before the colon.

FILE   `System_Interface.h`

```
 1  const DOESNOTEXIST = -1; (* Time returned if a file does not exist. *)
 2
 3  procedure TimeStamp(    FileName: integer;
 4                      var err: boolean; var time: integer); external;
 5    (* Return the time that the file  FileName  was last modified.  If the
 6       file does not exist indicate this fact with a flag.  If anything goes
 7       wrong  err  will be set to true.
 8    *)
 9
10  procedure ExecuteCommand(Command: integer; var err: boolean); external;
11    (* Execute the  Command .  If anything goes wrong  err  will be set
12       to true.
13    *)
```

FILE   `System_Interface.p`

[!] CAUTION   **System dependent code**

```
 1  #include "String.h"
 2  #include "Sys.h"
 3  #include "System—Interface.h"
 4
 5  (* procedure TimeStamp(    FileName: integer;
 6                        var err: boolean; var time: integer); *)
 7  procedure TimeStamp;
 8    (* Return the time that the file  FileName  was last modified.  If the
 9       file does not exist indicate this fact with a flag.  If anything goes
10       wrong  err  will be set to true.
11    *)
12  begin
13    GetFTime(StringPool[FileName],err,time)
14  end; (* TimeStamp *)
15
16  (* procedure ExecuteCommand(Command: integer; var err: boolean); *)
17  procedure ExecuteCommand;
18    (* Execute the  Command .  If anything goes wrong  err  will be set
19       to true.
20    *)
21  begin
22    Exec(StringPool[Command],err)
23  end; (* ExecuteCommand *)
```

If you compare these calls to the declarations in `Sys.h`, *it appears to Pascal as if we are passing a character by reference. As explained in Section 1.4, what we are really passing is the address of the character. The C routines* `GetFTime` *and* `Exec` *in* `Sys.c` *reinterpret this as the address of a string of characters ending with an ASCII NUL.*

In the UNIX view of `make`, *the C routines* `GetFTime` *and* `Exec` *are coded with knowledge of how Pascal stores* `boolean` *variables. The C routines need to know the size of a* `boolean` *variable and the conventions for* `true` *and* `false`.

FILE

 System dependent code

See the annotations in System—Interface.p.

```
1  procedure GetFTime(var FileName: char;
2                        (* From the point of view of C this is really
3                           char *FileName  or  ^packed array [1.. ] of char . *)
4                     var err: boolean; var time: integer); external;
5   (* Return the time that the file  FileName  was last modified.  If the
6      file does not exist indicate this fact with a flag.  If anything goes
7      wrong  err  will be set to true.
8   *)
9
10 procedure Exec(var Command: char; (* Same for  Command . *)
11              var err: boolean); external;
12  (* Execute the  Command .  If anything goes wrong  err  will be set
13     to true.
14  *)
```

GLOSSARY

Abstract Data Type (or ADT) (p. 106) A collection of values and related operations. The logical structure of an ADT is independent of the representation selected for its implementation.

Actual parameter (p. 42) The variable or expression passed to a procedure by the caller. Contrast with *formal parameter*.

Adjacency list (p. 284) A representation of a graph in which each vertex has associated with it a list of vertices to which it is connected by an edge (in an undirected graph) or an arc (in a directed graph).

Adjacency matrix (p. 284) A representation of a graph as a matrix, where

$$M_{ij} = \begin{cases} 1, & \text{if } v_i \text{ is connected to } v_j \text{ by an edge or arc;} \\ 0, & \text{otherwise.} \end{cases}$$

Algorithm (p. 1) A precise, abstractly stated method for solving a problem.

Aliasing (p. 123) Having two names for the same location in memory.

Alphabet (p. 225) A finite set of symbols without any associated interpretation.

Ambiguous grammar (p. 232) A grammar with the property that there exists at least one string with two derivation trees.

Arc See *graph*.

ASCII (p. 48) Literally, American Standard Code for Information Interchange. A commonly used internal representation of characters.

Automatic variable (p. 84) A variable whose lifetime is identical to the lifetime of the invocation of the procedure in which it is declared. Storage for the variable is allocated in the stack frame of the invocation.

Balanced search tree (p. 303) A search tree with a guaranteed worst-case performance for FIND, INSERT, and DELETE of $O(\log n)$. AVL trees, 2-3 trees, and red-black trees are some well-known types of balanced search trees.

Base case (p. 165) The simple situation that terminates a recursive definition or terminates the execution of a recursive procedure. It is also known as a *terminal condition* or *degenerate case*.

Base type (p. 33) The universe of discourse from which the objects of a Pascal set are drawn.

Big Oh See $O(\ )$.

Binary search (p. 4) An algorithm for searching a sorted list that cuts the size of the list to be searched in half with each step. It is very efficient, running in $O(\log n)$ time.

Binary search tree (p. 294) A binary tree containing keys comparable with the less-than operator, and which satisfies the following property for every node in the tree:

> *If the key of the node is k, then the keys of all the nodes to its left must be less than k and the keys of all the nodes to its right must be greater than k.*

This allows average-case $O(\log n)$ performance for searching and insertion.

Call-by-reference parameter (p. 27) A parameter passing mechanism where the address of the actual parameter, which must be a variable, is passed to the called procedure. References to the actual parameter are indirect and changes to the formal parameter are reflected back to the actual parameter immediately.

Call-by-value parameter (p. 27) A parameter passing mechanism where the value of the actual parameter is copied into a local variable of the called procedure.

Call-by-value/result parameter (p. 32) A parameter passing mechanism where the value of the actual parameter, which must be a variable, is copied into a local variable of the called procedure. When the called procedure returns, the current value of the formal parameter is copied back into the actual parameter. This method is also known as *call-by-copy/restore*.

Cast (p. 41) An operator that can be applied to a variable or expression and that informs the compiler to consider the result to be of a specified type. This can involve an actual conversion, as when an `integer` is cast to a `real`, or can just involve a change of perspective, as in Turbo Pascal when an untyped `var` parameter is cast to an array of integers.

Circular buffer (p. 62)   A data structure that implements a queue of bounded length in an array (as opposed to using a linked list). The array is treated as circular, with the first element following the last.

Collision (p. 305)   In hashing, when two keys have the same hash value.

Concatenation (p. 226)   An operator that takes two strings and combines them into one by writing them back to back.

Constant-time operation (p. 63)   An operation whose running time is independent of the size of the data structure to which it is applied. Also called an $O(1)$ operation.

Container type (p. 182)   An abstract data type, like Stack, Set, and Tree, that holds atoms of another ADT within a data structure.

Context-free grammar (p. 224)   A grammar in which each production has the form $A \to \alpha$. The nonterminal on the left is not surrounded by any "context," as it is in more general grammars. Contrast with *phrase-structure grammar*.

Context-free language (p. 233)   A language for which there exists a context-free grammar.

Cycle (p. 285)   In a graph, a sequence of edges or arcs that starts from a vertex and ultimately returns to the same vertex.

Dangling `else` *problem* (p. 248)   The ambiguous grammar fragment

$$SL \to SL \; ; \; S \mid S$$
$$S \; \to \text{begin } SL \text{ end} \mid$$
$$\text{if } BE \text{ then } S \mid$$
$$\text{if } BE \text{ then } S \text{ else } S$$

which models the `if ... then ... else ...` construct of Pascal and C. The ambiguity is resolved by imposing the extragrammatical rule: the `else` should be paired with the closest unmatched `then`.

Declaration (p. 59)   A programming language construct that defines a procedure interface or the characteristics of a variable, without actually giving the body of the procedure or allocating storage for the variable. It is what the compiler needs to know to compile calls to the procedure or references to the variable. Contrast with *definition*.

Definition (p. 59)   The point in a program where the body of a procedure is given or the storage for a variable is allocated. Every variable or procedure can have only one definition, but its declaration can be repeated in as many places as needed. The separation of the declaration of a procedure or variable from its definition is intimately tied up with independent compilation.

Degenerate case   See *base case*.

Depth-first search (p. 287)   A method for recursively walking a graph. The essence of the algorithm is

```
procedure DFS(p: ^Node);
  begin
    if not p^.Encountered
      then begin
            p^.Encountered := true;
            Recursively call DFS for each of
                the children of p
          end
  end; (* DFS *)
```

Derivation tree (p. 231)   A pictorial representation of a derivation that hides the exact order in which the productions were applied.

DFS numbering (p. 289)   A numbering imposed on the vertices of a graph by depth-first search. The vertices are numbered consecutively as they are encountered for the first time.

Directed acyclic graph (p. 285)   A directed graph with no cycles. Often abbreviated DAG.

Directed graph   See *graph*.

Double hashing (p. 306)   A method of resolving collisions where the hashing algorithm successively searches i, $i + k$, $i + 2k$, ... looking for an unoccupied slot. k is a second hash of the key and must be relatively prime to the size of the hash table.

Dynamic property (p. 26)   A property of a program that depends on how the program behaves during execution. An example is the sequence of activation records stored on the stack. Contrast with *static property*.

Dynamically allocated arrays (p. 46)   Arrays whose bounds can be specified at runtime. Both Ada and PL/I support dynamically allocated arrays. In C the same effect can be gotten by using `malloc`.

Edge   See *graph*.

Empty string (p. 226)   The string of zero length, usually denoted by ϵ or, sometimes, λ.

Formal parameter (p. 42)   A variable in the argument list of a procedure or function declaration. When a call is made, each formal parameter is associated with an *actual parameter*.

Full evaluation (p. 20)   The method of evaluating Boolean connectives in which both clauses are always evaluated. Contrast with *short-circuited evaluation*.

Garbage collection (p. 190)   A method of managing dynamically allocated memory where, when there is no more storage available, the system sweeps memory reclaiming any unreachable cells.

Graph (p. 283)   A graph, $G = (V, E)$, is a collection of *vertices* and *edges*. "Vertex" is an undefined concept, but can be thought of as a point. The edges connect pairs of vertices. If the edges have no directionality, the graph is *undirected*, whereas if the edges have directionality, the graph is *directed*. In a directed graph the edges are usually called *arcs*.

Greatest common divisor (p. 136) Given two positive integers, the largest integer that divides them both evenly. The greatest common divisor of 20 and 21 is 1, while the greatest common divisor of 30 and 36 is 6.

Hashing (p. 303) A technique for converting names into locations that has constant-time average-case performance if the hash table is not too heavily loaded.

Heap (p. 126) The region of memory where variables allocated by `new` are located. (A heap is also an implementation of the priority queue ADT. This is an unrelated concept.)

Immutable (p. 169) Used to describe an ADT in which the primitive operations do not change their operands.

Independent compilation (p. 59) The ability to compile the procedures of a program separately and then link the compiled pieces together into a single executable program. Independent compilation supports libraries and simultaneous development of logically independent portions of a large program.

Inherently ambiguous language (p. 358) A context-free language for which every grammar is ambiguous.

Integrated development environment (p. 73) A programming environment in which the editor, compiler, linker and runtime support system appear to the user as a unified whole. This allows the use of domain-specific information, something not possible when the editor, compiler, linker, and runtime support system are separate and generic.

Invariant (p. 6) A property of an algorithm, data structure, or collection of variables that is true when a piece of code is entered and remains true when the piece of code is exited, despite the fact that the values stored in the variables have been changed.

Invocation (p. 26) The act of calling a procedure. Also, the lifetime of a single call to a procedure, including any time during which it is suspended.

Language (p. 224) A set of strings drawn from some finite alphabet.

Left factoring (p. 242) A modification to a grammar designed to make it usable by the recursive descent parsing method. Productions of the form

$$A \rightarrow \alpha\beta$$
$$A \rightarrow \alpha\gamma$$

are converted into

$$A \rightarrow \alpha X$$
$$X \rightarrow \beta$$
$$X \rightarrow \gamma$$

Left-recursive grammar (p. 244) A grammar containing productions of the form $A \rightarrow A\alpha \mid \beta$.

Left recursion elimination (p. 244) A modification to a grammar designed to make it usable by the recursive descent parsing method. Productions of the form

$$A \rightarrow A\alpha$$
$$A \rightarrow \beta$$

are converted into

$$A \rightarrow \beta A'$$
$$A' \rightarrow \alpha A'$$
$$A' \rightarrow \epsilon$$

Leftmost derivation (p. 230) A derivation in which the nonterminal chosen for replacement is always the leftmost one.

Lexical analysis (p. 226) The process of converting a stream of characters drawn from one alphabet into a stream of characters drawn from another alphabet.

Library routine (p. 2) A procedure for a commonly occurring task, coded by an expert, and made available to the general user community. While the specification (procedure name and calling sequence) must be user visible, frequently the body of the procedure is provided only in compiled form.

Lifetime (p. 46) The period of time within the execution of a program that a variable exists, whether or not it can be referenced. Lifetime is a dynamic property of a program. In Pascal, variables declared within procedures have a lifetime that begins when the procedure is invoked and which ends when the procedure returns. In C and FORTRAN it is possible to declare a variable whose scope is limited to a procedure, but whose lifetime is the same as that of the entire program. In C this is done with the keyword `static`.

Line buffering (p. 54) An approach to input from the terminal where characters are delivered to the language subsystem a line at a time. This allows simple corrections to be made to the input as it is typed.

Linear congruential method (p. 91) A method of generating random numbers where

$$x_{i+1} = ax_i + c \pmod{m}$$

Linear probing (p. 305) A method of resolving collisions where the hashing algorithm successively searches i, $i + 1$, $i + 2$, ..., looking for an unoccupied slot.

Linking (p. 73) The process of assembling a collection of independently compiled object files into a single, executable program. The program which does this is called a *linker*. This is an essential step in independent compilation.

List (p. 165) The fundamental data type of the programming language LISP.

Loading factor (p. 307) The percentage of spaces in a hash table that are in use.

Name equivalence (p. 43) A rule for determining when two variables have the same type. The rule says that two variables have the same type when their type names are the same. It is insufficient for them to have the same structure. This is a strict approach. Compare with *structure equivalence*.

Nonrecursive shell (p. 196) A nonrecursive procedure that contains within itself a recursive procedure that does most of the work. The nonrecursive procedure typically does initialization, hides extra parameters to the recursive procedure, or does a few lines of special processing after the recursive procedure returns. By branching to the `end` of the nonrecursive procedure, the recursive procedure can terminate when it has completed its useful work, without going through a sequence of returns. (This is not possible in Turbo Pascal due to limitations placed on the `goto` statement.)

Nonterminal (p. 227) An alphabet-like symbol used in a grammar that appears in sentential forms, but which is not part of the alphabet. It denotes a class of strings. Nonterminals correspond to English language concepts like *noun*, *adjective*, and *clause*.

O( ) (p. 4) A notation used to express the approximate running time of a program. If an algorithm is $O(n^2)$, then it takes on the order of n^2 steps to complete. $O(n^2)$ is read aloud as "Big Oh of n squared."

Object code (p. 79) The machine language translation of a source file. It usually is not executable, because it typically contains unresolved external references. These are resolved by the linker when a complete executable is built.

Overloading (p. 3) Using one variable or operator for two different purposes. For example, + is overloaded in Pascal since it specifies both addition and set union.

Own variable (p. 89) A static variable whose scope is that of the procedure in which it is declared. The term comes from ALGOL.

Parser (p. 235) A program that uses a grammar to determine the derivations of strings. Building the derivation tree is known as *parsing*.

Period of a random number generator See *pseudorandom number generator*.

Phrase-structure grammar (p. 233) A grammatical system in which productions have the form $\alpha A \gamma \rightarrow \alpha \beta \gamma$. Contrast with *context-free grammar*.

Postorder traversal (p. 287) A recursive traversal of a tree (or graph) where a node is visited after making the recursive calls for its children. Contrast with *preorder traversal*.

Power set (p. 33) The set of all subsets of a set. The power set of $S = \{1, 2, 3\}$ is $\{\emptyset, \{1\}, \{2\}, \{3\}, \{1, 2\}, \{1, 3\}, \{2, 3\}, \{1, 2, 3\}\}$. The notation for the power set of S is 2^S.

Precondition (p. 3) A mathematical property of, or a relationship between, variables that is assumed true on entry to a procedure, loop, or block of code and whose correct functioning depends on its being true. Examples: a procedure for binary search assumes that its input is sorted; a primality testing procedure assumes its input is greater than zero.

Predefined type (p. 106) A type, such as `integer` or `boolean`, that is built into a programming language, but that can be overridden by a user-supplied type declaration that uses the same name. Contrast with *reserved word*.

Predictive parser See *recursive descent parsing*.

Preorder traversal (p. 287) A recursive traversal of a tree (or graph) where a node is visited before making the recursive calls for its children. Contrast with *postorder traversal*.

Production (p. 227) A rewriting rule of a grammar.

Proper subtraction (p. 108) The result of $\max(a - b, 0)$.

Pseudorandom number generator (p. 90) A mathematical routine for generating a sequence of numbers that pass statistical tests for randomness. The numbers are not truly random because they are reproducible. The number of calls to the generator before the random numbers repeat is called the *period* of the generator. The number used to start the generation of random numbers is called the *seed*.

Range checking (p. 21) The automatic checking of subscripts and values to see that they fall within the bounds of an array or limits of a subrange type. Most Pascal compilers implement range checking (in both UNIX and Turbo Pascal range checking can be turned off).

Real-time processing (p. 64) A programming paradigm in which the program must respond to regularly occurring external events as they occur. It requires that each action of the program take a limited amount of time.

Recursion (p. 27) The ability of a procedure to call itself, either directly or indirectly. Also, the act of calling itself.

Recursive descent parsing (p. 235) A method of parsing utilizing mutually recursive procedures. There is one procedure for each nonterminal. The parser must be able to select the production to apply based on which procedure/nonterminal is currently active and using a limited amount of lookahead.

Relatively prime (p. 306) Having a greatest common divisor of 1.

Reserved word (p. 106) An identifier, like `if` or `begin`, in a programming language whose use for any other purpose is forbidden. Contrast with *predefined type*.

Scope (p. 46) The region in a program where a variable can potentially be referenced. Scope is a static property of a program. Compare with *visibility*.

Seed of a random number generator See *pseudorandom number generator*.

Sentence symbol or start symbol (p. 227) The nonterminal with which a derivation begins.

Sentential form (p. 231)   Any string of terminals and nonterminals that can be derived from the sentence symbol.

Sequential file (p. 2)   A file where the primitive operation is `GetNextRecord` and where there is no capability to move directly to the *n*th record for arbitrary *n* or to locate a record by specifying its key. This is the kind of file supported by standard Pascal.

Short-circuited evaluation (p. 20)   The method of evaluating Boolean connectives in which the evaluation of the entire expression stops as soon as the result is known. In particular, for `and`, if the first clause is false, the second clause is not evaluated. Contrast with *full evaluation*.

Side effect (p. 20)   An incidental effect of a statement that affects the global state of the computation. Reading input or setting a global variable from inside a function are examples.

Sink (p. 284)   A vertex in a directed graph with only in-arcs.

Source (p. 284)   A vertex in a directed graph with only out-arcs.

Stack frame (p. 25)   A record, maintained in a stack, that contains storage for the parameters and local variables of a procedure or function. It also contains other information relating to a particular invocation, such as the return address. It is also known as an *activation record*.

Standard expression grammar (p. 230)   The grammar

$$E \rightarrow E + T \mid E - T \mid T$$
$$T \rightarrow T * F \mid T / F \mid F$$
$$F \rightarrow \text{num} \mid (\ E\ )$$

for generating arithmetic expressions.

Static property (p. 26)   A property of a program, like the scope of variables, that reflects the structure of the program as it appears on paper and to the compiler. Contrast with *dynamic property*.

Static variable (p. 89)   A variable whose lifetime extends over the entire run of the program.

String (p. 226)   A finite sequence of characters drawn from some alphabet.

Strong typing (p. 38)   A philosophy of programming language design in which every variable has a specific type and operations involving variables of two different types are strictly controlled. Strong typing allows the compiler to detect certain, hard-to-find bugs.

Structure equivalence (p. 43)   A rule for determining when two variables have the same type. This approach is less strict than *name equivalence* because it requires only that the two variables have the same layout in memory.

Terminal (p. 225)   A symbol from the alphabet of a language.

Terminal condition   See *base case*.

Topological sort (p. 313)   An ordering of the vertices of a directed acyclic graph such that for any vertex the immediate successors of the vertex follow it in the ordering.

Unambiguous grammar (p. 232)   A grammar with the property that every string in the language has exactly one derivation tree.

Unconstrained array (p. 44)   A type declaration of an array in which the component type is specified, but the bounds are not. C and Ada allow unconstrained arrays to be formal parameters of a procedure.

Undirected graph   See *graph*.

Vertex   See *graph*.

Visibility (p. 46)   The region in a program where a variable can actually be referenced. Visibility is a static property of the program. The visibility of a variable can be different from its *scope* because internal procedures can declare variables with the same name.

Work array (p. 47)   An auxiliary array passed into a procedure to provide temporary storage.

ANSWERS AND HINTS

To get the most out of any textbook you need to do the exercises, but if you don't know if your answers are correct, some of the value is lost. Here are the answers, or at least some hints, for most of the exercises and projects. (The solutions are organized on a chapter-by-chapter basis. Within each chapter the solutions to the exercises are followed by the solutions to the projects.)

EXERCISE 1–1 Try the sequence 1 2 6 7 9, searching for 8.

EXERCISE 1–2 Replace lines 36–39 with

Don't peek! To get the most out an exercise, do it before you look at the answer. You'll learn more by doing it and getting it wrong than by just reading the solution.

```
else begin (* A[m] = X -- found it *)
         r := m;
         while l < r do
           begin
             m := (l + r) div 2;
             if A[m] < X
               then l := m + 1
               else r := m
           end;
         Where := l;
         goto 99 (* return *)
      end
```

After finding an occurrence of X, the routine finds the leftmost occurrence by a special version of binary search. This second search performs only at most another $O(\log n)$ comparisons. Both searches can be combined into one by replacing the body of the procedure with

```
while l < r do
  begin
    m := (l + r) div 2;
    if A[m] < X
      then l := m + 1
      else (* A[m] >= X *)
            r := m
  end;
if A[r] = X
  then Where := r
  else Where := 0 (* not present *)
```

(This code does not handle the empty list correctly.)

EXERCISE 1–3   Either

```
if ...
   then begin
            if ...
               then ...
         end
   else ...
```

or

```
if ...
   then if ...
            then ...
            else (* do nothing *)
   else ...
```

works.

EXERCISE 1–4   The most common incorrect solution is discussed in For Your Information: Evaluation of Boolean Connectives. If A is not degenerate (that is, N is not zero), a tricky, but correct, solution is

```
i := 1;
while (i < N) and (A[i] <> X) do i := i + 1;
if A[i] = X (* needlessly recheck an element of  A[1..N-1]  or
               check  A[N]  for the first time *)
   then Where := i
   else Where := 0
```

The solution

```
            Where := 0;
            for i := 1 to N do
              if A[i] = X then Where := i
            (*  Where  still zero if  X  not present *)
```

is incorrect, because it finds the rightmost occurrence if X occurs more than once, while

```
            Where := 0;
            for i := N downto 1 do
              if A[i] = X then Where := i
            (*  Where  still zero if  X  not present *)
```

is correct, but inefficient, since it always searches the entire array.

EXERCISE 1–5   If X is not present in A, the code examines A[N+1] when it tests to see if A[i] = X. Even worse than a possible subscript-out-of-range error, if A[N+1] accidentally equals X, i will be set to N+1.

EXERCISE 1–6   Consider the output of the following program.

```
 1   program EvalOrder(input,output);
 2     procedure a(i, j: integer);
 3       begin
 4         (* No need to do anything. *)
 5       end; (* a *)
 6
 7     function f(i: integer): integer;
 8       begin
 9         writeln('In function f.');
10         f := i
11       end; (* f *)
12
13     function g(i: integer): integer;
14       begin
15         writeln('In function g.');
16         g := i
17       end; (* g *)
18
19     begin
20       a(f(1),g(1))
21     end. (* EvalOrder *)
```

EXERCISES 1–7 through 1–11 The answers are given in the text. The first of the two programs of Exercise 1–9 prints 50 when n is 50 and produces a runtime error message when n is 101. The second program does not compile.

EXERCISE 1–12   It will print

                    The sum was: 27

The blank line causes no problems. The call to readln(i) after the 3 has been read will skip over the blank line (that is, skip over the logical end-of-line character on that line), skip over the blank preceding the 2, read the 2, and finally throw away the logical end-of-line character after the 2.

EXERCISE 1–13   No. For each logical end-of-line (a carriage return/line feed combination) it will output a carriage return and two line feeds.

EXERCISE 1–14

```
    i := 1;
    while (i <= MAX) and not eoln do
      begin
        read(CustomerName.name[i]);
        i := i + 1
      end;
    if not eoln then report error; (* too many characters *)
    readln; (* throw away logical end-of-line character *)
    CustomerName.length := i - 1
```

This solution treats trailing blanks as part of the name. How would you fix this?

EXERCISE 2–1   Local variables don't retain their values from invocation to invocation. See Section 1.4 for an explanation. Section 2.4, More on Lifetime, Scope, and Visibility, discusses an alternative that standard Pascal does not support.

EXERCISE 2–2   The loop isn't needed, except to handle one special case. What if the first character typed by the user is illegal? In this circumstance there isn't any valid last character to use as a substitute. (`LastDirection` must also be initialized to an invalid character in the main program.)

EXERCISE 2–3   Determining if the worm has hit the wall or eaten the food can be done in constant time. If we let the new position of the head be (r, c), then to determine if the worm has hit the wall we need to compare r to `MINROW` and `MAXROW` and c to `MINCOL` and `MAXCOL`. The location of the food can be stored separately, in a record, and compared to the new position of the head. The easiest way to determine if the worm fills the screen is to make the length of the circular buffer equal to the number of cells on the board; if

$$\text{TailPos} = (\text{HeadPos mod BUFFERSIZE}) + 1$$

the buffer is full. Initialization requires placing the locations of the eight initial segments of the worm in `WormSeg[1..8]` and setting `TailPos` to 1 and `HeadPos` to 8.

EXERCISE 2–4   Declare `SeedSet` to be a `boolean` variable in the implementation section (outside of any procedure), set it `false` in the initialization section, and set it `true` when `xsubk` is set to `iseed` in `Seed`. It also needs to be set `true` by `Random`, since a call to `Random` before a call to `Seed` implies that the default seed of 1 has been accepted. The check for misuse occurs in `Seed`—on entry, the procedure checks `SeedSet` to see if it is `true`. If it is, then either `Seed` is being called for the second time or `Random` already has been called.

Pascal does not provide a good mechanism for informing the caller that it has used the package improperly. Stopping the program is probably too strong a measure, and setting a `boolean` call-by-reference parameter is too weak, since it can be ignored. Ada allows the package to raise an `exception`, an unignorable signal that something has gone wrong.

EXERCISE 2–5   It will depend on your compiler—you'll have to run it to find out.

EXERCISE 2–6   While `round((n-1)*Random) + 1` returns a random integer in the range $[1, n]$, 1 and n are only half as likely to be generated as the other integers.

PROJECT 2–1   Because all our operations take constant time, translating H into a sequence of at most 9 h's should pose no problems. The worm will complete its moves in well less than a second.

PROJECT 2–2   Make the worm move all the way down to the bottom row, over one space, all the way up to the next-to-top row, over one space, all the way down to the bottom row, over one space, all the way up to the next to top row, over one space, all the way down.... If you arrange for the worm to go down in the leftmost column, it will go up in the rightmost column. It can then go across the topmost row, which it carefully avoided, from right to left, and repeat this process forever. As it sweeps the board the worm will accidentally bump into the food, growing longer and longer as time goes on.

PROJECT 2–3   A nice approach is to place a piece of food every 25 to 75 moves, with the exact number of moves chosen randomly each time. The main difficulty with having more than one piece of food on the board at any one time is that using a single variable to mark its location is no longer possible. It is probably best to no longer treat the locations of food as free. We can just use a flag, like the negative of its value (change `NOTFREEFLAG` as well), to record in `Board` the presence of food. Not including the locations of food in `FreePool` has the advantage that we will not accidentally place food where some is already located. Making food disappear is harder. If you decide to have it disappear at random times, you can use an array, `FoodPool`, similar to `FreePool`, to make this a constant-time operation. The special case of the worm completely filling the board requires attention.

EXERCISE 3–1

```
 1 #include "Long_Arithmetic.h"
 2
 3 program Fibonacci(input,output);
 4   (* Compute the n'th Fibonacci number using an infinite precision
 5     arithmetic package. *)
 6   var Fn, Fnminus1, Fnminus2: LongInteger;
 7       i, n: integer;
 8   begin
 9     InitializeMemoryManagement;
10
11     Declare(Fn); Declare(Fnminus1); Declare(Fnminus2);
12
13     write('For what  n  do you wish to compute the n''th Fibonacci number: ');
14     readln(n);
15
16     if n = 0
17       then MakeLong(Fn,0)
18     else if n = 1
19       then MakeLong(Fn,1)
20     else begin
21           MakeLong(Fnminus1,0);
22           MakeLong(Fn,1);
23
24           (* Move the current F_[n-1] and F_[n] back one and compute
25              the next F_[n].
26           *)
27           for i := 2 to n do          (* for i := 2 to n do            *)
28             begin                     (*    begin                      *)
29               Assign(Fnminus2,Fnminus1); (*     F_[n-2] := F_[n-1];     *)
30               Assign(Fnminus1,Fn);    (*      F_[n-1] := F_[n];        *)
31               Add(Fn,Fnminus1,Fnminus2) (*    F_[n] := F_[n-1] + F_[n-2] *)
32             end                       (*    end                        *)
33         end;
34
35     writeln('F_',n:1,' ='); WriteNum(Fn)
36   end. (* Fibonacci *)
```

EXERCISE 3–2

```
 1 function Mult(m1, m2: LongInteger): LongInteger;
 2   (* Precondition: neither  m1  nor  m2  is zero. *)
 3   var n,     (* running sum of partial products *)
 4       prod: (* partial product *)
 5         LongInteger;
 6       i: integer;
 7   begin
 8     MakeLong(n,0);
 9     for i := 1 to m2.NumDigits do
10       if m2.Number[i] <> 0
11         then begin
12                 prod := MultByDigit(m1,m2.Number[i]);
13                 ShiftingOver(prod,i-1);
14                 n := Add(n,prod)
15              end;
16     Mult := n
17   end; (* Mult *)
```

EXERCISE 3–3   Depending on the speed and memory capacity of your machine, you may need to use an exponent larger than 1000. On a DECstation, evaluating $2^{10,000}$ took 148 seconds using repeated multiplication, but only 37 seconds using repeated squaring and multiplication. The performance of repeated squaring and multiplication can be improved slightly by making `odd` a primitive function, and by not copying the parameters `x` and `n` into local variables. (While the rules say that they should be copied, because `x` and `n` aren't changed the program still works correctly.)

EXERCISE 3–4   Let the number of digits in m and n, the two numbers being multiplied, be p and q. The lengths of the partial products, counting trailing zeros, are approximately p, $p+1$, $p+2$, …, $p+q-1$, so the total amount of work to perform a multiplication is roughly $2pq + q^2$, which shows that it pays to make the shorter number the multiplier. In "Big Oh" terms, the time to perform a multiplication is $O(pq)$ or, converting back to values from lengths, $O(\log m \cdot \log n)$.

Squaring m results in a number approximately twice as long. In computing x^n by repeated squaring and multiplication, we get a sequence of numbers whose lengths are p, $2p$, $4p$, …, $2^{\log_2 n} p$. Since $2^{\log_2 n} = n$, the predicted number of digits in the final answer is np, and the final multiplication will take $3n^2 p^2/4$ time all by itself. ($2^{10,000}$ is in fact only 3,011 digits long, not the predicted 10,000.) Counting all the multiplications, not just the final one, results in a running time of $O(n^2 p^2)$—the last multiplication essentially dominates all the others put together. Exponentiating by repeated multiplication does not do much worse, because the multiplicand stays relatively small until near the end of the computation.

An important application of extremely large numbers is the RSA public key cryptography algorithm. All arithmetic in this algorithm is performed modulo n, for a very large n; in practice, n is typically two hundred digits long. Rapid exponentiation is at the heart of the algorithm. Because all the numbers involved in the computations have their lengths limited by the number of digits in n, exponentiation by repeated squaring and multiplication really does pay off—the algorithm performs several hundred multiplications between numbers several hundred digits long, instead of 10^{200} multiplications, an impossible task.

PROJECT 3–1   No hint for this project!

PROJECT 3–2   The idea is to delay computing `PartialProds[i]` until its value is needed. First set all the elements of `PartialProds` to `nil`. When `PartialProds[i]` is called for, if it is still `nil`, compute it with a call to `MultByDigit` and store it in `PartialProds[i]` for future use. The remaining inefficiency now lies in the two sweeps of `PartialProds`, one to set all the entries to `nil` and the other, at the end of `Mult`, to call `DisposeNum` for all non-`nil` entries. These sweeps can be avoided by making `PartialProds` global, initializing all its elements to `nil` on program entry, keeping a list within `Mult` of just which elements have been set, and resetting only those specific elements to `nil` (by calling `DisposeNum`) on procedure exit. (The list is most easily stored in an array.) While efficient, does this really make the technique effective when the base is 1000?

PROJECT 3–3   Sometimes you need to use three digits of the dividend and sometimes you need to use only two. You must also consider the possibility that the next digit of the quotient is zero. Single-digit divisors are a special case. Also note that this algorithm requires being able to read numbers from left to right; another boost for the doubly linked list approach.

PROJECTS 3–4 through 3–7   No hints for these projects!

EXERCISE 4–1

```
((a) b c)
((a) (b c))
((a) (b) (c))
```

EXERCISE 4–2   The recursion will eventually reduce p and q to the case where one of them is ( ) and the other isn't.

EXERCISE 4–3   The recursion will peel off the elements of p until the call is append(( ),q), leaving a trail of pending cons operations. The base case will *not* fail; it will return q. But the first attempt to perform a cons while the recursion is unwinding will fail, since the second argument to cons cannot be an atom. The only way to avoid this error is to avoid the cons. This occurs only when p is initially ( ).

EXERCISE 4–4   It returns $(l_n \ l_{n-1} \ \ldots \ l_1 \ k_1 \ k_2 \ \ldots \ k_m)$.

EXERCISE 4–5   (a b e d c)

EXERCISE 4–6   It is correct, but it is less efficient. The result returned by this version of union is (b a e d c). The reason it is less efficient is that as the algorithm progresses member is searching a longer and longer list as elements of p are added on to the front of q.

EXERCISE 4–7   When called with (a b c) the procedure returns

$$((\ ) \ (c) \ (b) \ (b \ c) \ (a) \ (a \ c) \ (a \ b) \ (a \ b \ c))$$

EXERCISE 4–8   Change the union on line 68 to append. This works because we know a priori that the powerset(cdr(p)) and

$$insert(car(p),powerset(cdr(p)))$$

have no elements (subsets) in common.

EXERCISE 4–9

```
function islat(p: list): boolean;
  begin
    if null(p)
      then islat := true
    else if atom(car(p))
      then islat := islat(cdr(p))
    else    islat := false
  end; (* islat *)
```

EXERCISE 4–10

```
function last(p: list): list;
  begin
    if null(cdr(p))
      then last := car(p)
      else last := last(cdr(p))
  end; (* last *)
```

EXERCISE 4–11

```
function flat(p: list): list;
  begin
    if null(p)
      then flat := NILL
    else if atom(car(p))
          then flat := cons(car(p),flat(cdr(p)))
          else flat := append(flat(car(p)),flat(cdr(p)))
  end; (* flat *)
```

EXERCISE 4–12

```
function shape(p: list): list;
  begin
    if null(p)
      then shape := NILL
      else if atom(car(p))
              then shape := shape(cdr(p))
              else shape := cons(shape(car(p)),shape(cdr(p)))
  end; (* shape *)
```

EXERCISE 4–13

```
function pair(p, q: list): list;
  begin
    if null(p)
      then pair := NILL
      else pair := cons(cons(car(p),cons(car(q),NILL)),pair(cdr(p),cdr(q)))
  end; (* pair *)
```

EXERCISE 4–14

```
function firsts(p: list): list;
  begin
    if null(p)
      then firsts := NILL
      else firsts := cons(car(car(p)),firsts(cdr(p)))
  end; (* firsts *)
```

EXERCISE 4–15

```
function substitute(p, q, r: list): list;
  begin
    if null(r)
      then substitute := NILL
    else if atom(r)
      then if eq(q,r)
              then substitute := p
              else substitute := r
    else   substitute := cons(substitute(p,q,car(r)),substitute(p,q,cdr(r)))
  end; (* substitute *)
```

EXERCISE 4—16   The basic strategy throughout is that $\mathrm{car}\,(\mathrm{cdr}\,(n)) = n-1$ and $\mathrm{cons}\,((\ ),\mathrm{cons}\,(n,(\ ))) = n+1$.

```
function greater(p, q: list): boolean;
  begin
    if null(p)
      then greater := false (* zero isn't greater than anything, though  p
                                might be equal to  q  *)
      else if null(q)
        then greater := true
      else   greater := greater(car(cdr(p)),car(cdr(q)))
                          (* greater(p,q) = greater(p-1,q-1) *)
  end; (* greater *)

function add(p, q: list): list;
  begin
    if null(p)
      then add := q           (* 0 + q = q *)
      else add := add(car(cdr(p)),cons(NILL,cons(q,NILL)))
                          (* p + q = (p-1) + (q+1) *)
  end; (* add *)

function sub(p, q: list): list;
  begin
    if null(p)
      then sub := NILL       (* 0 - q = 0 -- proper subtraction *)
      else if null(q)
        then sub := p          (* p - 0 = p *)
      else    sub := sub(car(cdr(p)),car(cdr(q)))
                          (* p - q = (p-1) - (q-1) *)
  end; (* sub *)

function mul(p, q: list): list;
  begin
    if null(p)
      then mul := NILL        (* 0 * q = 0 *)
      else mul := add(q,mul(car(cdr(p)),q))
                          (* p*q = q + (p-1)*q *)
  end; (* mul *)

function IntToList(n: integer): list;
  begin
    if n = 0
      then IntToList := NILL
      else IntToList := add(cons(NILL,cons(NILL,NILL)),IntToList(n-1))
                          (* n = 1 + (n-1) *)
  end; (* IntToList *)
```

The functions divv, modd, and ListToInt are similar and left to the reader.

EXERCISE 4—17 If you are unfamiliar with binary search trees you can learn more about them in Section 6.4 and in For Your Information: When Not to Use Recursion. The code for INSERT is

```
function BSTInsert(x: list; p: list): list;
  (* Insert atom  x  into the binary search tree  p . *)
  begin
    if null(p)
      then BSTInsert := cons(x,cons(NILL,cons(NILL,NILL))) (* ( x ( ) ( ) ) *)
      else if eq(x,car(p)) (* already in the tree *)
           then BSTInsert := p
         else if lessthan(x,car(p))
           then BSTInsert := cons(car(p),
                                  cons(BSTInsert(x,car(cdr(p))),
                                  cons(car(cdr(cdr(p))),NILL)))
         else    BSTInsert := cons(car(p),
                                  cons(car(cdr(p)),
                                  cons(BSTInsert(x,car(cdr(cdr(p)))),NILL)))
  end; (* BSTInsert *)
```

The considerably more complex algorithm for DELETE can be found in books on data structures. In "Big Oh" terms, having to construct a new tree has no effect on the running time. The algorithm recursively walks down the tree, looking for the insertion point and then, during the sequence of returns, builds the new tree. As we will see in the next section, each of the building steps (the three `cons` operations) takes constant time. There is a penalty, however: the amount of memory consumed is proportional to the length of the path from the root of the tree to the insertion point.

EXERCISE 4—18 There are a number of different solutions. Here is one. It uses two auxiliary functions.

```
function doitforalistofatoms(p, a, q: list): list;
  (* p  is a list of atoms,  a  is an atom, and  q  is a list of atoms.
     doitforalistofatoms  returns a list of lists of atoms, where each list
     of atoms in the result is formed from  q  by first placing  a  in a
     different position within  q  and then appending the elements of  p  on
     to the front.  The call from the outside,  doitforalistofatoms(NILL,a,q) ,
     has the effect of returning a list of lists of atoms formed from  q
     by inserting  a  at each possible position.
  *)
  begin
    if null(q)
      then doitforalistofatoms := cons(append(p,cons(a,NILL)),NILL)
             (* return  ( (p1 p2 ... pn a) ) *)
      else doitforalistofatoms := cons(append(append(p,cons(a,NILL)),q),
             doitforalistofatoms(append(p,cons(car(q),NILL)),a,cdr(q)))S ()
           (* stick (p1 p2 ... pn a q1 q2 ... qm) onto the front of
                     ( (p1 p2 ... pn q1 a q2 q3 ... qm)
                       (p1 p2 ... pn q1 q2 a q3 ... qm) ...
                       (p1 p2 ... pn q1 q2 q3 ... qm a) )
           *)
  end; (* doitforalistofatoms *)

function addinallpositions(a, q: list): list;
  (* a  is an atom.  q  is a list of lists of atoms.  addinallpositions
     returns a list of lists of atoms.  Logically, each list in  q  is
     replicated as often as necessary to allow  a  to be placed in each
     possible position in every list in  q .
  *)
```

```
begin
  if null(q)
    then addinallpositions := NILL
    else addinallpositions := append(doitforalistofatoms(NILL,a,car(q)),
                                      addinallpositions(a,cdr(q)))
end; (* addinallpositions *)

function permute(p: list): list;
  begin
    if null(p)
      then permute := cons(NILL,NILL) (* permute( () ) = ( () ) *)
      else permute := addinallpositions(car(p),permute(cdr(p)))
  end; (* permute *)
```

EXERCISE 4–19   The following solution eliminates only duplicates at the top level. It won't find the duplicate in (a (b b)), which is supposed to represent the set {*a*, {*b*}}.

```
function elimdups(p: list): list;
  begin
    if null(p)
      then elimdups := NILL
      else if member(car(p),cdr(p))
              then elimdups := elimdups(cdr(p))
              else elimdups := cons(car(p),elimdups(cdr(p)))
  end; (* elimdups *)
```

How would you modify this function to handle (a (b b))? What does your modified solution return on ((a b) (b a))? (See Above and Beyond: A Small Problem in member for a discussion of the issues raised by this last example.)

EXERCISE 4–20   No. As pointers, cons(car(p),cdr(p)) and p are unequal. Memory looks like

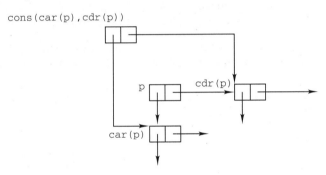

car(cons(p,q)) and cdr(cons(p,q)) point to the same places as p and q, however.

EXERCISE 4–21   Add to the program four globally accessed stacks, one for each spike and one for the stack frames. Adjust the stacks for the spikes whenever the program moves a disk and adjust the stack of stack frames just after procedure entry and before procedure exit. (Right before Towers is called recursively, the return address will have to be stored by the caller in the stack frame that is about to be created.)

EXERCISE 4–22   Change lines 329–355 to use `car` and `cdr`.

```
write out the left parenthesis;
RecWriteList(car(p));
p := cdr(p);
while not null(p) do
  begin
    write out a blank;
    RecWriteList(car(p));
    p := cdr(p)
  end;
write out the right parenthesis
```

We can lessen our dependence on knowledge of the internal representation further by defining an additional auxiliary procedure that recursively writes out a list, except for the leading parenthesis. This procedure and `RecWriteList` will be mutually recursive. This allows us to avoid the assignments `p := cdr(p)`.

EXERCISES 4–23 and 4–24   No hints for these exercises!

EXERCISE 4–25   It returns `(a b)` and `(cons a nil cons b nil)`. In the first expression `nil` returns `( )` and everything goes smoothly. In the second expression both `cons` and `nil` are interpreted as atoms, not functions.

PROJECT 4–1   The intended interface is

```
const MAXSTRING = 80;
type string = packed array [1..MAXSTRING] of char;
function quote(s: string): list;
```

In absolutely strict, standard Pascal this exercise is impossible because a Pascal string constant like `'(a b c)'` can be assigned to a variable of type `string` only if its length is MAXSTRING. Almost all compilers relax this restriction, truncating the string constant if it is too long, or padding it with blanks if it is too short. Another problem is that `'a'` will be interpreted by the compiler as a *character* constant and not a string constant—the user of our package can get around this problem by using `' a '`. Turbo Pascal contains a predefined `string` type, which can be used instead of the one given above.

PROJECT 4–2   Integers will have to be read in character by character, just like atoms, and converted to integers by your program. This can be done with the loop

```
i := 0;
while CurrentChar.ch in ['0'..'9'] do
  begin
    i := 10*i + ord(CurrentChar.ch) - ord('0');
    ReadClean(CurrentChar)
  end
```

PROJECT 4–3   No hint for this project!

EXERCISE 5–1   The derivation of 0001100000 is

(0)	S
(1)	0S0
(2)	00S00
(3)	000T000
(4)	0001T0000
(5)	0001100000

The derivation of 0100 is

(0)	S
(1)	0T0
(2)	0100

To get a string that begins 001... we must apply productions 1 and 2, followed by either production 3 or 4. This gives us the sentential forms 001*T*000 or 001000, neither of which can lead to a string ending with two 0's.

EXERCISE 5–2

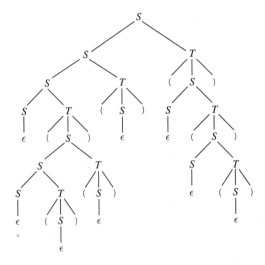

EXERCISE 5–3   The corresponding grammars are

$$S \to SS \mid (S) \mid (\,)$$

and

$$S \to ST \mid T$$
$$T \to (S) \mid (\,)$$

(The grammar

$$S \to SS \mid T$$
$$T \to (S) \mid (\,)$$

is an alternative answer for the first part of the question.)

EXERCISE 5–4

1. $S \to 0S1 \mid 01$ (not $S \to 0S1 \mid \epsilon$)

2. $S \to 1S \mid 1T$ or $S \to UT$
   $T \to 0T1 \mid 01$ $U \to 1U \mid 1$ (or $U \to U1 \mid 1$)
   $T \to 0T1 \mid 01$

3. $S \to 0S \mid T$ or $S \to 0S1 \mid T$
   $T \to 0T1 \mid \epsilon$ $T \to 0T \mid \epsilon$

4. $S \to TT$
   $T \to 0T1 \mid 01$

   There is no need to have

   $S \to TU$
   $T \to 0T1 \mid 01$
   $U \to 0U1 \mid 01$

5. $S \to 0S1 \mid 0T1$
   $T \to 1T0 \mid 10$

6. The solution to this problem suggests a general theorem: The union of two context-free languages is context free.

$$S \rightarrow T \mid U$$
$$T \rightarrow 0T1 \mid 01$$
$$U \rightarrow 0U11 \mid 011$$

7. Though it is difficult to find, it is possible to give an unambiguous grammar for this language. An ambiguous grammar that is not so difficult to find is

$$S \rightarrow 0S1S \mid 1S0S \mid \epsilon$$

An unambiguous grammar is

$$S \rightarrow 0AS \mid 1BS \mid \epsilon$$
$$A \rightarrow 0AA \mid 1$$
$$B \rightarrow 1BB \mid 0$$

8. The following grammar is ambiguous:

$$S \rightarrow 0S1A \mid 01A$$
$$A \rightarrow 1 \mid \epsilon$$

as is

$$S \rightarrow 0S1 \mid 0S11 \mid 01 \mid 011$$

An unambiguous grammar for this language is

$$S \rightarrow 0S1 \mid 01 \mid T$$
$$T \rightarrow 0T11 \mid 011$$

9. This language is very interesting because it can be proven that there is no unambiguous context free grammar for it. Such a language is called *inherently ambiguous*. The answer, using the approach taken to the sixth problem, combines the answers to problems 4 and 5. The strings with two derivations, no matter what grammar you invent, are those of the form $0^n1^n0^n1^n$.

EXERCISE 5–5   Define

```
type PtrToDTNode = ^DTNode;
     DTNode = record
                 Symbol: char; (* S, T, (, ), or e (for epsilon) *)
                 case NumChildren: integer of
                    0: ( ); (* leaves -- (, ), or epsilon *)
                    1: (Child: PtrToDTNode); (* S --> epsilon *)
                    2: (LeftChild, RightChild: PtrToDTNode); (* S --> T S *)
                    3: (FirstChild, SecondChild, ThirdChild: PtrToDTNode)
                          (* T --> ( S ) *)
              end;
```

and convert `Sprime`, `S`, and `T` to functions that return `PtrToDTNode`.

EXERCISE 5–6   There are several problems, both practical and theoretical. One problem is that code in the style of Figure 5–9 actually consumes input. When an attempt to apply $N \rightarrow A_1A_2 \cdots A_m$ fails, we need to back the input up to where it was at the start of the call to N, so that $N \rightarrow B_1B_2 \cdots B_{m'}$ starts in the right place. This is not difficult if the entire input is read into an array and `l` is passed explicitly. There are

still difficulties, however. First, even if $N \rightarrow A_1 A_2 \cdots A_m$ succeeds, it may be the wrong production to apply in the wider context. N must be prepared to keep trying alternatives when instructed to do so by whoever called it. This can be accomplished by passing to N a parameter indicating which production should be applied next. While now the method is capable of using a much wider range of grammars, the program can take exponential time to find the derivation, since it may need to repeatedly back up and restart. Even with all these "improvements" not all grammars can be used. The standard expression grammar is one such example. The problem is that E will call E without consuming any input, because the right-hand side of $E \rightarrow E + T$ begins with an E. This will lead to an infinite sequence of recursive calls.

EXERCISE 5–7   Run the program and find out.

EXERCISE 5–8   The output will be

```
VIII + IV**I
----------^
```

At or near the indicated point a number or left parenthesis was expected.
I - X

To produce output identical to that produced by the interactive version of the program, the location of the error must be recorded and the input line flushed before ReportError is called.

EXERCISE 5–9   The point of this exercise was to make you appreciate the method about to be described in the text.

EXERCISE 5–10   Any collection of I, V, X, L, C, and D has combined value less than M, any collection of I, V, X, L, and C has combined value less than D, and so on. This means that each run of negatives is more than canceled out by the following positive contribution.

PROJECTS 5–1 and 5–2   No hints for these projects!

EXERCISE 6–1   Repeat the second through fourth steps of the following algorithm over and over again.

- Pick any vertex.
- If it is a source, we are done.
- If not, there is at least one arc coming into this vertex.
- Walk backwards over this arc.

Eventually the process must stop, since otherwise, due to the finiteness of the graph, we will return to some vertex we have already visited. This implies the graph has a cycle, which we have walked backwards.

EXERCISE 6–2   The graph below has $3n + 1$ vertices and $4n$ edges, but the procedure makes $4 \cdot 2^n - 3$ calls.

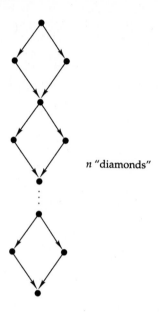

n "diamonds"

EXERCISE 6–3   In the pictorial representation of the depth-first search, dashed arrows indicate recursive calls that immediately backed out of the recursion. The order of the calls is indicated with lowercase letters.

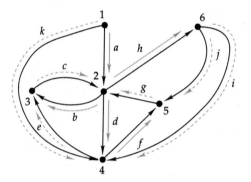

EXERCISE 6–4   The algorithm will visit each vertex once and traverse each edge twice, once in each direction.

EXERCISE 6–5   No. As the tree below shows, the two conditions are not the same. The search algorithm fails to find 18 because it searches the wrong subtree of 12.

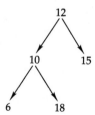

EXERCISE 6–6   The difficulty is that each edge, (i, j), is represented as two arcs, one from i to j and one from j to i. The algorithm will always find the cycle $i \rightarrow j \rightarrow i$, which does not exist in the abstract graph. The solution is to pass an additional parameter to `Walk`, one that indicates which vertex sent the algorithm to the

current vertex. When that vertex is encountered on the adjacency list of the current vertex, as it surely will be, the walk back can be suppressed.

EXERCISE 6–7   It is crucial that the hash function produce the same initial guess when given a key for the second time. A random number generator doesn't have this behavior.

EXERCISE 6–8   The probability of two people being born on different days is 364/365; the second person can be born on any day other than the one the first person was born on. (This ignores leap year.) The probability of three people all being born on different days is (364/365)·(363/365), since the third person can be born on any of the remaining 363 days. Continuing in this manner, we see that the probability of k people all being born on different days is

$$\frac{364}{365} \cdot \frac{363}{365} \cdot \ldots \cdot \frac{366 - k}{365}$$

When k equals 23 this drops below one-half. To generalize, replace 365 by m. For $m = 10000$, the value of this expression falls below one-half when $k = 119$. (The author used the infinite precision arithmetic package of Chapter 3 to compute these values.)

EXERCISE 6–9   One way to do this is to modify the makefile in the following manner:

```
worm:       worm.o pscr.o random.o clock.o date.h
            pc worm.o pscr.o random.o clock.o -ltermlib -o worm
            touch makefile

date.h:     makefile
            date +"(* \%c *)" > date.h
```

The command `touch makefile` forces the time stamp of `makefile` to be set to the present moment, which will be a fraction of a second later than when `date.h` was rebuilt. This sets the stage for the next time `make` is invoked. (This isn't foolproof either. If something goes wrong during the rebuilding of `worm`, the `touch makefile` will not execute.)

EXERCISE 6–10   By making the `.p` file depend on the `.h` files it includes, the `.p` file is forced to be more recent. The modified `makefile` looks like

```
worm.p:     pscr.h random.h
            echo "worm.p appears to be out of date"
            touch worm.p
```

Unfortunately, because of the `touch` command, it will not be out of date the next time `make` is run, even if the file is not updated. (Because our `make` utility checks to see that a file it attempts to rebuild has actually been rebuilt, without this `touch` command `make` will inform us that "even after attempting to rebuild `worm.p` it is out of date." This trick also fails if `worm.p` does not exist.)

EXERCISE 6–11   Essentially, `BuildGraph` treats the adjacency lists as a collection of stacks. It needs to treat them as a collection of queues, just like it treats the sequences of rebuilding commands.

EXERCISE 6–12

- Associate a `boolean` flag with each vertex, `IsSource`, initialized to `true`.
- Run down each adjacency list, setting the `IsSource` field of the vertices that are at the far end of arcs to `false`.
- Check the flag of each vertex, exactly one of them should still be `true`.

If either none or more than one of the `IsSource` flags is still `true`, then the graph is not single source. Even if it is, the graph might still contain a cycle. In all three steps the algorithm finds all the vertices by recursively walking the binary search tree.

EXERCISES 6–13 and 6–14   No hints for these exercises!

PROJECTS 6–1 and 6–2   No hints for these projects!

PROJECT 6–3   At an abstract level, the algorithm for topological sorting is

- ■ Repeat the following step until it no longer applies.
  - – Find a source, put it into the output, and remove it and the edges incident to it from the graph.
- ■ If the graph has not been completely eliminated, the original graph has a cycle.

By using a stack (or a queue) to hold all the sources that have been discovered but not yet eliminated from the graph, the algorithm can be made to run in $O(|V| + |E|)$ time, which is as efficient as possible. Associated with each vertex, we also keep the current in-degree. In more detail the algorithm is

- ■ Initialize the in-degrees. Do this in a "forward manner." In other words, first set them all to zero, and then run down each adjacency list: if (i, j) is an arc, then increment the in-degree of vertex j. This takes $O(|V| + |E|)$ time.
- ■ Initialize the stack. Check the in-degrees, putting those vertices that are sources on the stack. This takes $O(|V|)$ time.
- ■ If the stack is empty, go on to the next step. Otherwise, remove the top element from the stack, put it into the output, and remove it and the edges incident to it from the graph. Do this by decrementing the in-degree of each vertex on its adjacency list; if the in-degree of a vertex drops to zero, put it on the stack. Repeat this step. This takes $O(|V| + |E|)$ time over the life of the algorithm.
- ■ If not all the vertices have been output, the graph contains a cycle.

PROJECT 6–4   No hint for this project!

NOTES

NOTES

NOTES

NOTES

NOTES

NOTES

NOTES

NOTES